POWERSCORE® LSAT® LOGIC GAMES BIBLE

A Comprehensive System for Attacking the
Logic Games Section of the LSAT

Published by
PowerScore LLC
12222 Merit Drive
Suite 1340
Dallas, TX 75251

Author: David M. Killoran
Editorial Assistance: Jon M. Denning

Printed in the United States of America
12 15 20 22

ISBN: 978-0-98875-865-0

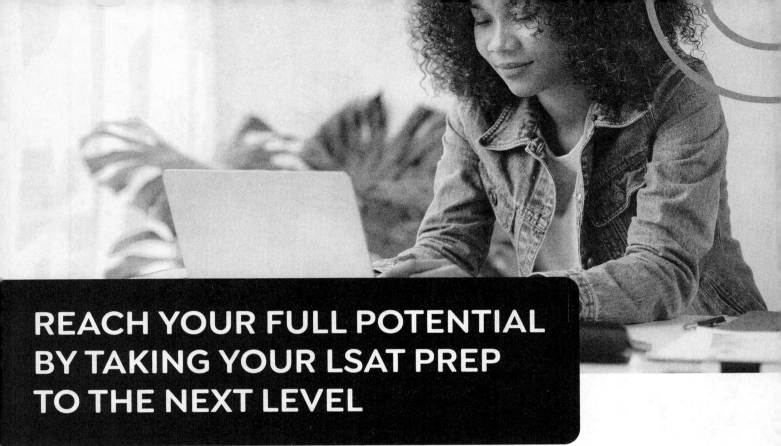

REACH YOUR FULL POTENTIAL BY TAKING YOUR LSAT PREP TO THE NEXT LEVEL

With our LSAT Bibles in hand, you are already building the strong foundation you'll need for LSAT success. The LSAT is manageable with the right plan of attack—and the next logical step is to build on your foundation and focus on making the leap from "good" to "great."

The PowerScore LSAT Course will bolster and refine the skills you're developing and elevate your chances to get into stronger law schools and qualify for favorable financial aid offers.

- Core syllabus, study roadmap, and in-depth LSAT lessons designed by LSAT Bible authors, Dave Killoran & Jon Denning
- Tailored to your learning style with live, interactive online or pre-recorded video lessons
- Digital practice test database containing every available official LSAT
- Full explanations and walkthroughs for all available past LSAT questions
- Insider info about upcoming LSATs and test content predictions

"I decided to go with PowerScore for online LSAT lessons to get an extra edge after receiving the basic groundwork from the LSAT Bibles. My instructor had unique insights and tricks that I couldn't get from the books, and I found the online tools to be outstandingly helpful for practice. Over time my practice scores crept up and I scored a 170 on my official test! I would recommend PowerScore's collection of LSAT prep services to any prospective test taker." —**Jack F.**

GET YOUR HIGHEST POSSIBLE LSAT SCORE NOW AT
powerscore.com/lsatprep

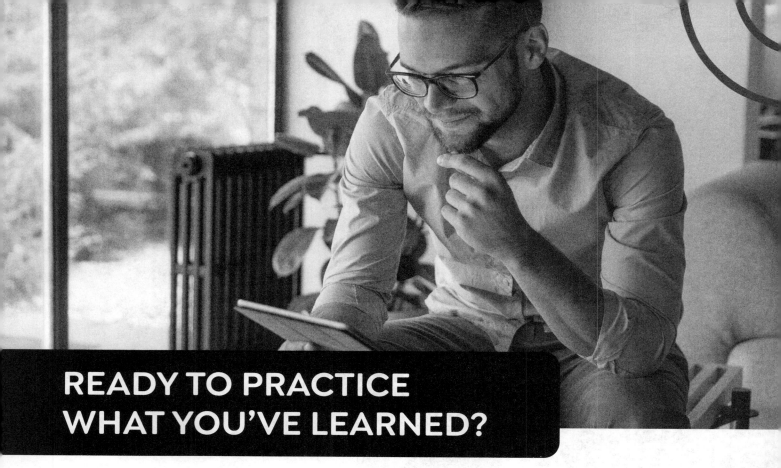

"I GOT IN"
You can do it. We can help.

PowerScore Admissions Consulting

- Our consultants are admissions experts, many of whom are lawyers and graduates of the top law schools in North America.

- We offer a multitude of packages. Whether you need help from start-to-finish or an in-depth evaluation and critique of your personal statement, we've got you covered.

- Need general guidance or help with specific parts of your application? Hourly admissions consulting is also available.

POWERSCORE
BY BARBRI

GET STARTED TODAY! GO ONLINE OR CALL TODAY TO START AN INQUIRY.
powerscore.com/lsat/law-school-admissions
1-800-845-1750

CONTENTS

CHAPTER ONE: INTRODUCTION

CHAPTER TWO: ANALYTICAL REASONING BASICS

Chapter Three: Linear Games

CHAPTER FOUR: ADVANCED LINEAR GAMES

CHAPTER FIVE: GROUPING GAMES

CHAPTER SIX: GROUPING/LINEAR COMBINATION GAMES

Chapter Seven: Pure Sequencing Games

Chapter Eight: The Forgotten Few

CHAPTER NINE: ADVANCED FEATURES AND TECHNIQUES

CHAPTER TEN: SECTION STRATEGY AND MANAGEMENT

LOGIC GAMES RECHALLENGE

APPENDICES

GLOSSARY AND INDEX

About PowerScore

PowerScore is one of the nation's largest test preparation companies. Founded in 1997, PowerScore offers LSAT, GMAT, GRE, SAT, and ACT preparation classes in over 150 locations in the U.S. and abroad. Preparation options include In Person courses, Accelerated courses, Live Online courses, On Demand courses, and private tutoring. For more information, please visit our website at powerscore.com or call us at (800) 545-1750.

For supplemental information about this book, please visit the Logic Games Bible website at powerscore.com/gamesbible. The website contains supplementary information including expanded concept explanations, LSAT articles and discussions, and a complete classification of every released LSAT game.

About the Author

Dave Killoran, a graduate of Duke University, is an expert in test preparation with over 25 years of teaching experience and a 99th percentile score on an LSAC-administered LSAT. In addition to having written PowerScore's legendary LSAT Bible Series and many other popular publications, Dave has overseen the preparation of thousands of students and founded two national LSAT preparation companies. Find him on Twitter at http://twitter.com/DaveKilloran or on the PowerScore LSAT Forum at http://forum.powerscore.com.

Chapter One:

Introduction

Chapter One: Introduction

Introduction

Welcome to the *PowerScore LSAT Logic Games Bible*! The purpose of this book is to provide you with a complete and cohesive system for attacking the Analytical Reasoning section of the Law School Admission Test (LSAT). By carefully studying and correctly applying the techniques we employ, we are confident that you will increase your Analytical Reasoning score.

In an effort to clearly explain the fundamental principles of the Analytical Reasoning section (also known as *Logic Games*), each chapter of this book contains a variety of drills, explanations, and Logic Games. The explanations and drills have been created by the development team at PowerScore, makers of the world's best LSAT preparation courses and materials. The techniques in this book have been tested in live classes, through individual tutoring, and on the LSAT itself. Each Logic Game comes from an actual LSAT and is used with the permission of LSAC, the producers of the LSAT. We feel the use of real Logic Games is essential to your success on the LSAT, and none of the content of the games in this book has been modified from its original form.

Each part of this book has been designed to reinforce your understanding of the concepts behind the Logic Games section. In order to effectively and efficiently apply our methods, we strongly recommend that you:

- Carefully read and then re-read each of the discussions regarding game recognition, rule diagramming, and inference production;

- Look at each problem and determine which elements led to the correct answer, then study the analyses provided in the book and check them against your own work;

- Track every question that you miss or that you struggle with, and record each problem in a performance tracker (see the Study Plans referenced on page 5 for more information).

By doing the above you will greatly increase your chances of performing well on the Logic Games section.

If you are looking to further improve your LSAT score, we also recommend that you pick up copies of the renowned PowerScore LSAT Logical Reasoning Bible and LSAT Reading Comprehension Bible. When combined with the Logic Games Bible, you will have a formidable methodology for attacking the entire test. The other LSAT Bibles are available through our website at powerscore.com and at fine retailers.

While none of the content of the games in this book has been modified, the layout of some games has been changed. Starting with the June 2012 LSAT, every Logic Game began appearing on two pages, and thus we have replicated that format with all of the games in this book.

How LSAT Studying is Different From "Regular" Studying

Studying for the LSAT is different from studying for a history or chemistry test. In those disciplines, when you learn a fact or formula there is often a direct increase in your score on the exam. However, the LSAT is not a fact-based test; it is a test of reasoning processes, and so the correlation between learning an idea and seeing an immediate score increase is not as strong. In a sense, it is like learning to drive a car: even after you learn the rules of the road, the first several times you go driving you probably are not a good driver at all. Nothing is familiar or comes easily, and you are likely more of a menace on the road than anything (I certainly was!).

Many of the tools we talk about in this book are fundamental to the LSAT, but they take time to integrate into how you approach the test, so at first they will seem slow and time-consuming. It will get better! For the time being, focus more on learning the ideas, and less on how they impact your practice tests results. Once you have completed most of the book, you should shift into a practice testing mode that will allow you to work with the ideas and to make them second nature. This practice will cement the ideas and show the greatest scoring impact.

A Note About Timing

As will be discussed in more detail later, time pressure is one of the defining challenges of taking the LSAT. Thus, when studying LSAT questions, there can be an overwhelming urge to focus on the clock. But for now you must resist that impulse. When you are first learning new concepts, take your time to understand what is being said and focus on the mechanics of how to apply the techniques presented. Don't worry about the clock! Once you have internalized the concepts and methodology, then you can start slowly working in timing as an element of study. The old adage about learning to walk before you can run applies perfectly to LSAT preparation, so worry more about how key strategies and ideas work than about your initial speed.

Additional Resources

This book has been carefully designed to explain the concepts behind the Logic Games section, and we are confident you will increase your Logic Games score by thoroughly studying and correctly applying the system explained herein. Because new LSATs are administered regularly, we always strive to present the most accurate, up-to-date, and helpful information available. Consequently, *LSAT Logic Games Bible* students have access to a variety of resources to help with their preparation:

1. **The *Logic Games Bible* book site**. This free online resource area offers:

   • Extensive supplements to the book, including important discussions on Rule Substitution Questions, Flawed Setups, and full book Glossary and Index.

   • A comprehensive classification of all released LSAT Logic Games.

   • *LSAT Bible* study plans based on how much time you have available to prepare, and in conjunction with the other LSAT Bibles.

   • An LSAT Prep Mentality guide that outlines critical components for establishing an ideal mindset.

   The exclusive *LSAT Logic Games Bible* online area can be accessed at:

   powerscore.com/lsatprep

   Once there, create an account and then use the code on the inside front cover of this book to gain access.

2. **The PowerScore LSAT Discussion Forum**, where you can talk to the author of this book and ask questions about the material:

 forum.powerscore.com

Staffed regularly by our LSAT instructors, the Forum offers thousands of searchable answers to student questions, including many lengthy explanations of individual LSAT questions, and additional concept and strategy discussions.

3. And please feel free to connect with me directly via **Twitter** and **our PodCast**:

 @DaveKilloran

 powerscore.com/lsat/podcast

I frequently post about the LSAT and developments with the test, and provide breaking news on test days and score release days.

We are happy to assist you in your LSAT preparation in any way, and we look forward to hearing from you!

Now that we've discussed some of the prep resources available to you, let's talk about the LSAT itself.

A Brief Overview of the LSAT ■■■■

The Law School Admission Test is administered multiple times each year. This standardized test is often required for admission to American Bar Association-approved law schools. According to LSAC, the producers of the test, the LSAT is designed "to measure skills that are considered essential for success in law school: the reading and comprehension of complex texts with accuracy and insight; the organization and management of information and the ability to draw reasonable inferences from it; the ability to think critically; and the analysis and evaluation of the reasoning and arguments of others."

The LSAT consists of the following four sections:

1 Section of Logical Reasoning	short arguments, 24-26 total questions
1 Section of Reading Comprehension	3 long reading passages, 2 short comparative reading passages, 26-28 total questions
1 Section of Analytical Reasoning	4 logic games, 22-24 total questions
1 Experimental Section	one of the above three section types

You are given 35 minutes to complete each section. The experimental section is unscored and is not returned to the test taker. An optional break of 10 minutes is given between the 2nd and 3rd sections.

The Logical Reasoning Section

The Logical Reasoning Section is composed of approximately 24 to 26 short prompts. Every short passage is followed by a question such as: "Which one of the following weakens the argument?" "Which one of the following parallels the argument?" or "Which one of the following must be true?"

The keys to this section are time management and an understanding of the reasoning types and question types that frequently appear.

The Analytical Reasoning Section

This section, also known as Logic Games, is typically the most difficult for students taking the LSAT for the first time. The section consists of four games or puzzles, each followed by a series of five to eight questions. The questions are designed to test your ability to evaluate a set of relationships and to make inferences about those relationships.

To perform well on this section you must understand the types of games that frequently appear and develop the ability to properly diagram the rules and make inferences.

The Reading Comprehension Section

This section is composed of three long reading passages, each approximately 450 words in length, and two shorter comparative reading passages. The passage topics are drawn from a variety of subjects, and each passage is followed by a series of five to eight questions that ask you to determine viewpoints in the passage, analyze organizational traits, evaluate specific sections of the passage, or compare facets of two different passages.

The Experimental Section

Each LSAT contains one undesignated experimental section, which does not count towards your score. The experimental can be any of the three section types described above, and the purpose of the section is to test and evaluate questions that will be used on *future* LSATs. By pretesting questions before their use in a scored section, the experimental helps the makers of the test determine the test scale.

LSAT Writing

For many years the writing section was administered before the LSAT, and then later after the LSAT. Now known as "LSAT Writing," the section is administered separately from the test.

A 35-minute writing section is administered *separately* from the LSAT, using secure online proctoring software. LSAT Writing is not scored, but law schools will have access to a candidate's three most recent samples.

In LSAT Writing, you are asked to write a short essay that defends one of two possible courses of action. There is no correct or incorrect answer, and your goal is to write the most coherent essay possible. Essays are typed, and you have access to basic word processing tools such as spell check, and cut, copy, and paste.

The LSAT Scoring Scale

Each administered LSAT contains approximately 75 scored questions, and each LSAT score is based on the total number of questions a test taker correctly answers, a total known as the raw score. After the raw score is determined, a unique Score Conversion Chart is used for each LSAT to convert the raw score into a scaled LSAT score. Since June 1991, the LSAT has utilized a 120 to 180 scoring scale, with 120 being the lowest possible score and 180 being the highest possible score. Notably, this 120 to 180 scale is just a renumbered version of the 200 to 800 scale most test takers are familiar with from the SAT and GMAT. Just drop the "1" and add a "0" to the 120 and 180.

Although the number of questions per test is relatively constant, the overall logical difficulty of each test varies. This is not surprising since the test is made by humans, and there is no precise way to completely predetermine logical difficulty. To account for variances in test "toughness," the test makers adjust the Scoring Conversion Chart for each LSAT in order to make similar LSAT scores from different tests mean the same thing. For example, the LSAT given in June may be logically more difficult than the LSAT given in December, but by making the June LSAT scale "looser" than the December scale, a 160 on each test would represent the same level of performance. The looser scale would translate into needing to answer fewer questions correctly to achieve that 160 (and thus also allowing more questions to be missed). Perhaps, to achieve a 160 on the "harder" June LSAT would require answering only 54 questions correctly (meaning one could miss 21 questions on a 75 question test). For the "easier" December LSAT, to achieve a 160 perhaps one would have to answer 56 questions correctly (allowing only 19 questions missed on a 75 question test).

This scale adjustment, known as equating, is extremely important to law school admissions offices around the country. Imagine the difficulties that would be posed by unequated tests: admissions officers would have to not only examine individual LSAT scores, but also take into account which LSAT each score came from. This would present an information nightmare.

The LSAT Percentile Table

Since the LSAT has 61 possible scores, why didn't the test makers change the scale to 0 to 60? Probably for merciful reasons. How would you tell your friends that you scored a 3 on the LSAT? 123 sounds so much better.

It is important not to lose sight of what LSAT scaled scores actually represent. The 120 to 180 test scale contains 61 different possible scores. Each score places a student in a certain relative position compared to other test takers. These relative positions are represented through a percentile that correlates to each score. The percentile indicates where the test taker ranks in the overall pool of test takers. For example, a score of 166 represents the 92nd percentile, meaning a student with a score of 166 scored better than 92 percent of the people who have taken the test in the last three years. The percentile is critical since it is a true indicator of your positioning relative to other test takers, and thus law school applicants.

Charting out the entire percentage table yields a rough "bell curve." The number of test takers in the 120s and 170s is very low (only 2.4% of all test takers receive a score in the 170s), and most test takers are bunched in the middle, comprising the "top" of the bell. In fact, approximately 40% of all test takers score between 145 and 155 inclusive, and about 65% of all test takers score between 140 and 160 inclusive.

There is no penalty for answering incorrectly on the LSAT. Therefore, you should guess on any questions you cannot complete, and the last chapter of this book contains a discussion of proper guessing strategy.

The median score on the LSAT scale is approximately 153. The median, or middle score, is the score at which approximately 50% of test takers have a lower score and 50% of test takers have a higher score. Typically, to achieve a score of 153, you must answer between 43 and 46 questions correctly from a total of approximately 75-76 questions. In other words, to achieve a score that is perfectly average, you can typically miss between 29 and 33 questions. To obtain a score of 170 (which is uniformly considered an excellent score), you can typically miss between 6 and 10 questions. Thus, it is important to remember that you don't have to answer every question correctly to obtain an excellent LSAT score. There is room for error, and accordingly you should never let any single question occupy an inordinate amount of your time.

The Digital LSAT

As opposed to the traditional paper-and-pencil format used by many other tests, the LSAT is administered digitally. The digital interface allows for certain advantages such as automated section timing with a visible countdown timer, and a navigation bar that shows your progress through the section and allows for the flagging of individual questions.

On the next page there is a graphic of how a typical question appears in the Logic Games section, with the most relevant parts labelled. We will talk about these elements later in the book, but as an overview they include:

- Buttons for Directions, Text Size, Line Spacing, and Screen Brightness;

- An onscreen timer that counts down from the initial allotted time to 0, and provides a warning when 5 minutes remain;

- The choice of underlining text, or highlighting using any of three colors: yellow, pink, or orange. Plus, an eraser to remove any underlining or highlighting;

- Lettered bubbles to select each answer choice, as well as an "eye" icon to grey out the answer and strike through its letter bubble;

- A flag for each question that allows you to mark selected problems for further review;

- A navigation bar across the bottom of the screen that shows the question you are currently on, which questions have been answered and which remain to be answered, as well as which questions have been flagged.

To interact with and control the on-screen content, you simply use a mouse when testing remotely. However, you cannot annotate on the screen in any other fashion aside from the controls above, including freehand writing. In other words, you can't draw on problems, make notes on the screen, or otherwise mark up questions. You are limited to using the annotation tools provided by the test makers. To make any separate notes or diagrams, you must instead use separate scratch paper and a pen or pencil.

Here is a look at LSAC's digital interface, with its key features noted:

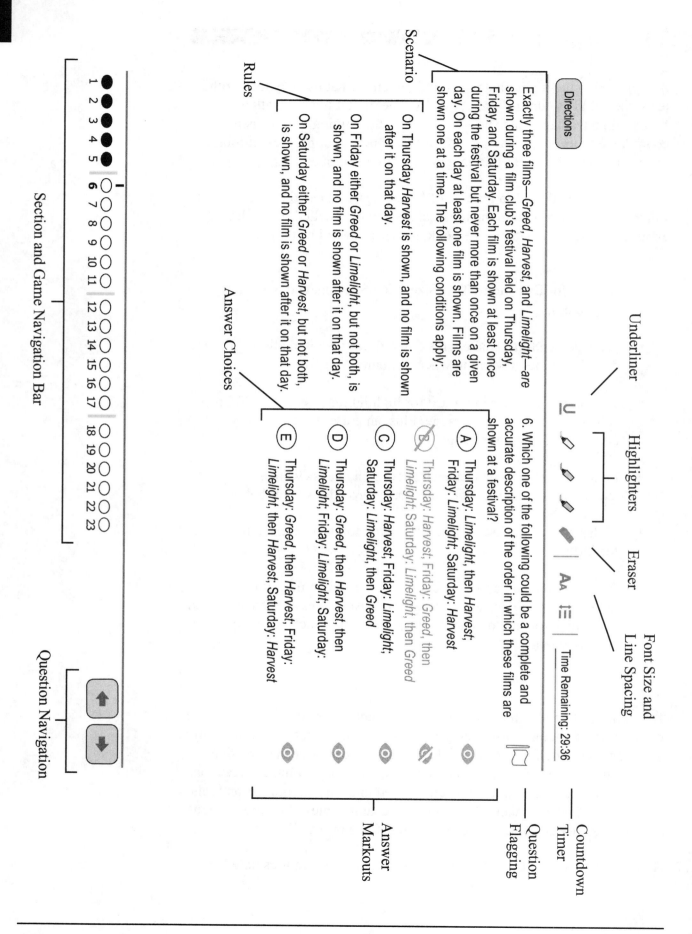

Directions

Underliner

Highlighters

Eraser

Font Size and Line Spacing

Countdown Timer

Question Flagging

Time Remaining: 29:36

Scenario

Exactly three films—*Greed*, *Harvest*, and *Limelight*—are shown during a film club's festival held on Thursday, Friday, and Saturday. Each film is shown at least once during the festival but never more than once on a given day. On each day at least one film is shown. Films are shown one at a time. The following conditions apply:

Rules

On Thursday *Harvest* is shown, and no film is shown after it on that day.

On Friday either *Greed* or *Limelight*, but not both, is shown, and no film is shown after it on that day.

On Saturday either *Greed* or *Harvest*, but not both, is shown, and no film is shown after it on that day.

6. Which one of the following could be a complete and accurate description of the order in which these films are shown at a festival?

(A) Thursday: *Limelight*, then *Harvest*; Friday: *Limelight*; Saturday: *Harvest*

(B) Thursday: *Harvest*; Friday: *Greed*, then *Limelight*; Saturday: *Limelight*, then *Greed*

(C) Thursday: *Harvest*; Friday: *Limelight*; Saturday: *Limelight*, then *Greed*

(D) Thursday: *Greed*, then *Harvest*, then *Limelight*; Friday: *Limelight*; Saturday:

(E) Thursday: *Greed*, then *Harvest*; Friday: *Limelight*, then *Harvest*; Saturday: *Limelight*, then *Harvest*

Answer Choices

Answer Markouts

Question Navigation

Section and Game Navigation Bar

1 2 3 4 5 6 7 8 9 10 11 12 13 14 15 16 17 18 19 20 21 22 23

For students used to paper-and-pencil exams, the separation of the problems and the scratch paper can present a challenge, since scratch paper notes and test content are physically independent of one another. This setup can initially be disconcerting, but as you practice you will find that it becomes less of a difficulty.

In your practice (especially with paper tests or prep materials), **you should use *separate* scratch paper at all times in order to prepare for the actual testing environment**, and refrain from making notes and diagrams directly on the test content itself.

LSAC provides some free, official tests online (lsac.org/lsat/prep/lawhub) that are delivered via their digital interface, and we strongly encourage you to spend as much time as possible practicing within the digital environment. Simply put, you must be extremely familiar with the platform before test day if you want to perform your best!

As we progress through this book we will further discuss aspects of the digital interface as well as diagramming strategies, so keep an eye out for those discussions. Now, with some of the basics of the LSAT out of the way, let's move on to discussing Logic Games questions in detail!

Our Testing & Analytics package offers every released LSAT in digital form. It is the ideal way to prepare for this unique testing experience!

Chapter Two:
Analytical
Reasoning Basics

Chapter Two: Analytical Reasoning Basics

The Analytical Reasoning Section ■

As you know, the focus of this book is on the Analytical Reasoning section of the LSAT. Each Analytical Reasoning section contains four games and a total of 22-24 questions. Because you have thirty-five minutes to complete the section, you have an average of eight minutes and forty-five seconds to complete each game. Of course, the amount of time you spend on each game will vary with the difficulty and the number of questions per game. For many students, the time constraint is what makes Logic Games the most difficult section on the LSAT, and as we progress through this book, we will discuss time management techniques as well as timesaving techniques that you can employ within the section.

Let us start by briefly examining the basic elements of a logic game. Each logic game contains three separate parts:

1. The scenario

2. The rules

3. The questions

The Scenario

Each game scenario introduces sets of variables—people, places, things, or events—involved in an easy-to-understand activity or exercise such as sitting in seats or singing songs in order. Here is an example of a game scenario:

> Seven comics—Janet, Khan, Leticia, Ming, Neville, Olivia, and Paul—will be scheduled to perform in the finals of a comedy competition. During the evening of the competition, each comic, performing alone, will give exactly one performance.

In the above scenario there are two variable sets: the comics J, K, L, M, N, O, and P, and the seven performance positions, which would be numbered 1 through 7 (this type of game is a known as a Linear game; more on this type of game in the next chapter).

In basic terms, the scenario "sets the stage" for the game and provides you with a quick picture of the situation to be analyzed. Although many game scenarios simply introduce the variables, on occasion the test makers place numerical information in the scenario, and this information is critical to understanding the possibilities inherent in the game.

This is an extremely brief introduction to the Logic Games section. The remainder of the book will expand on how to approach games and how to put the pieces together.

On average, you have 8 minutes and 45 seconds to complete each game.

The last chapter of this book contains an extensive discussion of overall section time management.

Always write down and keep track of each variable set.

As you work through this book, if you forget any of the terms, or if you would like to review a concept, use the Glossary and Index on page 715.

Because you cannot afford to misunderstand any of the basics of the game, you *must* read the game scenario very closely. You should look for the following elements as you read through each scenario:

1. What is the nature of the exercise? For example, are you lining variables up in order? Grouping variables together? Fitting them into a specified arrangement? ... and so on.

   In our scenario on the prior page about the comics, the nature of the exercise is creating an order for the seven performances.

   We will discuss the different types of games as we progress through this book, but as you read, you should always be trying to ascertain the fundamental nature of the activity at the heart of each game.

2. The number and type of variable sets. How many variable sets appear in the game? What elements make up each set?

   In our comic performances scenario, there are two sets of variables: one set is the seven performances, and the other set is the seven comics who will fill each performance.

3. If two or more variable sets come into play, how are the sets connected?

   In the example about the comics, the performance variable set provides order, and the comic variable set then fills each of those ordered spaces.

   Of course, different game scenarios will produce different relationships. For example, are clothing types connected to specific colors? Are different employees assigned to each seminar?

4. Numerical information, including: Are all the variables used? Are all the spaces filled? Can only one variable be placed into a space? ...and so on. Numerical information often appears to be a minor part of the scenario, but the truth is that *all* numerical information can be critical, and you should not assume that certain conditions hold just because they often apply in other Logic Games.

   Referencing the comic performances scenario, each comic performs exactly once, all of the spaces are filled by exactly one comic, and there are no unused or extra spaces or comics. This relationship—where the numbers match perfectly—is known as a one-to-one relationship, and will be examined later in this book.

The Rules

The second part of every game, just below the scenario, is the rules—a set of indented statements that describe and control the relationships between the variables. Here are the rules that accompany the comics game scenario presented on the first page of the chapter:

> Seven comics—Janet, Khan, Leticia, Ming, Neville, Olivia, and Paul—will be scheduled to perform in the finals of a comedy competition. During the evening of the competition, each comic, performing alone, will give exactly one performance. The performances are subject to the following constraints:
>> Neville performs either second or sixth.
>> Paul performs at some time after Leticia performs.
>> Janet performs at some time after Khan performs.
>> There is exactly one performance between Neville's performance and Olivia's performance, whether or not Neville performs before Olivia performs.

— The rules

The initial rules in a game apply to each and every question (unless otherwise stated, an occurrence we will address later).

The rules are critical because they control the possible placements of the variables. As such, you must devote a considerable amount of your attention to understanding the rules, and the way the rules interact. As we cover each game type, we will discuss the various rules and rule representations that accompany each game.

The Step Between the Rules and the Questions

The next part of every Logic Game is the questions. However, after reading the scenario and the rules, you should create a diagram of the relationships *before* moving on to the questions. Thus, we will focus briefly on those steps before addressing the questions.

Approaching the Games in General ■

2

Always read through the entire scenario and each rule before you begin diagramming.

As you begin each game you should carefully and completely read through the entire game scenario and all of the rules *before* you begin writing or making notes. This initial reading will help you determine the type of game you are facing, as well as what variable sets exist and what relationships govern their actions. This advice will also save you time by allowing you to formulate an exact plan of action, and it will save you from diagramming a rule and then re-diagramming if you find a later rule that alters the situation.

At this point in the game you must also fix the rules in your memory because it will save you valuable time during the questions. Students who fail to identify strongly with the rules inevitably struggle with the questions. You must also identify the most powerful rules in a game and consider how the rules interact with one another. Of course, we will discuss how to do this throughout our analysis.

In general, these are the initial, very basic steps you must take to move efficiently through each game:

Try to memorize the rules during the setup if possible, and be willing to spend an extra 10-20 seconds to do so if needed. This will save you time during the questions because you will not have to constantly refer back to the rule list. The more rules you can memorize, the more time you can save during the questions.

1. Read through the game scenario and all of the rules. Look for rules that either connect to other rules, or modify other rules.

2. Diagram the scenario and the rules on your scratch paper. Number the rules if that helps you organize the information. Attempt to fix your rule diagrams in your mind; memorize them if possible!

3. Make inferences (previously unknown or unstated facts about the game) by dynamically linking rules together, and by comparing each rule to previous rules. Note that steps 2 and 3 often occur in tandem.

4. Consider the structure of the game, including numerical options and the overall limitations present in the game.

5. Use the rules and inferences to attack the questions.

We will of course expand on these points as we discuss each game type!

Setups and Diagramming

When you take the digital LSAT, you will be given a booklet of scratch paper to use for note-taking and diagramming. Especially in the Logic Games section, you should use the scratch paper for your main diagram and individual question work!

Your initial reading of the game will also indicate what setup to use to attack the game. Many students are not aware of the best ways to set up Logic Games, and waste far too much time during the actual exam wondering what approach to take. Because you must read the rules and set up a diagram quickly and efficiently, the key to succeeding on the Logic Games section is to know the ideal approach to every game type before walking into the exam.

You should use the space at the top of one of the scratch paper pages to diagram your *initial* setup. This main setup should include:

1. A list of the variables referenced by initial, and their exact number. For example: J K L M N O P [7]

2. An identification of any randoms in the game (randoms are variables that do not appear in any rules) by using an asterisk.

3. A diagrammatic representation of the variable sets.

4. A diagrammatic representation of the rules.

5. A list of inferences. Making inferences involves deducing hidden rules or facts from the given relationships between variables. Inferences almost always follow from a combination of the rules or limiting structural factors within the game.

By following the above steps and using the scenario and rules from the previous pages, you can produce a basic setup for the game in your scratch paper booklet. That booklet can be placed either next to the tablet, or lined up directly below the tablet between you and the screen (a position most similar to that of the old paper-and-pencil testing format, where the game text and your setup are "grouped" together for a coherent, vertical view).

The following is a sample setup for the comic performances game, provided only as an example; you are *not* expected to know how (or why) to diagram this game in this fashion at this point!

One of the goals of this book is to teach you how to create the ideal setup for any game you encounter.

Randoms are variables that do not appear in any of the rules. You should notate them with an asterisk (*) below the variable.

You are not
expected to
produce the
game setup to
the right just
yet! It is just
an example; the
remainder of the
book will discuss
diagramming
choices and rule
representation.

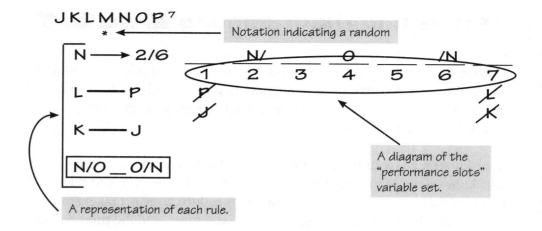

A representation of each rule.

A diagram of the "performance slots" variable set.

Notation indicating a random

This comic scenario setup is linear in nature, and in the next chapter, we will further discuss this type of linear game, as well as how to create this type of diagram.

Let us discuss some of the broader strategic elements of games and diagramming.

The Focus on Inferences

Most students can understand the nature of the game scenario and the basic working of the rules. Thus, perhaps the most important aspect of a strong Logic Games performance is the ability to make inferences. Inferences result when you combine two or more pieces of information to create a new, previously unstated insight into the game. These insights can be very specific, as in "J cannot perform first," or they could be broader, such as "An accountant must always serve on the Finance committee" or "Accountants and Managers never serve on a committee together." Inferences are tested frequently in the questions, and the harder the inference, the more likely it is to be tested in a question.

Every Logic Game scenario and rule set results in inferences, and as you create your main diagram you must examine the relationships between the rules, variables, and spaces to find those inferences that will help you answer the questions more quickly and accurately. Given the importance of this topic, one of the major points of emphasis in this book will be to show you how to make inferences.

Your Main Diagram vs Individual Question Diagrams

Once you have completed your main game setup, you should *not* draw or otherwise write on your main diagram again (except to add new information that applies to all questions, such as new inferences).

After making the initial setup, do not write on your main diagram.

2

What, then, should you do when additional work is required for individual questions? After you complete the main diagram, draw a line underneath it to indicate that you should not use it again. Then, as you do each question, use a separate numbered space to reproduce a miniature diagram with the basic structural features of your main diagram.

You should *not* use your main diagram for the work of individual questions. Instead, write out the work for each problem separately on your scratch paper (for example, place a "5" next to the work if you are creating a diagram in response to question #5).

For example, if a question introduces the condition that Leticia performs sixth out of the seven comics, draw the seven spaces next to the question number on your scratch paper, make a note about the new condition, place L in the sixth space, make inferences, and then proceed with answering the question. Refer to your main setup for the details of the relationships between the variables if needed. The result would then appear on your scratch paper as follows:

$$1. \; L = 6 \qquad \underset{\cancel{J}}{\underline{\text{K/M}}} \quad \underline{\text{N}} \quad \underline{} \quad \underline{} \quad \underline{\text{O}} \quad \underset{\cancel{K}}{\underline{\text{J/M}}} \quad \underline{\text{L}} \quad \underline{\text{P}}$$

There are several important benefits that you derive from recording your work separately from the main diagram:

1. Should you need to return to the question later, your work will be readily available and accessible.

2. Keeping the individual conditions of each question separate from the main setup reduces the possibility that you will mistake a local condition for a global rule.

3. You will be able to more clearly see which conditions produced which results.

Some students say that they save time by using their main diagram for each question. While they may save a bit of time in the short run, the overall costs always outweigh the benefits, particularly since those same students have a tendency to erase during the game.

We will discuss diagramming for games and individual questions in the next section, but for now keep in mind that all diagramming happens on separate sheets of scratch paper. Consequently, a sample setup and individual work for a game would appear along the following lines:

Don't worry about any of these question notations at this point. This is just an example of how your scratch paper might appear after you finish a game. We'll go into more detail on these diagrams soon!

Erasing Work

As you complete each question, it is absolutely essential that you *not* erase your previous work (both on the main diagram and on individual questions). There are several important reasons not to erase your work:

1. You can sometimes accidentally erase work you did not intend to erase, thus eliminating parts of your work you meant to keep. This unfortunately becomes more likely under the time pressure of the test.

2. Erasing work does not allow you to return to the question and review your work, which is especially damaging in those cases where you discover new information in a later question that alters your view of the game.

So, there are clear benefits to not erasing your work. Is there ever a time you should erase? Yes, if you make a mistake, you should definitely erase that work and start again!

Do not erase unless you make a mistake.

Reusing Work

There is actually a third excellent reason not to erase your work:

3. Each question that you complete adds to your repository of game knowledge, and that knowledge can be invaluable when answering other questions. Thus, as you progress through the game, you learn more about the game, and that information can be used to attack subsequent questions (and sometimes earlier questions, as we will see).

The work done on some questions can be used to help solve other questions.

For example, suppose the first question in a game produces a scenario where A is in the first position. Then, the second question asks for a complete and accurate listing of the positions A can occupy. Based on the first question, A can clearly be in the first position, and therefore you can eliminate any answer in the second question which does not contain the first position as a possibility. Thus, the work you do in *some* questions can be used to help answer other questions. This is true as long as the work you are referencing conforms to the conditions in the question you are currently answering. For example, suppose the third question in the same game states, "If A is in the third position, which one of the following could be true?" You *cannot* use the information from the first question to help answer the third question because A was in the first position in the first question, and thus does not fit the condition imposed in the third question.

Reusing prior work is one of the advanced elements of attacking questions that we will discuss in this book, and we will bring this topic up again later when looking at actual LSAT games.

The Questions—Part 1

The third and final part of each logic game is a set of five to eight questions that test your knowledge of the relationships between the variables, the structural features of the game, and the way those relationships and features change as conditions in the game change.

Once you have completed your diagram and made inferences, you will be ready to answer the questions. Keep in mind that each question has exactly the same value and that there is no penalty for guessing. Thus, if you cannot complete the section you should guess on the questions that remain (more on this in the Time Management chapter). If you cannot complete an individual question, do not spend an undue amount of time on the question. Instead, move on and complete the other questions.

The wording of each question (which is called the question stem) is extremely important, and you must pay careful attention to the details of each question. Each question in the Logic Games section is either Global or Local:

Guessing strategy is discussed in the last chapter of this book.

Global Questions

Global questions ask about information derived only from the initial rules, such as "Which one of the following must be true?" or "Which one of the following is a pair of comics that could perform consecutively, in the given order?" As such, Global question stems do not generally reference individual variables (but they can, as we will see later).

Because no additional conditions are imposed by Global questions, you must use the rules, your main diagram, and the answer choices themselves to answer Global questions. Applying these ideas will be discussed once we begin looking at specific game types.

Local Questions

Local questions generally begin with the words "if," "when," or "suppose," and impose a new condition in addition to the initial rules, such as "If Leticia performs sixth, which one of the following could be true?" Thus, Local question stems typically include one or more variables (often mentioned by name) involved in the new condition.

The additional conditions imposed by Local questions apply to that question only and do *not* apply to any of the other questions. It is essential that you focus on the implications of the new conditions. Ask yourself how this condition affects the variables and the existing rules. For Local questions (and some Global questions), reproduce a mini-setup on your scratch paper, apply the local condition, and proceed. We will discuss how to do this in our games discussion in the next chapter.

Local questions almost always require you to produce a "mini-setup" on your scratch paper.

The Range of Truth

Within the Global/Local designation all questions ultimately ask for one of four things: what must be true, what is not necessarily true, what could be true, and what cannot be true. Every question is a variation of one of these four basic ideas, which we will discuss in greater detail in Chapter Three. In essence, however, these questions (in various combinations) cover the full range of truth possibilities within LSAT logic.

Falsity and Modifiers

Although all LSAT Logic Game questions take on one of the four truth characteristics discussed in the previous paragraph, the producers of the LSAT have an arsenal of tricks to disguise and change the nature of the question.

The first trick is to present questions in terms of false. Most LSAT questions are presented in terms of "true," such as, "Which one of the following must be true?" However, because "true" and "false" are opposites, an LSAT author can very easily transform a question into terms of false. For example, instead of asking "Which one of the following cannot be true?" a question might instead ask "Which one of the following must be false?" The two questions clearly look quite different, but they are, in fact, functionally identical. Understanding this aspect is critical to a solid Games performance

The second trick is to add a modifier to a question stem, the most common modifier being "except." "Except" changes the entire nature of the question (and transforms it into the opposite of the original version).

Because both of these tricks are so important, yes, once again, we will discuss them in more detail in the next chapter.

Tracking the Nature of the Question

At all times, you must be aware of the exact nature of the question you are being asked. If you find that you are missing questions because you miss words such as "false," "least," or "except" when reading, then take a moment at the beginning of each question to underline or highlight the key words as "must," "could," etc.

The key to quickly answering questions is to identify with the rules and inferences in a game. This involves both proper diagramming of the rules and simple memorization. If you often find yourself rereading the rules during a game, you are failing to identify with the rules. And do not forget to constantly apply your inferences to each question!

 If you frequently misread questions, underline or highlight the key part of each question before you begin answering the question. You will not forget about a word like "except" if you have it marked!

Attacking the Section ▰▰▰▰

The key to optimal performance on Logic Games is to be focused and organized. This involves a number of factors:

1. **The Games are not presented in order of difficulty, so play to your strengths and away from your weaknesses**

   You are not required to do the games in the order presented on the test, and you should not expect that the test makers will present the games in the best order for you. Students who expect to have difficulty on the games section should attack the games in order of their personal preferences and their particular strengths and weaknesses.

   You can implement this strategy by quickly previewing each of the four games as you start the section (use the navigation bar at the bottom of the screen to quickly jump to the first question in each game). By doing so you can select a game that you feel is the best fit for your strengths (you will discover your strengths as you progress through this book).

2. **Create a strong setup for the game**

   Often, the key to powerful games performance is to create a good setup diagram of the rules and inferences using your scratch paper. At least 80% of the games on the LSAT are "setup games" wherein the quality of your setup dictates whether or not you are successful in answering the questions. In the following chapters, make sure to focus on the guidelines given for diagramming and inference-making. Mastering those elements will help you become an expert in handling any of the many types of games.

3. **Look to make inferences**

   As mentioned previously, there are always inferences in a game, and the test makers expect you to make at least a few of them. Always check the rules and your setup with an eye towards finding inferences, and then relentlessly use those inferences to attack the questions.

Although test takers have found the first game on many LSATs to be the easiest, there is no set order of difficulty, and you cannot predict where the easiest or hardest game will appear. On some tests the first game has been the hardest and the last game has been the easiest. With that said, for the majority of LSATs, the hardest game usually appears third or fourth, and the easiest game usually appears first.

4. Be smart during the game

If necessary, skip time-consuming questions and return to them later. Remember that it is sometimes advisable to do the questions out of order. For example, if the first question in a game asks you for a complete and accurate list of the positions "R" could occupy, because of time considerations it would be advisable to skip that question and complete the remaining questions. Then you can return to the first question and use the knowledge you gained from the other questions to quickly and easily answer the first question.

5. Neatness counts

Sloppy writing on your scratch paper can lead to errors and mistakes, especially under the time pressure of the exam. Make sure to write in a neat and orderly manner, so that you can access your information easily and clearly.

Know these points! They are basic principles you must know in order to perform powerfully.

6. Do not be intimidated by size

A lengthy game scenario and a large number of initial rules do not necessarily equal greater difficulty. Some of the longest games are easy because they contain so many restrictions and limitations.

7. Keep an awareness of time

As stated previously, you have approximately eight minutes and forty-five seconds to complete each game and bubble in your answers. There is a timer in the upper left-hand corner of the tablet screen so you will always know how much time remains. Do not let one game or question consume so much time that you suffer later on!

8. Maintain a positive attitude, and concentrate

Above all, you must attack each game with a positive and energetic attitude! If you do not believe you will do well, you won't do well.

Try to see the Logic Games section as an enjoyable exercise (as hard as that may seem). The games themselves are often challenging and interesting, and students who actively involve themselves in the games generally perform better overall.

Chapter Two Quick Review ▮▮▮▮▮

Chapter Two is a basic overview of the Logic Games section; subsequent chapters will explain and expand upon the ideas presented in this chapter.

If you do all four games, you have 8 minutes and 45 seconds to complete each game, inclusive of answer transferring. If you do only three games, you have 11 minutes and 40 seconds to complete each game. If you do just two games, you have 17 minutes and 30 seconds to complete each game.

You can do the games out of order and according to your strengths and weaknesses.

There are three parts to every Logic Game: the scenario, the rules, and the questions.

Always read the scenario and rules once through before you begin diagramming.

Fix the rules in your mind—try to memorize them if possible!

Make a main diagram for each game on your scratch paper. Include the following:

- List the variables and their exact total number
- Identify randoms
- Diagram the variable sets
- Diagram the rules
- Make inferences—they always exist
- Identify the powerful rules and variables

Write neatly.

You can do the questions out of order if it saves time or is more efficient.

Always look to use your inferences when answering questions.

Do not erase unless you have made a mistake.

Do not forget that work from one question might be useful on other questions.

Maintain a positive attitude, concentrate, and try to enjoy yourself!

Chapter Three:
Linear Games

Chapter Three: Linear Games

The Concept of Linearity ▨

Linearity involves the fixed positioning and ordering of variables (often in numerical order, but sometimes as days of the week, letter grades, or some other ordered scheme). In every Linear game, one of the variable sets is chosen as the "base" and is diagrammed in a straight line, either horizontally or vertically, and the remaining variable sets are placed into slots above or next to the base. For example, consider the following game scenario:

> A tutor is planning a daily schedule of individual tutoring sessions for each of six students—S, T, W, X, Y, and Z. The tutor will meet with exactly one student at a time, for exactly one hour each session. The tutor will meet with students starting at 1 P. M., for six consecutive hours.

In this game, the hours would be chosen as the base because they have an inherent sense of order (2 P. M. comes immediately after 1 P. M., and immediately before 3 P. M., etc.). The six students would then be placed into individual slots above the six hours, as follows:

$$\text{S T W X Y Z}^6 \longrightarrow \quad \underline{} \quad \underline{} \quad \underline{} \quad \underline{} \quad \underline{} \quad \underline{}$$
$$\qquad\qquad\qquad\quad 1 \quad\; 2 \quad\; 3 \quad\; 4 \quad\; 5 \quad\; 6$$

The game could also be set up vertically, and the six students would be placed into individual slots next to the hours:

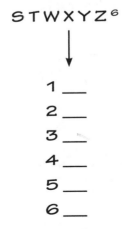

Linearity and Grouping are the two core concepts that appear in the Games section. Grouping will be discussed in Chapter Five.

Most of the examples in this chapter will assume the use of a horizontal diagram with six slots, like the one to the left.

Always choose a
base which has
an inherent sense
of order.

3

Variable sets with the greatest sense of inherent order almost always create the best base, because they provide a logical framework within which to place all other variable sets. Certain types of variable sets are always chosen as the base—days of the week, for example. In the prior game, if you decide to choose the six students as the base, throughout the questions you will have to keep in mind an extra consideration: the order of the hours. Since choosing the hours as the base eliminates this problem, it is a superior choice.

It is your choice whether to diagram the game horizontally or vertically, although some games demand a vertical setup (such as a game about floors of an office building), and some games demand a horizontal setup (such as a game about houses on an East-West street). Throughout this book we will typically present games in a horizontal fashion unless the game dictates otherwise.

One-to-One Relationships

The prior two diagrams reflect what is known as a one-to-one variable set relationship. In a one-to-one relationship, each variable fills exactly one slot and there are the same number of slots as variables to be placed. For example, there are six hour-long slots and six students, and one student is tutored each hour. Thus, there is one student for each hour, and a total of six students for six hours (which is a numerical distribution of 1-1-1-1-1-1. More on numerical distributions will be covered later in this book).

Not every game's variable sets have a one-to-one relationship, and thus you must closely track the number of variables and available spaces in each game. The numerical relationship of the variable sets is one of the key indicators of the difficulty of a game, and we will discuss this concept again later in this chapter. In the meantime, for the remainder of this chapter, assume a one-to-one relationship exists in each example unless otherwise stated.

Linear Base Representation Diagramming Drill ▪▪▪

Each of the following items contains a game scenario that features two separate variable sets. Using the given information, choose a base for the game and create a linear diagram. To the side, specify the variable set that will fill the linear slots. *Answers on page 40*

Example Scenario:

Six sprinters—Hu, Natchez, O'Dell, Prince, Sato, and Tran—are assigned to six separate running lanes on a track. The lanes are numbered from 1 through 6.

Answer:

H N O P S T⁶

$$\underline{} \quad \underline{} \quad \underline{} \quad \underline{} \quad \underline{} \quad \underline{}$$
1　　2　　3　　4　　5　　6

---

1. A dancer must choose a single outfit to wear to rehearsal on each of five consecutive days—Monday, Tuesday, Wednesday, Thursday, and Friday. Each outfit is a single color—black, gray, purple, red, and white—and no outfit can be worn more than once.

variable is the clothing

base is the day of the week

$$\overline{M} \quad \overline{T} \quad \overline{W} \quad \overline{T} \quad \overline{F}$$

B M P R W

2. A hotel manager assigns six guests—Riley, Santos, Tanaka, Vu, Xicu, and Yee—to six separate floors of the hotel, floors 20 through 25. Each guest is assigned to a different floor.

bases people variable people

R S T V X Y

$\overline{20}$

$\overline{21}$

$\overline{23}$

$\overline{24}$

$\overline{25}$

Linear Base Representation Diagramming Drill

3. The organizer of a singing competition must determine the order in which seven competitors— Abbas, Baruch, Cara, Demir, Frank, Hatsuko, and Jasmine—will perform. Each competitor performs exactly once, one after another.

[handwritten notes]

5. A child stacks five lettered boxes on top of one another, with the first box on the bottom and the fifth box on the top. The boxes are lettered A through E, not necessarily in that order.

[handwritten notes]

4. A student receives a lettered grade—A, B, C, and D—in each of four different subjects: Anthropology, Biology, Computer Science, and Economics. The student is given a grade in each subject, and no two subjects receive the same grade.

[handwritten notes]

6. A film festival manager is scheduling show times for four movies in a single day: *Flare*, *Gusto*, *Helpless*, and *Jinxed*. Each movie is shown exactly once, and the movies are shown one after another in the same theater. Each film is allotted exactly two hours on the day's schedule, which begins at noon and ends at 8:00 p.m.

[handwritten notes]

Linear Base Representation Diagramming Drill

7. From west to east, the five houses on one side of a
   street are numbered consecutively 111, 113, 115,
   117, and 119 respectively. Each house is occupied by
   exactly one of five families: the Milanos, the Ogawas,
   the Painters, the Raos, and the Sanders.

   M O P R S

   ‾‾‾   ‾‾‾   ‾‾‾   ‾‾‾   ‾‾‾
   111   113   115   117   119

8. A museum clerk places six objects into the six
   drawers of a vertical storage cabinet. The drawers are
   labeled in order from A through F, with drawer A at
   the top and drawer F at the bottom. The six objects are
   a cup, a flagon, a mask, a plate, a statue, and a tablet.
   Each drawer holds only one of the objects, and each
   object is placed into exactly one drawer.

   C F M P S

   ‾a‾
   ‾B‾
   ‾ ‾ ‾ ‾ ‾ ‾ ‾ ‾ ‾C‾
   1   2   3   4   5   6
   ‾D‾
   ‾e‾
   ‾F‾

Linear Base Representation Diagramming Drill Answer Key

1. A dancer must choose a single outfit to wear to rehearsal on each of five consecutive days—Monday, Tuesday, Wednesday, Thursday, and Friday. Each outfit is a single color—black, gray, purple, red, and white—and no outfit can be worn more than once.

B G P R W⁵

___	___	___	___	___
M	T	W	Th	F

Because the days of the week have an inherent sense of order, they should be chosen as the base. The outfit colors are then the variable set that is distributed over the five days. The diagram can be horizontal or vertical, depending on your preference.

2. A hotel manager assigns six guests—Riley, Santos, Tanaka, Vu, Xicu, and Yee—to six separate floors of the hotel, floors 20 through 25. Each guest is assigned to a different floor.

R S T V X Y⁶

25 ___

24 ___

23 ___

22 ___

21 ___

20 ___

Because the floors of the hotel have an inherent sense of order, they should be chosen as the base. And, because the floors of a hotel are vertically aligned, the diagram is vertical as well. The guests are then the variable set that is distributed over the six floors.

Linear Base Representation Diagramming Drill Answer Key

3. The organizer of a singing competition must determine the order in which seven competitors—Abbas, Baruch, Cara, Demir, Frank, Hatsuko, and Jasmine—will perform. Each competitor performs exactly once, one after another.

    A B C D F H J^7

    $\underline{\quad}$ $\underline{\quad}$ $\underline{\quad}$ $\underline{\quad}$ $\underline{\quad}$ $\underline{\quad}$ $\underline{\quad}$
     1   2   3   4   5   6   7

    While not directly stated, the singers must perform in order, and hence the logical base for this game is the variable set of 1 through 7 representing the order of the performances. The competitors are then the variable set that is distributed over the seven performances. The diagram can be horizontal or vertical depending on your preference.

4. A student receives a lettered grade—A, B, C, and D—in each of four different subjects: Anthropology, Biology, Computer Science, and Economics. The student is given a grade in each subject, and no two subjects receive the same grade.

    A B C E^4

    $\underline{\quad}$ $\underline{\quad}$ $\underline{\quad}$ $\underline{\quad}$
     A   B   C   D

    Because the grades have an inherent sense of order (A is better than B, B is better than C, C is better than D), they should be chosen as the base. The subjects then make up the variable set that is distributed over the grades. The diagram can be horizontal or vertical depending on your preference.

5. A child stacks five lettered boxes on top of one
    another, with the first box on the bottom and the fifth
    box on the top. The boxes are lettered A through E,
    not necessarily in that order.

    A B C D E⁵

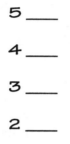

    5 ___

    4 ___

    3 ___

    2 ___

    1 ___

    Because the five box numbers have an inherent sense of order, they should be chosen as
    the base, and arranged vertically as specified in the scenario. The letters then make up the
    variable set that is distributed over the boxes. Even though the letters have inherent order,
    note that the scenario removes that order ("not necessarily in that order").

6. A film festival manager is scheduling show times for
    four movies in a single day: *Flare, Gusto, Helpless,*
    and *Jinxed*. Each movie is shown exactly once, and
    the movies are shown one after another in the same
    theater. Each film is allotted exactly two hours on the
    day's schedule, which begins at noon and ends at 8:00
    p.m.

    F G H J⁴

    ___ ___ ___ ___
    12   2   4   6

    Because the movie show times have an inherent sense of order, they should be chosen as
    the base, and in this case the movies show at 12, 2, 4, and 6. The movies then comprise
    the variable set that is distributed over the times. The diagram can be horizontal or vertical
    depending on your preference.

7. From west to east, the five houses on one side of a
   street are numbered consecutively 111, 113, 115,
   117, and 119 respectively. Each house is occupied by
   exactly one of five families: the Milanos, the Ogawas,
   the Painters, the Raos, and the Sanders.

   MOPRS⁵

   <u>111</u> <u>113</u> <u>115</u> <u>117</u> <u>119</u>

   Because the house numbers have an inherent sense of order, they should be chosen as the
   base, and in this case the houses are odd-numbered from 111 to 119. The families are then
   the variable set that is distributed over the house numbers. Because the street runs from west
   to east, the diagram should be horizontal.

---

8. A museum clerk places six objects into the six
   drawers of a vertical storage cabinet. The drawers are
   labeled in order from A through F, with drawer A at
   the top and drawer F at the bottom. The six objects are
   a cup, a flagon, a mask, a plate, a statue, and a tablet.
   Each drawer holds only one of the objects, and each
   object is placed into exactly one drawer.

   CFMPST⁶

   A ____

   B ____

   C ____

   D ____

   E ____

   F ____

   Because the drawers are lettered A though F and thus have an inherent sense of order, they
   should be chosen as the base. The objects are then the variable set that is distributed over the
   drawers. Because the drawers are vertically stacked, the diagram is vertical, with A—the top
   drawer—on top, and F—the bottom drawer—on the bottom.

Rule Representation ▐▬▬▬▬▬

Now that we have looked at the concept of linearity briefly, let us turn to the rules that typically accompany a linear game scenario.

Your representation of the rules is critical to your success on any game. Many students diagram the rules ineffectively, and pay a heavy price when attempting to answer the questions. In representing the rules, there are two primary considerations: how to diagram the rule itself, and how to show the implications of the rule on your main diagram.

There are four main types of Linear rules:

1. Variable placement rules

2. Fixed position rules

3. Sequencing or relative placement rules

4. Conditional rules

The following sections will discuss each of these rule types.

1. Variable Placement Rules ▐▬▬▬▬

Variable placement rules specify where a variable or variables must be placed or cannot be placed. For example, if a rule states:

R must be the first singer.

Then this condition can be represented by placing R in the first slot:

$$\frac{R}{1} \quad \frac{}{2} \quad \frac{}{3} \quad \frac{}{4} \quad \frac{}{5} \quad \frac{}{6}$$

This placement eliminates R from further consideration for any other position (assuming R is used only once), and immediately reduces the variable options for all other positions.

Of course, some rules specify where a variable or variables *cannot* be placed:

Not Laws™

Not Laws physically notate where a variable cannot be placed. For example, if a rule states:

As you begin setting up each game, always search for what must be true and what cannot be true.

T cannot be placed first.

Then this can be represented with a Not Law underneath the first slot:

$$\underline{} \quad \underline{} \quad \underline{} \quad \underline{} \quad \underline{} \quad \underline{}$$
$$1 \quad\;\; 2 \quad\;\; 3 \quad\;\; 4 \quad\;\; 5 \quad\;\; 6$$
$$\cancel{T}$$

Unfortunately, many students have a tendency to focus initially on what could be true instead of what must or cannot be true. The problem with this approach is that there can be many possibilities within a game. If you spend time showing what can occur, this time may end up being wasted if the questions never test those possibilities. You can focus on what could be true as you work through each question.

By crossing out (also known as "negating") T under the first slot, you can easily see that T cannot be placed in that slot. Not Laws are very useful since it is essential that you establish the events that cannot be true in a game. In fact, in representing the rules, you should always search for what must be true and what cannot be true. These two characteristics represent the "endpoints" of the spectrum of possibilities within a game, and by defining the endpoints you define the range of possibilities within a game. Additionally, Global questions often appear in order to test your knowledge of what must and what cannot be true, such as "Which one of the following must be true?" (Answer: T cannot be in the first slot). Interestingly, with the above rule, the Not Law is the representation of the rule itself. In many other cases, however, Not Laws will follow after the rule has been separately represented (as we will see with Blocks shortly).

One note about Not Laws: in certain games we will examine (notably Sequencing games), there can be so many Not Laws present that drawing them all out is not the right approach. The general guideline to use is thus one of moderation and of value for time spent. Drawing out five or ten Not Laws is helpful and reasonable. But twenty or thirty? That is too many and loses focus of what really matters—the rules and consequences. There will be more on this idea as we cover various game types but for the time being, focus on seeing what cannot occur and properly representing that with a Not Law in each case.

Dual Options

When only two variables can occupy a slot, this is known as a dual-option.

Certain variables or slots have a limited number of possibilities. When there are only two variables that can be placed in a single slot, this can be shown with a Dual Option. Consider the following rule:

Either H or J must be inspected on the third day.

$$\underline{}\quad \underline{}\quad \overset{\text{H/J}}{\underline{}}\quad \underline{}\quad \underline{}\quad \underline{}$$
$$1 \qquad 2 \qquad 3 \qquad 4 \qquad 5 \qquad 6$$

In this case, since it must be true that H or J is inspected on the third day, H/J is placed on the third day. As you can see, what must be true is represented by placing the variables above the slots, and what cannot be true is represented by Not Laws below the numbers:

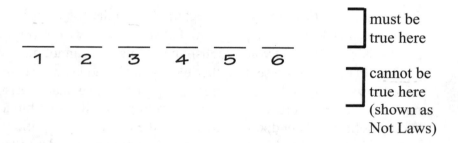

In the case of the dual-option above, it is also true that no other variable besides H or J can appear third, so it might seem appropriate to show Not Laws on that slot for all other variables. This representation would be correct, but since H and J are already placed on the third day, it is obvious that no other variable can be placed on that day, and therefore showing Not Laws on the third day would be redundant. However, if you find it helpful to show the Not Laws, by all means do what works best for you.

Split Dual-Options

Occasionally, a single variable will have only two possible positions. This is known as a Split Dual-Option. Consider the following rule:

When a single variable is limited to only two potential slots, this is known as a split dual-option, or sometimes as a split-option.

3

H must be inspected on either the third day or the fifth day.

$$\underline{\hspace{1em}} \quad \underline{\hspace{1em}} \quad \underset{1}{\underline{\text{H/}}} \quad \underset{\;}{\underline{\hspace{1em}}} \quad \underset{\;}{\underline{\text{/H}}} \quad \underline{\hspace{1em}}$$
$$\;\;1 \quad\;\; 2 \quad\;\; 3 \quad\;\; 4 \quad\;\; 5 \quad\;\; 6$$

Of course, if H can only be inspected on the third or fifth day, H cannot be inspected on the first, second, fourth, or sixth days. Since the positioning of H is still a bit uncertain, in this case it makes sense to show H Not Laws on the other days:

$$\underline{\hspace{1em}} \quad \underline{\hspace{1em}} \quad \underline{\text{H/}} \quad \underline{\hspace{1em}} \quad \underline{\text{/H}} \quad \underline{\hspace{1em}}$$
$$\;\;1 \quad\;\; 2 \quad\;\; 3 \quad\;\; 4 \quad\;\; 5 \quad\;\; 6$$
$$\;\;\cancel{H} \quad\;\; \cancel{H} \quad\;\;\;\;\; \cancel{H} \quad\;\;\;\;\; \cancel{H}$$

Triple Options

Sometimes a rule or an inference will lead you to determine that a single space can contain only one of three variables. This is known as a Triple Option. Consider the following rule:

A, B, or C must be displayed on the first day.

This rule would be represented directly on the diagram as follows:

$$\underset{1}{\underline{\text{A/B/C}}} \quad \underline{\hspace{1em}} \quad \underline{\hspace{1em}} \quad \underline{\hspace{1em}} \quad \underline{\hspace{1em}} \quad \underline{\hspace{1em}}$$
$$\;\;1 \quad\;\; 2 \quad\;\; 3 \quad\;\; 4 \quad\;\; 5 \quad\;\; 6$$

Split triple-options can also occur, but they are extremely tricky to work with, and generally we do not recommend that you use them as part of your rule representation arsenal.

2. Fixed Position Rules

Fixed position rules specify where a variable must be placed or cannot be placed in relation to another variable. Prior to looking at those rules, let us clarify a point about the language used in individual rules.

Left/Right Diagramming Terminology

One point of confusion when diagramming with Linear scenarios is the language used by the test makers regarding variables being to the left of, or to the right of, other variables. In the typical Linear diagram, numbered spaces on the left side of the diagram are "ahead," "earlier," or "before" the spaces on the right side:

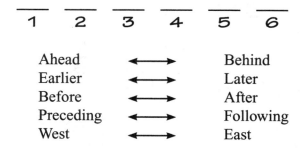

These left/right designators can refer to any numbered space unit, including performances, places, days, weeks, etc. For example, a scenario could say, "J performs one day earlier than R," and then J would be to the left of R by one day.

So, are there exceptions? Yes, when the test makers reference "higher" or "lower" numbered situations. In those situations, the lower numbers are on the left, and the higher numbers are on the right:

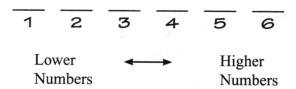

The use of "lower-numbered" and "higher-numbered" in LSAT rules can be challenging because "lower" seems equivalent in meaning to "later" and "after," and "higher" seems equivalent in meaning to "earlier" and "before." However, the "lower" and "higher" refer to actual numerical value, and under that construct, 1 is lower than 2, 2 is lower than 3, etc. When the spaces are not numbered, the relationships become contextual. For example, bases that are listed as days or months use the natural order of those sets, which is typically the same as a regular numbered set. For example, with a days-of-the-week base, the following holds true:

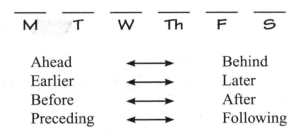

But, the context of the variable set can affect the nature of the relationships. For example, when grades are used as the base, grades listed to the left are "higher" or "better:"

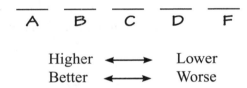

The guiding principle is that you should always carefully scrutinize the variable set, and the language used by the test makers to convey the relationships between variables. That language will tell you how to interpret each rule.

Blocks

Basic blocks
indicate
adjacency.

In Linear games, blocks reflect the idea of a fixed spatial relationship between variables. Blocks represent variables that are next to one another, not next to one another, or separated by a fixed number of spaces. The most basic block indicates that two variables are adjoining, as shown by the following rule:

Y is tutored during the hour immediately before Z is tutored.

This rule should be diagrammed using the block notation:

In Linear games,
the "front" or
"first" slot is
typically on the
left hand side.
Thus, the variable
that is at the
front or "ahead,"
will be to the left
of other variables.

In the representation, Y is immediately to the left of Z because the "hour immediately before" is always to the left on our diagram. Furthermore, since Y is always ahead of Z, Z can never be first and therefore a Z Not Law should be placed under the first slot, as indicated below. And, since Z is always behind Y, Y can never be last, and a Y Not Law should be placed under the last slot (using the example on page 48, it is the sixth slot):

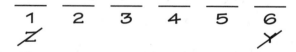

The block created here is just one example of a block. There are many other types of blocks, as will be shown in the next sections.

Split-Blocks

A split-block indicates that the variables are separated by a fixed number of spaces, as shown by this rule:

D is inspected two days before E is inspected.

The rule should be diagrammed as $\boxed{\text{D} \underline{} \text{E}}$ (Even though D is inspected two days before E, that means that there is exactly one day between D and E). As in the previous rule, Not Laws can again be drawn based on the restrictions created by the rule:

3

$$\begin{array}{cccccc} \underline{} & \underline{} & \underline{} & \underline{} & \underline{} & \underline{} \\ 1 & 2 & 3 & 4 & 5 & 6 \\ \cancel{E} & \cancel{E} & & & \cancel{D} & \cancel{D} \end{array}$$

Note that in the linear stream, day 1 is "before" day 2, and day 2 is before day 3, and so on.

The language used by the test makers to indicate the presence of a split-block can be confusing, and you must pay close attention to wording used. Here are three of the most frequently used language constructions in split-block rules:

1. Spaces Ahead or Spaces Before

   When the phrase "spaces ahead" or one of its synonyms appears, count the spaces *from* one variable to the other. Consider again the rule from the prior example:

   D is inspected exactly two days before E is inspected.

   The phrase "two days before" indicates the presence of a split-block. In this instance, D is established as being ahead of E, by exactly two days. Starting from E, count forward (to the left):

$$\underline{} \quad \text{E}$$

$$\uparrow$$

1 day before

Then:

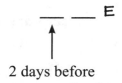

2 days before

Resulting in the final block representation:

Note that during the test you would not physically draw out each step; we do this simply to illustrate the mental process you would go through.

2. Spaces Behind or Spaces After

With this wording, simply reverse the process given above. For example, consider the following rule:

F marches exactly three groups behind G.

The phrase "three groups behind" indicates the presence of a split-block. In this instance, F is established as being behind G (that is, to the right of G), by exactly three groups. Starting from G, count to the right:

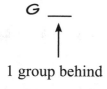

1 group behind

Then:

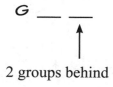

2 groups behind

Note that "spaces ahead" and "spaces behind" can be attacked in the same way. For example, in the "spaces behind" example to the right (where the "spaces" are represented by "groups"), the rule could have been viewed as stating that G was 3 groups ahead of F. In both cases the diagram is identical.

And finally:

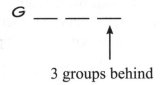

3 groups behind

Resulting in the final block representation:

The diagrams here are presented horizontally, but they could just have easily been presented vertically.

3. Spaces Between or Spaces Separated By

With the phrase "spaces between" or any synonymous phrase, simply put that exact number of spaces between the two variables. Consider the following rule:

> There are exactly three spaces between L and M, and M is examined before L.

The phrase "three spaces between" indicates the presence of a split-block. In this instance, M is established as being ahead of L, with exactly three examinations between them. Diagram as follows:

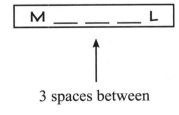

3 spaces between

Always read carefully—the test makers will place wrong answers that will check to see if you correctly interpreted the wording of a split-block rule (for example, did you see the "between," or did you misinterpret it as "before" or "after"?).

Rotating Blocks

The previous blocks all addressed fixed relationships in which the order of the variables was known. Rotating blocks present an extra consideration: the order of the variables is not given. For example, consider the following rule:

S and T are displayed on consecutive days.

Rotating blocks require special attention because the two options are easy to forget under the time pressure of the test.

This rule establishes two possibilities:

and

For the sake of absolute clarity, we prefer to write out both possibilities when diagramming this rule, as follows:

We use this representation because during the time pressure of the test it is easy to forget the exact meaning of the rule or get confused if you do not have it diagrammed in an easy-to-read fashion. If you are striving for the fastest rule representation possible, diagram rotating blocks with a circle:

The circle is meant to convey the idea that the two variables can "go back and forth." Throughout this book, however, we will typically diagram rotating blocks by showing both options in block form in order to reinforce the idea of multiple possibilities.

Rotating Split-blocks

Rotating split-blocks can typically be diagrammed in more compact form than regular rotating blocks. Consider the following split-block rule:

> There are two days between the day Q is inspected and the day R
> is inspected.

In this case, the rule specifies that there must be two days between Q and R, but it does not specify whether Q or R is inspected first. Thus, there are two possible configurations for Q and R:

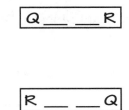

and

However, we can diagram this rule in more compact form:

The "/" notation indicates that there are two options for that space of the block. And, it is no mistake that the first option is Q/R and that the second option is R/Q. This notation allows for an efficient representation of both possibilities:

The option represented by the variables before the slash, which is:

and

The option represented by the variables after the slash, which is:

Not-blocks™

In Linear games,
blocks tend to
be much more
useful than not-
blocks since the
placement of
blocks is always a
concern, whereas
not-blocks only
come into play
once one of the
variables has
been placed.

Not-blocks, or negative blocks, indicate that variables cannot be next to one another, or cannot be separated by a fixed amount of space. Consider the following rule:

Q is not inspected the day before R is inspected.

This rule should be diagrammed with a slash over the block, as in , which means that Q can never appear in the slot before R. Interestingly, no Not Laws can be drawn from this rule until either Q or R is placed into the setup by another rule or by one of the questions.

Not-blocks can also appear with split-blocks. For example:

D is not inspected exactly two days before E is inspected.

This rule would be diagrammed as:

$$\boxed{D \;\;/\;\; E}$$

Always read the
rules carefully
to make sure
you do not miss
the word "not."
The presence
of the word
"not" typically
produces an
opposite diagram
from rules that
do not contain
the word "not."

Verticality and Horizontality in Blocks

Once you decide to diagram a game horizontally or vertically, make sure your blocks properly reflect the orientation of the setup. As we have seen, in horizontal setups a block such as Q R indicates adjacency. But in a vertical setup, a block diagrammed the same way would indicate similarity or overlap, that is, the variables would both be placed in the same slot:

Q R

1 ____

2 ____

3 ____

4 ____

5 ____

6 ____

In the diagram above, the QR block indicates that Q and R will both be on the same day, not adjoining days. To indicate that Q is placed the day before R in the above diagram, the block should be diagrammed as:

Q
R

This block is known as a vertical block. Again, Not Laws (R not in 1, Q not in 6) would follow as before.

In a horizontal setup, vertical blocks indicate identicalness or similarity:

Q
R

____ ____ ____ ____ ____ ____
1   2   3   4   5   6

In games with vertical setups, vertical blocks indicate adjacency. In games with horizontal setups, vertical blocks indicate similarity or overlap.

In the diagram above, the QR block indicates that Q and R will both be on the same day, not adjoining days. No Not Laws would follow from this block.

3. Sequencing Rules

This section is only a short introduction to sequencing rules. Chapter Seven will address games based entirely on sequencing rules, and therein we will discuss the diagramming of sequencing rules in greater detail.

Sequencing rules establish the relative positioning of variables. The key to differentiating a sequencing rule from a block rule is that block rules precisely fix the variables in relation to each other (for example, one space ahead, or two spaces in between) and sequencing rules do not. For example, a rule might state that:

Q is inspected before R is inspected.

To represent sequential relationships, we use a straight line between the two variables, and thus we diagram this rule as Q ——— R.

When we use the " ——— " symbol, we consider it to be a relative positioning indicator, not an absolute distance or value indicator. Thus, "A ——— B" indicates that A is to the left of B in a horizontal diagram, no more and no less. The distance between the two variables could be no spaces, one space, or up to the maximum allowed in the game. It's a relative indicator, and thus the position of the two variables is not fixed. In this book, we will diagram all sequential relationships with a " ——— " symbol, to reflect that the variable in front of the sign must be placed to the left of the other variable.

Returning to the Q ——— R rule, we only know that Q is inspected before R, but not by how many days. However, since Q is always inspected before R, in a diagram with six variables for six spaces, R can never be inspected first, and because R is always inspected after Q, Q can never be inspected last. Thus, the following Not Laws result:

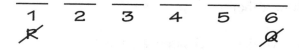

If the rule stated that:

Q is inspected before R is inspected but after H is inspected.

The diagram for the rule would be H ——— Q ——— R, and the following Not Laws would result:

$$\overline{\underset{\substack{\cancel{R}\\\cancel{Q}}}{1}} \quad \overline{\underset{\cancel{R}}{2}} \quad \overline{3} \quad \overline{4} \quad \overline{\underset{\cancel{H}}{5}} \quad \overline{\underset{\substack{\cancel{H}\\\cancel{Q}}}{6}}$$

On occasion, a rule such as the following will appear:

H and Q are both inspected before R is inspected.

This rule should be diagrammed as:

This representation is known as a Double-Branched Sequence. The two separate lines—one to H and one to Q—functionally indicate that H and Q do not have a direct relationship with each other. Visually, the lines create two "branches," one involving H, and one involving Q. The multiple lines serve as a reminder that the relationship between H and Q is uncertain: H may be inspected before Q, Q may be inspected before H (or, if more than one variable can be placed in a space, H and Q may be inspected at exactly the same time). The only known relationship is that both H and Q must be inspected before R. From this sequence several Not Laws result in a one-to-one relationship game:

$$\overline{\underset{\cancel{R}}{1}} \quad \overline{\underset{\cancel{R}}{2}} \quad \overline{3} \quad \overline{4} \quad \overline{5} \quad \overline{\underset{\substack{\cancel{H}\\\cancel{Q}}}{6}}$$

In the above diagram, R cannot be placed either first or second because there must be room for H and Q, and neither H nor Q can be placed sixth, since there must be room for R.

Three variables linked in a sequence such as the one to the left will always yield six Not Laws.

Within the Logic Games Bible we often use proprietary terms (e.g. "Not Law") to represent various concepts and techniques. The terms are used as simple shorthand to represent complex ideas (for example, imagine how much more work you would have to do if every time you wanted to reference the idea of a "car" you had to describe exactly what a car does and how it works).

You are not required to memorize the terms we use, but a working knowledge of their meaning will allow you to gain more value from this book. What is most important, however, is that you understand the concept that underlies each term, because these concepts appear on many of the LSAT games you will encounter.

3

The following rule also produces a Branched Sequence:

A is inspected before B, C, and D are inspected.

This Triple-Branched Sequence should be diagrammed as:

In this representation, the three lines create three separate branches, one for B, one for C, and one for D. Again, we cannot ascertain the exact relationship between B, C, and D other than to say that all three are inspected after A is inspected.

From this sequential rule several Not Laws result in the typical one-to-one relationship game:

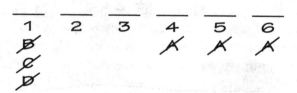

Although this short section only addresses sequential rules, do not forget that the test makers can combine rules. For example, a block can be combined with a sequential rule:

F is displayed immediately prior to G, and G is displayed at some point before I.

This rule should be diagrammed as:

FG — I

The following Not Laws would result from the rule:

In Chapter Seven, we will discuss sequencing rules in more depth.

4. Conditional Rules

The final type of Linear game rule is the most complex. Conditional reasoning is a fundamental component of both the Logical Reasoning and Logic Games sections of the LSAT, and thus you will encounter it frequently on the test. In the Logic Games section, conditional rules appear most often in Grouping games, and thus we will also discuss conditional reasoning in the Grouping chapter. However, because basic conditional rules appear frequently in Linear games, we will begin our discussion here. Let us start with a broad discussion of conditionality, one not directly linked to Logic Games.

Conditional reasoning involves sufficient and necessary conditions. These are elements that you may not have heard by name, but that you are actually familiar with from everyday use. For example, conditional statements are often brought up using the "if...then" construction. So, let's start by first defining what the conditions mean from a logical standpoint:

> A sufficient condition can be defined as an event or circumstance whose occurrence indicates that a necessary condition must also occur.

> A necessary condition can be defined as an event or circumstance whose occurrence is required in order for a sufficient condition to occur.

That's quite a mouthful, so let's try that in English! In other words, if a sufficient condition occurs, you automatically know that the necessary condition also occurs, *every time*. If a necessary condition occurs, then it is *possible* that the sufficient condition will occur, but not certain.

The PowerScore LSAT Logical Reasoning Bible has an extensive discussion of conditional reasoning as it applies to the Logical Reasoning section of the LSAT.

Let us see how that works in practice, using the following statement:

If a person gets an A+ on a test, then he or she must have studied.

If the above statement is true, then anyone who receives an A+ on a test must have studied. Because getting an A+ *automatically* indicates that studying must have occurred, "get an A+" is the sufficient condition, and it follows that "must have studied" is the necessary condition.

To make working with this relationship easier, we can reduce the sentence above to a basic diagram that involves the use of an arrow. In the diagram of a conditional statement, the sufficient condition always comes at the "beginning" of the arrow, and the necessary condition always comes at the "end" of the arrow. Instead of writing each condition out in detail, we symbolize each condition with words or initials. Thus, in this example the two conditions can be symbolized as follows:

A+ = get an A+ on a test

Study = must have studied

Then, we use those symbolizations in an arrow diagram, with "A+" at the beginning of the arrow because it is the sufficient condition:

Sufficient	Necessary
A+ ⟶	Study

Working with this symbolization is easy: anytime the condition at the beginning of the arrow is met, then you also know that the condition at the end of the arrow will be met, without exception (thus, once the condition at the start of the arrow is met, you "travel" down the arrow to the other condition). So, for example, if Joaquin received an A+ in a class and the above conditional statement was in force, then we would also know that Joaquin must have studied as well.

Although the above example may seem relatively easy, the makers of the LSAT often use conditional reasoning to ensnare unwary test takers, primarily because it is easy to draw invalid statements from conditional statements. Let us first look at some statements that can be possibly drawn from our example, and then afterwards examine the conditional relationship in more detail.

Taking the original statement as true:

> True: If a person gets an A+ on a test, then he or she must have studied.

Sufficient		Necessary
A+	$\longrightarrow$	Study

Let us now consider four separate statements. Two of the four statements that follow are invalid, and two of the four statements are valid. Can you tell which two are valid?):

1. John received an A+ on the test, so he studied for the test.

2. John studied for the test, so he must have received an A+ on the test.

3. John did not receive an A+ on the test, so he must not have studied for the test.

4. John did not study for the test, so he must not have received an A+ on the test.

Statement 1 is *valid*. If receiving an A+ is the sufficient condition, and John received an A+, then according to the original statement John must have also studied. Because this statement follows the original form of the conditional relationship, it is known as a Restatement, and would appear as follows when diagrammed:

Sufficient		Necessary
$A+_J$	$\longrightarrow$	$Study_J$

The subscript J above stands for "John."

Statement 2 is *invalid*. Just because John studied for the test does not mean he actually received an A+. He may have only received a B, or perhaps he even failed. This error is referred to as a Mistaken Reversal™, because it appears to have reversed the terms of the original diagram:

<u>Sufficient</u>   <u>Necessary</u>

Study$_J$ $\longrightarrow$ A+$_J$

The reason this is flawed (that is, that this statement cannot be known to be undeniably true based on the original statement alone), is that just because the original necessary condition occurs does not mean that the sufficient condition must also occur. Therefore, when John studied for the test, there was no way to know if he received an A+.

Statement 3 is also *invalid*. Just because John did not receive an A+ does not mean he did not study. He may have studied but did not happen to receive an A+. Perhaps he received a B instead. This error is referred to as a Mistaken Negation™, because it appears to have negated the terms of the original diagram:

<u>Sufficient</u>   <u>Necessary</u>

A̶+̶$_J$ $\longrightarrow$ S̶t̶u̶d̶y̶$_J$

The reason this is flawed (again, that is that this statement cannot be known to be undeniably true based on the original statement alone), is that just because the sufficient condition does not occur does not mean that the necessary condition did not also occur.

A contrapositive denies the necessary condition, thereby making it impossible for the sufficient condition to occur. Contrapositives can often yield important insights into a game.

Statement 4 is *valid*. If, in the original statement, studying is the necessary condition for getting an A+, and John did not study, then according to the original statement there is no way John could have received an A+. This inference is known as the contrapositive, and diagrammatically, you can see that when the necessary condition fails to occur, then the sufficient condition cannot occur:

<u>Sufficient</u>   <u>Necessary</u>

S̶t̶u̶d̶y̶$_J$ $\longrightarrow$ A̶+̶$_J$

The form here takes the original terms, and then reverses *and* negates the Study and A+ elements. When you are looking to find the contrapositive, do not think about the elements and what they represent. Instead, simply reverse and negate the two terms.

There is a contrapositive for every conditional statement, and if the initial statement is true, then the contrapositive is also true. The contrapositive is simply a different way of expressing the initial statement. To analogize, it is like examining a penny: both sides look different but intrinsically the value is the same.

Because the contrapositive both reverses and negates, it is a combination of a Mistaken Reversal and Mistaken Negation. Since the contrapositive is valid, it is as if two wrongs do make a right.

Understanding Conditional Statements

Let us expand on some of the ideas in the previous section.

At first glance, conditional statements appear to be easy to work with, but as you may have seen from the four statements, they can be tricky. This is especially highlighted by the fact that the original statement we used involved grades and studying, two concepts that every LSAT taker is familiar with from school. When the conditions involve more abstract elements—such as the variables in a Logic Game—properly understanding and manipulating the conditions gets even more challenging.

Let us take another look at the conditional relationship, with an eye towards understanding how the concept works on the LSAT.

In one sense, a sufficient condition is an indicator: when the sufficient condition is fulfilled, it indicates that the necessary condition must also be fulfilled at some point. Simply put, if the sufficient happens, then you know without question that the necessary happens as well.

This fact means that you can set up any relationship between two variables, and as long as you accept the relationship as true (as you do when you read Logic Game rules), once the sufficient condition is fulfilled you *must* also have the necessary condition. For example, consider these rules that are then paired with known facts:

The parameters of conditional reasoning allow the necessary condition to be filled before, during, or even after the sufficient condition is fulfilled. For example,

Necessary occurs before: To reach the top of the building, one must climb the stairs.

Necessary occurs at same time: If I can think, then I must exist.

Necessary occurs after: If we win the war, we will have world peace.

However, in Logic Games you typically never need to worry about the time element of the relationship.

Rule: If P performs third, then R performs fourth.

Known: P performs third.

Conclusion: R performs fourth.

P performing third is the sufficient condition, and when it is known that this condition is met, then the necessary condition (R performs fourth) must also occur.

Let's look at another, similar example:

Rule: If G is not the second truck, then H is the first truck.

Known: G is not the second truck.

Conclusion: H is the first truck.

G *not* being the second truck is the sufficient condition, and when it is known that this condition is met, then the necessary condition (H is the first truck) must also occur.

So, when the sufficient condition is met, it is a signal that the necessary condition is met. But, the relationship does *not* go backwards. Let us consider why.

A necessary condition is just that—something that must occur or be true for another condition (the sufficient) to occur. The occurrence of a necessary condition tells you nothing about whether the sufficient condition has occurred, just that it *could* occur. For example, consider the following relationship:

If one is human, then one is a mammal.

In this relationship, "human" is the sufficient condition, and "mammal" is the necessary condition. Thus, if you knew someone to be human, you would automatically know he or she was also a mammal. But, consider the relationship from the other side: if you know something is a mammal, what does that tell you?

The answer is, not much really. While it could still be human, it doesn't have to be. It could be a cat, or a wolf, or an elephant, or one of the many other mammals.

Consider that thinking in the context of Logic Games:

Rule: If W speaks first, then Y speaks sixth.

Known: Y speaks sixth.

Conclusion: None. W could speak first, but does not have to
                    speak first.

Thus, while the fulfilment of a sufficient condition is a sign that the necessary condition has occurred, the fulfilment of the necessary condition alone does not signify anything other than that the sufficient condition could occur.

As previously mentioned, the error associated with thinking that the occurrence of a necessary condition automatically means that the sufficient condition has occurred is called a Mistaken Reversal. Mistaken Reversals are very dangerous on the LSAT, and you must make sure to avoid making them at all times.

While fulfilling the necessary condition doesn't make the sufficient condition happen, if the necessary condition does *not* occur, then the sufficient condition also cannot occur. Consider again the mammal example:

If something is human, then it is a mammal.

If you can definitively say that something is not a mammal, then you would also know that it could not be human. As mentioned previously, this is the contrapositive, which is a powerful inference that is present in *all* conditional statements. Consider the following example:

Rule: If M is the fifth session, then O is the third session.

Known: O is not the third session.

Conclusion: M is not the fifth session.

This is a powerful insight into the workings of the rule, and would likely be tested during the game.

Identifying Conditional Statements

One of the confusing elements in recognizing conditional statements is that so many different terms can be used to introduce sufficient or necessary conditions. Consider the following statements:

    1. To get an A+ you must study.

    2. Studying is necessary to get an A+.

    3. When someone gets an A+, it shows they must have studied.

    4. Only someone who studies can get an A+.

    5. Unless you study, you cannot get an A+.

    6. You will get an A+ only if you study.

Take a moment to examine the above statements. Interestingly, each of the statements would be diagrammed exactly the same way:

It is essential that you be able to recognize the many terms that identify and precede sufficient and necessary conditions. In Logic Games, the test makers typically use the following terms:

To introduce a sufficient condition:	To introduce a necessary condition:
If	Then
When	Only
Whenever	Only if
Every	Must
All	Required/Precondition
Any	Unless
People who	Except
In order to	Until
	Without

Thus, many of the Logic Game rules that you see can be quickly diagrammed by recognizing these words, and the role they play.

Using the words from the indicator lists, let's re-examine each of the six statements on the previous page. In each sentence, the conditional indicator is in italics:

1. To get an A+ you *must* study.

2. Studying is *necessary* to get an A+.

3. *When* someone gets an A+, it shows they *must* have studied.

4. *Only* someone who studies can get an A+.

5. *Unless* you study, you *cannot* get an A+.

6. You will get an A+ *only if* you study.

Comparing the six sentences reveals two critical rules about how conditional reasoning appears in a given sentence:

1. Either condition can appear first in the sentence.

   The order of presentation of the sufficient and necessary conditions is irrelevant. In statements 1, 3, and 6 the sufficient condition appears first in the sentence; in statements 2, 4, and 5 the necessary condition appears first. Thus, when you are reading, you cannot rely on encountering the sufficient condition first, and instead you must keep an eye out for conditional indicators.

2. A sentence can have one or two indicators.

   Sentences do not need both a sufficient condition indicator and a necessary condition indicator in order to have conditional reasoning present. As shown by statements 1, 2, 4, and 6, a single indicator is enough. Note that once you have established that one of the conditions is present, you can examine the remainder of the sentence to determine the nature of the other condition. For example, in statement 6, once the "only if" appears and you establish that "study" is the necessary condition, return to the first part of the sentence and establish that "A+" is the sufficient condition.

The Unless Equation™

In the case of "unless" (and its analogues "except," "until," and "without"), a special two-step process called the Unless Equation is applied to the diagram:

1. Whatever term is modified by "unless," "except," "until," or "without" becomes the necessary condition.

2. The remaining term is negated and becomes the sufficient condition.

For example, consider the following:

Unless a person studies, he or she will not receive an A+.

Since "unless" modifies "a person studies," "Study" becomes the necessary condition. The remainder, "he or she will not receive an A+," is negated by dropping the "not" and becomes "he or she will receive an A+." Thus, the sufficient condition is "A+," and the diagram is as follows:

Another way to handle terms like "unless" is to substitute the phrase "if not" for "unless." The only drawback to this method is that it tends to produce diagrams containing negatives.

Sufficient   Necessary

A+ $\longrightarrow$ Study

Here is an example in the context of the typical Logic Games rule:

S is not fourth unless T is fifth.

"Unless" modifies T is fifth, and thus T is fifth is the necessary condition. The remainder ("S is not fourth") is negated and becomes the sufficient condition:

Sufficient   Necessary

$S_4 \longrightarrow T_5$

Conditional Rules in Linear Games

When conditional reasoning is applied to Linear Logic Games, the rules often specify exact place assignments for the variables. For example:

Laron performs second only if Nancy performs sixth.

In this rule, the phrase "only if" introduces a necessary condition. Rewording the sentence may help to make the relationship clearer, "If Laron performs second then Nancy performs sixth." This rule should be diagrammed as:

$$L_2 \longrightarrow N_6$$

Thus, any game situation where Laron performed second would force Nancy to perform sixth. However, do not make the error of mistakenly reversing the relationship. That is, if Nancy performs sixth, that does not automatically mean that Laron performs second. He *could* perform second, but he does not have to perform second. The test makers will have attractive wrong answer choices ready for you if you make a Mistaken Reversal of this nature.

Of course, via the contrapositive, if Nancy does *not* perform sixth, then Laron cannot perform second:

$$\cancel{N}_6 \longrightarrow \cancel{L}_2$$

Therefore, any situation where Nancy did not perform sixth would then preclude Laron from performing second.

You must rigorously guard against reversing the terms in a conditional relationship. Unfortunately, many students make this error, and the test makers are well-prepared for this mistake with attractive wrong answer choices.

Conditional rules can also involve some of the other rule representations that we have encountered thus far, for example:

Conditionality and Blocks

Examine the following rule:

If V is displayed immediately before W, then S must be displayed third.

This rule would be diagrammed as:

$$\boxed{\text{V W}} \longrightarrow S_3$$

Conditionality and Sequencing

Consider the following rule:

If Kahlil performs first, then Martin performs at some time before Paulo.

This rule would be diagrammed as:

$$K_1 \longrightarrow M \text{---} P$$

You can also place parentheses around the sequence if you wish to make the distinction even clearer, or avoid confusion when using arrows and lines together:

$$K_1 \longrightarrow (M \text{---} P)$$

Dead vs Active Rules ▮▮▮▮▮

At times we will mention the concept of "dead" and "active" rules in our discussions. A dead rule is one that either has been fully encompassed within your diagram or that no longer needs to be actively considered when solving the questions. For example, a rule such as "X performs second" in a standard Linear game can be fully captured by placing X in the second position, thus rendering the rule effectively dead for the remainder of the game. Or, a rule stating that "Exactly one senior is assigned to each group" can be shown on a diagram by reserving a space in each group for a senior. In each instance, once the rule is properly represented on the diagram, you do not have to actively think about it since the diagram fully represents the rule's implications.

Active rules, on the other hand, must still be considered when solving questions. The majority of rules in a game tend to be active, and typically involve degrees of uncertainty that must be tracked in each question. For example, rules such the following are likely to be "active" rules as you move through the questions:

> "Farhad cannot sing the same type of song as Kwon."

> "Luz must arrive earlier than Sandrine."

> "T must be presented immediately before V is presented."

The distinction here is useful because it allows you to better prioritize and allocate your focus when attacking games. Whereas you might initially look at a game with five rules and worry about juggling all of them, if two of them are dead then you can direct your attention to the three active rules, relying on them to help you power through the questions.

Conditional Rule Satisfaction

An interesting set of "dead rule" circumstances arises when working with conditional rules where the necessary condition is known to be satisfied, or, alternately, when the sufficient condition is known to be unsatisfied.

These circumstances typically occur during the questions as other variables are placed (and thus affect the conditions mentioned above). Let's take a look at a rule that might occur in a standard 1-to-1 Basic Linear game and use it to illustrate the idea:

> "If S is placed 3rd, then T must be placed 6th."

This is the type of conditional rule that appears frequently in Linear games, and thus you should eventually be comfortable working with all aspects of the rule. First, let's show the standard rule representation:

$$S_3 \longrightarrow T_6$$

When working with this rule in a question, the result of S being placed 3rd is straightforward: T must then be placed 6th. And, via the contrapositive, if T is *not* placed 6th, then automatically S cannot be placed 3rd. Those two situations should be clear. Let's look at two other situations:

1. T is placed 6th.

    When T is 6th, we cannot assume that S is 3rd. To do so would be a Mistaken Reversal, and lead you into a trap the test makers are hoping you will fall into. So, when T is placed 6th, what is the effect on S? While we know that S is not forced into 3rd, the operating effect is that the entire rule is dead. Once the necessary condition is satisfied (T placed 6th), then anything can happen with the sufficient condition. In other words, in our example S could go in any open position (including 1st, 2nd, 3rd, 4th, etc). So, once the necessary condition occurs, you can effectively stop worrying about the rule and its effects!

2. S is *not* placed 3rd.

    When S is not placed 3rd, we cannot assume that T is *not* 6th. To assume so would be a Mistaken Negation, and would lead you into a different trap the test makers are hoping you will fall into. However, once S is placed somewhere other than 3rd, the sufficient condition is not met (and will not be met for that question), meaning T is free to move about without restriction (restriction from this particular rule, at least). Thus, once the sufficient condition does not occur, anything can happen with the necessary condition. In this case, T could be 6th, or it could be elsewhere. The sufficient condition not occurring kills the rule and frees you up to stop thinking about the rule entirely for the remainder of that question.

In abstract terms, when the necessary condition is satisfied, the rule becomes irrelevant; you can stop thinking about it because it is impossible to contradict the rule for the entirety of that question.

When the sufficient condition is *not* met, again the rule no longer matters—it has been effectively "turned off," and you can stop thinking about its impact for that question.

Now that you are familiar with some rule basics, try your hand at some rule representation drills.

Conditional Reasoning Diagramming Drill

Each of the following statements contains a sufficient condition and a necessary condition; therefore, each of the following statements can be described as a "conditional statement." In the spaces provided write the proper arrow diagram for each of the following conditional statements. Then write the proper arrow diagram for the contrapositive of each of the following conditional statements. Assume a Basic Linear 1-to-1 setup is in effect, with no ties possible. *Answers on page 77*

Example:

If R is delivered first, then X is delivered fourth.

Answer:

original diagram: $R_1 \longrightarrow X_4$

contrapositive: $\cancel{X_4} \longrightarrow \cancel{R_1}$

---

1. If R is inspected on the third day, S is not inspected on the fifth day.

    original diagram: $R_3 \longrightarrow \cancel{S_5}$

    contrapositive: $\cancel{S_5} \longrightarrow \cancel{R_3}$

2. G does not speak fourth unless Q speaks second.

    original diagram: $\cancel{G_4} \longrightarrow Q_2$

    contrapositive: $\cancel{Q_2} \longrightarrow \cancel{G_4}$

3. If F's delivery is earlier than M's, then L's delivery is earlier than H's.

    original diagram: $FM \longrightarrow LH$

    contrapositive: $\cancel{LH} \longrightarrow \cancel{FM}$

4. T dances sixth only if P dances third.

    original diagram: $T_6 \longrightarrow P_3$

    contrapositive: $\cancel{P_3} \longrightarrow \cancel{T_6}$

Conditional Reasoning Diagramming Drill

5. B swims immediately before C only if D does not swim immediately before E.

original diagram: BC ⟶ ~DE

contrapositive: ED ⟶ ~CB

6. If X arrives second, Y cannot arrive third.

original diagram: X₂ ⟶ ~Y₃

contrapositive: Y₃ ⟶ ~X₂

7. F sings immediately before K if G sings immediately after K.

original diagram: F-K ⟶ ~KG

contrapositive: KG ⟶ ~FK

8. R is published after P only if P is published fifth.

original diagram: P₅ ⟶ R

contrapositive: ~R ⟶ ~P₅

9. N does not perform first unless P performs second.

original diagram: ~P₂ ⟶ ~N

contrapositive: N ⟶ P₂

10. If J takes off later than K, it takes off immediately after K.

original diagram: KJ ⟶ K̲J̲

contrapositive: ~K̲J̲ ⟶ ~KJ

11. G cannot be cleaned until F is cleaned, unless F is cleaned second.

original diagram: ~F₂ ⟶ FG

contrapositive: GF ⟶ F₂

12. The A train cannot arrive until the C train arrives, unless it arrives immediately before the C train.

original diagram: CA ⟶ AC

contrapositive: AC ⟶ CA

Conditional Reasoning Diagramming Drill Answer Key

1. If R is inspected on the third day, S is not inspected on
    the fifth day.

    original: $R_3 \longrightarrow \cancel{S}_5$

    (If R is inspected third, then S is not inspected fifth.)

    contrapositive: $S_5 \longrightarrow \cancel{R}_3$

    (If S is inspected fifth, then R is not inspected third.)

2. G does not speak fourth unless Q speaks second.

    original: $G_4 \longrightarrow Q_2$

    (G does not speak fourth unless Q speaks second.)

    Note: "Unless" introduces the necessary condition.
          (So if G speaks fourth, then Q must speak second)

    contrapositive: $\cancel{Q}_2 \longrightarrow \cancel{G}_4$

    (If Q does not speak second, then G does not speak fourth.)

3. If F's delivery is earlier than M's, then L's delivery is
    earlier than H's.

    original: (F —— M) $\longrightarrow$ (L —— H)

    (If F —— M, then L —— H.)

    contrapositive: (H —— L) $\longrightarrow$ (M —— F)

    (If not L —— H (and so H —— L), then not F —— M (and so M —— F).)

Conditional Reasoning Diagramming Drill Answer Key

4. T dances sixth only if P dances third.

    original:

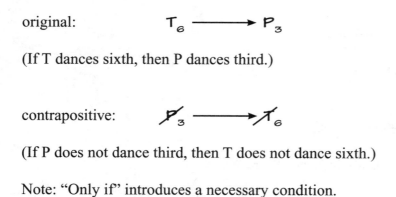

    (If T dances sixth, then P dances third.)

    contrapositive:

    (If P does not dance third, then T does not dance sixth.)

    Note: "Only if" introduces a necessary condition.

---

5. B swims immediately before C only if D does not
    swim immediately before E.

    original:

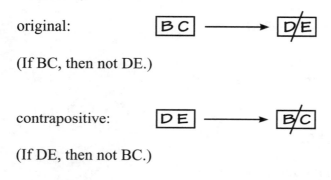

    (If BC, then not DE.)

    contrapositive:

    (If DE, then not BC.)

    Note: "Only if" introduces a necessary condition.

As you may have noticed in the mini-drill, the contrapositive can yield some interesting insights into the relationship between the variables. You should always be on the lookout for conditional statements in Logic Games, and when you identify them, be sure to consider the implications of the contrapositive. We will discuss conditional reasoning and the contrapositive in further detail in the chapter on Grouping games.

Conditional Reasoning Diagramming Drill Answer Key

6. If X arrives second, Y cannot arrive third.

   original: $X_2 \longrightarrow \cancel{Y}_3$

   (If X arrives second, then Y does not arrive third.)

   contrapositive: $Y_3 \longrightarrow \cancel{X}_2$

   (If Y arrives third, then X does not arrive second.)

---

7. F sings immediately before K if G sings immediately
   after K.

   original:

   (If G sings immediately after K, then F sings immediately before K (which consequently
   forms an FKG block).)

   contrapositive:

   (If F does not sing immediately before K, then G does not sing immediately after K.)

---

8. R is published after P only if P is published fifth.

   original: $(P \rule{1em}{0.4pt} R) \longrightarrow P_5$

   (If R is published after P, then P is published fifth.)

   contrapositive: $\cancel{P}_5 \longrightarrow (R \rule{1em}{0.4pt} P)$

   (If P is not published fifth, then R is not published after P (and thus R must be published
   before P—remember, no ties!).)

Conditional Reasoning Diagramming Drill Answer Key

9. N does not perform first unless P performs second.

   original: $N_1 \longrightarrow P_2$

   (If N performs first, then P must perform second (forming an NP block in 1-2).)

   contrapositive: $\cancel{P}_2 \longrightarrow \cancel{N}_1$

   (If P does not perform second, then N does not perform first.)

   Note: "Unless" determines the necessary condition.

---

10. If J takes off later than K, it takes off immediately after K.

    original: $(K \longrightarrow J) \longrightarrow \boxed{KJ}$

    (If J takes off later than K, then J takes off immediately after K (forming a KJ block).)

    contrapositive: $\cancel{\boxed{KJ}} \longrightarrow (J \longrightarrow K)$

    (If J does not take off immediately after K, then J does not take off after K (and thus J must take off before K—remember, no ties).)

    Note: In a typical linear setup of, for instance, 7 total spaces, this rule produces important inferences at the end points:

    $J_7 \longrightarrow K_6$

    $K_1 \longrightarrow J_2$

11. G cannot be cleaned until F is cleaned, unless F is
    cleaned second.

original: $(G \text{ ---- } F) \longrightarrow F_2$

(If G is cleaned before F, then F is cleaned second.)

contrapositive: $\cancel{F}_2 \longrightarrow (F \text{ ---- } G)$

(If F is not cleaned second, then F is not cleaned after G (and thus F is cleaned before G—
remember, no ties).)

Note: This rule produces the following inference:

$$G_1 \longrightarrow F_2$$

Also, if G is cleaned second, then clearly F is not cleaned second. By the contrapositive
(above), F must be cleaned before G. Therefore, F must be cleaned first:

$$G_2 \longrightarrow F_1$$

---

12. The A train cannot arrive until the C train arrives,
    unless it arrives immediately before the C train.

original: $(A \text{ ---- } C) \longrightarrow \boxed{A\ C}$

(If the A train arrives before the C train, then it must arrive immediately before the C train
(creating an AC block).)

contrapositive: $\cancel{\boxed{A C}} \longrightarrow (C \text{ ---- } A)$

(If the A train does not arrive immediately before the C train, then the A train does not arrive
before the C train (and thus the C train arrives before the A train since there are no ties).)

Linear Games Rule Diagramming Drill

In the space provided, supply the best symbolic representation (if any) of each of the following rules. If applicable, show any corresponding implications (Not Laws, dual-options, etc.) on the linear diagram provided. Assume a one-to-one relationship for each item, with no ties possible. *Answers on page 84*

1. G is recorded earlier than H.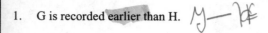

recording positions = __1__ __2__ __3__ __4__ __5__ __6__

2. Z is selected during one of the first two days.

days = __1__ __2__ __3__ __4__ __5__ __6__

3. C must sit 4 chairs behind D, and E must sit 3 chairs before C.

chairs = __1__ __2__ __3__ __4__ __5__ __6__

4. Either S or T must speak on the third day.

days = __1__ __2__ __3__ __4__ __5__ __6__

5. Tom can sit neither immediately before nor immediately after Pat.

seats = __1__ __2__ __3__ __4__ __5__ __6__

THE POWERSCORE LSAT LOGIC GAMES BIBLE

Linear Games Rule Diagramming Drill

6. If J is performed fourth, K is performed sixth.

$$\text{performances} = \frac{}{1} \quad \frac{}{2} \quad \frac{}{3} \quad \frac{\cancel{J}}{4} \quad \frac{}{5} \quad \frac{\cancel{K}}{6}$$

7. A is not shorter than B.

$$\text{height (tallest first)} = \frac{}{1} \quad \frac{}{2} \quad \frac{}{3} \quad \frac{}{4} \quad \frac{}{5} \quad \frac{}{6}$$

8. If A sits next to B, then B does not sit next to C.

$$\text{seats} = \frac{}{1} \quad \frac{}{2} \quad \frac{}{3} \quad \frac{}{4} \quad \frac{}{5} \quad \frac{}{6}$$

9. Y is inspected before both X and Z are inspected.

$$\text{inspections} = \frac{}{1} \quad \frac{}{2} \quad \frac{}{3} \quad \frac{}{4} \quad \frac{}{5} \quad \frac{}{6}$$

10. M and T must be performed on consecutive days.

$$\text{days} = \frac{}{1} \quad \frac{}{2} \quad \frac{}{3} \quad \frac{}{4} \quad \frac{}{5} \quad \frac{}{6}$$

1.   G is recorded earlier than H.

Rule diagram: G ——— H

Diagram inferences:

recording positions = $\overline{\underset{\cancel{H}}{1}}$ $\overline{2}$ $\overline{3}$ $\overline{4}$ $\overline{5}$ $\overline{\underset{\cancel{G}}{6}}$

Because G is always recorded earlier than H, G can never be recorded last and H can never be recorded first.

---

2.   Z is selected during one of the first two days.

Rule diagram: Z ———⟶ 1 or 2

The rule is shown in conditional fashion since Z must always be selected during the first two days.

Diagram inferences:

days = $\overset{Z/}{\overline{1}}$ $\overset{/Z}{\overline{2}}$ $\overline{\underset{\cancel{Z}}{3}}$ $\overline{\underset{\cancel{Z}}{4}}$ $\overline{\underset{\cancel{Z}}{5}}$ $\overline{\underset{\cancel{Z}}{6}}$

Because Z must always be selected first or second, Z can never be selected for days 3, 4, 5, or 6.

3. C must sit 4 chairs behind D, and E must sit 3 chairs
    before C.

Rule diagram:

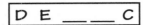

Diagram inferences:

Due to the size of the block, it can only be placed in two different positions: 1-5 or 2-6. The
best strategy from here would be to show those two possibilities (or templates):

	D	E			C	
Template #2:						
Template #1:	D	E			C	
chairs =	1	2	3	4	5	6
	C̸	C̸	C̸	C̸	E̸	E̸
	E̸		D̸	E̸	D̸	D̸
				D̸		

The two templates alone would be sufficient to move forward in the game. Thus, the Not
Laws above are shown for information purposes as drawing them out during the game would
be wasteful. More on templates will be presented later in the book.

---

4. Either S or T must speak on the third day.

Rule diagram: 3 ⟶ S/T

Diagram inferences:

			S/T			
days =	1	2	3	4	5	6

5. Tom can sit neither immediately before nor immediately after Pat.

Rule diagram:

Diagram inferences:

None. No Not Laws or variable placements can be drawn from this rule.

6. If J is performed fourth, K is performed sixth.

Rule diagram: J₄ ⟶ K₆

Contrapositive: K̶₆ ⟶ J̶₄

Diagram inferences:

None. No Not Laws or variable placements can be drawn from this rule.

7. A is not shorter than B.

Rule diagram: A —— B

If this was *not* a one-to-one relationship, this would be a trick question with no Not Laws, and a diagram of A ══ B (the two lines indicate that the variables *can* be equal; if the variables are known to be equal, then a vertical block would be used). However, according to the rule, A is *not* shorter than B, which means A is either taller than B, or A is the same height as B. In a one-to-one relationship where each variable completely fills a single space, A and B cannot be the same height, and thus you can infer that B is not first and A is not last, and the proper diagram for this rule is A —— B.

Diagram inferences:

height (tallest first) =
$$\overline{\underset{\cancel{B}}{1}} \quad \overline{2} \quad \overline{3} \quad \overline{4} \quad \overline{5} \quad \overline{\underset{\cancel{A}}{6}}$$

Because A is taller than B, A can never be last and B can never be first.

---

8. If A sits next to B, then B does not sit next to C.

Rule diagram:

Most students diagram this rule as: **AB ⟶ B̸C**. This is *not* incorrect, it is just less efficient! The application of the rule reveals that you can *never* have ABC or CBA in a row, and thus the optimal rule diagram shows those two impossible outcomes as not-blocks. Note, however, that ACB, BCA, BAC, and CAB are still possible. Again, no Not Laws can be drawn.

If you represented the rule in conditional form, that representation requires more work than the diagram we have chosen above. The conditional form shows the individual pieces of the rule whereas our diagram shows the full consequences of the statement.

Diagram inferences:

None. No Not Laws or variable placements can be drawn from this rule.

9. Y is inspected before both X and Z are inspected.

    Rule diagram:

    Diagram inferences:

    inspections =

1	2	3	4	5	6
X̸ Z̸				Y̸	Y̸

    Because Y must be inspected before both X and Z, Y can never be inspected on day 5 or 6, and neither X nor Z can be inspected on day 1.

10. M and T must be performed on consecutive days.

    Rule diagram:

M	T

T	M

    Diagram inferences:

    None. No Not Laws or variable placements can be drawn from this rule.

    Final Note: In most cases not-blocks and rotating blocks do not allow you to make initial inferences. However, once other rules are added to the blocks, inferences often follow.

Internal versus External Diagramming

Up to this point we have focused on creating efficient and useful representations of the rules. Before moving on to a discussion of making inferences, let's examine one additional rule diagramming consideration.

Many rules are automatically diagrammed in "external" fashion, that is, away from or off to the side of the part of the diagram that contains the slots or spaces. Certain rules are diagrammed "internally," that is, directly on the part of the diagram that contains the slots or spaces. For example, consider the following rule:

> R cannot be inspected first.

This rule is best represented with a Not Law underneath the first slot:

$$\frac{\quad}{1} \quad \frac{\quad}{2} \quad \frac{\quad}{3} \quad \frac{\quad}{4} \quad \frac{\quad}{5} \quad \frac{\quad}{6}$$
$$\not{R}$$

This is considered an internally diagrammed rule because the representation is immediately next to or within the slots. Other rules, such as dual-options, are also best represented directly on the diagram.

Some rules, of course, cannot be diagrammed internally. A rule stating that, "When X is third then Y is sixth" must be separated from the slots and diagrammed off to the side because this rule only comes into play in certain instances.

The general rule is that if you can represent a rule efficiently within the slotted part of the diagram, then do so. Diagramming the rule internally gives you a powerful visual reminder of the presence of the rule and lowers the chances that you will forget that rule. Consider the following situation:

> Three speakers—F, G, and H—give six consecutive one-hour speeches, two speeches per speaker. Exactly one speaker speaks during each hour.
>> The speaker that gives the first speech must also give the second speech.

Most students, when faced with this scenario, would create a setup similar to the following:

F F G G H H [6]

1 ——→ 2   ___ ___ ___ ___ ___ ___
            1   2   3   4   5   6

This external rule representation, while perfectly reasonable, does not have the same visual power as an internally diagrammed representation. At the least, the rule should also be represented directly on the diagram:

F F G G H H [6]

1 ——→ 2   ___ ___ ___ ___ ___ ___
            1→ 2   3   4   5   6

This "internal" representation assures that you will never forget that rule, and it will make your analysis process during the questions faster and more compact.

Of course, if you further consider the nature of this game, since all six spaces must be filled and the speaker that gives the first speech must also give the second speech, you can infer that the first and second speakers must always be the same. This could be shown on the diagram in even more powerful fashion as a block:

F F G G H H [6]

1 ——→ 2   [1   2] ___ ___ ___ ___
                        3   4   5   6

This representation would assure that any time you assigned the first or second speech you would automatically assign the other speech as well.

As we move forward, you will see other instances where rules are diagrammed internally. Keep in mind that although not all rules can be diagrammed in this manner, you will gain speed and accuracy advantages when you recognize the correct situations to diagram this way.

Note that this is an unusual but valid reversal of the conditional rule given in the scenario. Conditional rules do not normally reverse in this manner, but the circumstances in this scenario allow you to infer that the first two speakers must be the same. If you are wondering why this works, think about the contrapositive and the limited number of speakers available, as well as the fact that all speech slots must be assigned.

Making Inferences ▬▬▬

Inferences are relationships that must be true in a game but are not explicitly stated by the rules or game scenario. One of the keys to powerful games performance is making inferences after you have diagrammed all of the rules. In some games, a single inference can be the difference between the game seeming easy or difficult. For some people inference making is intuitive, and for others it is very difficult. Here are three basic but time-tested strategies for making inferences:

1. Linkage

Linkage is the simplest and most basic way to make inferences. Linkage involves finding a variable that appears in at least two rules and then combining those two rules. Often that combination will produce an inference of value. Consider the following two rules:

> K must be played before L.
> L must be played before M.

Individually the two rules would be diagrammed as follows:

$$K — L$$
$$L — M$$

If we represented Not Laws from each rule, we would have the following:

Clearly, "L" is common to both rules. By combining the rules we come up with the following relationship:

$$K — L — M$$

Linkage should always be the first step you take to make inferences.

Three variables in a sequence similar to the one to the left always yield 6 Not Laws.

We can now infer that K must be played before M, and this information helps us to establish all of the applicable Not Laws:

Linkage between the rules should always be the first place you look to discover inferences. Incidentally, the above example again proves the value of reading all of the rules before you begin diagramming. If you had diagrammed each rule individually, then later discovered the linkage, you would then have had to return to the two rules and diagram the additional implications of the linkage. That would be an inefficient approach and thus detract from your performance.

Here is another example featuring linkage:

> If Q is displayed fourth, then R must be displayed first.
> R and S are displayed consecutively.

These examples of linkage all relate to Linear games. Other linkage examples will appear in the chapters devoted to other game types.

Individually the two rules would be diagrammed as follows:

$$Q4 \longrightarrow R1$$

$$\boxed{R\ S} \atop \boxed{S\ R}$$

However, if R is first, then according to the second rule S must be second, which should be written as:

$$Q4 \longrightarrow R1, S2$$

Thus, combining the two rules leads to the further inference that S must be second when Q is fourth. Although this cannot be represented directly on the diagram, this relationship can and should be displayed as above, as an addition to the original representation of the first rule.

Here is a final example featuring linkage:

> W and X cannot speak consecutively.
> X must speak third or fifth.

Individually the two rules would be diagrammed as follows:

Although these three examples each feature linkage between two rules, there are situations that arise where three rules are linked.

$$\boxed{\begin{array}{|c|}\hline W/X \\ \hline X/W \\ \hline \end{array}}$$

$$\underline{}_{1} \quad \underline{}_{2} \quad \underline{X/}_{3} \quad \underline{}_{4} \quad \underline{/X}_{5} \quad \underline{}_{6}$$

At first, it may appear that linking the two rules yields no inference, but if X is always third or fifth, then W can never be placed fourth (to do so would cause a violation regardless of whether X was third or fifth). This leads to a W Not Law on 4:

$$\underline{}_{1} \quad \underline{}_{2} \quad \underline{X/}_{3} \quad \underline{}_{4} \quad \underline{/X}_{5} \quad \underline{}_{6}$$
$$\text{\sout{W}}$$

2. Rule Combinations

As we study more and more game types, your arsenal of rule recognition skills will increase. In certain games, there are classic combinations which always yield certain inferences. In contrast to linkage, however, making inferences from rule combinations does not rely upon the connection of a variable common to two or more rules. For example, consider this scenario:

> Six lawyers—H, J, K, L, M, and O—must speak at a convention. The six speeches are delivered one at a time, consecutively, according to the following restrictions:
> K and L must speak consecutively.
> O must speak fifth.

From the scenario and rules above, we can draw the following diagram:

HJKLMO⁶

| KL |
| LK |

___	___	___	___	O	___
1	2	3	4	5	6
					K̸
					L̸

Because of the interaction of the two rules, we can infer that K and L can never speak sixth (there is not enough room for K and L to be next to each other). In addition, because O must speak fifth, only H, J, and M remain as possible candidates to speak sixth. This could be shown as a triple-option (H/J/M):

HJKLMO⁶

| KL |
| LK |

___	___	___	___	O	H/J/M
1	2	3	4	5	6
					K̸
					L̸

This type of rule combination is one of many we will discuss in this book.

3. Restrictions

In Logic Games always look to the restricted points for inferences. Restricted points are the areas in the game where only a few options exist—for example, a limited number of variables to fill in a slot, a block with a limited number of placement options, or a slot with a large number of Not Laws. If you can identify a restriction, generally there are inferences that will follow from your examination of that point. The trick is to determine exactly where the restrictions in a game actually occur.

Note that rule combination inferences are normally produced by a restriction that results from combining the two rules.

Consider the following example:

> A salesman must visit five families—the Browns, the Chans, the Duartes, the Egohs, and the Feinsteins—one after another, not necessarily in that order. The visits must conform to the following restrictions:
> > The Browns must be visited first or fifth.
> > The Feinsteins cannot be visited third.
> > The Chans must be visited fourth.

Using the scenario and rules above, we can produce the following diagram:

B C D E F⁵

The easiest way to find restrictions in a game is to examine the Not Laws for each slot. The slot with the most Not Laws may be so restricted that it has a limited number of possibilities. In this case, the third slot is the most restricted active slot since it has two Not Laws. Technically, the fourth slot is the most restricted since it has only one option, the Chans. But, since the fourth slot has already been filled by the Chans, it is no longer "active" and we can disregard it from further consideration. However, since the Chans have been placed, they cannot go in any other slot, and so it is now true that neither B, C, nor F can be visited third. Since there are only five families to visit and B, C, and F have been eliminated from contention, it follows that either D or E must be visited third. That inference should be shown with a D/E dual-option on the third slot:

BCDEF[5]

```
 B/  ___  D/E   C   /B
 1    2    3    4    5
      B̸    B̸    B̸
           F̸
```

Restrictions also frequently occur with blocks, especially split-blocks. Consider the following scenario:

> A child must play five games—P, Q, R, S, and T—one after another, not necessarily in that order. The games must be played according to the following conditions:
> The child plays exactly two games between playing S and playing T, whether or not S is played before T.
> P is played immediately before Q is played.

Once again, using the scenario and rules, we can produce the following initial setup:

PQRST[5]

```
┌─────────────────┐
│ S/T ___  ___ T/S │
└─────────────────┘

┌────┐          ___  ___  ___  ___  ___
│ PQ │           1    2    3    4    5
└────┘           Q̸         S̸         P̸
                            T̸
```

Blocks have a
reduced number
of spacing
options and
as such they
can play a very
powerful role in
games.

As usual, P cannot be played fifth since Q must be played behind it, and Q cannot be played first since P must always be played ahead of it. However, the S and T split-block is more interesting because it has a limited number of spacing options. In fact, the ST split-block can only be placed into positions 1-4 or 2-5. Thus, neither S nor T can be played third. At this point it appears that we have our inferences and that we are ready to continue on. But consider the interaction of the two blocks. If S and T are in the 1-4 position, then P and Q must be in 2-3. If S and T are in the 2-5 position, then P and Q must be in the 3-4 position. That means that either P or Q must always be played third. Additionally, we can infer that R must always be played first or fifth:

PQRST[5]

S/T __ __ T/S	R/	__	P/Q	__	/R
	1	2	3	4	5
PQ	Q̸		S̸		P̸
			T̸		

Given these inferences, there are only two possible "templates" to the game based on the placement of the two blocks:

Template #2:	R	S/T	P	Q	T/S
Template #1:	S/T	P	Q	T/S	R
	1	2	3	4	5

These two templates encompass four solution sets to the game and make it abundantly clear how the interaction of some rules and game restrictions can set off a series of powerful inferences. In a later chapter we will discuss templates in detail, but you will see references to this approach throughout the book. Templates result from restrictions within the game, and in many games the best setup is one that shows these possibility blueprints.

Consider one more example:

> A doctor must see six patients—C, D, E, F, G and H—one after another, not necessarily in that order. The patients must be seen according to the following conditions:
> E is seen exactly three patients after C.
> D is seen immediately before F is seen.

Using the scenario and rules, we can produce the following initial setup:

CDEFGH[6]

C __ __ E						
DF	1	2	3	4	5	6
	Ɇ	Ɇ	Ɇ	Ȼ	Ȼ	Ȼ
	F̸					D̸

Although this game has restrictions—the placement of the CE split-block is limited to 1-4, 2-5, or 3-6—there are still many different solutions. However, suppose for a moment that the test makers asked a question that contained a specific condition, such as:

If G is seen third, which one of the following must be true?

The addition of this new condition affects the restrictions in the basic diagram to such an extent that only one solution is possible:

Step One: G is seen third

$$\frac{\quad}{1} \quad \frac{\quad}{2} \quad \frac{G}{3} \quad \frac{\quad}{4} \quad \frac{\quad}{5} \quad \frac{\quad}{6}$$

Step Two: The CE split-block must be placed into slots 1-4 because if it is placed in slots 2-5 there will be no room for the DF block

$$\frac{C}{1} \quad \frac{\quad}{2} \quad \frac{G}{3} \quad \frac{E}{4} \quad \frac{\quad}{5} \quad \frac{\quad}{6}$$

Step Three: The DF block must be placed into 5-6

$$\frac{C}{1} \quad \frac{\quad}{2} \quad \frac{G}{3} \quad \frac{E}{4} \quad \frac{D}{5} \quad \frac{F}{6}$$

Step Four: H must be placed into 2

$$\frac{C}{1} \quad \frac{H}{2} \quad \frac{G}{3} \quad \frac{E}{4} \quad \frac{D}{5} \quad \frac{F}{6}$$

Randoms are weaker variables that typically are placed after more powerful variables have been placed.

Note that the random H, a variable with little power, is placed last.

After completing these steps in response to the question, you could then use the single solution to easily select the correct answer choice.

The point is that restrictions, when present in a game, never go away. You must always track them and be prepared for questions that will force you to address the restriction.

Avoiding False Inferences

The test makers always check to see if you have interpreted the rules correctly, and some rules are easier to misinterpret than others. Here are four mistakes that students often make:

<u>Conditional Rule Reversal</u>

As previously discussed, a conditional rule is triggered when the sufficient condition occurs. For example, consider the following rule:

When M is shown first, then O is shown sixth.

This rule would be diagrammed as:

$$M_1 \longrightarrow O_6$$

When M appears in the first slot, then O *must* appear in the sixth slot. However, many test takers make the mistake of reversing the relationship, and when faced with O in the sixth slot, they assume that M must be in the first slot. This is not a valid inference, and this mistake is known as a Mistaken Reversal.

<u>Misinterpreting Block Language</u>

As discussed on pages 50 through 57, the test makers will use different language to denote different types of blocks. "Before" and "after" are used in one manner, whereas "between" has an entirely different meaning. Many students make the mistake of misreading this language, and then they draw inferences based on a relationship that is actually incorrect. You must always read each rule very carefully because making a mistake in the rules will almost always cause a high number of missed questions.

False Blocks

The test makers are savvy, and they know that the average student does not carefully read the language of the rules. Consider the following rule from a Linear game:

> Each rock classic is immediately preceded on the CD by a new composition.

In this game, songs were being selected for a demo CD, and each song was classified as either a rock classic (R) or a new composition (N), and there were multiple songs classified as each type. Most students, upon reading the rule above, immediately diagrammed the rule as follows:

$$\boxed{\text{N R}}$$

Why doesn't this rule create a classic block like the one presented on page 50? Because the scenario on that page is based on a 1-to-1 setup where exactly one of each variable exists. In the example to the right, there are multiple rock classics and new compositions. That changes the situation significantly.

However, this representation is not fully correct. The diagram above implies that N and R are always in a standard block formation—that is, every time N appears then R immediately follows, and every time R appears then N immediately precedes. But take a moment to re-read the rule. Does the rule state that the two variables are in block formation? No, what the rules states is that every rock classic is preceded by a new composition. There is no corresponding statement that every new composition is also followed by a rock classic. So, this rule is only triggered when a rock classic is present. Thus, the rule is conditional, and should be diagrammed as follows:

This representation correctly indicates that the relationship in the rule occurs when a rock classic is present. Under this representation, it becomes possible for two or more new compositions to appear in a row (NN, NNN, etc.).

False Not-Block Inferences

As discussed on page 56, not-blocks indicate that variables cannot be next to one another, or cannot be separated by a fixed amount of space. Some students make the mistake of combining not-blocks with Not Laws to arrive at false inferences. Consider the following two rules:

> B is not inspected the day before C is inspected.
> C cannot be inspected second.

The diagram for these two rules would be:

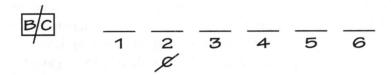

Many students, after reviewing these two rules, make one of the following two errors:

1. They mistakenly conclude that B cannot be inspected first, and then place a B Not Law under slot 1. These students erroneously act as if the BC relationship is a regular (or positive) block: because C cannot be inspected second, if BC was a regular block, then B could not be inspected first.

2. They mistakenly conclude that B must be inspected second, and then place B into slot 2. The error here is to act as if the C Not Law on slot 2 then forces B into slot 2. That outcome does not have to occur, although, of course, B could be inspected second.

Remember, not-blocks only come into play when one of the variables in the not-block is placed on the diagram.

Balanced versus Unbalanced Games

Up to this point we have been discussing what are known as "Balanced" games, where the number of supplied variables equals the number of available slots, resulting in a one-to-one numerical relationship of variables to slots. As you might expect, not every Linear game features a Balanced scenario, and since Unbalanced games are generally more difficult than Balanced games, it is to your advantage to be able to recognize what type of numerical situation you are facing.

There are two types of Unbalanced Linear games: Underfunded and Overloaded. Underfunded games feature fewer variables than available slots, for example, seven passengers assigned to nine seats on a plane. Overloaded games feature a greater number of variables than available slots, for example, eight piano lessons to be taught over five days. Overloaded scenarios often produce the most difficult Linear games.

Inherent in the discussion of Balanced and Unbalanced games is the idea of numerical distributions. A numerical distribution allocates one set of variables among another set of variables. For example, consider the game scenario from page 35:

> A tutor is planning a daily schedule of individual tutoring sessions for each of six students—S, T, W, X, Y, and Z. The tutor will meet with exactly one student at a time, for exactly one hour each session. The tutor will meet with students starting at 1 P. M., for six consecutive hours.

As mentioned previously, this sets up a 1-1-1-1-1-1 numerical distribution where there is a single different student to be tutored each hour, and there are exactly enough students to fill in all of the hours. Most Linear games have a numerical distribution that can be represented along similar lines. However, Overloaded games must be represented a bit differently. Consider the following game scenario:

> Dr. Saitawa schedules six patients—G, H, L, M, O, and P—for surgery during a single week on Monday through Friday. Dr. Saitawa will operate on exactly one patient each day, except for one of the days when Dr. Saitawa will operate on two patients in separate, non-simultaneous sessions.

In this game there are six patients to be placed into five days. So instead of having a 1-1-1-1-1 numerical relationship (5 into 5), we have a 2-1-1-1-1 relationship (6 into 5), and it is uncertain which day receives two patients. This uncertainty is very important and has a tremendous impact on the game. For example, once a patient has been assigned to a day, it is still possible that another patient could be assigned to that day and thus the day is not "closed off" from further consideration. This makes the game more difficult because there are more options to consider.

Given the numerical distribution for Overloaded games, you might wonder how Underfunded games can be represented. Actually, it depends on the nature of the game. For example, consider a game where just five students are assigned to seven chairs. In such a game, the "deficit" of variables can be countered by creating two "E" placeholder variables to represent the two empty chairs. Thus, in our example you would write down the five students and then two additional "E" variables, bringing the total number of variables to account for to seven, and the numerical distribution would be 1-1-1-1-1-1-1, just like in a normal one-to-one game. In other Underfunded games the rules make it clear you should double at least some of the variables, and by doing so there are enough variables to fill all of the spaces (for a sample of a game like this, see the example on page 89—in that game, F, G, and H are doubled, and in that way there are six variables for six spaces). We will see more of these games later when we further discuss numerical distributions.

Numerical Distributions occur in every type of game except Mapping games.

The Step Between Diagramming and the Questions

After you diagram all of the rules and before you head into the questions, take a moment to consider the nature of the scenario, rules, and inferences. Specifically, consider the following:

1. What is the numerical nature of the game? Balanced or unbalanced?

2. Which variables are the most powerful and have the greatest effect on the other variables? Which variables are weaker and will likely play a lesser role in the game?

3. Which rules are most powerful, and are the first rules you will seek to reference when attacking the questions?

4. Which inferences are most notable, or most controlling?

5. What portion of the game is the most confusing? Expect the test makers to attack those sections that you perceive as most challenging to understand.

Taking a moment to evaluate the various strengths, weaknesses, and peculiarities of each game before you attack the questions will give you a better sense of how to attack each question, and which rules and formations to rely upon.

Now that we have discussed some of the basic concepts of Linear Games, here is a Linear Games setup drill that will test your understanding of the concepts and help develop your diagramming skills. The purpose of this drill is to gain a clear understanding of the principles we have discussed, so speed is not a consideration. Your speed will naturally develop as your ability to analyze the components of each game increases.

Linear Setup Practice Drill

Each of the following items presents a scenario and corresponding rules similar to those found in actual Logic Games. Using the space provided, diagram the setup and include a representation of all sequences, blocks, not-blocks, and Not Laws. Occasionally, a problem will contain a corresponding question. Use your knowledge of the rules and the setup to answer the question. After you complete *each* item, check your work against the diagram in the answer key, and carefully read the comments concerning each diagram. *Answers on page 112*

1. Six swimmers—H, J, K, L, N, and P—are assigned to six swimming lanes numbered 1 though 6. Exactly one swimmer is assigned to each lane. The lane assignments conform to the following conditions:
    Swimmer K is assigned a lower-numbered lane than is swimmer J.
    Swimmer P is assigned a lower-numbered lane than is swimmer K.

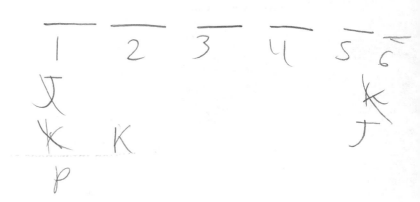

2. Five dogs—an Akita, a Bulldog, a Cocker Spaniel, a Doberman, and an English Setter—compete in the final round of a dog show. Each dog will be shown alone to the judges exactly once, in accordance with the following conditions:
    The Doberman can be shown neither immediately before nor immediately after the English Setter.
    The Akita must be shown exactly two places before the Doberman.

Question 2.1. Which one of the following must be true?

(A) If the Akita is shown third, the English Setter must be shown second.
(B) If the Bulldog is shown fourth, the Akita must be shown third.
(C) If the Cocker Spaniel is shown third, the English Setter must be shown first.
(D) If the Doberman is shown third, the Bulldog must be shown second.
(E) If the English Setter is shown second, the Cocker Spaniel must be shown fourth.

Linear Setup Practice Drill

3. A manager must schedule five meetings—
   Accounting, Finance, Management, Resources, and
   Training—during a single week, Monday through
   Friday. Each meeting will be scheduled for exactly
   one day, and exactly one meeting is held each day.
   The meeting schedule must observe the following
   constraints:

   The Management meeting is held the day before
   the Finance meeting.
   The Resources meeting is held at some time after
   the Finance meeting.
   The Accounting meeting is held second.

4. Six students—T, V, W, X, Y, and Z—are scheduled
   to speak in a debate contest. Each student will speak
   exactly once, and no two speakers will speak at the
   same time. The schedule must satisfy the following
   requirements:

   T speaks at some time before W.
   X must be the fourth speaker.
   V speaks immediately after T.

Linear Setup Practice Drill

5. A jazz band director is selecting the songs for an evening's performance. Seven songs—F, G, H, J, Q, R, and S—will be played one after another, not necessarily in that order. Each song will be played exactly once, according to the following conditions:

    F must be played immediately before or immediately after G.

    H must be played immediately before or immediately after J.

    S must be played fourth.

    G must be played after F.

    H must be played before J.

Question 5.1. Which one of the following cannot be true?

(A) F and R are played consecutively.
(B) G and Q are played consecutively.
(C) H and R are played consecutively.
(D) J and Q are played consecutively.
(E) Q and R are played consecutively.

6. A college dormitory manager must assign five students—P, Q, R, S, and T—to five different floors of the dormitory—floors 1, 2, 3, 5, and 6. The assignments must comply with the following restrictions:

    P must be assigned to the floor directly above Q.

    R must be assigned to floor 6.

Linear Setup Practice Drill

7. Seven attorneys—C, D, F, G, H, J, and K—are
scheduled to interview for a position with a local
law firm. The seven interviews are conducted on six
different days, Monday through Saturday. On one of
the days two attorneys will be interviewed and on all
other days exactly one attorney will be interviewed.
The interview schedule must conform to the following
conditions:

    F and K must be interviewed on the same day.
    J must be interviewed on Thursday.
    F must be interviewed after C but before G.
    D and H cannot be interviewed on consecutive
    days.
    K must be interviewed on either Tuesday or
    Friday.

Question 7.1. Which one of the following could be true?

    (A)   C is interviewed on Wednesday.
    (B)   C is interviewed on Friday.
    (C)   D is interviewed on Tuesday.
    (D)   G is interviewed on Wednesday.
    (E)   G is interviewed on Friday.

8. Each of six patrons—L, M, N, O, P, and Q—will be
assigned to exactly one of seven tables. The tables are
arranged consecutively and are numbered 1 through
7, and each table is assigned no more than one
patron. Table assignments must meet the following
requirements:

    N cannot be assigned to table 3, 5, or 7.
    P and Q must sit at lower-numbered tables than M.
    Tables 5, 6, and 7 must be occupied by a patron.
    O must sit at a higher-numbered table than M.

Linear Setup Practice Drill

9. There are exactly seven office buildings numbered 1 through 7 on a street. Each building is occupied by exactly one of seven companies: A, B, C, D, E, F, and G. All of the buildings are on the same side of the street, which runs from west to east. Building 1 is the westernmost building. The following restrictions apply:

Company A does not occupy building 1, 3, 5, or 7.

Company C occupies the building immediately to the west of Company D.

Company B occupies one of the three westernmost buildings.

Company F is the third building to the east of Company E.

The easternmost building is not occupied by Company G.

10. A dance academy instructor must schedule eight dance classes—a charleston class, a foxtrot class, a jitterbug class, a limbo class, a polka class, a rumba class, a tango class, and a waltz class—for a single day. Exactly two classes will be scheduled at a time, and the scheduling must be made according to the following conditions:

The limbo class and the rumba class are not scheduled for the same time.

The charleston class and the polka class must be scheduled for the same time.

The tango class and the rumba class are not scheduled for the same time.

The limbo class is scheduled at some time after the polka class.

The rumba class and the waltz class are not scheduled for the same time.

Question 10.1. If the tango class is scheduled for the same time as the foxtrot class, which one of the following must be true?

(A) The jitterbug class and the limbo class must be scheduled for the same time.

(B) The jitterbug class and the rumba class must be scheduled for the same time.

(C) The jitterbug class and the waltz class must be scheduled for the same time.

(D) The limbo class and the rumba class must be scheduled for the same time.

(E) The rumba class and the waltz class must be scheduled for the same time.

Linear Setup Practice Drill

11. A driver must pick up exactly eight passengers—P, R, S, T, V, X, Y, and Z—one at a time, not necessarily in that order. The pickups must be made in accordance with the following conditions:

Either T or V must be picked up fifth.

Either Y or Z must be picked up third.

The driver picks up exactly one passenger between picking up T and picking up Z.

S is picked up eighth when Y is picked up third.

Z must be picked up ahead of T.

Question 11.1. If V is picked up fifth, which one of the following must be true?

(A) P is picked up first.
(B) R is picked up sixth.
(C) S is picked up eighth.
(D) X is picked up seventh.
(E) Z is picked up sixth.

Linear Setup Practice Drill

12. A doctor must schedule nine patients—L, M, O, P, R, S, T, V, and X—during a given week, Monday through Sunday. At least one patient must be scheduled for each day, and the schedule must observe the following constraints:

    M and S must be scheduled for the same day.

    On the day P is scheduled, P must be the only patient scheduled to see the doctor.

    Exactly one patient is scheduled for Wednesday.

    T cannot be scheduled for Thursday.

    If P is scheduled for Monday, then V and X must be scheduled for Saturday.

    R is not scheduled for Thursday unless L is scheduled for Monday.

Question 12.1. If L is scheduled for Monday, which one of the following must be true?

    (A)   R is scheduled for Thursday.
    (B)   V is scheduled for Saturday.
    (C)   S is scheduled for Saturday.
    (D)   P is not scheduled for Monday.
    (E)   V is not scheduled for Monday.

Question 12.2. Which one of the following statements about the doctor's schedule must be true?

    (A)   The maximum number of patients scheduled for Monday is one.
    (B)   The maximum number of patients scheduled for Tuesday is two.
    (C)   The maximum number of patients scheduled for Friday is three.
    (D)   The minimum number of patients scheduled for Saturday is two.
    (E)   The minimum number of patients scheduled for Sunday is two.

3

Linear Setup Practice Drill Answer Key

Note: Most of the problems in this drill are diagrammed with horizontal setups. In many cases these problems could be alternatively diagrammed with vertical setups, although some games should only be shown horizontally, such as one about houses on a street. Also, if you encounter a Not Law in the answer key that appears incorrectly placed, put that variable into that position and observe the consequences. This will allow you to better understand the interaction taking place between the variables and the rules.

1. Six swimmers—H, J, K, L, N, and P—are assigned to six swimming lanes numbered 1 though 6. Exactly one swimmer is assigned to each lane. The lane assignments conform to the following conditions:
    Swimmer K is assigned a lower-numbered lane than is swimmer J.
    Swimmer P is assigned a lower-numbered lane than is swimmer K.

There are two variable sets in this problem: the six swimmers and the six swimming lanes. Because the swimming lanes have an inherent sense of order, they are chosen as the base. Since each lane will be filled by exactly one swimmer, a single slot is drawn above each lane number, and the swimmers are connected to the lanes in a one-to-one relationship (In this case, 1-1-1-1-1-1).

HJKLNP⁶

P—K—J

$$\underline{\quad}\ \ \underline{\quad}\ \ \underline{\quad}\ \ \underline{\quad}\ \ \underline{\quad}\ \ \underline{\quad}$$
  1   2   3   4   5   6

The two sequencing rules can be linked together to form one "super" rule. The A —— B —— C format of the super rule appears frequently on the LSAT and always yields exactly six Not Laws.

2. Five dogs—an Akita, a Bulldog, a Cocker Spaniel,
    a Doberman, and an English Setter—compete in the
    final round of a dog show. Each dog will be shown
    alone to the judges exactly once, in accordance with
    the following conditions:
    > The Doberman can be shown neither immediately
    > before nor immediately after the English Setter.
    > The Akita must be shown exactly two places
    > before the Doberman.

There are two variable sets in this problem: the five dogs and the five positions in which they are shown. Since the positions in which the dogs are shown has an inherent sense of order, they are chosen as the base. Again, the two variable sets are in a one-to-one relationship (1-1-1-1-1).

A B C D E^5

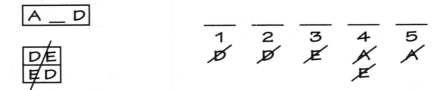

E can never appear in slot 3 or 4 because E and D cannot be consecutive, and when this rule is combined with the $\boxed{A \_\_ D}$ rule, we run into the following problems:

> If $\boxed{A \_\_ D}$ is in the first and third slots, then the third slot is occupied, and since D is third, E can't be (second or) fourth.

> If $\boxed{A \_\_ D}$ is in the second and fourth slots, then the fourth slot is occupied, and since D is fourth then E can't be third (or fifth).

> If $\boxed{A \_\_ D}$ is in the third and fifth slots, then the third slot is occupied by A, and since D is fifth then E can't be fourth.

Thus, since $\boxed{A \_\_ D}$ must be in one of the three positions outlined above, and in none of those scenarios can E be third or fourth, we can eliminate E from those two slots. The best way to understand an inference of this nature is to reverse-engineer it; that is, put E in third slot and see what problems occur, then put E in the fourth slot see what happens. You will quickly see why placing E in either position causes difficulty.

From a visual standpoint, the unwieldy block has only three spacing options: 1-3, 2-4, and 3-5. The following diagram shows each option drawn out:

	1	2	3	4	5	
Template #3:	E/	/E	A	___	D	Block in 3-5
Template #2:	E	A	___	D	___	Block in 2-4
Template #1:	A	___	D	___	E	Block in 1-3

Although this problem is too simple to appear as an entire Logic Game, it is indicative of the type of "endgame" situations that occur after several variables have already been placed in a question.

In Templates #1 and #3, the third position is occupied by D and A, respectively. In Template #2, D is shown fourth and from the rules it follows that E cannot be shown third or fifth. Thus, in each of the three templates, the third position is either occupied or otherwise off-limits to E. Since these are the only three templates for the game, it follows that E can never be shown third.

In Template #2, the fourth position is occupied by D. In Template #1, D is shown third and thus E cannot be shown fourth. In Template #3, D is shown fifth and so E cannot be shown fourth. Thus, in each template the fourth position is either occupied or otherwise unavailable to E. It therefore follows that E can never be shown fourth.

The inference that E cannot be shown third or fourth would certainly be tested during the game. To find such an inference in the future, be on the lookout for split-blocks (which have limited placement options) and not-blocks that link to one of the variables in the split-block.

Question 2.1. Which one of the following must be true?

   (A)   If the Akita is shown third, the English Setter must be shown second.
   (B)   If the Bulldog is shown fourth, the Akita must be shown third.
   (C)   If the Cocker Spaniel is shown third, the English Setter must be shown first.
   (D)   If the Doberman is shown third, the Bulldog must be shown second.
   (E)   If the English Setter is shown second, the Cocker Spaniel must be shown fourth.

Question 2.1. The correct answer is (C). If C is shown third, then A must be shown second and D must be shown fourth. Since D and E cannot be shown consecutively, it must be true that E is shown first.

Answer choice (A) is incorrect since E could be shown first instead of second.

Answer choice (B) is incorrect since A could be shown first instead of third.

Answer choice (D) is incorrect since B could be shown fourth instead of second.

Answer choice (E) is incorrect since C could be shown first instead of fourth.

3. A manager must schedule five meetings—
    Accounting, Finance, Management, Resources, and
    Training—during a single week, Monday through
    Friday. Each meeting will be scheduled for exactly
    one day, and exactly one meeting is held each day.
    The meeting schedule must observe the following
    constraints:
    The Management meeting is held the day before
      the Finance meeting.
    The Resources meeting is held at some time after
      the Finance meeting.
    The Accounting meeting is held second.

Whenever a game introduces the days of a week as a variable set, always use the days of the week as the base. As in the first two problems, the two variable sets are in a one-to-one relationship (1-1-1-1-1).

A F M R T⁵

$\boxed{\text{M F}}$ —— R

T	A	M	F	R
M	Tu	W	Th	F
~~M~~			~~M~~	~~M~~
~~F~~				~~F~~
~~R~~				

This problem provides an excellent example of why you should always read each rule before beginning your diagram. Because A must be held on Tuesday, it follows that F, M, and R cannot be held on Monday. Accordingly, T must be held on Monday, and the MFR sequence must fill in Wednesday, Thursday, and Friday.

4. Six students—T, V, W, X, Y, and Z—are scheduled
to speak in a debate contest. Each student will speak
exactly once, and no two speakers will speak at the
same time. The schedule must satisfy the following
requirements:

  T speaks at some time before W.
  X must be the fourth speaker.
  V speaks immediately after T.

In this problem the speaking order should be chosen as the base, and the variables are in a one-to-one
relationship (1-1-1-1-1-1).

TVWXYZ⁶

$$\boxed{TV} \longrightarrow W$$

	T/V		X		
1	2	3	4	5	6
W̶	W̶	T̶		T̶	T̶
X̶	X̶			X̶	X̶
	Z̶				

The first point of interest in this problem is in the representation of X. Since X must speak fourth,
it automatically follows that X cannot speak first, second, third, fifth, or sixth. As mentioned
previously, an argument could thus be made that X Not Laws should be shown on those slots. This
representation would be correct, but since X is already placed, and, therefore, out of consideration,
this would be redundant. However, if you find yourself continually missing these types of inferences,
you can certainly show the X Not Laws.

The second point of interest is in the placement of the TV block. Since T and V cannot speak fifth or
sixth, it follows that the TV block must be either 1-2 or 2-3. Accordingly, either T or V must always
speak second and no other student can speak second. This "dual option" is represented by T/V in the
second slot. It is interesting to note that in both problem #3 and this problem, the limited placement
options of the block ultimately yield the key inferences. In any logic game that contains a block,
always make sure to account for the possibilities presented by that block.

The final piece of relevant information in this problem concerns W, Y, and Z. Although we cannot be
sure of the exact placement of these three variables, we can deduce that they will never be ordered
consecutively. In fact, one of the group must always occupy the first or third slot, and the remaining
two variables must occupy the fifth and sixth slots. In logic games it is almost always fruitful to
examine the possibilities among those variables that have yet to be placed by a question.

5.   A jazz band director is selecting the songs for an
     evening's performance. Seven songs—F, G, H, J,
     Q, R, and S—will be played one after another, not
     necessarily in that order. Each song will be played
     exactly once, according to the following conditions:
     F must be played immediately before or
        immediately after G.
     H must be played immediately before or
        immediately after J.
     S must be played fourth.
     G must be played after F.
     H must be played before J.

In this problem the order of performance is chosen as the base, and the variable sets are in a one-to-
one relationship (1-1-1-1-1-1-1).

F G H J Q R S⁷

| FG |

| HJ |

```
                              S
___   ___   ___       ___   ___   ___
 1     2     3     4   5     6     7
 Ǥ     Ǫ     F̶         Ǥ     Ǫ     F̶
 ȷ     R̶     Ⱨ         ȷ     R̶     Ⱨ
```

Again, this problem proves that you must thoroughly read all of the rules before starting your
diagram. The first and fourth rules set up an FG block, and the second and fifth rules set up an HJ
block. The two blocks ultimately prove to be the key to the problem. Since S effectively splits the
diagram into two equal parts, one of the blocks must be placed into the first three slots and the other
block must be placed into the last three slots. Since one block always appears in slots 1-2 or 2-3, slot
2 must always be occupied by one of the four block variables and therefore can never be occupied by
Q or R. Additionally, since the other block must always appear in slots 5-6 or 6-7, slot 6 also cannot
be occupied by Q or R. Finally, since S is already in slot 4, F and H cannot be played third, and G
and J cannot be played fifth. Regarding the third and fifth slots, whenever a variable (such as S) is
placed into the middle of a one-to-one linear diagram, any fixed blocks will yield Not Laws before
and after that variable.

Question 5.1. Which one of the following cannot be true?

(A)   F and R are played consecutively.
(B)   G and Q are played consecutively.
(C)   H and R are played consecutively.
(D)   J and Q are played consecutively.
(E)   Q and R are played consecutively.

Question 5.1. The correct answer is (E). If Q and R are played consecutively, there would not be enough room to place the FG and HJ blocks.

Answer choice (A) is incorrect because R could be first and F could be second. There is another possibility (R could be fifth and F could be sixth) but one hypothetical is sufficient to disprove the answer choice and the same is true for the other incorrect answer choices.

Answer choice (B) is incorrect because G could be second and Q could be third.

Answer choice (C) is incorrect because R could be first and H could be second.

Answer choice (D) is incorrect because J could be second and Q could be third.

Note that this game would probably contain some question or answer choice that would test your knowledge of the fact that the two blocks can never stand consecutively. Since there is not enough room to place the blocks side-by-side, the following inferences can be made:

---

6. A college dormitory manager must assign five students—P, Q, R, S, and T—to five different floors of the dormitory—floors 1, 2, 3, 5, and 6. The assignments must comply with the following restrictions:

    P must be assigned to the floor directly above Q.
    R must be assigned to floor 6.

Of the two variable sets, the floors should be chosen as the base because they have the greatest sense of inherent order. When displaying the floors, even though the listed floors do not include floor 4, the fourth floor should be shown anyway. The value of this decision will prove itself in a moment. The variable sets are in a one-to-one relationship (1-1-1-1-1), and in this case the best representation is vertical since that is the way the floors of buildings exist in the real world.

PQRST[5]

```
6  _R_
5  S/T  P̶  Q̶
4  XXX
3  ___  Q̶
2  P/Q  S̶/T̶
1  ___  P̶
```

By showing floor 4, it becomes apparent that neither P nor Q can be assigned to floor 5 (in addition, Q cannot be assigned to floor 3). It then follows that the PQ block must be on either floors 3-2 or floors 2-1. Thus, either P or Q must be assigned to floor 2 and S and T cannot be assigned there.

In any game where one of the internal spaces is skipped, still show that space on your diagram, but mark it through with an "X." The test makers *always* test you to see if you understand the implications of the missing space.

---

7.   Seven attorneys—C, D, F, G, H, J, and K—are scheduled to interview for a position with a local law firm. The seven interviews are conducted on six different days, Monday through Saturday. On one of the days two attorneys will be interviewed and on all other days exactly one attorney will be interviewed. The interview schedule must conform to the following conditions:

    F and K must be interviewed on the same day.
    J must be interviewed on Thursday.
    F must be interviewed after C but before G.
    D and H cannot be interviewed on consecutive days.
    K must be interviewed on either Tuesday or Friday.

As discussed in problem #3, the days of the week should always be chosen as the base. Interestingly, in this problem there are only six days but seven attorneys to be scheduled. Thus, this is an Unbalanced game that is Overloaded. Ordinarily this would be a cause for concern because Linear games are easier when each space is filled by just one variable (e.g. Balanced games). In problems such as this one where the number of variables is Unbalanced (7 into 6), the extra uncertainty often increases the overall difficulty. Here that uncertainty is somewhat alleviated since the first rule schedules F and K to be interviewed together. With F and K as a block, there are just six separate "variables" to assign (FK, C, D, G, H, and J). Thus, the distribution could be characterized as a 1-1-1-1-1-1 relationship of attorneys to days of the week, where it just happens that one of the "1's" is the FK block.

Most students set this game up as follows:

CDFGHJK⁷

While this partial representation is accurate, it does not characterize the full scope of the possibilities. Since the FK block is limited to Tuesday or Friday, and the FK block is involved in a sequence with other variables, why not draw out two separate templates that show the possibilities when the FK block is placed? This technique, known as Identifying the Templates™, occasionally produces startling inferences and usually provides you with a greater understanding of the game. Identifying the Templates should generally be used when certain variables or blocks have a limited number of placement options (usually two or three) and their placement correspondingly affects other variables. Here are the two templates in this problem:

With F and K on Tuesday, C must be interviewed on Monday. This leaves D, G, and H to be interviewed on Wednesday, Friday, and Saturday. Since D and H cannot be interviewed on consecutive days, either D or H must be interviewed on Wednesday, and the remainder interviewed on Friday or Saturday. Since Friday and Saturday are limited to G and D or H, this option is shown in parentheses. Thus, the (G, H/D) notation helps to represent four possibilities: G on Friday and H on Saturday; G on Friday and D on Saturday; G on Saturday and D on Friday; and G on Saturday and H on Friday.

Linear Setup Practice Drill Answer Key

With F and K on Friday, G must be interviewed on Saturday. This leaves C, D, and H to be interviewed on Monday, Tuesday, and Wednesday. Since D and H cannot be interviewed consecutively, C must be interviewed on Tuesday. Since D and H can be interviewed on either Monday or Wednesday, this template therefore represents two possibilities. By combining both templates, we find that this problem contains only six unique solutions and we have identified each one.

3

Question 7.1. Which one of the following could be true?

    (A)   C is interviewed on Wednesday.
    (B)   C is interviewed on Friday.
    (C)   D is interviewed on Tuesday.
    (D)   G is interviewed on Wednesday.
    (E)   G is interviewed on Friday.

Question 7.1. Answer choice (E) is correct and is proven by the first of the two templates.

Answer choice (A) cannot be true since only D or H can be interviewed on Wednesday.

Answer choice (B) cannot be true since C can be interviewed only on Monday or Tuesday.

Answer choice (C) cannot be true since only K, F, and C can be interviewed on Tuesday.

Answer choice (D) cannot be true since only D or H can be interviewed on Wednesday.

---

8.   Each of six patrons—L, M, N, O, P, and Q—will be assigned to exactly one of seven tables. The tables are arranged consecutively and are numbered 1 through 7, and each table is assigned no more than one patron. Table assignments must meet the following requirements:

        N cannot be assigned to table 3, 5, or 7.
        P and Q must sit at lower-numbered tables than M.
        Tables 5, 6, and 7 must be occupied by a patron.
        O must sit at a higher-numbered table than M.

Of the two variable sets, the tables should be chosen as the base since they are numbered and stand consecutively. At first it appears that this problem is Unbalanced in the same way as problem #7, but in this case the game is Underfunded with only six patrons for the seven tables (6 into 7). However, this shortage can be alleviated by representing the "missing" patron with an "E" for empty. Whenever there is a shortage of variables (in this case, the patrons) available to fill a set number of spaces (in this case, the tables), you can always combat this problem by representing the missing variable with an E (or if the given variables already include E, use another letter, such as X). With the shortage of variables eliminated, the variable set relationship can be seen as a one-to-one (1-1-1-1-1-1-1).

L M N O P Q E⁷

As discussed earlier, in all game types, one of the basic methods for identifying inferences is to examine the points of restriction in the game. In games with Not Laws, that involves looking closely at the slots with the greatest number of Not Laws. In this case, it becomes apparent that table 7 is the most restricted table in the problem. In fact, since five of the seven variables cannot sit at table 7 (E is counted as a variable for this purpose), only two patrons—L and O—are available to sit at table 7. This inference would most likely be tested in a game by a question such as, "If L is assigned to table 3, which one of the following must be true?" The correct answer would be "O must be assigned to table 7." In one-to-one Linear games, always examine any space that has a large number of Not Laws, and do not forget that any variable that is already placed is automatically eliminated from all other slots!

In addition, the "O" Not Law on table 4 is correct because placing O on 4 causes a violation of the third rule:

> When O is placed at table 4, then tables 1, 2, and 3 must be occupied by patrons P, Q, and M (not necessarily in that order). This forces the Empty table (variable "E") to be assigned to table 5, 6, or 7. Unfortunately, that assignment is a violation of the third rule that states that tables 5, 6, and 7 must be occupied by a patron.

9. There are exactly seven office buildings numbered 1 through 7 on a street. Each building is occupied by exactly one of seven companies: A, B, C, D, E, F, and G. All of the buildings are on the same side of the street, which runs from west to east. Building 1 is the westernmost building. The following restrictions apply:

    Company A does not occupy building 1, 3, 5, or 7.
    Company C occupies the building immediately to the west of Company D.
    Company B occupies one of the three westernmost buildings.
    Company F is the third building to the east of Company E.
    The easternmost building is not occupied by Company G.

Linear Setup Practice Drill Answer Key

The buildings should be chosen as the base since they are numbered and stand on the same side of the street. The two variables sets are in a one-to-one relationship (1-1-1-1-1-1-1), and the game should be set up horizontally since that is the way streets exist in the real world. This is the initial setup, with just the immediate Not Laws from the rules:

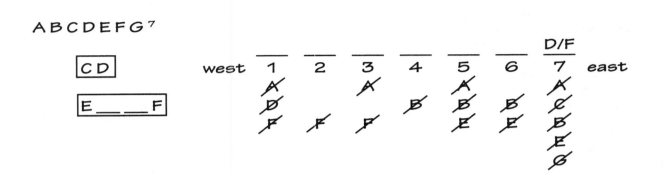

ABCDEFG⁷

As in the previous problem, the abundance of Not Laws on the seventh building leads to the inference that only companies D and F can occupy building 7. Since D and F are both involved in block rules, it makes sense to apply the Identify the Templates technique used previously in problem #7:

D in 7:

B/G	E	G/B	A	F	C	D
E	A	B	F	G	C	D
1	2	3	4	5	6	7

F in 7:

B/G	A	G/B	E	C	D	F
B	C	D	E	G	A	F
C	D	B	E	G	A	F
1	2	3	4	5	6	7

As you can see, the two major templates have themselves been split into smaller sub-templates. This method is the most efficient since the placement of each of the two blocks then limits the placement of the other block. It is interesting to note that, although the Identify the Templates method of attack often consumes more time than the average setup, it also allows you to answer the questions more quickly. In this problem there are only seven different solutions, and identifying each one would allow you to answer any question quickly and easily.

As a note of warning, the majority of Linear games cannot be attacked with the Identify the Templates method since their rules simply do not combine to produce enough restrictions. However, part of the purpose of this drill is to challenge you to identify the dominant features of any linear setup and concomitantly employ the correct techniques to attack the game most effectively. There will be times when your ability to employ certain techniques at the right moment is critical, and this drill helps prepare you for those moments.

10. A dance academy instructor must schedule eight dance classes—a charleston class, a foxtrot class, a jitterbug class, a limbo class, a polka class, a rumba class, a tango class, and a waltz class—for a single day. Exactly two classes will be scheduled at a time, and the scheduling must be made according to the following conditions:

> The limbo class and the rumba class are not scheduled for the same time.
>
> The charleston class and the polka class must be scheduled for the same time.
>
> The tango class and the rumba class are not scheduled for the same time.
>
> The limbo class is scheduled at some time after the polka class.
>
> The rumba class and the waltz class are not scheduled for the same time.

The dance class times should be selected as the base since they have a consecutive nature. There are eight dance classes and eight time slots, and therefore the two variable sets are in a one-to-one relationship (1-1-1-1-1-1-1-1). However, since two dance classes are scheduled for each time slot the distribution could also be seen as 2-2-2-2. The two representations essentially mean the same thing.

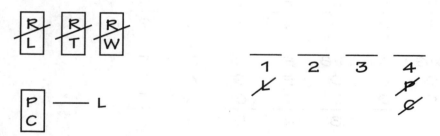

Since there are two classes in each time slot, we can represent the second class in each time period with another "stack" of slots. Blocks that represent the same time period can be drawn vertically, and blocks that represent consecutive time periods can be drawn horizontally. Thus, because L and R cannot be scheduled for the same time period, that not-block must be drawn vertically (whether R or L is on top is irrelevant for this problem).

Some students attempt to use the following representation for the time slots:

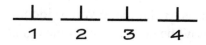

Linear Setup Practice Drill Answer Key

The prior representation is flawed and will lead to problems in the future. Do not use it! The primary problem is that blocks cannot be meaningfully represented. A block that shows the same time period would be drawn horizontally, and a block that shows consecutive time periods would also be drawn horizontally. Thus, there would be no way to determine the exact meaning of a block during a game other than through memory or a rereading of the rule. This is obviously inefficient, and therefore a weak representation.

The key feature of the problem is the three not-blocks. In games with a large number of not-blocks, powerful inferences can often be made regarding which variables can and cannot go together. In this case, R appears in each of the not-blocks, and that eliminates R from being paired with L, T, or W. Since P and C must be scheduled together, it follows that R cannot be scheduled with C, L, P, T, or W. Therefore, R can only be paired with F or J:

$$R \longrightarrow \text{or} \quad \begin{matrix} F \\ \\ J \end{matrix}$$

This inference is tested in the accompanying question:

Question 10.1. If the tango class is scheduled for the same time as the foxtrot class, which one of the following must be true?

    (A)   The jitterbug class and the limbo class must be scheduled for the same time.

    (B)   The jitterbug class and the rumba class must be scheduled for the same time.

    (C)   The jitterbug class and the waltz class must be scheduled for the same time.

    (D)   The limbo class and the rumba class must be scheduled for the same time.

    (E)   The rumba class and the waltz class must be scheduled for the same time.

Question 10.1. Answer choice (B) is correct. If F is scheduled with T, then only J remains to be paired with R.

Answer choice (A) is incorrect since if J and L are scheduled for the same time, there would be no class to schedule with R.

Answer choice (C) is incorrect since if J and W are scheduled for the same time, there would be no class to schedule with R.

Answer choice (D) is incorrect since according to the first rule L and R can never be scheduled together.

Answer choice (E) is incorrect since according to the fifth rule R and W can never be scheduled together.

---

11. A driver must pick up exactly eight passengers—P, R, S, T, V, X, Y, and Z—one at a time, not necessarily in that order. The pickups must be made in accordance with the following conditions:

    Either T or V must be picked up fifth.
    Either Y or Z must be picked up third.
    The driver picks up exactly one passenger between picking up T and picking up Z.
    S is picked up eighth when Y is picked up third.
    Z must be picked up ahead of T.

The order of pickup should be chosen as the base in this problem, and the variable sets are in a one-to-one relationship (1-1-1-1-1-1-1-1).

PRSTVXYZ^8

The interaction of the first, second, third, and fifth rules establishes that there are only two possibilities for the third and fifth pickups: Z in three and T in five, or Y in three and V in five. Using this information the best attack is to Identify the Templates:

Z in three:	1	2	Z 3	4	T 5	6	7	8

		Z	Y	Z	V	T		S
			Y	T	V			S
Y in three:	1	2	3	4	5	6	7	8

This form of Identify the Templates, where only some of the variables are placed, is more likely to occur on a Linear game than the form seen in problems #7 and #9, where all of the variables are placed.

The hardest Not Laws in this game to identify are that Z cannot be picked up sixth and T cannot be picked up eighth. These occur because when Z is picked up sixth, then from the second rule Y must be picked up third, and then from the fourth rule S must be picked up eighth. But, when Z is picked up sixth, then from the third and fifth rules T must be picked up eighth, causing a conflict.

Note also that the fourth rule is conditional, and uses the conditional indicator "when." We did not show the contrapositive because over time you should begin to understand that the contrapositive inherently follows from any conditional relationship. The rule of thumb is to write out the contrapositive, when you feel that doing so will make the game easier for you.

Question 11.1. If V is picked up fifth, which one of the following must be true?

(A)   P is picked up first.
(B)   R is picked up sixth.
(C)   S is picked up eighth.
(D)   X is picked up seventh.
(E)   Z is picked up sixth.

Question 11.1. Answer choice (C) is correct. If V is picked up fifth, Y must be picked up third, and when Y is picked up third then S must be picked up eighth.

Answer choice (A) is incorrect since it could be true, but it does not have to be true.

Answer choice (B) is incorrect since it could be true, but it does not have to be true.

Answer choice (D) is incorrect since it could be true, but it does not have to be true.

Answer choice (E) is incorrect since it cannot be true.

12. A doctor must schedule nine patients—L, M, O, P, R, S, T, V, and X—during a given week, Monday through Sunday. At least one patient must be scheduled for each day, and the schedule must observe the following constraints:

    M and S must be scheduled for the same day.
    On the day P is scheduled, P must be the only patient scheduled to see the doctor.
    Exactly one patient is scheduled for Wednesday.
    T cannot be scheduled for Thursday.
    If P is scheduled for Monday, then V and X must be scheduled for Saturday.
    R is not scheduled for Thursday unless L is scheduled for Monday.

As discussed in previous problems, the days of the week should be chosen as the base. The patients should be distributed across the days, and similar to problem #7, there is an unbalanced relationship between the patients and the days of the week (9 to 7). Whenever an unbalanced relationship such as this one occurs in a game, it should always be examined closely. In this case there are two numerical distributions possible for spreading the nine patients across the seven days:

Distribution #1:   3 - 1 - 1 - 1 - 1 - 1 - 1
                        M   P
                        S

Distribution #2:   2 - 2 - 1 - 1 - 1 - 1 - 1
                        M   P
                        S

In distribution #1, one of the seven days receives three scheduled patients, and each of the other six days receives one patient. In distribution #2, two of the seven days receive two patients each, and each of the other five days receives one patient. Numerical distributions will be discussed in more detail later in the course, but for the time being the following is a quick analysis of this numerical distribution.

There are seven days, and each day must have at least one scheduled patient. Thus, the minimum requirements for each day require seven of the patients:

$$7 = \frac{1}{M} \quad \frac{1}{Tu} \quad \frac{1}{W} \quad \frac{1}{Th} \quad \frac{1}{F} \quad \frac{1}{Sa} \quad \frac{1}{Su}$$

This arrangement leaves two patients as "free agents" that can be scheduled for any day. If both free agents are scheduled together, say on Monday, the following arrangement would appear:

$$
9 = \quad
\begin{array}{ccccccc}
1 & & & & & & \\
1 & & & & & & \\
1 & 1 & 1 & 1 & 1 & 1 & 1 \\
\hline
M & Tu & W & Th & F & Sa & Su
\end{array}
$$

Thus, we arrive at the 3-1-1-1-1-1-1 distribution. Note that the "3" does not have to be on Monday. It is just easier to represent the distribution with the 3 at the beginning, and so technically this is called an unfixed distribution. The distinction will be further explained later in this book.

To arrive at distribution #2, simply split up the two free agents and schedule them for different days:

$$
9 = \quad
\begin{array}{ccccccc}
1 & 1 & & & & & \\
1 & 1 & 1 & 1 & 1 & 1 & 1 \\
\hline
M & Tu & W & Th & F & Sa & Su
\end{array}
$$

Thus, we arrive at the 2-2-1-1-1-1-1 distribution. As before, the groups of "2" do not have to appear on Monday and Tuesday.

Some students object that the 3-1-1-1-1-1-1 distribution cannot occur since the first rule establishes that M and S must be scheduled together. However, the rule does not state that M and S are the *only* two patients scheduled for the same time and thus it is possible that another patient could be scheduled along with M and S. Of course, in the 3-1-1-1-1-1-1 distribution M and S must be part of the group of 3 and in the 2-2-1-1-1-1-1 M and S must form one of the groups of 2.

Now that we have discussed the numbers (which are always primary in Logic Games), let's diagram the rules:

L M O P R S T V X^9

<u>Question 12.1</u>. If L is scheduled for Monday, which one of
the following must be true?

(A)   R is scheduled for Thursday.
(B)   V is scheduled for Saturday.
(C)   S is scheduled for Saturday.
(D)   P is not scheduled for Monday.
(E)   V is not scheduled for Monday.

Question 12.1. Answer choice (D) is the correct answer. If L is scheduled for Monday, then according to the second rule P cannot be scheduled for Monday.

Answer choice (A) is incorrect because it reverses the last rule and is therefore not necessarily true.

Answer choice (B) is incorrect because it is not necessarily true.

Answer choice (C) is incorrect because it is not necessarily true.

Answer choice (E) is incorrect because it is not necessarily true.

This question can be confusing, and many students mistakenly select answer choice (A). Although answer choice (A) could occur, it does not have to occur, and because this is a Must Be True question, answer choice (A) is thus incorrect. Let's take a moment to analyze the last rule:

"R is not scheduled for Thursday unless L is scheduled for Monday."

The critical part of the sentence is the word "unless," and when "unless" appears it introduces the necessary condition, and then the rest is negated and becomes the sufficient condition. Hence, the proper diagram for the rule is:

$$R_{Th} \longrightarrow L_M$$

Let's review that again. To diagram a statement involving "unless" (or its analogues "except," "until," or "without"), take the following two steps:

1. The clause modified by "unless" becomes the necessary condition.

2. The remainder is negated—which normally involves removing or adding a "not"—and becomes the sufficient condition.

Thus, in the rule under consideration, "unless" modifies "L is scheduled for Monday" and that becomes the necessary condition; the remainder, "R is not scheduled for Thursday," is negated to "R is scheduled for Thursday" and becomes the sufficient condition. Hence the diagram

$$R_{Th} \longrightarrow L_M.$$

So, with this diagram in mind for question 12.1, when L is scheduled for Monday, the necessary condition is met. This does NOT mean, however, that R must be scheduled for Thursday (it is possible but not certain). To infer R is on Thursday would be a Mistaken Reversal of the statement and erroneous (this error is covered in the Avoiding False Inferences section on page 99). Since (A) tries to say that it must be true that R is on Thursday, answer choice (A) is therefore wrong.

Question 12.2. Which one of the following statements about the doctor's schedule must be true?

(A)   The maximum number of patients scheduled for Monday is one.
(B)   The maximum number of patients scheduled for Tuesday is two.
(C)   The maximum number of patients scheduled for Friday is three.
(D)   The minimum number of patients scheduled for Saturday is two.
(E)   The minimum number of patients scheduled for Sunday is two.

Question 12.2. Answer choice (C) is correct since the maximum number of patients that can ever be scheduled for a single day is three (3-1-1-1-1-1-1).

Answer choice (A) is incorrect since three is the maximum number of patients that could be scheduled for Monday.

Answer choice (B) is incorrect since three is the maximum number of patients that could be scheduled for Tuesday.

Answer choice (D) is incorrect since one is the minimum number of patients that could be scheduled for Saturday.

Answer choice (E) is incorrect since one is the minimum number of patients that could be scheduled for Sunday.

Most games that feature a Numerical Distribution have at least one question that tests to see if you identified the distribution.

The Questions—Part 2

Now that you have had an opportunity to hone your setup and inference making skills, it is time to discuss the questions in detail. As mentioned in the second chapter (in the Questions—Part 1), all LSAT Logic Games questions are either Global or Local:

Global Questions

Global questions ask about information that can be derived from the initial rules. Global questions are easily identifiable because they ask broad questions without adding any new conditions. For example, a Global question might ask, "Which one of the following cannot be true?" or "Which one of the following is a pair of songs that must occupy consecutive tracks?"

If you have a strong setup, many of the Global questions should be relatively easy, and will in many cases not require further work. Regardless, the first step to attacking Global questions is always to consider the nature of what is being asked, a point that will be examined more closely later.

Local Questions

Local questions impose a new condition in addition to the initial rules. Local questions generally can be identified by the "if" (or "when" or "suppose") at the beginning of the question stem. The "if" clause provides a new rule for you to consider *for that question only*. Most Local questions will require you to make a mini-diagram next to the question itself or below the questions (we will discuss this point later).

Always read to
the end of the
"if" clause in a
question and
then stop to
consider the
implications
of the new
information.

When encountering a Local question, always read to the end of the "if" clause in a question and then enact the condition being added (for example, if L must be third—then place L in the third space). Then, consider the implications of this new information before moving on. Considering the implications will typically involve one of the standard inference-making methods discussed earlier in this chapter (for example, Linkage: perhaps a rule in the game states that if L is third then Q must be sixth. That would result in Q being placed sixth, and so on).

The Global and Local designations broadly categorize every question on the games section, so let us take a moment to complete a short classification drill.

Global/Local Question Identification Drill

Each of the following items contains a sample question stem. Using the given information, identify each question stem as Global or Local. *Answers on page 134*

Example Stem:

> If Reynaud speaks fifth, which one of the following must be true?

Answer: Local question

---

1. Which one of the following CANNOT be true?

    _____

2. If Lu is the only employee to take a break during the week, which one of the following must be true?

    _____

3. Which one of the following is an acceptable schedule of performances?

    _____

4. Each of the following could be true EXCEPT:

    _____

5. If the mayor is on the same committee as the business owner, which one of the following must be false?

    _____

6. Which one of the following lists three doctors that could perform surgery together?

    _____

7. If none of the families live in Rivertown, which one of the following could be false?

    _____

8. In the lineup of suspects, Q could be in any of the following spots EXCEPT:

    _____

Global/Local Question Identification Drill Answer Key

1. Which one of the following CANNOT be true?

    Global question

---

2. If Lu is the only employee to take a break during the week, which one of the following must be true?

    Local question

---

3. Which one of the following is an acceptable schedule of performances?

    Global question

---

4. Each of the following could be true EXCEPT:

    Global question

---

5. If the mayor is on the same committee as the business owner, which one of the following must be false?

    Local question

---

6. Which one of the following lists three doctors that could perform surgery together?

    Global question

---

7. If none of the families live in Rivertown, which one of the following could be false?

    Local question (this question imposes an additional condition, and hence it is Local)

---

8. In the lineup of suspects, Q could be in any of the following spots EXCEPT:

    Global question (although Q is named, no additional restriction is imposed)

Truth and Logical Opposition

In addition to being Global or Local, each question can be specifically categorized by its logical truth characteristics. Although this may sound formidable, it simply refers to whether a question asks for what cannot be true, what could be true, what is not necessarily true, or what must be true. Those four questions cover the range of logical possibilities when discussing the truth, and the correct answer to *every* Logic Game question has one of those four characteristics. Let us take a moment to discuss those possibilities and their meaning in more detail.

Let's say you were to put the truth possibilities on a scale from 0 to 100:

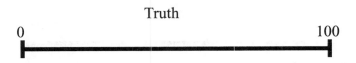

On such a scale, Must Be True and Cannot Be True would be easy to identify, as they are the "ends" or "extremes" of truth:

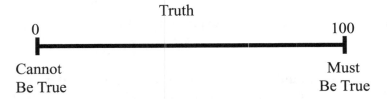

Because we have put truth on a 0 to 100 scale, Cannot Be True, which is similar to "none of the truth," equals 0; Must Be True, which is similar to "all of the truth," equals 100. In this sense, Cannot Be True and Must Be True are polar opposites—at the far ends of the scale.

Thus far, most students intuitively understand what is occurring. And when asked in a question for what Must Be True or Cannot Be True, the nature of the correct answer is easy to understand. But, as you know, each problem on the LSAT has only one correct answer. The other four answer choices are incorrect, which is the *logical* opposite of correct. Thus, because correct and incorrect answers are logical opposites, it can be said that each incorrect answer choice has the exact logical opposite characteristic of the correct answer choice. Understanding the nature of each incorrect answer is also useful, because there will be many instances in which eliminating incorrect answers is critical.

The logical opposite is different from the polar opposite mentioned above, and we will discuss the difference shortly.

So, if we can identify the logical characteristic of the correct answer choice, then because the incorrect answer has the opposite characteristic, we can immediately determine the characteristic of the four incorrect answers as well.

Let us start with Cannot Be True, which represents 0 on our scale. If the correct answer to a question has the characteristic that it Cannot Be True, then the four incorrect answers will have the logically opposite characteristic. In terms of truth, the opposite of Cannot Be True is Could Be True. Numerically speaking, Could Be True is equivalent to the range of 1 to 100:

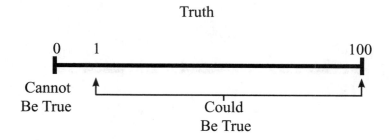

Cannot Be True = 0   (None of the truth, so to speak)

Could Be True = 1 to 100 (everything but Cannot Be True)

Cannot Be True and Could Be True are logical opposites that encompass all possibilities. Since Cannot Be True is so specific, that means that Could Be True encompasses every other possibility (maybe, probably, must, etc).

So, if a question asks for what Cannot Be True, the correct answer must be one that is never the case in the game, and the four incorrect answers each Could Be True, where each answer could be true in the game (or possibly even must be true in the game—more on this point shortly).

Of course, since these two terms are logical opposites, the reverse is true as well. If a question asks for what Could Be True, the one correct answer Could Be True, and the four incorrect answers must have the logically opposite quality, which is Cannot Be True. Thus, we can very easily classify the nature of all of the answers depending on the question being asked:

Question Characteristic	Logical Opposite
1. Cannot Be True	Could Be True
If a question asks for what cannot be true:	
One correct answer: Cannot Be True	Four incorrect answers: Could Be True
2. Could Be True	Cannot Be True
If a question asks for what could be true:	
One correct answer: Could Be True	Four incorrect answers: Cannot Be True

Note that in our truth scale, Cannot Be True and Could Be True have divided the truth spectrum into two parts, and those two parts contain the entire range of truth. Thus, once you have a question that asks for Cannot Be True or Could Be True, you know *all* the possibilities for the correct answer and the four incorrect answers. However, the Cannot/Could pair is not the only pair that exists to classify truth. Because the Cannot/Could pair looks at truth starting from one "end" of the truth scale, it is just one way of looking at truth. If we look at truth from the other end of the scale (Must Be True), a new pair emerges.

Let us now start with Must Be True, which represents 100 on our scale. If the correct answer to a question has the characteristic of Must Be True, then the four incorrect answers will have the logically opposite characteristic. In terms of truth, the opposite of Must Be True is Not Necessarily True. Numerically speaking, Not Necessarily True is equivalent to the range of 0 to 99:

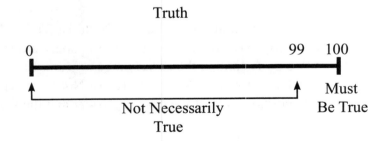

Must Be True = 100 (if something Must Be True then it is 100% of the truth, so to speak)

Not Necessarily True = 0 to 99 (everything but Must Be True)

Must Be True and Not Necessarily True are logical opposites that encompass all possibilities. Since Must Be True is so specific, that means that Not Necessarily True encompasses every other possibility (maybe, possibly, cannot, etc).

So, if a question asks for what Must Be True, the correct answer must be one that is always the case in the game, and the four incorrect answers each are Not Necessarily True, where each answer does not have to be true all of the time in the game (or possibly even cannot be true in the game—more on this point shortly).

Of course, since these two terms are logical opposites, the reverse is true as well. If a question asks for what is Not Necessarily True, the one correct answer is not necessarily true, and the four incorrect answers must have the logically opposite quality, which is Must Be True. Thus, we can again very easily classify the nature of all of the answers depending on the question being asked:

Question Characteristic	Logical Opposite
1. Must Be True	Not Necessarily True
If a question asks for what must be true:	
One correct answer: Must Be True	Four incorrect answers: Not Necessarily True
2. Not Necessarily True	Must Be True
If a question asks for what is not necessarily true:	
One correct answer: Not Necessarily True	Four incorrect answers: Must Be True

In our truth scale, just as with Cannot Be True and Could Be True, Must Be True and Not Necessarily True have divided the truth spectrum into two parts, and those two parts contain the entire range of truth. Thus, once you have a question that asks for what Must Be True or Not Necessarily True, you know *all* the possibilities for the correct answer and the four incorrect answers.

Because the range of truth only extends from Cannot Be True to Must Be True, the four characteristics above represent all of the possible questions you can be asked. And, because the four items naturally divide into two pairs—Could Be True vs. Cannot Be True, and Must Be True vs. Not Necessarily True—when you are analyzing questions, the correct and incorrect answer choices will all be classified into one of these two pairs.

Logical Opposition vs Polar Opposition

Let's take a moment to step back from the abstract discussion of truth. Earlier, we mentioned that the polar opposite of a statement is different from the logical opposite of a statement. Here are the LSAT definitions of each term:

Logical Opposite: Any statement that contradicts the statement in question. Literally, anything different from the statement.

Polar Opposite: A statement that contradicts the statement in question as completely as possible.

When discussing any item that has a range of outcomes (such as truth), these concepts come into play. Let us use temperature as an example.

When discussing temperature, hot and cold are often thought of as the natural "poles," or endpoints, of the scale. These poles are on the extreme ends of the scale, and thus, hot and cold are considered polar opposites. But, in between hot and cold there are many gradations. For example, there is warm, lukewarm, mild, temperate, chilly, etc. A term such as warm is not the polar opposite of hot, but it is different from hot. And, any term that is different from hot will be its logical opposite. That "difference" is the essence of contradiction, and you can imagine how a conversation about temperature that involves contradiction might go:

Speaker 1: Wow, it's hot outside today.

Speaker 2: No, it's just warm.

The "no" at the beginning of the second speaker's sentence signifies that he or she is contradicting the first speaker, and thus providing a logical opposite.

Viewed from this angle, you can also see how the polar opposite qualifies as a logical opposite (just at the extreme): because cold is the polar opposite of hot, it also is a logical opposite of hot.

Truth, like temperature, exists on a gradable scale with many elements, but not all elements exist on a similar scale. Some items have only a few, pre-defined states. For example, marriage: you are either single or married, with no in-between. Thus, single and married are both logical opposites and polar opposites.

Other elements have no polar opposites, only logical opposites. Colors, for example, do not have a pre-defined scale where there are known "ends" (which is why you often see color "wheels"). So, there is no polar opposite of "blue." But, there are many logical opposites of blue, and anything "not blue" would qualify (red, orange, green, etc).

Returning to the scale of truth, because Cannot Be True and Must Be True stand at the ends of the scale, they are polar opposites. The logical opposite of a term like Cannot Be True is then anything but Cannot Be True, which is Could Be True (and Could Be True includes Must Be True, the polar opposite of Cannot Be True).

In Logic Games, polar opposition does not play a large role. Instead, logical opposition is typically the focus, and as long as you understand the logical opposites on the truth scale, you can interpret any Logic Games question with accuracy.

Could Be True vs Not Necessarily True

Let's return to the 0 to 100 truth scale presented earlier in this section. By looking closely at the quantities each possibility represents, we can see that Could Be True (1 to 100) actually includes Must Be True (100). This makes sense because Could Be True, if it is to be the exact logical opposite of Cannot Be True, should include every other possibility besides Cannot Be True. The same relationship also holds true for Not Necessarily True (0 to 99) and Cannot Be True (0)—Not Necessarily True includes Cannot Be True. The operational effect of this fact is that wrong answer choices *can* have characteristics that "go beyond" the simple logical opposite of the correct answer to include the polar opposite. For example, if a question asks for what Cannot Be True, then all four of the incorrect answer choices must have the characteristic of Could Be True (the logical opposite). However, within those four Could Be True answers, some may go even further and have the characteristic of Must Be True (the polar opposite). The same holds true for a question that asks for what Must Be True. The four incorrect answers choices will have the characteristic of Not Necessarily True (the logical opposite), and within those four Not Necessarily True answers some may go further and have the characteristic of Cannot Be True (the polar opposite).

Some students reasonably ask if Could Be True and Not Necessarily True mean the same thing. Could Be True (1 to 100) and Not Necessarily True (0 to 99) are largely the same (between 1 and 99 they are identical), but they differ significantly at the extremes (0 and 100). Could Be True actually includes Must Be True, the opposite of Not Necessarily True, and Not Necessarily True includes Cannot Be True, the opposite of Could Be True. So, despite being similar in many respects, each term actually includes the exact opposite of the other term.

This paragraph confuses some students at first, but there is no anomaly here. For example, consider that Cannot Be True encompasses Not Necessarily True. In other words, if a thing Cannot Be True, it automatically is also Not Necessarily True. Thus, for example, if two answers are Cannot Be True, they are also Not Necessarily True and thus all four are actually under the Not Necessarily True banner.

Logic Game Question Stems

Using the following examples, let's consider how the truth characteristic applies to Logic Game questions, which have been additionally categorized as Global or Local:

If R is seated second, which one of the following could be true?
Categorization: Local, Could Be True
(the 4 incorrect answers Cannot Be True)

Which one of the following cannot be true?
Categorization: Global, Cannot Be True
(the 4 incorrect answers Could Be True)

If R is selected fifth, which one of the following must be true?
Categorization: Local, Must Be True
(the 4 incorrect answers are Not Necessarily True)

For the most part, understanding the questions above should not be too difficult. However, the test makers often append the word "except" to questions similar to those above in order to confuse test takers. In these cases, "except" functions to logically turn the question upside down. Consider the following two examples:

Always be on the lookout for the word "except."

Which one of the following must be true?
Categorization: Global, Must Be True
(the 4 incorrect answers are Not Necessarily True)

Each of the following must be true EXCEPT:
Categorization: Global, Not Necessarily True
(the 4 incorrect answers Must Be True)

In the second example, the presence of "except" inverts the question. Now, the four incorrect answers Must Be True. The correct answer is the opposite of Must Be True, which is Not Necessarily True.

As a rule, the LSAT makers always capitalize "except" when it appears in a question stem. They do so because they are aware of how dramatically it changes the meaning of a question.

Falsity

Another confusing ploy the test makers use is to pose questions in terms of falsity, such as "Which one of the following cannot be false?" Most students are unaccustomed to thinking in terms of false, and thus lose valuable time trying to understand the exact meaning of the question. Since false and true are opposites, whenever you are faced with a question posed in terms of falsity, convert it into one of the four "true" questions we have already reviewed. Here is the conversion table:

Question in False		True Equivalent
1. Must Be False	⟶	Cannot Be True
2. Not Necessarily False	⟶	Could Be True
3. Could Be False	⟶	Not Necessarily True
4. Cannot Be False	⟶	Must Be True

When a question is posed in terms of falsity, convert it to terms of truth. When a question is posed in terms of truth, use it that way.

In using this table, **always convert from False to True**. Never convert from true into false. If the question asks, "Which one of the following could be false?" immediately convert that question to "Which one of the following is not necessarily true?" and then proceed, knowing that the four incorrect answers Must Be True.

Once again, here are some categorized examples:

> Which one of the following could be false?
> > Categorization: Global, Not Necessarily True
> > > (the 4 incorrect answers Must Be True)

> If J speaks third, which one of the following must be false?
> > Categorization: Local, Cannot Be True
> > > (the 4 incorrect answers Could Be True)

> Each of the following cannot be false EXCEPT:
> > Categorization: Global, Not Necessarily True (remember, convert false to true and then apply the "except")
> > > (the 4 incorrect answer Must Be True)

We know what you are thinking: why should I really care about these Global/Local, Cannot/Could/Not Necessarily/Must, and True/False designations? The answer is simple: if you do not know what you are being asked, you cannot answer the question. The LSAT is a precision exam, and to excel you must know as much as possible about the test before you walk in. There are students out there who will see a question such as, "Each one of the following could be false EXCEPT" and they will freeze while trying to determine exactly what the question means (the correct answer Must Be True). By memorizing the tables above, you will save time and gain confidence.

Question Stem Classification Drill

For each of the following items, classify the question stem as Global or Local, and then identify the truth characteristic of the correct answer and then the truth characteristic of the four incorrect answers. Remember, always convert false into true. *Answers on page 148*

Example:

Which one of the following must be true?

Answer:

Classification: Global, Must Be True
Four Incorrect Answers: Not Necessarily True

3

---

1. If G is the second most expensive suite, then which one of the following could be true?

    Classification:

    _____

    Four Incorrect Answers:

    _____

2. If K is displayed third, then each of the following could be true EXCEPT:

    Classification:

    _____

    Four Incorrect Answers:

    _____

3. Which one of the following could be false?

    Classification:

    _____

    Four Incorrect Answers:

    _____

4. If R is delivered earlier than S, then which one of the following cannot be false?

    Classification:

    _____

    Four Incorrect Answers:

    _____

5. Each of the following must be false EXCEPT:

    Classification:

    _____

    Four Incorrect Answers:

    _____

Question Stem Classification Drill

6. Which one of the following CANNOT be the list of elements in the mixture?

   Classification:

   _____

   Four Incorrect Answers:

   _____

7. If Liam selects history, then which one of the following could be true?

   Classification:

   _____

   Four Incorrect Answers:

   _____

8. If H is the last building inspected, it must be true that

   Classification:

   _____

   Four Incorrect Answers:

   _____

9. Each of the following must be true EXCEPT:

   Classification:

   _____

   Four Incorrect Answers:

   _____

10. If the four developments each are new, then which one of the following is allowed?

    Classification:

    _____

    Four Incorrect Answers:

    _____

11. Which one of the following must be false?

    Classification:

    _____

    Four Incorrect Answers:

    _____

12. If Juan is a manager, then each of the following cannot be true EXCEPT:

    Classification:

    _____

    Four Incorrect Answers:

    _____

13. Which one of the following statements can be false?

    Classification:

    _____

    Four Incorrect Answers:

    _____

14. Which one of the following must be a history major?

Classification:

_____

Four Incorrect Answers:

_____

15. Assuming Janet is the first speaker, each of the following cannot be false EXCEPT:

Classification:

_____

Four Incorrect Answers:

_____

3

Question Stem Classification Drill Answer Key

1. If G is the second most expensive suite, then which
    one of the following could be true?

    Classification: Local, Could Be True

    Four Incorrect Answers: Cannot Be True

2. If K is displayed third, then each of the following
    could be true EXCEPT:

    Classification: Local, Cannot Be True

    Four Incorrect Answers: Could Be True

3. Which one of the following could be false?

    Classification: Global, Not Necessarily True

    Four Incorrect Answers: Must Be True

    Remember, "could be false" is equivalent to "not necessarily true."

4. If R is delivered earlier than S, then which one of the
    following cannot be false?

    Classification: Local, Must Be True

    Four Incorrect Answers: Not Necessarily True

    Remember, "cannot be false" is equivalent to "must be true."

5. Each of the following must be false EXCEPT:

    Classification: Global, Could Be True

    Four Incorrect Answers: Cannot Be True

    Remember, "must be false" is equivalent to "cannot be true."

6. Which one of the following CANNOT be the list of elements in the mixture?

    Classification: Global, Cannot Be True

    Four Incorrect Answers: Could Be True

7. If Liam selects history, then which one of the following could be true?

    Classification: Local, Could Be True

    Four Incorrect Answers: Cannot Be True

8. If H is the last building inspected, it must be true that

    Classification: Local, Must Be True

    Four Incorrect Answers: Not Necessarily True

9. Each of the following must be true EXCEPT:

    Classification: Global, Not Necessarily True

    Four Incorrect Answers: Must Be True

10. If the four developments each are new, then which one of the following is allowed?

    Classification: Local, Could Be True

    Four Incorrect Answers: Cannot Be True

11. Which one of the following must be false?

      Classification: Global, Cannot Be True

      Four Incorrect Answers: Could Be True

---

12. If Juan is a manager, then each of the following
    cannot be true EXCEPT:

      Classification: Local, Could Be True

      Four Incorrect Answers: Cannot Be True

---

13. Which one of the following statements can be false?

      Classification: Global, Not Necessarily True

      Four Incorrect Answers: Must Be True

---

14. Which one of the following must be a history major?

      Classification: Global, Must Be True

      Four Incorrect Answers: Not Necessarily True

---

15. Assuming Janet is the first speaker, each of the
    following cannot be false EXCEPT:

      Classification: Local, Not Necessarily True

      Four Incorrect Answers: Must Be True

Six Specific Question Types ▬▬▬

The general characteristics of Logic Games questions that we just discussed will cover the majority of questions you encounter. However, there are six very specific question types that you will also see:

This is a brief introduction to these six types. In a later chapter some of the types will be discussed in more detail.

1. List Questions

List questions present a list of variables that can either fill an individual slot or possibly solve the game. Here are the two basic types of List questions:

Complete Solution List question

Here is an example of a Complete Solution List question, the most common type of List question:

The first question in a game is often a List question.

> Which one of the following could be a list of the students in the order of their tutoring sessions, from 1 P.M. to 6 P.M.?
>
> (A)   S, T, Z, W, X, Y
> (B)   T, W, X, Y, Z, S
> (C)   T, X, W, Y, S, Z
> (D)   W, X, Y, S, Z, T
> (E)   X, T, W, Y, Z, S

This type of List question asks you to select the answer choice that contains a solution to the game that does not violate any of the rules. The best technique for attacking this type of List question is to take a *single* rule and apply it to each of the five answer choices, one at a time. Eliminate any answer choice that violates the rule. Then, choose another rule and apply the same procedure to the remaining answer choices. Do this until you have only one answer choice left. If you run out of rules and there is still more than one answer choice remaining, look to see if the game scenario contains some limiting feature that you overlooked, such as that one variable is used multiple times, or that some numerical restriction exists.

Games featuring numerical distributions often test the distribution in a List question.

When choosing a game rule to apply to this type of question, do not choose randomly! Instead, consider the following elements:

---

1. Choose rules that are simple and thus visually easy to apply.

   For example, a rule that states that "S cannot be tutored at 6 P.M." involves only one variable and would be very easy to apply, whereas a rule such as "X must be tutored earlier than Y and Z" involves three variables and would be more time-consuming to apply.

2. Begin by choosing rules that are as concrete as possible, and have as few options as possible.

   For example, a rule that states that "X is tutored immediately before Y" would be preferable to a rule that states that "S and T are tutored consecutively," because the first rule has only one configuration whereas the second rule has two configurations.

   Similarly, a rule such as "X is tutored immediately before Y" would be preferable to a rule such as "W is tutored earlier than Z," again because the first rule has only one configuration whereas the second rule has multiple configurations.

3. In any game that contains one or more rules that specify an exact number, any Complete Solution List question will typically test you on at least one side of the number rule, and often on both sides of the number rule.

   For example, consider a rule that states that "N performs exactly twice during the show." In such a game (which then would not be a 1-to-1 relationship game), you would expect a List question to have incorrect answers that present N performing exactly once, or exactly three times. In other words, something other than the number of times specified by the rule. In certain games, checking these numerical restrictions can eliminate pesky incorrect answers that otherwise appear correct.

List questions of this sort are usually Global but can be Local (if, for example, a variable was placed and then the rest of the solution was required). As a reference, the above question would be designated as a Global, Could Be True, List question.

When we begin examining actual LSAT games, we will discuss List questions in detail in the explanations, and walk through the optimal steps for solving each question.

Important Digital LSAT diagramming note: When you identify the correct answer to a Complete Solution List question (and you are sure it is correct), write down the solution *separately* on your scratch paper, for example:

    1. L N M O K J P

This will allow you to see this solution when working on any other question in the game, and as we will discuss later in this chapter, this can be a valuable aid when solving other questions.

Complete Variable List question

Another type of List question supplies a list of all of the variables that could be placed in a single slot, as in the following example:

> Which one of the following is a complete and accurate list of the singers any of which could be the first to perform?
>
> (A)   P, S
> (B)   P, Q, R, S
> (C)   P, Q, R, V
> (D)   Q, R, S, V
> (E)   Q, R, S, T, V

The question above is not suggesting that each answer supplies a list of variables that starts at the first space and goes out from there; rather, the question asks you to identify every variable that could be first in *some* scenario in the game. Thus, if in one solution to the game P could be first, then P *must* appear in the correct answer choice (and, in our sample question, if P could be first, answer choices (D) and (E) would immediately be eliminated, because neither contains P). If in another scenario Q could be first, then Q must also appear in the correct answer choice, and so on.

To solve these questions, first check the rules to see if any of the variables cause a violation when placed in the slot. Second, check all Not Laws for that slot and scan all the answer choices to see if any answers can be eliminated on that basis. Finally, make hypothetical solutions (as discussed in the upcoming Attacking the Questions section) to prove or disprove any remaining answers.

2. Maximum/Minimum Questions

Maximum/Minimum questions generally ask you to identify the greatest or least number of possibilities in a certain scenario, and these questions typically fall into one of two types:

- Questions that ask for the maximum or minimum number of possible variables that can fill a certain position, or the maximum or minimum number of positions a variable can fill.

- Questions that ask for the maximum or minimum number of variables that can be placed between two particular variables, or ask for the maximum or minimum number of spaces from one variable to another.

In answering Maximum/Minimum questions, you must control the variables in order to produce the optimal situation to either maximize the situation or minimize the situation. Essentially, you get to play LSAT god for the purposes of the question, altering and adjusting each situation to produce the desired results.

Consider the following example question stems:

> What is the maximum possible number of speeches any one of which could be the one given on the third day?

> What is the minimum number of different procedures that can be used by the six surgeons?

> What is the minimum possible number of houses between the Tanners and the Carrolls, counting from east to west?

For the above examples, the first question is a Global, Must Be True, Maximum, and the second and third questions are Global, Must Be True, Minimum questions.

In evaluating Maximum/Minimum questions, consider the following points:

1. The answer choices often feature numbers as the answer (for example, 2 or 5). However, there are a number of Maximum/ Minimum questions that first require you to create a Maximum/ Minimum situation and then ask about an aspect of the situation. For example:

> If as many of the parents attend the meeting as possible, that group will consist of

In this question, you first have to establish the maximum number, and then examine the characteristics of that group.

2. Maximum/Minimum questions are often Global but can be Local. The three question stem examples provided on the previous page are Global, but the example provided in point 1 above is Local (because it specifies that you must make the group as large as possible before proceeding).

3. These questions appear to trade on a degree of uncertainty because they often use the word "could" in the stem, and thus the initial inclination is to classify them as Could Be True questions. However, because these questions ask you to identify an absolute truth in the game (the maximum or minimum of a relationship), they are actually Must Be True questions.

For example, in the first example question stem on the previous page, because there is only one possible number that can represent the maximum number of speeches, the correct answer *must be* the maximum number, and thus it is a Must Be True question.

4. Regardless of whether a question is posed in terms of Maximum or in terms of Minimum, each question has both a Maximum and Minimum component. For example, a question that asks "What is the *maximum* number of clowns *ahead* of Q?" is basically the same as a question that asks, "What is the *minimum* number of clowns *behind* Q?"

In general, to solve these questions, you should take the following steps:

1. Check prior work to eliminate any incorrect answers or to confirm a correct answer (more on this process later in this chapter).

2. Consider the abstract relationships created by the rules in order to establish the general Maximum/Minimum number in play.

3. If multiple answers remain in contention, in order to decide which answer is correct, attempt to create a solution that matches the greatest/least possible number remaining among the answers.

We will discuss how to solve Maximum/Minimum questions in additional detail when we encounter them in the actual Logic Games in this book.

3. "5 If" Questions

"5 if" questions are identifiable not by an element in the question stem, but by the language in the five answer choices. Here is an example from an actual game that appears later in the book:

Which one of the following statements must be true?

(A) If P is in group 1, then T must be in group 2.
(B) If Q is in group 1, then P must be in group 1.
(C) If R is in group 2, then V must be in group 2.
(D) If R is in group 2, then S must be in group 3.
(E) If S is in group 3, then T must be in group 1.

"5 if" problems are dangerous because they can be quite time-consuming.

In this question, each of the five answer choices begins with the word "if," hence the "5 if" designation. The "if" in each answer choice adds a new condition to the scenario that must be taken into account, and thus each answer choice is essentially a whole new question. Consequently, test takers are forced to work out a new scenario or solution for each (or most) of the five answer choices. Because these questions are basically five questions in one, they can be incredibly time consuming. If you struggle with time issues at all in the Logic Games section, you would be well advised to either skip these questions entirely or wait to do them until after you have completed the other questions in a game.

4. Justify Questions

Justify questions ask you to select the answer choice that forces a specified result. For example:

P must be the first singer to perform if which one of the following is true?

(A) Q performs second
(B) R performs fourth
(C) S performs fifth
(D) T performs fifth
(E) V performs seventh

In this question, the desired result is for P to be the first singer to perform. You must then select the one answer choice that forces this result to occur. While in theory this may sound easy, in practice these questions can be quite difficult. In part, this is because the question is "upside down:" in normal questions, information from the question stem has certain effects, and then you choose the answer that reflects one of these effects. In Justify questions, the answer choices create the effects, and the result is the one specified by the question stem.

To solve a Justify question, the first step is to carefully analyze the result that is specified in the question stem. Because producing this final result is your goal, in a sense you have to work backwards in order to determine which answer choice will produce that result. This process typically centers around which variables are the most powerful (the variables that have the greatest impact on other variables) and which spaces are the most restricted (spaces with more restrictions are often at the center of question solutions). The second step involves analyzing the answer choices to determine which is most likely to create the type of limitations that will result in the desired outcome.

One recurrent type of incorrect answer choice has been an answer that *could* create the desired outcome, but does not *have* to create the outcome. For example, in the question above, an incorrect answer might allow P to be the first singer, but also allow P to perform in a different position. Because the question stem specifies that P *must* be the first singer to perform, such an answer would be incorrect.

5. Suspension Questions

Suspension questions always appear at the end of the game, and they suspend one of the rules from the game. These questions, although relatively rare, are also very time consuming because usually you must redraw most of the diagram and re-evaluate the relationship of the rules.

Here is an example:

> Suppose that the condition that the Marketing conference is scheduled immediately after the Finance conference is removed. If all the other conditions remain the same, then which of the conferences could be the Sales conference?
>
> (A) the first
> (B) the second
> (C) the third
> (D) the fifth
> (E) the seventh

The removal of a rule from the original setup of the game almost always forces you to reconsider the game from the beginning. Typically, removing a rule changes the inferences you have made, and usually creates a greater number of solutions to the game than originally existed. Thus, if you are struggling with time, this is a question type that you might want to skip, or return to at the end of the section if you have time.

6. Rule Substitution Questions

Rule Substitution questions are an unusual combination of Suspension and Justify questions. In a Rule Substitution question, one of the original rules of the game is suspended, and you are asked to select an answer choice that contains language that has an identical effect as the original rule. In short, you must find an answer that presents a perfect equivalent of the original rule.

Here is an example:

> Which one of the following, if substituted for the condition that F and G must be separated by exactly one session, would have the same effect in determining the order of the sessions?
>
> (A)   F must be scheduled for the second, third, or fourth session.
> (B)   F cannot be scheduled for an earlier session than G.
> (C)   G cannot be scheduled for the last session.
> (D)   H must be scheduled for a session somewhere between F and G.
> (E)   J and K cannot be scheduled for consecutive sessions.

Rule Substitution questions are a relatively new phenomenon in the Logic Games section, having first appeared in 2009. Like regular Suspension questions, when they have appeared in a game, they have always appeared as the last question in the game.

These questions can be very challenging, and thus we will cover them (and Justify questions) in more detail in a second section about question types later in the book. For now, note that if you are struggling with time at this point in your preparation, this is a question type that you might want to skip, or return to at the end of the section if you have time.

Attacking the Questions ■■■■■■

One of the critical elements in attacking the questions is the ability to classify the questions as Global or Local, and then to designate each question as one of the "truth" characteristics discussed on pages 135-144. Classifying each question will tell you exactly what you are being asked, thereby making your task easier. And, as time goes by, this process will become second nature, and you will no longer have to actively think about the fundamentals of each question as you work through each game—you will simply recognize each question type almost instantly. Once you understand the question that is being asked, you must then seamlessly slip into a mode that allows you to solve the question as quickly and as easily as possible. Let us discuss some of the elements involved in making that occur.

Learn from the Question Stem When Possible

Because of the language used in asking questions, some question stems reveal useful information about the game, information that can then be used later to your advantage. This information is typically delivered in one of two ways:

1. The question stem indicates that a variable can be placed into a certain position or that certain variables can be grouped together.

   Example stem:

   > If the L is exhibited sixth, then which one of the following must be true?

   In a question stem such as the one above, you automatically know that L can be exhibited sixth. This information, while seemingly innocuous, could be useful elsewhere in the game, such as in a List question asking for variables that could appear in the sixth position (such occurrences may sound surprising, but have happened before).

2. The question stem indicates that a global truth is present in the game.

On occasion, the way a question stem is phrased indicates that certain events must always occur in the game. In those instances it is imperative that you solve the question, as it is likely that the answer will greatly increase your ability to answer the other questions more quickly.

Example stem:

> Which one of the following managers must work during the first week?

In this question stem, the test makers indicate that there is a manager who is *always* working during the first week. Hopefully, your initial game setup contains that information, and answering this question becomes a simple process of checking your setup. However, in the event that you did not make this inference during the setup, it is critical that you complete this question when you encounter it (meaning, do not skip this question and decide to return to it later!). Because the question stem indicates that there is a universal truth in the game, it will appear in *every* solution to the game, and thus it is a piece of information you need to have before answering any other questions.

Of course, not every question stem provides you with useful information. While most Local questions give you some information, there are a number of Global questions that do not provide any information about the game. For example:

> Which one of the following could be true?

> Each of the following must be true EXCEPT:

These questions only ask about universal aspects of the game without providing additional information about the variables, and thus there is no information to be derived from them.

Question Solution Strategies

In general, the fastest way to find the correct answer is to read the question stem, process the implications mentally, and then identify the correct answer from among the five answer choices. Of course, this does not always happen so easily! Usually, much more work is involved.

In the likely scenario that you do not immediately see the correct answer, keep in mind that there are several simple methods of attacking the questions, as outlined below.

Solve for the Correct Answer

In Global questions, solving for the correct answer typically involves referring to the inferences you made during the setup of the game. When one of your inferences answers the question, the result is the most optimal as virtually no time passes between the start of the question and finding the correct answer.

The first step in any Local question is to consider the effects of the condition posed in the question stem. This usually involves drawing out a skeletal version of the main diagram (more on this in the next section) and then working out the problem. Although this may take a few moments, this approach, which may already be intuitive, is often the most effective.

Process of Elimination

As you encounter questions on the LSAT, keep in mind that you do not always have to prove that the right answer is indisputably correct. At times you will be able to easily find the correct answer, especially when using Not Laws or inferences. But, it can be equally rewarding to eliminate each of the incorrect answers and then be left with the correct answer. This process of elimination is extremely useful and can be the most efficient technique for finding the correct answer, especially if you are having difficulty with solving a problem. For example, even if you cannot clearly prove that answer choice (B) is correct, if you can disprove answer choices (A), (C), (D), and (E), you will know that (B) is correct.

Use process of elimination when applicable.

For example, consider a question that asks the following:

Which one of the following could be true?

(A)   D performs third
(B)   F performs fourth
(C)   J performs second
(D)   M performs sixth
(E)   O performs seventh

Perhaps from your initial analysis of the game, none of the answers immediately jumps out as a potential winner. But, when you examine the Not Laws in the game, you notice that every answer but one is eliminated from contention (for example, you see a D Not Law on the third position, and that eliminates answer choice (A), etc). This method, although slightly more time-consuming than simply seeing the correct answer right off the bat, is equally effective in helping you arrive at the correct answer choice.

Process of elimination is an important tool in answering LSAT questions, and even when you cannot eliminate all four incorrect answers, the ability to eliminate even one or two incorrect answer choices is very important because it will save time overall. If you are forced to consider each answer choice on its own merits, the fewer answer choices you have to consider, the better.

Hypotheticals

Whenever you find yourself stumped by a problem, instead of just aimlessly pondering what the right answer might be, try to solve the question with a hypothetical. A hypothetical is one possible solution to the question that *you quickly create* to gain insight into the answers. Some questions can be solved entirely with hypotheticals, and in other questions hypotheticals can help you quickly eliminate several incorrect answer choices from contention.

Consider the following question:

Which one of the following could be true?

(A) P speaks first.
(B) Q speaks second.
(C) R speaks third.
(D) S speaks fourth.
(E) T speaks fifth.

Assume that initially you did not see an obvious answer, and then you checked your inferences, Not Laws, etc, and were only able to eliminate two incorrect answers, answer choices (A) and (B). You are now left with three remaining answer choices. What should you do at this point?

In this problem, a single hypothetical could prove the correct answer choice. Let us say you came up with the following hypothetical:

$$\frac{T}{1} \quad \frac{P}{2} \quad \frac{R}{3} \quad \frac{Q}{4} \quad \frac{S}{5} \quad \frac{V}{6} \quad \frac{W}{7}$$

Because this is a Could Be True question, just showing that any one of the answer choices could occur is enough to prove that answer correct. Thus, because this hypothetical shows R speaking third, it alone proves answer choice (C) correct.

Of course, a natural question comes up at this point: why that particular hypothetical? A hypothetical is just a single, self-made solution to the game. Some hypotheticals are easy to create because you might already have them in hand, or you may need to add only one or two more variables to a diagram in order to create a full solution. In other instances, you may be trying to prove a certain point and thus you "engineer" the hypothetical to appear a certain way. When engineering a hypothetical, your goal is to create maximal effect: either confirm a correct answer, or eliminate as many incorrect answers as possible.

Let us look at another, more difficult example. Consider the following question:

Which one of the following must be true?

(A)   C speaks third.
(B)   D speaks fourth.
(C)   E speaks fifth.
(D)   F speaks sixth.
(E)   G speaks seventh.

Suppose you were not sure which one of the answers had to be true, and you saw no easy way to solve the problem. Instead of skipping the problem or wasting valuable time, you could quickly create a hypothetical solution to help eliminate at least some of the incorrect answer choices (if you could create a hypothetical to eliminate every answer choice that would be optimal, but that is generally unlikely to occur!). Let us say you came up with the following hypothetical on your scratch paper:

$$\frac{C}{1} \quad \frac{E}{2} \quad \frac{D}{3} \quad \frac{A}{4} \quad \frac{B}{5} \quad \frac{F}{6} \quad \frac{G}{7}$$

Because the question was a Must Be True question, any hypothetical that shows a named variable in a position other than the one referenced in the answer choice can then be used to eliminate that answer.

Using the above hypothetical, you can immediately eliminate three answers:

Answer choice (A):   Because C is first in the hypothetical and (A) claims it *must* be third, (A) does not have to be true.

Answer choice (B):   Because D is third in the hypothetical and (B) claims it *must* be fourth, (B) does not have to be true.

Answer choice (C):   Because E is second in the hypothetical and (C) claims it *must* be fifth, (C) does not have to be true.

Thus, from this one hypothetical, we have eliminated three incorrect answer choices, leaving only answer choices (D) and (E) in contention.

At this point, the hypothetical can look confusing, because it appears that it proves both answer choices (D) and (E) correct. Of course, there are never two correct answers to an LSAT problem, so what is happening here?

In the question at the top of page 165, one of the five answer choices *must always* occur. That does not mean that the other four never occur; it just means that they do not always occur. So, between answer choices (D) and (E), one must always occur, and the other clearly can occur, but will not always occur (this fact is known because the question stem asks for what Must Be True). If necessary, you could produce another hypothetical to determine whether answer choice (D) or (E) is correct. Although this method will take a bit of time, it is worth it if you can get the question correct. Plus, each hypothetical you create adds to your arsenal of game information, and makes you more comfortable with the way the rules interact. In many cases, one of the hypotheticals you make can later be used to answer another question.

Oftentimes, the process of simply creating the hypothetical is enough to not only solve the question, but also shed additional light on how the game operates. If you find yourself spending a lot of time thinking about a question, a better approach would probably be to try a few hypotheticals. By coming up with hypotheticals, you are at least making some progress in answering the question.

Important Digital LSAT diagramming note: When you create hypotheticals on your scratch paper and they are a viable solution to the game, make a notation to that effect (such as putting a star next to the hypothetical) so that you are aware that the solution was viable if you review that work later; additionally, make sure to mark out any solution that isn't viable. This approach helps eliminate confusion when you attempt to reuse work!

For example:

The process of creating hypotheticals is easier in practice than it may sound in theory, and this book often refers to hypothetical scenarios to explain why certain answers are right or wrong.

5. Gbl   K   N   M   O   J   L   P   *

~~   N   O   K   L   M~~

Re-Using Information

As you work with each question, your understanding of the game naturally increases. Thus, as you approach each question, do not forget that you may have already gained information in a previous question that might apply to the question you are working on. Some students, upon hearing this advice, respond by saying, "But isn't the information in each question relevant to that question only?" Yes, the conditions in the question stem apply directly to that question only, but the work done for that question *may* apply elsewhere. Consider the following scenario:

Reusing applicable information is one of the most powerful techniques available to students.

The first question of the game is a Global, Could Be True, List question, such as this one:

1. Which one of the following is an acceptable schedule for the six speakers?

	Mon.	Tues.	Wed.	Thurs.	Fri.	Sat.
(A)	B	C	D	E	G	H
(B)	E	B	D	C	G	H
(C)	C	G	D	B	E	H
(D)	B	C	D	G	E	H
(E)	G	B	D	E	C	H

Let us say that the correct answer to this question is (E), and that this question is considered "very easy." Note that once you have established (E) as the correct answer (and it is likely that you would be extremely confident in selecting answer choice (E) because List questions are generally quite easy), you know that the sequence of G—B—D—E—C—H is a workable solution to the game. In other words, the solution in answer choice (E) is a valid hypothetical given to you *for free* by the test makers!

Continuing on in the game, question #2 asks:

Once you know that (E) is a viable solution, write down that solution on your scratch paper next to the question number (as discussed previously). This will make it far easier to return to that work when you do other questions.

2. Which one of the following is a complete and accurate list of those speakers each of whom CANNOT speak on Tuesday?

    (A) C, G, H
    (B) D, H
    (C) B, C, H
    (D) B, D, H
    (E) D, G, H

Since this Global, Cannot Be True, List question asks about which speakers cannot speak on Tuesday, the information we derived in question

Only reuse previous answers and work in which you have complete confidence. For instance, if you answer a List question and you are not sure you have chosen the correct answer, do not re-use the information from that question!

The question to the right is a Local, Could Be True question.

#1 is applicable (since question #1 gave us information about Tuesday as part of the overall answer). In fact, since we know from question #1 answer choice (E) that B *can* speak on Tuesday, any answer in question #2 that contains B is automatically incorrect. Since both answer choices (C) and (D) contain B, they are both incorrect. Thus, the answer choice to question #1 can be used to eliminate two of the answers in question #2. This certainly reduces the amount of work you have to do in question #2 and it has the added benefit of increasing your speed and confidence as you work through the question.

And, the benefits of using work from question #1 in this game do not stop there. Consider question #3 from the same game:

3. If E speaks on Thursday, B could speak on

    (A)   Monday, but on no other day
    (B)   Thursday, but on no other day
    (C)   Monday or else on Tuesday, but on no other day
    (D)   Tuesday or else on Wednesday, but on no other day
    (E)   Wednesday or else on Thursday, but on no other day

Because E is scheduled for Thursday in question #1 answer choice (E), the solution to question #1 meets the condition given in question #3. Thus, we know from question #1 that when E speaks on Thursday, it is possible that B speaks on Tuesday. We can now use this information to attack some of the answer choices in question #3. Specifically, we can eliminate answer choices (A), (B), and (E) since they do not allow for the possibility that B can speak on Tuesday. We are now left with only answer choice (C) and (D) to consider, and it will not take very long to determine which one is correct.

Remember, to reuse work it must meet the criteria given in the question stem of the question on which you are working.

To summarize, it is possible to reuse information from previous questions on subsequent questions, *as long as the work you use meets the criteria in the question you are working on.* The application of this technique to the game under discussion eliminates 5 of the 10 answer choices in questions #2 and #3 without requiring any other work besides referring back to question #1. This technique can be immensely powerful and you should always look to apply it when doing Logic Games. In our discussion of the games in this book, you will see a number of references to this approach.

Placing Diagrams ▮▮▮

As discussed briefly back in Chapter Two, you should use the space at the top of a scratch paper page to diagram your *initial* setup, and then make mini-diagrams as needed below that for each question:

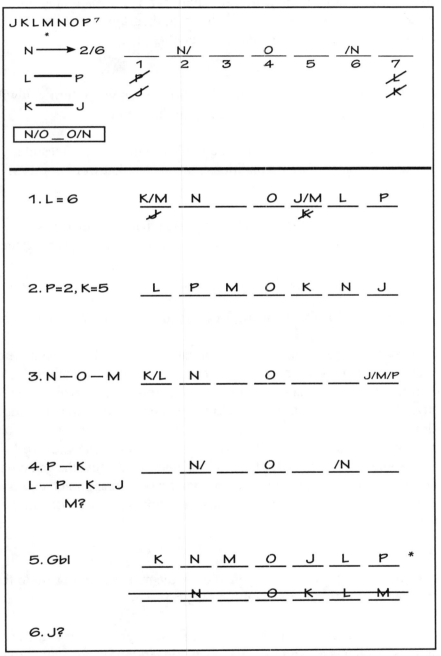

When creating your main diagram, make sure your writing is not too small or too large, do not crowd the rules together, and do not orient your diagram too far to the left or right. The reason for this advice is that in some instances you may find that you need more room on one side than you initially plan for, and it is helpful if you still have some room on each side of the diagram to work with.

Diagramming Local Questions

For many Global questions, the work you do in creating your main setup and making inferences will be sufficient to answer the question. Local questions, which supply a new piece of information specific to that question only, *generally* require additional work. When extra work is required, you should do this work separately *below* the main diagram on your scratch paper (as opposed to on the main diagram itself or as part of a unified grid). This yields you some key benefits:

1. If you need to come back to a question, when you return you will be able to see the work you did up to that point.

2. Should you be able to reuse the work you did for the question, you will be able to see the conditions that created that work more easily.

There are two alternate theories to this approach that are sometimes suggested and we believe each is flawed. Let us take a moment to examine why:

Flawed Approach #1: Do the work for each question on the main diagram

This approach suggests that the work for each question should be done on the main diagram. In order to use this method, you must erase your previous work before beginning each question. Erasing your work has a number of negative effects: you could accidentally erase important information that applies to all questions, you could accidentally leave information that applies only to one question, and most importantly, every time you erase your work you lose some of the knowledge that you had uncovered about the game. This method also destroys your ability to reuse your work, an approach discussed previously. As a rule, *never* erase any of your work unless you have made a mistake.

If you use a pencil to make your diagrams (and you should), do not erase any of your work unless you have made a mistake.

Flawed Approach #2: Create a "grid" below the main diagram and do the work for each question in rows within the grid

While this approach is superior to the first flawed approach, it still has limitations. Students attempting this technique tend to create matrix-like charts, such as:

	1	2	3	4	5	6
Question #1	T	V	W	Z	X	S
Question #2	V	W		Z		
Question #3		S	X	Z	T	

Although this method is superior to using the first flawed approach above, it too has several negative effects:

1. Using the grid tends to train students to use horizontal setups that do not contain a vertical component. As will be discussed in the Advanced Linear games section, this is particularly problematic because the most complex Linear games have both vertical and horizontal components. For example, consider the following game. In this game four music classes, four teachers, and four students were each assigned to one of four consecutive days. This produced a setup akin to the following:

   Student: ___ ___ ___ ___   (R, S, T, V)

   Teacher: ___ ___ ___ ___   (G, H, J, K)

   Class: ___ ___ ___ ___   (B, C, D, E)

            1   2   3   4

   Trying to reproduce a similar diagram within a grid is a nightmare, as each question requires three rows, something the grid is ill-equipped to handle. Any technique you use should work equally well for the hard games and the easy games. This is not the case for the grid!

2. As Linear games become more complex, the grid tends to work less and less efficiently. In contrast, working separately with each question is always efficient, as doing so allows you to draw the most appropriate diagram for the conditions.

3. In games that are non-Linear (such as Grouping games or Circular games), a grid often is too cumbersome or space inefficient to be a viable approach. As mentioned before, you want a diagramming system that handles *any* type of game, not just certain types.

Setups that use an X, O, or check are weak. See Appendix Three for more information.

The game setup to the right is provided to give you a sense of the difference between the main diagram and the mini-diagram you would create next to an individual question, and so the discussion that follows about "diagramming under the question" makes sense. It is not intended to be an actual game diagramming exercise (if it had been, we would have provided the entire text of the game for you).

The key point is that when work is done for a specific question, only the bare basics of the diagram should be re-created under the main diagram.

By the way, it seems that some proponents of the grid also use notations such as "X," "O," and "✓." This type of notation is relatively useless because it abstracts the representation process. Variables are always better represented by directly placing them on the diagram and using Not Laws, etc.

Now that we have discussed some flawed methods of diagramming the questions, let us return to the discussion of working next to the question itself. Working next to the question often requires you to re-create the basics of the main setup. This re-creation will be in skeletal form only; there is no need to redraw the entire diagram or all of the rules. Consider the following example:

Main diagram from a Logic Game:

Question #2 from the same game:

2. If P performs second and K performs fifth, the third performer must be

(A) J
(B) L
(C) M
(D) N
(E) O

Do the work on your scratch paper under the main diagram!

2. P=2, K=5   L   P   M   O   K   N   J

Note that the work is done on a diagram that reflects just the simple base of the game—none of the rules are redrawn and you can even skip numbering the spaces if you feel comfortable.

Tricks of the Trade ▬■▬▬▬▬

The Digital LSAT: Problem Flagging and Answer Marking

There are two tools available to you in the digital interface that work well together when you are working with questions and answer choices:

Flagging

To the right of each question stem is a small flag icon that, when selected, marks the question for you. The flag darkens, and, more importantly, a small blue flag appears above the question number at the bottom of the screen in the navigation bar. This allows you to instantly see all the problems you have flagged, and using the navigation bar, to return to them instantly. Simply click on the flagged question at the bottom and you will immediately return to that problem.

Answer Markout

Another tool available to you on the Digital LSAT allows you to "mark out" individual answer choices that you deem incorrect. By selecting the circle with a slash through it that sits to the right of each answer, the entire answer will be greyed out (readable still, but clearly dimmed on-screen). The answer choice bubble itself then appears with a slash through it, indicating that you have chosen to eliminate the answer (this can be overridden by tapping the answer bubble).

For many students, the markout tool is a helpful substitute for their normal approach to eliminating answers visually: simply crossing through the lettered answer choice in their test booklet. Perhaps most useful, if you leave the question and return to it later, the markouts remain, which helps you quickly identify the answers you disliked on your first read-through. This tool, when combined with the flagging of questions, allows you to instantly return to uncertain questions and re-engage with the problem.

Because these tools allow you to navigate both questions and answer choices more easily, we strongly recommend that you use them both!

Flagging Questions vs Dwelling on Problems

The individuals who construct standardized tests are called *psychometricians*. We know this job title sounds ominous, but it's actually quite revealing: breaking the word into its two parts tells you a great deal about the nature of the LSAT!

While we could make a number of jokes about the *psycho* part (and often do in class!), this portion of the word merely refers to psychology; the *metrician* piece relates to metrics or measurement. Thus, the purpose of these individuals is to create a test that measures you in a precise, psychological way.

As part of this process, the makers of the LSAT carefully analyze reams of data from every test administration in order to assess the tendencies and behavior of test takers. As Sherlock Holmes observed, "You can, for example, never foretell what any one man will do, but you can say with precision what an average number will be up to." By studying the actions of all past test takers, the makers of the exam can reliably predict where you will be most likely to make errors. And throughout this book we will reference those pitfalls as they relate to specific game and question types.

For the moment, we would like to highlight one mental trap you must avoid at all times in any LSAT section: the tendency to dwell on past problems and allow them to subvert your concentration going forward. Many students fall prey to "answering" a question, and then continuing to replay it in their minds as they start the next question, and the next. Obviously, this is distracting and creates an environment where missing subsequent problems becomes far more likely. So be sure to separate the notions of reusing your prior work within a game or passage set and learning as you go—approaches that are crucial for success!—from the psychological pitfall we're describing here: when you finish a question, you must move to the next question with 100% focus, clarity, and confidence.

Remember, if you are uncertain of your answer on a problem, simply flag that question electronically and then, time permitting, return to it later for further review (use the navigation bar at the bottom of the screen to quickly jump to your flagged questions). This allows you to track any difficulties that may arise, but also immediately set them aside as you move on to the remaining questions and the continued insights and assistance they often provide.

Final Pregame Note

At this point we have covered many of the basic concepts that appear in Linear games, and more importantly, we have defined much of the terminology that we will use in our analyses of the games to come. On the next page is the first of five Linear game challenges. Each game comes from an actual LSAT and has been reproduced exactly as it first appeared, down to the original question numbering. Thus, if a game originally appeared last in the Analytical Reasoning section, we have numbered it appropriately, perhaps as questions #18-24. The date the game appeared is also noted in the header. On the pages immediately following each game, there is a comprehensive explanation of the setup, the inferences, and each question, along with strategy and technical notes. Please be sure to read the explanations carefully, as they explain many of the finer points of our approaches and they will give you a true sense of how to best attack each game.

If you would like to test yourself under timed conditions, you should give yourself 8 minutes and 45 seconds for each game. However, with the first few games we recommend that you worry less about time and focus more on properly diagramming and analyzing the game. In that vein, before continuing on, now would be a great time to go back and review this chapter, at least briefly. Regardless, good luck on the games!

Two Notes:

> Every game from each chapter is presented again at the end of the book in the ReChallenge section. This section gives you the opportunity to try each game again.

> In doing these games, **use scratch paper instead of writing directly on the game!** This will prepare you for the Digital LSAT format where you cannot write directly on the screen.

3

In our explanations we often include points of interest outside the game, as well as general strategy tips. Therefore, even if you answered the question correctly, reading the explanation can still be quite valuable.

Games from the LSATs that were administered in the most recent years have been avoided in order to preserve those tests for use as fresh practice exams.

During a period of six consecutive days—day 1 through day 6—each of exactly six factories—F, G, H, J, Q, and R—will be inspected. During this period, each of the factories will be inspected exactly once, one factory per day. The schedule for the inspections must conform to the following conditions:

F is inspected on either day 1 or day 6.

J is inspected on an earlier day than Q is inspected.

Q is inspected on the day immediately before R is inspected.

If G is inspected on day 3, Q is inspected on day 5.

1. Which one of the following could be a list of the factories in the order of their scheduled inspections, from day 1 through day 6?

(A)   F, Q, R, H, J, G
(B)   G, H, J, Q, R, F
(C)   G, J, Q, H, R, F
(D)   G, J, Q, R, F, H
(E)   J, H, G, Q, R, F

GO ON TO THE NEXT PAGE.

2. Which one of the following must be false?

   (A)   The inspection of G is scheduled for day 4.
   (B)   The inspection of H is scheduled for day 6.
   (C)   The inspection of J is scheduled for day 4.
   (D)   The inspection of Q is scheduled for day 3.
   (E)   The inspection of R is scheduled for day 2.

3. The inspection of which one of the following
   CANNOT be scheduled for day 5?

   (A)   G
   (B)   H
   (C)   J
   (D)   Q
   (E)   R

4. The inspections scheduled for day 3 and day 5,
   respectively, could be those of

   (A)   G and H
   (B)   G and R
   (C)   H and G
   (D)   R and J
   (E)   R and H

5. If the inspection of R is scheduled for the day
   immediately before the inspection of F, which one of
   the following must be true about the schedule?

   (A)   The inspection of either G or H is scheduled
         for day 1.
   (B)   The inspection of either G or J is scheduled for
         day 1.
   (C)   The inspection of either G or J is scheduled for
         day 2.
   (D)   The inspection of either H or J is scheduled for
         day 3.
   (E)   The inspection of either H or J is scheduled for
         day 4.

6. If the inspections of G and of H are scheduled, not
   necessarily in that order, for days as far apart as
   possible, which one of the following is a complete and
   accurate list of the factories any one of which could
   be scheduled for inspection for day 1?

   (A)   F, J
   (B)   G, H
   (C)   G, H, J
   (D)   F, G, H
   (E)   F, G, H, J

7. If the inspection of G is scheduled for the day
   immediately before the inspection of Q, which one of
   the following could be true?

   (A)   The inspection of G is scheduled for day 5.
   (B)   The inspection of H is scheduled for day 6.
   (C)   The inspection of J is scheduled for day 2.
   (D)   The inspection of Q is scheduled for day 4.
   (E)   The inspection of R is scheduled for day 3.

GO ON TO THE NEXT PAGE.

This was the first game on the June 1996 LSAT, and for most students it was a perfect game to begin the section. The game should be set up as follows:

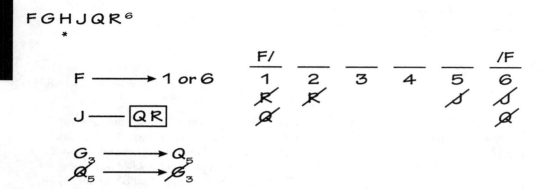

This game is perfectly Balanced, with 6 variables each filling one of 6 slots. The great benefit of doing Balanced games is that as you use a variable, that variable is eliminated from the list and can no longer be used; when you fill a space, that space is unavailable to all other variables. In contrast, Unbalanced games have variables that can sometimes be used again (as in the sixth game in this set), and sometimes a space can contain two or more variables. This tends to make things much more confusing as all of the variables could be used again even if already placed once, and spaces that contain a single variable might still be able to accommodate another.

An analysis of the variables reveals that H is a random, and this is indicated by the "*" notation. The first thing that jumps out regarding the rules is the linkage that can be made between the second and third rule. This allows us to make a JQR super rule that yields six Not Laws (if you are unsure why a particular Not Law is given, attempt to place the variable in that space and observe the consequences. This should help you better understand why certain Not Laws appear). Furthermore, since Q appears in both the super rule and the last rule, we can make the following inference:

> If G is inspected on day 3, then Q is inspected on day 5 and R is inspected on day 6. Since R is inspected on day 6, F must be inspected on day 1. This inference leads to the further inference that only two possible scenarios exist when G is inspected on day 3: F-H-G-J-Q-R or F-J-G-H-Q-R.

The other issue to consider is the interaction between F and the Not Laws. If F is inspected first, then the Not Laws shift over one space, and neither R nor Q can be inspected second, and R cannot be inspected third. The same logic in reverse can be applied to F in 6.

Rule Diagramming Note: The rule that states, "If G is inspected on day 3, Q is inspected on day 5" is conditional in nature and is represented with an arrow. The second diagram, with the slashes, is the contrapositive of the first diagram, and indicates that if Q is not inspected on day 5, then G is not inspected on day 3. Remember, the contrapositive of a statement is simply another way of expressing the original statement. The famous analogy we use is one that involves a penny: the two sides of a penny look different, but each side refers to the same intrinsic value. The same is true for a statement and its contrapositive.

Also remember, as with all conditional rules, to avoid making a Mistaken Reversal: when Q is inspected on day 5, G can be, but does not have to be, inspected on day 3.

With the above analysis, you should be ready to attack the questions.

Question #1: Global, Could Be True, List. The correct answer choice is (B)

This is a Global List question, so apply the proper technique! Generally, the first rule to apply is one that can be seen easily from a visual perspective. In this case you have the choice of several rules that fit that criterion. Let us start with the rule that states F is inspected on either day 1 or day 6. Applying this rule eliminates answer choice (D). Next, apply the rule that states that Q must be inspected the day before R is inspected. This eliminates answer choice (C). Now apply the rule that states that J is inspected on an earlier day than Q is inspected. This eliminates answer choice (A). Now we are down to answer choices (B) and (E). By applying the last rule about G in 3, we can eliminate answer choice (E), and thus answer choice (B) must be the correct answer.

Notice how easy this technique makes this question. There is no stress involved and very little mental energy has been expended. In other words, a perfect way to start the game. Fortunately, many games begin with List questions. One of the further benefits of this type of question is that you have now produced one workable hypothetical, G-H-J-Q-R-F, that you know is valid. Always do List questions first if possible because they are generally easy and always provide you with helpful information.

Question #2: Global, Cannot Be True. The correct answer choice is (E)

This question has been phrased in terms of falsity. Remember, always convert "false" questions into terms of "true." As discussed earlier in this chapter, "must be false" is identical to "cannot be true," and so this question simply asks which one of the following cannot be true. In Global Cannot Be True questions, always look to your Not Laws first for an answer since Not Laws reflect which variables have global restrictions. In this case, our initial Not Laws tell us that answer choice (E) must be correct since R can never be inspected on day 2. Again, Global Cannot Be True questions and Global Must Be True questions lend themselves very well to the use of Not Laws. You did the work for the setup, so why not enjoy the results?

Question #3: Global, Cannot Be True. The correct answer choice is (C)

This question is almost the same as #2, except now the focus is specifically on day 5. According to our Not Laws, J cannot be inspected on day 5, and so it must be that answer choice (C) is correct. This is an excellent example of what "attacking the question" means. By using the Not Laws, you should already know what the answer is before looking at the answer choices. Instead of slowly looking at answer choice (A), then (B), and so on, why not immediately look for "J" as one of the choices? This saves time, and more importantly, builds your confidence as you find the answer that you are looking for.

An interesting aside: the worst answer choice for a student to select in this question is answer choice (E). Why? Because from the hypothetical we produced in question #1 we know that R *can* be scheduled for day 5. Even if you cannot figure out which answer was definitely correct in this problem, you could use that hypothetical to kill answer choice (E) and improve your odds of answering correctly. And, although this information is not of very great value on this question, in future games this technique will prove to be very helpful indeed.

Question #4: Global, Could Be True. The correct answer choice is (E)

Since this question focuses specifically on days 3 and 5, again apply the Not Laws from day 3 and day 5. There are none for day 3, but we see that J cannot be inspected on day 5, and so we can kill off answer choice (D), which attempts to place J in day 5. Now, apply linkage to help eliminate more answer choices: Day 3 appears in the question and it also appears in the last rule. Thus, as you should recall, if G is inspected on day 3, then Q must be inspected on day 5. This information is sufficient to eliminate answer choices (A) and (B) since both have G on day 3 but another variable besides Q on day 5. Now we are down to only two remaining answer choices, yet we have only had to do a minimal amount of work. At this point, quickly scan the two remaining answer choices to see if you can identify the correct answer without doing further work. If you cannot, why not use one of the answer choices to help make a hypothetical that will solve the problem? To prove a "Could Be True" answer, all that is needed is one hypothetical that shows that one of the scenarios is possible, or alternately, a hypothetical that shows that one of the scenarios is impossible. Let us try answer choice (C) first. Make the following notation *right beside the problem*:

$$\underline{\quad} \quad \underline{\quad} \quad \underline{H} \quad \underline{\quad} \quad \underline{G} \quad \underline{\quad}$$

Diagramming note: We did not write out the numbers since most people do not need the numbers when they work next to the question. Had this been the main diagram you would most certainly have wanted to write out the number for each space.

As you might see, this scenario presents a problem because there is no room for the QR block. If F is inspected on day 1, there are not two consecutive spaces available for the QR block. If F is inspected on day 6, the only two spaces available for Q and R are days 1 and 2, but that leaves no room for J and so answer choice (C) cannot be correct. By process of elimination this means answer choice (E) must be correct. Notice that we do not need to prove that (E) is possible since we have already eliminated each of the other answer choices. Since the other four are incorrect, answer choice (E) must be correct. Mark it and continue. For those of you wondering if answer choice (E) can fit in a valid solution, here is a hypothetical that fits (E) and fits all of the rules of the game: J-Q-R-G-H-F.

Question #5: Local, Must Be True. The correct answer choice is (D)

The local condition specifies that R is inspected the day before F, which creates this block sequence:

$$J \text{———} \boxed{Q R F}$$

Of course, you should draw out that block sequence right next to the problem. At this point, there are several different ways to proceed with this question. One approach is to check any previous hypothetical to see if it conforms to the requirements in this question. Fortuitously, the only hypothetical we have—from question #1 answer choice (B)—actually conforms to the local condition imposed in this question. Thus, we can use that hypothetical, G-H-J-Q-R-F, to help answer this question. Accordingly, we can eliminate answer choices (C) and (E) since the hypothetical proves that neither *must* be true. Note how the hypothetical partially agrees with answer choices (A), (B), and (D), but it does not prove that they *must* be true.

The other method of attack is to use the linkage involving F. Since F must be in day 1 or day 6, and in this question F is scheduled behind R, we can infer that F must be inspected on day 6. Accordingly, we can make the following hypothetical right next to the problem:

$$\frac{\quad}{1} \quad \frac{\quad}{2} \quad \frac{\quad}{3} \quad \frac{Q}{4} \quad \frac{R}{5} \quad \frac{F}{6}$$
$$\cancel{G}$$

Although you may not realize it, this hypothetical solves the problem. If Q, R, and F are already placed, and G cannot be inspected third (that would violate the G3 then Q5 rule), that leaves only H or J to fill day 3. That inference is reflected in the wording of answer choice (D) and thus (D) is correct.

Question #6: Local, Must Be True, Maximum, List. The correct answer choice is (D)

Note that the question stem asks for a complete and accurate list, and the correct answer must list *all* of the factories that could appear on day 1. So, the correct answer must contain each and every factory that is possible for day 1. As strange as it may sound, the question asks for what must be true about what is possible.

If G and H are to be scheduled as far apart as possible (that is, the distance between them is maximized), this would likely place G and H in days 1 and 5 or days 2 and 6 (do not forget that F must be in either day 1 or day 6). Again, there are several ways to approach this question depending on your level of game understanding. At the most advanced level, answer choices (A), (C), and (E) can likely be eliminated since each contains J. If J is inspected on day 1, then F would be inspected on day 6 and G and H would not be as far apart as possible—a violation of the "if" clause in the question. Only F differentiates answer choice (B) from answer choice (D), and since F is a day 1 or day 6 player, it seems likely that answer choice (D) is correct, and in fact it *is* the correct answer. If that type of theoretical analysis makes you a bit nervous, you can always resort to the other form of attack on this question: make a few quick hypotheticals. Here is one that eliminates answer choices (B) and (C): F-G-J-Q-R-H. Another that eliminates answer choice (A) is: G-J-Q-R-H-F. And again, the inclusion of J in answer choice (E) should be a tip-off that answer choice (E) is likely incorrect.

Question #7: Local, Could Be True. The correct answer choice is (C)

The last question in a game is often the most difficult, and that general rule holds true here. Let us take a moment to examine why LSAC so often makes the last question difficult. The key to understanding this phenomenon is to look at it from a psychological perspective. As you near the end of a game, your mind naturally begins to focus on quickly finishing the game at hand and preparing for the next game. At just this point, when you want to go more quickly, LSAC throws in a difficult question. This tends to have the effect of slowing you down considerably, and that usually leads to a degree of frustration. Once you become frustrated, your chances of missing the question increase. And when you go to the next game, you may still be thinking about what happened on the last question, and that can contribute to a poor start on the new game, causing further trouble. In a nutshell, do not forget about the importance of psychology on the test. You must remain positive, focused, and calm throughout each section. If you become upset or frustrated, take a moment to relax and regain your equilibrium.

The local condition in the question stem sets up the following relationship:

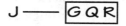

This sequential relationship automatically produces several Not Laws:

```
   1      2      3      4      5      6
  ___    ___    ___    ___    ___    ___
   R̸      R̸      R̸      R̸      R̸      R̸
   Q̸      Q̸                    G̸      G̸
   G̸                                  Q̸
```

In addition, the interaction of the last rule and the sequence further establishes that G cannot be inspected on day 3 since it would then be impossible for Q to be inspected on day 5 (in this question if G is inspected on day 3 then R would be inspected on day 5). Also, because of the block produced by the question stem, if G cannot be inspected on day 3, then Q cannot be inspected on day 4 and R cannot be inspected on day 5. Using these inferences and the Not Laws above, we can eliminate answer choices (A), (D), and (E) from consideration. At this point, unless you see what distinguishes answer choice (B) from answer choice (C), the best strategy would probably be to try a quick hypothetical using either answer choice. As it turns out, answer choice (B) is incorrect, since if H is inspected on day 6 the following *impossible* scenario results:

```
  F    J    G    Q    R    H
 ___  ___  ___  ___  ___  ___
  1    2    3    4    5    6
```

As shown above, G is inspected on day 3, but Q is not inspected on day 5—a violation of the last rule. By process of elimination, answer choice (C) is proven correct.

Some students question whether answer choice (C) can be valid since it leads to a solution (F-J-H-G-Q-R) where Q is inspected on day 5 but G is not inspected on day 3. Remember, the conditional rule only activates if G is inspected on day 3. If Q is inspected on day 5, nothing necessarily happens (to think otherwise would be a Mistaken Reversal).

A messenger will deliver exactly seven packages—L, M, N, O, P, S, and T—one at a time, not necessarily in that order. The seven deliveries must be made according to the following conditions:

P is delivered either first or seventh.

The messenger delivers N at some time after delivering L.

The messenger delivers T at some time after delivering M.

The messenger delivers exactly one package between delivering L and delivering O, whether or not L is delivered before O.

The messenger delivers exactly one package between delivering M and delivering P, whether or not M is delivered before P.

8. Which one of the following is an order in which the messenger could make the deliveries, from first to seventh?

(A)   L, N, S, O, M, T, P
(B)   M, T, P, S, L, N, O
(C)   O, S, L, N, M, T, P
(D)   P, N, M, S, O, T, L
(E)   P, T, M, S, L, N, O

GO ON TO THE NEXT PAGE.

3

9. Which one of the following could be true?

    (A)   N is delivered first.
    (B)   T is delivered first.
    (C)   T is delivered second.
    (D)   M is delivered fourth.
    (E)   S is delivered seventh.

10. If N is delivered fourth, which one of the following could be true?

    (A)   L is delivered first.
    (B)   L is delivered second.
    (C)   M is delivered third.
    (D)   O is delivered fifth.
    (E)   S is delivered first.

11. If T is delivered fourth, the seventh package delivered must be

    (A)   L
    (B)   N
    (C)   O
    (D)   P
    (E)   S

12. If the messenger delivers M at some time after delivering O, the fifth package delivered could be any one of the following EXCEPT:

    (A)   L
    (B)   M
    (C)   N
    (D)   S
    (E)   T

GO ON TO THE NEXT PAGE.

Analysis of Linear Game #2: September 1998 Questions 8-12

This was the second game on the September 1998 LSAT, and many of our students were able to score a perfect 5-0 on the questions. The game should be set up as follows:

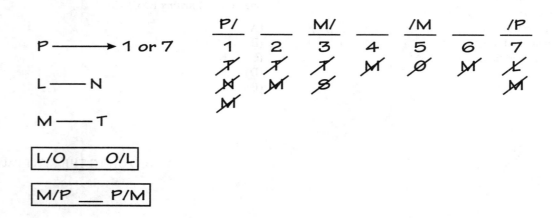

This game is perfectly Balanced, with 7 variables each filling one of 7 slots. An analysis of the variables reveals that S is a random, and this is indicated by the "*" notation. The first inference that can be made comes from the linkage of M and P. Since P must be delivered first or seventh, and exactly one package is delivered between P and M, it follows that M must be delivered third or fifth. Therefore, M cannot be delivered first, second, fourth, sixth or seventh. Since the earliest M can be delivered is third, that affects the delivery of T, and it can be inferred that T cannot be delivered first, second, or third.

Two other Not Laws also bear further examination. First, S cannot be delivered third because it sets off the following chain: M would be delivered fifth and P would be delivered seventh; in turn L and O have to be delivered second and fourth, with L being delivered second; this causes a problem since there is no room for N, which must be delivered after L. Second, O cannot be delivered fifth because of the problems it causes: M would have to be delivered third and P would have to be delivered first; since O and L must be separated by one package, L would have to be delivered seventh, and that is impossible since L must be delivered ahead of N.

Additionally, since the MP split-block is reduced to exactly two spacing options, one approach to setting up the game involves drawing out the two options (Identify the Templates™—to be discussed in greater detail in a later chapter), which are labeled #1 and #2 below:

#1: ___ ___ ___ ___ M T P

#2: P ___ M ___ ___ ___ ___
     1   2   3   4   5   6   7

In option #1, we can link rules and apply the M —— T rule, which yields the inference that T must be sixth when P is seventh and M is fifth. At this point, it should be apparent that you will have to keep an eye on L, N, and O since they are linked together. In general, the variables L, M, and P are the most powerful since each appears in two separate rules.

Question #8: Global, Could Be True, List. The correct answer choice is (C)

This type of question is your best friend when it comes to Games questions. Always make sure to apply the proper List question technique. The best rule to start with is the rule that states that P is delivered either first or seventh. Applying this rule eliminates answer choice (B). Next apply the rule that states that L —— N. This eliminates answer choice (D). Now apply the M —— T rule, and you can eliminate answer choice (E). Of course, so far we have applied the rules in order, but that also happens to be the preferred order from a visual standpoint. The last two rules are less desirable, because they force you to deal with variables that can switch back and forth, and so they are harder to see within the answer choices. That is why we have held them until the end, not because they are the last two rules. The order in which you apply the rules to a List question should not be determined by the order of the presentation of the rules. Finally, by applying the LO split-block rule, we can eliminate answer choice (A), and it follows that answer choice (C) is correct by process of elimination. This question is very easy and you should have had no trouble with it.

Question #9: Global, Could Be True. The correct answer choice is (E)

This question can easily be attacked by applying the Not Laws deduced in the setup. The Not Laws eliminate answer choices (A), (B), (C), and (D), and thus answer choice (E) is correct.

Question #10: Local, Could Be True. The correct answer choice is (A)

This is a Local question, and thus you should reproduce a mini-setup next to the question. Since this is a Could Be True question, and we have two major templates produced by the MP split-block (one template with P delivered first, and another template with P delivered last), why not reproduce both templates, and show each with N delivered fourth, as follows:

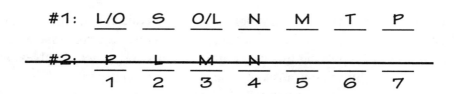

Note that the "#1" and "#2" designations are for our discussion purposes only; during the game you would not want to waste the time writing these designations out. An analysis of the two templates reveals that template #2 can never occur, and thus, that template is crossed out. If N is delivered fourth, then L would have to be delivered second (remember, we are only discussing template #2), but if L is delivered second, then the LO split-block dictates that O must be delivered fourth, and O cannot be delivered fourth in template #2 because N is already delivered there. Thus, in checking the answers, we should only refer to template #1.

In template #1 the only uncertainty involves L and O, and because this is a Could Be True question, you should immediately look at any answer that references L or O. Answer choice (A) references L, and since (A) could be true, it is the correct answer. Answer choice (B) also references L, but (B) cannot be true, and so it is incorrect. Answer choice (D) references O, but (D) cannot be true, and so it is also incorrect. Remember, once you make your mini-diagram in a Could Be True question, attack the answers by ignoring the variables that are placed. Instead, you can gain time by looking only at those answers that contain unplaced or moving variables (such as L and O in this problem).

Question #11: Local, Must Be True. The correct answer choice is (C)

Again, this is a Local question, and we can make a mini-setup in the space next to the question. Start with the condition given in the question stem:

$$\underset{1}{\underline{\quad}} \quad \underset{2}{\underline{\quad}} \quad \underset{3}{\underline{\quad}} \quad \underset{4}{\underline{\overset{T}{\quad}}} \quad \underset{5}{\underline{\quad}} \quad \underset{6}{\underline{\quad}} \quad \underset{7}{\underline{\quad}}$$

Since M ——— T, we can infer that P must be delivered first, and M must be delivered third:

$$\underset{1}{\underline{\overset{P}{\quad}}} \quad \underset{2}{\underline{\quad}} \quad \underset{3}{\underline{\overset{M}{\quad}}} \quad \underset{4}{\underline{\overset{T}{\quad}}} \quad \underset{5}{\underline{\quad}} \quad \underset{6}{\underline{\quad}} \quad \underset{7}{\underline{\quad}}$$

And, since L and O are in a split-block, we can continue to add inferences:

$$\underset{1}{\underline{\overset{P}{\quad}}} \quad \underset{2}{\underline{\quad}} \quad \underset{3}{\underline{\overset{M}{\quad}}} \quad \underset{4}{\underline{\overset{T}{\quad}}} \quad \underset{5}{\underline{\overset{L/O}{\quad}}} \quad \underset{6}{\underline{\quad}} \quad \underset{7}{\underline{\overset{O/L}{\quad}}}$$

However, since L ——— N, we can infer that L must be delivered fifth, N must be delivered sixth, and O must be delivered seventh. And since six variables have been placed, it follows that S must be delivered second:

$$\underset{1}{\underline{\overset{P}{\quad}}} \quad \underset{2}{\underline{\overset{S}{\quad}}} \quad \underset{3}{\underline{\overset{M}{\quad}}} \quad \underset{4}{\underline{\overset{T}{\quad}}} \quad \underset{5}{\underline{\overset{L}{\quad}}} \quad \underset{6}{\underline{\overset{N}{\quad}}} \quad \underset{7}{\underline{\overset{O}{\quad}}}$$

Accordingly, the correct answer choice must be (C).

Note how S, the random variable, is the last variable to be placed. Randoms are typically the least powerful variables in a game because they are not involved in any rules and therefore when they are placed they do not affect other variables directly. Randoms do take up space and so they have some power, but a variable such as L or M is much more powerful in this game because each of those variables directly affects two variables. Consider this point a bit more closely by comparing variables S and L:

Variable Placed	Effect
S	1. Takes up the assigned space, thereby prohibiting other variables from occupying that space.
L	1. Takes up the assigned space, thereby prohibiting other variables from occupying that space. 2. Limits the placement of N. 3. Limits the placement of O.

Aside from the fact that L has fewer placement options due to its relationships with other variables, once L is placed it has powerful effects on those variables. S, on the other hand, has no direct effect on other variables. So, when solving a problem, S would not be one of the first variables you should look at. Instead, you should look to the power variables within a game to help you solve the questions. One side effect of the lesser power of randoms is that you often see them placed last within individual solutions. Since they are largely "free," they can often float until the end before they need to be placed.

Question #12: Local, Could Be True, Except. The correct answer choice is (A)

The inclusion of "Except" in the question stem turns the meaning of the question "upside down," and so the four incorrect answer choices have the characteristic of Could Be True, and the one correct answer choice has the characteristic of Cannot Be True. In this way, the question can be analyzed as a simple Cannot Be True question, and in doing so we have negated the confusing effect of the word "except."

By adding the "if" statement in the question stem to our original rules, we arrive at the following chain sequence:

$$O \text{———} M \text{———} T$$

Once again, this is a Local question and the best approach is to make a mini-diagram next to the question, again accounting for the two basic templates created by the MP split-block:

#1: (L, N, O, S) M T P

#2: P   O   M   L (N, S, T)
     1   2   3   4   5   6   7

In the first template, P is delivered last and M is delivered fifth. According to the third rule, T must then be delivered sixth. The remaining four variables—L, N, O, and S—must then be delivered in the first four positions, in accordance with the remaining rules. The parentheses around L, N, O, and S are an efficient notation that indicates the enclosed variables are to be placed in the consecutive spaces in some order.

In the second template, P is delivered first and M is delivered third. According to the condition in the question stem, O must then be delivered second. And, because O is delivered second, L must then be delivered fourth as dictated by the fourth rule. The remaining three variables—N, S, and T—must then be delivered in the final three spaces in some order.

Since the question stem specifically focuses on the fifth package delivered, we can use our mini-diagram to quickly deduce which packages can be delivered fifth and then use that information to eliminate answer choices. From the first template it is proven that package M can be delivered fifth, and thus answer choice (B) can be eliminated. From the second template, it can be determined that packages N, S, and T can be delivered fifth, and this information eliminates answer choices (C), (D), and (E). At this point, the only remaining answer choice is (A), and it follows that response (A) is correct.

An alternate way to use the two templates is to say that the list of variables that could possibly appear fifth includes M from the first template, and N, S, and T from the second template. An examination of the answer choices reveals that only L in answer choice (A) does not appear as a possibility, and thus answer choice (A) must be correct.

3

Charlie makes a soup by adding exactly six kinds of foods—kale, lentils, mushrooms, onions, tomatoes, and zucchini—to a broth, one food at a time. No food is added more than once. The order in which Charlie adds the foods to the broth must be consistent with the following:

   If the mushrooms are added third, then the lentils are added last.

   If the zucchini is added first, then the lentils are added at some time before the onions.

   Neither the tomatoes nor the kale is added fifth.

   The mushrooms are added at some time before the tomatoes or the kale, but not before both.

1. Which one of the following could be the order in which the foods are added to the broth?

   (A) kale, mushrooms, onions, lentils, tomatoes, zucchini

   (B) kale, zucchini, mushrooms, tomatoes, lentils, onions

   (C) lentils, mushrooms, zucchini, kale, onions, tomatoes

   (D) zucchini, lentils, kale, mushrooms, onions, tomatoes

   (E) zucchini, tomatoes, onions, mushrooms, lentils, kale

GO ON TO THE NEXT PAGE.

2. Which one of the following foods CANNOT be added first?

(A) kale
(B) lentils
(C) mushrooms
(D) onions
(E) tomatoes

3. If the lentils are added last, then which one of the following must be true?

(A) At least one of the foods is added at some time before the zucchini.
(B) At least two of the foods are added at some time before the kale.
(C) The mushrooms are added third.
(D) The zucchini is added third.
(E) The tomatoes are added fourth.

4. Which one of the following could be an accurate partial ordering of the foods added to the broth?

(A) lentils: second; mushrooms: third
(B) mushrooms: fourth; lentils: last
(C) onions: second; mushrooms: fifth
(D) zucchini: first; lentils: last
(E) zucchini: first; mushrooms: second

5. If the zucchini is added first, then which one of the following CANNOT be true?

(A) The kale is added second.
(B) The tomatoes are added second.
(C) The lentils are added third.
(D) The lentils are added fourth.
(E) The onions are added fourth.

3

GO ON TO THE NEXT PAGE.

This game—a balanced basic linear game—provides a great start to the June 2003 LSAT. The game features six foods added one at a time, and thus we have created a diagram with six spaces. Because no food can be added more than once, the variables are in a one-to-one relationship with the spaces:

3

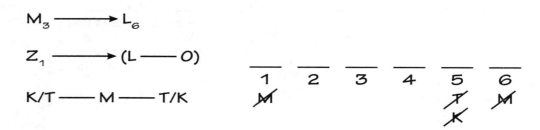

KLMOTZ^6

$M_3 \longrightarrow L_6$

$Z_1 \longrightarrow (L \longrightarrow O)$

K/T $\longrightarrow$ M $\longrightarrow$ T/K

1	2	3	4	5	6
M̸				T̸ / K̸	M̸

The first two rules of this game are conditional, and Linear games that feature conditional rules often are slightly harder than games that feature only Not Law, block, and sequencing rules. A close examination of the first two rules yields some useful inferences:

When Z is added first, L must be added before O. Thus, when Z is added first, L cannot be added sixth and O cannot be added second:

$$Z_1 \longleftarrow\!\!\!+\!\!\!\longrightarrow L_6$$

$$Z_1 \longleftarrow\!\!\!+\!\!\!\longrightarrow O_2$$

Note: The "$\longleftarrow\!\!\!+\!\!\!\longrightarrow$" symbol will be discussed in more detail in chapter Five, but it means that the two events at the ends of the arrow cannot both occur.

From the first rule, we know that when M is added third, L must be added sixth. Thus, if M is added third, then L could not come before O, and therefore when M is third, Z cannot be first:

$$Z_1 \longleftarrow\!\!\!+\!\!\!\longrightarrow M_3$$

Clearly, when Z is added first, the number of solutions to the game is limited. These scenarios are tested in question #5 and will be discussed in more detail then.

The last rule also bears examination. The rule is sequential, but contains an element of uncertainty because you cannot determine the exact relative order of the variables. There are only two possible orders that result from the rule:

$$T \text{—} M \text{—} K$$
$$or$$
$$K \text{—} M \text{—} T$$

Regardless of the exact order, we can infer that M is never added first or last (this is shown on our diagram with Not Laws). Additionally, if M is added second, either T or K must be added first; if M is added fifth, either T or K must be added sixth.

Combining the third and fourth rules, we can infer that if M is added fourth, then T or K must be added sixth.

If we combine the first and last rule, we can infer that if M is added third, then either T or K must be added fourth.

The above discussion should help you focus on M and Z as key variables in this game. Of additional note is the fact that there are no randoms in this game.

Question #1: Global, Could Be True, List. The correct answer choice is (D)

Answer choice (A) is incorrect because T cannot be added fifth.

Answer choice (B) is incorrect because if M is added third then L must be added sixth.

Answer choice (C) is incorrect because either K or T must be added before M.

Answer choice (D) is the correct answer.

Answer choice (E) is incorrect because if Z is added first then L must be added before O.

Question #2: Global, Cannot Be True. The correct answer choice is (C)

From our Not Laws we know that M cannot be added first, and thus answer choice (C) is correct.

Question #3: Local, Must Be True. The correct answer choice is (A)

If L is added last, from our first inference we know that Z cannot be added first. Thus, as stated in answer choice (A), at least one of the foods is added at some time before Z.

Question #4: Global, Could Be True. The correct answer choice is (C)

This is an unusual partial List question.

Answer choice (A) is incorrect because when M is added third then L must be added sixth.

Answer choice (B) is incorrect because the proposed scenario would force K or T to be added fifth, and that would be a violation of the third rule.

Answer choice (C) is the correct answer.

Answer choice (D) is incorrect because if Z is added first then L cannot be added last.

Answer choice (E) is incorrect because if Z is added first then M cannot be added second.

Note that answer choices (B), (D), and (E) are all violations of the inferences discussed above.

Question #5: Local, Cannot Be True. The correct answer choice is (D)

This question tests the limited scenarios that result when Z is added first. When Z is added first, M cannot be second, third, or last. Hence, we can create two hypotheticals based on the position of M:

Hypothetical #2:   Z   ___   ___   ___   M   ___

Hypothetical #1:   Z   ___   ___   M   ___   ___
             1   2   3   4   5   6

Because the position of M is restricted, we should first apply the last rule (and the third rule because it affects K and T) :

Hypothetical #2:   Z   (K/T, ___ ___)   M   T/K

Hypothetical #1:   Z   (K/T,)   M   ___   T/K
             1   2   3   4   5   6

Finally, by applying the second rule, we can fill in each hypothetical:

Hypothetical #2:   Z   (K/T, L———O)   M   T/K

Hypothetical #1:   Z   (K/T, L)   M   O   T/K
             1   2   3   4   5   6

When applying the second rule, in Hypothetical #1 we can infer that O must be added fifth by taking the following steps:

1. There are only three open spaces.

2. Since K/T ——— M, we know that K/T must be added second or third.

3. Since L ——— O, L must then be second or third.

4. The only remaining space for O is the fifth.

Both hypotheticals must be considered when answering the question. Answer choice (D) is correct because in Hypothetical #1 we know M is fourth, and in Hypothetical #2 we know L cannot be fourth because L ——— O. Thus, L cannot be added fourth when Z is added first.

Question #5 is probably the most difficult question, and the only effective way to attack the question is to use hypotheticals. Hopefully, by quickly answering questions #1 through #4 you will build enough time to comfortably work through question #5.

In the course of one month Garibaldi has exactly seven different meetings. Each of her meetings is with exactly one of five foreign dignitaries: Fuentes, Matsuba, Rhee, Soleimani, or Tbahi. The following constraints govern Garibaldi's meetings:

    She has exactly three meetings with Fuentes, and exactly one with each of the other dignitaries.

    She does not have any meetings in a row with Fuentes.

    Her meeting with Soleimani is the very next one after her meeting with Tbahi.

    Neither the first nor last of her meetings is with Matsuba.

1.   Which one of the following could be the sequence of the meetings Garibaldi has with the dignitaries?

  (A)   Fuentes, Rhee, Tbahi, Soleimani, Fuentes, Matsuba, Rhee

  (B)   Fuentes, Tbahi, Soleimani, Matsuba, Fuentes, Fuentes, Rhee

  (C)   Fuentes, Rhee, Fuentes, Matsuba, Fuentes, Tbahi, Soleimani

  (D)   Fuentes, Tbahi, Matsuba, Fuentes, Soleimani, Rhee, Fuentes

  (E)   Fuentes, Tbahi, Soleimani, Fuentes, Rhee, Fuentes, Matsuba

GO ON TO THE NEXT PAGE.

2. If Garibaldi's last meeting is with Rhee, then which one of the following could be true?

    (A) Garibaldi's second meeting is with Soleimani.
    (B) Garibaldi's third meeting is with Matsuba.
    (C) Garibaldi's fourth meeting is with Soleimani.
    (D) Garibaldi's fifth meeting is with Matsuba.
    (E) Garibaldi's sixth meeting is with Soleimani.

3. If Garibaldi's second meeting is with Fuentes, then which one of the following is a complete and accurate list of the dignitaries with any one of whom Garibaldi's fourth meeting could be?

    (A) Fuentes, Soleimani, Rhee
    (B) Matsuba, Rhee, Tbahi
    (C) Matsuba, Soleimani
    (D) Rhee, Tbahi
    (E) Fuentes, Soleimani

4. If Garibaldi's meeting with Rhee is the very next one after Garibaldi's meeting with Soleimani, then which one of the following must be true?

    (A) Garibaldi's third meeting is with Fuentes.
    (B) Garibaldi's fourth meeting is with Rhee.
    (C) Garibaldi's fifth meeting is with Fuentes.
    (D) Garibaldi's sixth meeting is with Rhee.
    (E) Garibaldi's seventh meeting is with Fuentes.

5. If Garibaldi's first meeting is with Tbahi, then Garibaldi's meeting with Rhee could be the

    (A) second meeting
    (B) third meeting
    (C) fifth meeting
    (D) sixth meeting
    (E) seventh meeting

6. If Garibaldi's meeting with Matsuba is the very next meeting after Garibaldi's meeting with Rhee, then with which one of the following dignitaries must Garibaldi's fourth meeting be?

    (A) Fuentes
    (B) Matsuba
    (C) Rhee
    (D) Soleimani
    (E) Tbahi

GO ON TO THE NEXT PAGE.

Analysis of Linear Game #4: October 2004 Questions 1-6

This is a basic linear game featuring five dignitaries placed in seven meetings. Because there are only five dignitaries, this game is underfunded, but the very first rule establishes that F must meet with Garibaldi three times, and so the composition of the group of dignitaries is precisely defined and balanced.

After reviewing the game scenario and the rules, you should make the following basic setup for this game:

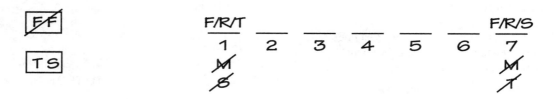

Note that the fourth rule involving M is represented by Not Laws on meetings 1 and 7. Let's take a moment to discuss the second and third rules.

Rule #2. This rule establishes that none of the three meetings with F can be consecutive. At a minimum, then, the three meetings with F require five spaces (meaning that among other things that if the TS block created by rule #3 is placed at the beginning or end of the meeting schedule then the placement of the three Fs will automatically be determined). Given the open-ended nature of this rule, and the fact that it addresses three of the seven meetings, this rule will play a major role in the game.

Rule #3. This rule creates a fixed block involving T and S. Because S is always the next meeting after T, S can never be Garibaldi's first meeting; because T is always the meeting before S, T can never be Garibaldi's last meeting. These two inferences are shown as Not Laws on the diagram above.

This game does not present a large amount of information in the scenario and rules, and you should expect to see a high number of Local questions, which will supply the additional information needed to place some of the variables. Given the dearth of information generated in the setup, we have elected to show the triple-options present for the first and last meetings. Since there are only five dignitaries, and the Not Laws eliminate two of those dignitaries from attending the first or last meeting, only three possible dignitaries could attend either meeting.

One other point of note is that R is a random in this game, and R can attend the first or last meeting.

Question #1: Global, Could Be True, List. The correct answer choice is (C)

As with any List question, simply apply the rules to the answer choices. Remember to apply the rules in order of the easiest to "see" within the answers. In this game, that order would be rule #4, rule #3, rule #2, and then rule #1 (rule #2 and rule #3 are equally easy to see, but we chose to apply rule #3 first since that allows rules #2 and #1—both of which involve F— to be applied together).

Answer choice (A): This answer is eliminated by the first rule. In this instance, there are only two meetings with F, instead of three.

Answer choice (B): This answer choice is incorrect because two of the meetings with F are consecutive, a violation of the second rule.

Answer choice (C): This is the correct answer choice.

Answer choice (D): Because T and S are not a block, this answer choice violates the third rule, and is therefore incorrect.

Answer choice (E): Because M is last, this answer choice violates the fourth rule and is incorrect.

Question #2: Local, Could Be True. The correct answer choice is (D)

This question is best attacked with hypotheticals. The question stem establishes that R is Garibaldi's seventh meeting:

$$\frac{\quad}{1} \quad \frac{\quad}{2} \quad \frac{\quad}{3} \quad \frac{\quad}{4} \quad \frac{\quad}{5} \quad \frac{\quad}{6} \quad \frac{R}{7}$$

From our discussion of the first and last meetings, we know that either F or T must now be Garibaldi's first meeting. However, the placement of R has limited the options for F, and if T is placed first then from the third rule S must be the second meeting, and there would not be sufficient room to separate the three meetings with F (meetings 1, 2, and 7 would be occupied, leaving only meetings 3-6 for the three Fs). Consequently, we can infer that F must be Garibaldi's first meeting:

$$\frac{F}{1} \quad \frac{\quad}{2} \quad \frac{\quad}{3} \quad \frac{\quad}{4} \quad \frac{\quad}{5} \quad \frac{\quad}{6} \quad \frac{R}{7}$$

At this point, the placement of the TS block and the two remaining Fs must be considered. The TS block cannot occupy meetings #3-4 or #5-6 because that would force two of the three Fs to be consecutive (if this does not appear logical, try placing the TS block in either of those positions and observe the results). Consequently, there are only two possible scenarios:

1. TS occupies the second and third meetings and the remaining two Fs occupy the fourth and sixth meetings. M is then forced into the fifth meeting.

2. TS occupies the fourth and fifth meetings and the remaining two Fs occupy the third and sixth meetings. M is then forced into the second meeting.

The two scenarios can be diagrammed as follows:

Scenario #2:	F	M	F	T	S	F	R
Scenario #1:	F	T	S	F	M	F	R
	1	2	3	4	5	6	7

Answer choices (A), (C), and (E): According to the two solutions to this question, Garibaldi's meets with S in either the third or fifth meetings. Consequently, each of these answer choices is incorrect.

Answer choice (B): As shown by the two diagrams, Garibaldi's third meeting must either be with F or S, and thus this answer choice is incorrect.

Answer choice (D): This is the correct answer choice.

Question #3: Local, Could Be True, List. The correct answer choice is (E)

The assignment of F to the second meeting has an immediate impact on the choices for the *first* meeting. We know that only F, R or T could be Garibaldi's first meeting. With F as the second meeting, the first meeting cannot be with F as that would violate the second rule. The first meeting also cannot be with T as there is no room to place S immediately after T. Consequently, when F is Garibaldi's second meeting, R *must* be Garibaldi's first meeting:

$$
\underset{1}{\underline{\text{R}}} \quad \underset{2}{\underline{\text{F}}} \quad \underset{3}{\underline{\quad}} \quad \underset{4}{\underline{\quad}} \quad \underset{5}{\underline{\quad}} \quad \underset{6}{\underline{\quad}} \quad \underset{7}{\underline{\quad}}
$$

~~M~~
~~S~~
~~F~~
~~T~~

This powerful deduction immediately eliminates answer choices (A), (B), and (D), each of which contain R. A very insightful test taker might realize at this point which of the foreign dignitaries could be Garibaldi's fourth meeting, but let's continue analyzing this problem as if we did not have that insight.

Comparing the remaining two answer choices, (C) and (E), both contain S, so the comparison should focus on M and F, the unique variables in each of the remaining answer choices.

Answer choice (C): A quick test of this answer would be to create a hypothetical that places M into the fourth meeting:

$$
\underset{1}{\underline{\text{R}}} \quad \underset{2}{\underline{\text{F}}} \quad \underset{3}{\underline{\quad}} \quad \underset{4}{\underline{\text{M}}} \quad \underset{5}{\underline{\quad}} \quad \underset{6}{\underline{\quad}} \quad \underset{7}{\underline{\quad}}
$$

Placing M fourth immediately forces the two remaining Fs into the fifth and seventh meetings:

$$
\underset{1}{\underline{\text{R}}} \quad \underset{2}{\underline{\text{F}}} \quad \underset{3}{\underline{\quad}} \quad \underset{4}{\underline{\text{M}}} \quad \underset{5}{\underline{\text{F}}} \quad \underset{6}{\underline{\quad}} \quad \underset{7}{\underline{\text{F}}}
$$

At this point there is no room for the TS block, and so we can eliminate this answer choice since placing M fourth does not allow us to create a viable solution.

Answer choice (E): This is the correct answer choice. The following hypothetical proves that F can be Garibaldi's fourth meeting:

$\underline{R}$	$\underline{F}$	$\underline{M}$	$\underline{F}$	$\underline{T}$	$\underline{S}$	$\underline{F}$
1	2	3	4	5	6	7

Question #4: Local, Must Be True. The correct answer choice is (E)

The condition in the question stem creates an SR block. Adding this to the third rule, we arrive at the following super-block:

$$\boxed{T\ S\ R}$$

The size of this block presents immediate problems for the three Fs, and you must consider the placement options of the block prior to attacking the answer choices. First, the block cannot be placed at the beginning or the end of the series of meetings because that would not leave sufficient room to separate the three meetings with F (if meetings 1-3 are occupied by the block, then only meetings 4-7 are available for the three Fs; if meetings 5-7 are occupied by the block, then only meetings 1-4 are available for the three Fs). Consequently, the TSR block must be placed in either meetings 2-4, 3-5, or 4-6. We can also deduce that F must be Garibaldi's first meeting because only F, R, or T could be Garibaldi's first meeting, and with T and R involved in the block neither can be first. With this fact in hand, you should quickly create hypotheticals reflecting each placement option:

Option #1: TSR as the second, third, and fourth meetings

When the TSR block is placed as the second, third, and fourth meetings, the remaining two Fs must be placed as the fifth and seventh meetings, leaving M as the sixth meeting.

$\underline{F}$	$\underline{T}$	$\underline{S}$	$\underline{R}$	$\underline{F}$	$\underline{M}$	$\underline{F}$
1	2	3	4	5	6	7

Option #2: TSR as the third, fourth, and fifth meetings

Hopefully you realized that this placement option would be unworkable prior to drawing out the diagram. When the TSR block is placed as the third, fourth, and fifth meetings, there is no way to place the other two Fs so that they do not violate the second rule. Consequently, TSR cannot be placed in this position and a viable hypothetical cannot be created.

$$\frac{F}{1} \quad \frac{}{2} \quad \frac{T}{3} \quad \frac{S}{4} \quad \frac{R}{5} \quad \frac{}{6} \quad \frac{}{7}$$

F̶

Option #3: TSR as the fourth, fifth, and sixth meetings

When the TSR block is placed as the fourth, fifth, and sixth meetings, the remaining two Fs must be placed as the third and seventh meetings, leaving M as the second meeting.

$$\frac{F}{1} \quad \frac{M}{2} \quad \frac{F}{3} \quad \frac{T}{4} \quad \frac{S}{5} \quad \frac{R}{6} \quad \frac{F}{7}$$

Thus, the condition in the question stem only allows for two solutions to the question:

TSR in 4-5-6: $\quad \frac{F}{} \quad \frac{M}{} \quad \frac{F}{} \quad \frac{T}{} \quad \frac{S}{} \quad \frac{R}{} \quad \frac{F}{}$

TSR in 2-3-4: $\quad \frac{F}{1} \quad \frac{T}{2} \quad \frac{S}{3} \quad \frac{R}{4} \quad \frac{F}{5} \quad \frac{M}{6} \quad \frac{F}{7}$

Answer choices (A), (B), (C), and (D): Each of these answer choices could be true. However, this is a Must be true question, and thus each of these answers is incorrect.

Answer choice (E): This is the correct answer choice. As proven by the two solutions above, F is always the last meeting.

Question #5: Local, Could Be True. The correct answer choice is (D)

This is one of the easier questions in the game. If Garibaldi's first meeting is with T, then according to the third rule, Garibaldi's second meeting must be with S:

$$\frac{T}{1} \quad \frac{S}{2} \quad \frac{}{3} \quad \frac{}{4} \quad \frac{}{5} \quad \frac{}{6} \quad \frac{}{7}$$

At this juncture, the three Fs must be placed in such a way that they are not consecutive. There is only one way that this can occur, by placing F in the third, fifth, and seventh meetings:

$$\frac{T}{1} \quad \frac{S}{2} \quad \frac{F}{3} \quad \frac{}{4} \quad \frac{F}{5} \quad \frac{}{6} \quad \frac{F}{7}$$

The remaining two variables—M and R—form a dual-option in the fourth and sixth meetings:

$$\frac{T}{1} \quad \frac{S}{2} \quad \frac{F}{3} \quad \frac{M/R}{4} \quad \frac{F}{5} \quad \frac{R/M}{6} \quad \frac{F}{7}$$

Consequently, Garibaldi's meeting with R could be either the fourth or sixth meeting, and answer choice (D) is correct.

Answer choices (A), (B), (C), and (E): Each of these answer choices is proven incorrect by the diagram above.

Question #6: Local, Must Be True. The correct answer choice is (A)

The condition in this question stem creates an RM block. Initially, it may seem as though this block has a wide number of placement options, but take a moment to consider the five variable groups created by this rule:

The interaction of the RM block, the TS block, and the second rule limits the placement options of each variable (creating a classic Separation Principle scenario, a concept that will be discussed in more detail in the next chapter). For example, because the Fs cannot be consecutive, they must be separated by the two blocks. Consider this for a moment—if you have to separate the three Fs with just two blocks, where must the Fs be placed? One of the blocks has to separate the first two Fs, and the other block has to separate the last two Fs, like so:

If the two blocks are not placed as they are above, at least two of the Fs will be consecutive, violating the second rule. Consequently, the Fs are forced into the first, fourth, and seventh meetings. The two blocks are interchangeable, and either TS or RM could be in either position 2-3 or 5-6.

Answer choice (A): This is the correct answer choice. If you are still uncertain about this answer choice, try placing a variable other than F into the fourth meeting. You will quickly see that any variable other than F in the fourth meeting will not allow for a workable solution.

Answer choices (B), (C), (D), and (E): Each of these answer choices is incorrect because they would not yield a viable solution for the question.

An apartment building has five floors. Each floor has either one or two apartments. There are exactly eight apartments in the building. The residents of the building are J, K, L, M, N, O, P, and Q, who each live in a different apartment.

    J lives on a floor with two apartments.
    K lives on the floor directly above P.
    The second floor is made up of only one apartment.
    M and N live on the same floor.
    O does not live on the same floor as Q.
    L lives in the only apartment on her floor.
    Q does not live on the first or second floor.

6. Which one of the following must be true?

(A)   Q lives on the third floor.
(B)   Q lives on the fifth floor.
(C)   L does not live on the fourth floor.
(D)   N does not live on the second floor.
(E)   J lives on the first floor.

GO ON TO THE NEXT PAGE.

3

7. Which one of the following CANNOT be true?

   (A) K lives on the second floor.
   (B) M lives on the first floor.
   (C) N lives on the fourth floor.
   (D) O lives on the third floor.
   (E) P lives on the fifth floor.

8. If J lives on the fourth floor and K lives on the fifth floor, which one of the following can be true?

   (A) O lives on the first floor.
   (B) Q lives on the fourth floor.
   (C) N lives on the fifth floor.
   (D) L lives on the fourth floor.
   (E) P lives on the third floor.

9. If O lives on the second floor, which one of the following CANNOT be true?

   (A) K lives on the fourth floor.
   (B) K lives on the fifth floor.
   (C) L lives on the first floor.
   (D) L lives on the third floor.
   (E) L lives on the fourth floor.

10. If M lives on the fourth floor, which one of the following must be false?

   (A) O lives on the fifth floor.
   (B) J lives on the first floor.
   (C) L lives on the second floor.
   (D) Q lives on the third floor.
   (E) P lives on the first floor.

11. Which one of the following must be true?

   (A) If J lives on the fourth floor, then Q does not live on the fifth floor.
   (B) If O lives on the second floor, then L does not live on the fourth floor.
   (C) If N lives on the fourth floor, then K does not live on the second floor.
   (D) If K lives on the third floor, then O does not live on the fifth floor.
   (E) If P lives on the fourth floor, then M does not live on the third floor.

12. If O lives on the fourth floor and P lives on the second floor, which one of the following must be true?

   (A) L lives on the first floor.
   (B) M lives on the third floor.
   (C) Q lives on the third floor.
   (D) N lives on the fifth floor.
   (E) Q lives on the fifth floor.

GO ON TO THE NEXT PAGE.

Analysis of Linear Game #5: October 1991 Questions 6-12

This game comes from the second LSAT of the modern era, the October 1991 LSAT. The Logic Games section on the October 1991 exam was interesting because for the typical student, the games were presented in order of difficulty. On a related note, you will sometimes hear that older LSATs from the early 1990s are no longer relevant and that they need not be studied. This is simply not true. Games from the 1990s are useful due to two important considerations:

1. The types of games and the language of the rules in the 1990s games are the same as they are today. Thus, by using these games, you have access to over 100 additional, official games directly from LSAC.

2. In many cases, the average difficulty of the sections in the 1990s is *higher* than that of today, making these sections ideal preparation tools. The theory is that if you can prepare by taking harder games sections, when you get to the real thing it will not feel so difficult.

Now that you have completed this game from 1991, we are sure you can see that these older tests still have great value.

In the context of our overall discussion of Linear games, this game differs from the first four because this game is not Balanced. Instead, this is an Unbalanced game that is Overloaded, since we have eight apartments that must be distributed over five floors. The given rules and restrictions can then be used to create a 2-2-2-1-1 unfixed numerical distribution. Unfortunately, this distribution proves to be of little value in the game. This occurrence should not deter you from seeking numerical distributions in the future. There are many examples of games where the numerical distribution proved to be the key to answering one or more questions.

The game should be set up as follows:

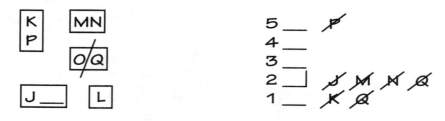

Unlike the previous four games, this game requires a vertical setup because buildings are vertical. One difficult aspect of this game is the uncertainty over which floors contain two apartments. Since it is certain that there is at least one apartment per floor, we have placed slots on each of the five floors of our diagram. In the case of the second floor, which is known to have only one apartment, a short vertical line has been placed at the end of the slot. This vertical line serves as a visual reminder that the second floor contains one and only one apartment. Also of note in this game is the importance of correctly diagramming each rule. In the case of K, who lives one floor above P, the block must be shown vertically since the main diagram is vertical. On the other hand, the rule involving M and N must be shown horizontally because they live on the same floor. By diagramming these rules correctly, you gain a powerful advantage over the game, and you also eliminate a possible source of confusion. Also note that if this game were set up horizontally, then the diagramming of each rule would shift accordingly. For example, the KP block would be horizontal, whereas the MN block would be vertical. In essence you align the blocks with the diagram in order to make the most visual sense. On a vertical diagram a vertical block suggests one variable on top of another, but on a horizontal diagram a vertical block suggests that the two variables share the same space.

Let us take a moment to examine the Not Laws in the game:

> The occupancy limitation on the second floor produces Not Laws for J, M, and N, each of which is involved in a block rule.

> Because K must live on the floor *directly* above P, P cannot live on the fifth floor and K cannot live on the first floor.

> The last rule creates Q Not Laws on the first two floors. Also note that although Q cannot live on the first and second floors, this does not affect the placement of O. In Linear games, not-blocks tend to be relatively weak rules (this will not be the case when discussing grouping games), because the not-block cannot be applied until one of the variables in the block is placed. Since Q has not been placed, it has not yet had an effect on O. This type of relationship was discussed in the Avoiding False Inferences section earlier in the chapter (see page 101).

One of the keys to doing well on the questions is to remember all of the different rules, each of which is unique in form (this is, of course, why we represent rules visually—doing so makes them easier to remember).

Question #6: Global, Must Be True. The correct answer choice is (D)

This question is tailor-made for a Not Law attack. Since M and N must live on the same floor, and the second floor contains only one apartment, answer choice (D) must be correct.

Question #7: Global, Cannot Be True. The correct answer choice is (E)

This question is also suited for a Not Law attack. Since P must live one floor below K, it follows that P cannot live on the fifth floor, and therefore answer choice (E) must be correct. As you may have noticed, with many Global questions, especially the ones that appear early in a game, the first avenue of attack is to check the existing Not Laws. Make sure you always follow this guideline!

Question #8: Local, Could Be True. The correct answer choice is (A)

After completing the first two questions with relative ease, you should arrive at this question feeling confident. Since this is a Local question, you should as always make a mini-diagram next to the question. The "if" statement in the question, in combination with the second rule, produces the following setup:

```
5 K        M̶  N̶
4 P   J |
3 __
2 __|
1 __
```

Several of the answer choices can be eliminated by using the rule that states that each floor has either one or two apartments. Since both J and P live on the fourth floor, no other residents can live on the fourth floor, and answer choices (B) and (D) can be eliminated. Since K lives on the fifth floor, the M and N block cannot live on the fifth floor, and answer choice (C) can be eliminated. Answer choice (E) can be eliminated since P must live on the fourth floor. Accordingly, answer choice (A) is correct.

Question #9: Local, Cannot Be True. The correct answer choice is (E)

This question is more difficult than any of the first three questions in this game, and it is based upon one of the test maker's favorite modes of attack, the use of uncertainty.

If O lives on the second floor, then the second floor is completely occupied, and no other resident can live on the second floor. For some variables, such as the MN block or the J block, this has no effect. For the KP block, however, the placement options are significantly reduced. Since the second floor is now "closed off," the KP block must be placed on the third and fourth floors (3-4) or on the fourth and fifth floors (4-5). At this point, many test takers stop their analysis under the mistaken impression that since the exact position of the block cannot be determined, further examination is worthless. In fact, to get past this situation you must use a technique called Hurdle the Uncertainties™: in games situations with limited solutions, it is often possible to make inferences in spite of the uncertainty. In this case, since the KP block is always on 3-4 or 4-5, it can be concluded that K or P is *always* on the fourth floor. *So, even though we cannot be certain of the exact KP block placement, we can deduce that in this question K or P must be on the fourth floor, and we must account for the space taken up by the K/P dual option:*

```
5 __
4 K/P  __|
3 __
2 O |
1 __
```

Thus, since K or P must always live on the fourth floor, L cannot live on the fourth floor since L must live in the only apartment on her floor. Therefore, answer choice (E) is correct. Note that an answer that attempted to place either M or N on the fourth floor would also have been correct as the presence of K or P on the fourth floor would have eliminated the MN block from the fourth floor.

Essentially, the placement of O builds a "wall" on the second floor. This wall affects the placement of any block which takes up adjoining spaces, such as the KP block. In Linear games where blocks are present, always closely examine the placement of a variable (such as O) into an interior space (such as the second floor). There may be inferences that follow from the reduced placement options of a block (such as either K or P must live on the fourth floor).

Opportunities to Hurdle the Uncertainty™ will appear in a number of games (including questions #10, #11, and #12 in this game), and this is the first introduction to this concept. In the Grouping games chapter, we will discuss the concept again, more formally.

Question #10: Local, Cannot Be True. The correct answer choice is (C)

Do not forget to convert Must Be False into Cannot Be True! This question uses the same Hurdle the Uncertainties™ principle seen in question #9. If M lives on the fourth floor, then the MN block completely occupies the fourth floor, again creating a wall in the interior of the game. This affects the placement of the KP block, which is now limited to floors one and two (1-2) or floors two and three (2-3). Accordingly, either K or P must live on the second floor:

```
5  __
4  M   N |
3  __
2  K/P|
1  __
```

Thus, no other variable can live on the second floor, and answer choice (C) must be correct.

Question #11: Global, Must Be True. The correct answer choice is (B)

If you have difficulty finishing the Logic Games section, or if you find yourself in trouble on a game, this "5 if" question format is one you should avoid. Observe the construction of the question: a Global Must Be True question stem where each of the five answer choices begins with an "if" statement. Essentially, each of the answer choices is a new scenario, and for the most part information cannot be shared among the answer choices in this question. This type of question is designed to consume time! Avoid it if you have time problems in the Logic Games section.

In a possible oversight by the test makers, this question contains an Achilles heel which allows the observant test taker to answer the question quickly. Whenever you encounter a Logic Games question where each answer choice begins with the word "if," always make sure to check your previous work in case some of the information can be reused. In this case, the information from question #9 is duplicated in answer choice (B). Since question #9 proves that, when O lives on the second floor, L cannot live on the fourth floor, and that is what answer choice (B) states in question #11, it must be true that answer choice (B) is correct.

Honestly, it is a stroke of good fortune that the information from question #9 solves this question. Generally, on questions where each answer choice begins with "if," using the information from previous questions would perhaps eliminate one or two answer choices at most. Of course, that would still provide a great advantage. Here, that technique answers a very time-consuming question quite quickly. Always remember to check your previous work to see if it applies to the question you are working on, especially when you know the question is specifically designed to consume time. Should you wish to complete this question, and you fail to refer to previous work, your only choice is to work through each answer until you come to one you can prove correct.

Question #12: Local, Must Be True. The correct answer choice is (C)

The Local conditions in the question stem establish the following partial setup:

```
5 __
4  O      L̸ Ø̸ M̸ N̸
3  K      L̸ M̸ N̸
2  P⌉     L̸ M̸ N̸ Ø̸
1 __
```

Because L, M, and N cannot live on the second, third, or fourth floors, they must live on either the first or fifth floors, and because the MN block and L each require a floor of its own, it can be inferred that L, M, and N will completely occupy the first and fifth floors, creating a L/MN dual split-option:

```
5 MN / L
4  O
3  K
2  P⌉
1  L/ MN
```

Given this information, you can Hurdle the Uncertainties™ and come to the realization that only floor three and floor four are available for J and Q, and since Q cannot live on the same floor as O, Q must live on the third floor and thus J must live on the fourth floor, resulting in the following setup:

```
5 MN / L
4  O      J
3  K      Q
2  P⌉
1  L/ MN
```

It follows that answer choice (C) is correct. Also of interest is the fact that this is the first question in the game to directly address the OQ not-block. The test makers probably left this rule out of the game until the end in an effort to see whether careless test takers would forget about the rule and then miss the question. You must fix the rules in your mind at the beginning of the game and never forget them!

Final Chapter Note

We strongly urge you to look at this entire chapter again before moving on to the next chapter. In particular, make sure you feel comfortable with the initial discussions of rule diagramming, sufficient and necessary conditions, numerical distributions, and especially the game explanations. There are many subtle Games points spread throughout this chapter, and we will encounter them again as we move deeper into our discussion.

Chapter Four: Advanced Linear Games

Chapter Four: Advanced Linear Games

Multiple Stacks ▬▬▬▬▬▬▬▬▬▬▬▬

In the previous chapter, we discussed games that involved just two variable sets: one variable set classified as the base, and another variable set controlled by the base. This chapter examines Linear games that feature three or more variable sets. As before, one of the variable sets will be classified as the base, and the other variable sets will generally be "stacked" in rows above the base. In this sense, Advanced Linear games are identical to the games in the last chapter. However, the presence of three or more variable sets creates a far greater degree of complexity in the game. For example, there are 5040 different solutions to a basic Linear game featuring seven variables placed into seven ordered positions (for you math majors, the number of combinations can be expressed by 7 factorial (7!)). Of course, the 5040 solutions are only possible *prior* to the consideration of the rules of the game. As soon as the rules are considered, the number of possible solutions decreases significantly. Now examine an Advanced Linear game featuring two variable sets of seven being placed into a base created by a third variable set (in other words, a single variable set has been added to the previous example): there are now 25,401,600 possible solutions to the game. Thus, the addition of just one variable set can exponentially increase the number of possible solutions to the game. Again, the rules will reduce the number of possible solutions, but the fact remains that Advanced Linear games inherently have more solutions and thus greater complexity.

When working with this increased complexity, you must organize your information as efficiently as possible. When you diagram multiple variable sets, choose a base and then "stack" each variable set on top of one another, as follows:

Three variable sets:

Variable set #3:	___ ___ ___ ___
Variable set #2:	___ ___ ___ ___
Variable set #1 (base):	1 2 3 4

Advanced Linear games are the same as the games in the last chapter, but there are now more variable sets with which to contend.

4

An Advanced Linear game with four separate variable sets of seven elements each will have over 128 billion solutions before the rules are applied. No wonder everyone thinks Games are challenging!

Create a new stack for each additional variable set.

Four variable sets:

Variable set #4:	___	___	___	___
Variable set #3:	___	___	___	___
Variable set #2:	___	___	___	___
Variable set #1 (base):	1	2	3	4

Of course, there will be times when one (or more) of the variable sets naturally fills in the spaces and does not need its own row, as in the following game scenario:

> During three days—Monday through Wednesday—a compliance officer will inspect exactly six companies—three banks: Amity, Bonded, and Community; and three brokerages: Xenon, Yarra, and Zenith. Each day, exactly two companies are inspected: one in the morning and one in the afternoon.

Accordingly, there are five variable sets:

> Set #1: the three days—Monday, Tuesday, and Wednesday
> Set #2: the three banks—A, B, and C
> Set #3: the three brokerages—X, Y, and Z
> Set #4: the three morning inspections
> Set #5: the three afternoon inspections

Since the days of the week have the greatest sense of inherent order, they should be chosen as the base, and since the morning and afternoon inspections naturally correspond to the days, they should be shown as stacks:

In multi-stack games one variable set is often used to "fill in" the spaces in the diagram created by another variable set.

Afternoon Inspections: ___ ___ ___

Morning Inspections: ___ ___ ___
                               M   T   W

The remaining two variable sets—the banks and the brokerages—can now be placed into the six spaces representing the days and times. In this way all five variable sets are displayed, and the diagram is orderly and logical.

Repeated Variable Sets

Most games use each variable set just a single time. However, some games repeat variable sets. Consider the following game scenario:

> At a small newspaper, over a period of six consecutive weeks, six restaurants—A, B, C, D, E, and F—will each be reviewed once by the editor, Gomez, and once by the head writer, Hughes. Each reviewer reviews exactly one restaurant per week.

In this game, the restaurant variable set will be assigned once to Gomez, and then assigned again to Hughes:

Hughes: ___ ___ ___ ___ ___ ___ (A, B, C, D, E, F)

Gomez: ___ ___ ___ ___ ___ ___ (A, B, C, D, E, F)
Weeks: 1   2   3   4   5   6

The one disadvantage of a variable set being repeated is that the variables in the set will appear more than once, and that repetition must be tracked. For example, in the game above, you must track "A" when it is assigned to Gomez and also when it is assigned to Hughes, and so you must be able to differentiate between those assignments. When diagramming the rules, the best technique to track individual assignments with repeated variable sets is to use subscripts (more on this in a bit).

Diagramming with Multiple Stacks ■

Linked Variable Set Rules

In addition to rules addressing individual variable sets, the test makers will also include rules that interrelate different variable sets. Consider the following partial game:

> Exactly six runners—P, Q, R, S, T, and U—compete in a marathon. Each runner completes the race, and no two runners finish at the same time. The information that follows is all that is known about the six runners:
>> Each runner is either an amateur or a professional, but not both.
>> Four of the runners are female and two are male.

In this game there are four variable sets: the six finishing places (which are chosen as the base due to their inherent natural order), the set of runners, the amateur/professional set, and the male/female set.

With the base chosen, "stack" each variable set on top of one another, as follows:

```
M/F:      ___  ___  ___  ___  ___  ___   F F F F  M M

A/P:      ___  ___  ___  ___  ___  ___

Runners:  ___  ___  ___  ___  ___  ___   P Q R S T U
Places:    1    2    3    4    5    6
```

Now that the variable sets have been established, let us continue. The next rule presented was as follows:

> The two male runners are professionals.

As would be expected, this rule connects two of the variable sets: the male/female variable set and the amateur/professional set. Rules that connect different variable sets are extremely common in Advanced Linear games, and you should always be prepared for them. In this case, the rule above creates two linked vertical blocks where M (male) connects to P (professional):

Not all the blocks will be simple vertical or horizontal blocks. The test makers like to challenge test takers with more complex blocks that have both vertical and horizontal components. Consider a game about five cars coming off an assembly line, where each car has a different exterior color, a different interior color, and a different type of transmission. Let us say that the basic setup for the game appears as follows:

In games with more than two variable sets, always be prepared for rules that link the variable sets together.

Trans:	___	___	___	___	___
Int Color:	___	___	___	___	___
Ext Color:	___	___	___	___	___
Cars:	1	2	3	4	5

Now, suppose that a rule is presented that states:

> The car with the blue exterior is assembled immediately before the car with the red interior but immediately after a car with a manual transmission.

Some students might be tempted to diagram this rule as a horizontal block with subscripts, as follows:

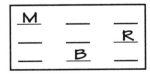

This approach would be a mistake because it does not take into account the multi-stacked aspect of the game. A better representation is a block that also takes into account the vertical aspect of the game:

This second representation is far superior to the first because it displays both the horizontal separation and the vertical separation of the individual elements. Visually, this representation is much more powerful.

The rules that link variable sets are not always block-oriented—the test makers also like to insert sequencing rules that link multiple variable sets. For example, the following rule from a different game sequentially links two different variable sets:

Exactly two of the taxis that arrive before D are yellow.

This rule links a variable set about color to a variable set about taxis. Because each variable set is placed in a different row, tracking rules like this one can be challenging. Some students use subscripts to track each variable set in Advanced Linear sequencing rules, but that is a decision that should be made based upon the complexity of the game and how confident you feel. For example, with this rule, most students feel comfortable with this representation:

The following sequencing rule, however, requires the use of subscripts:

Ronald receives a better grade in chemistry than in French.

In this game, chemistry and French were each different variable sets, and Ronald (and six other students) was assigned a grade for *each* class. The best representation of the rule is as follows:

$$R_C \longrightarrow R_F$$

The rule to the right does not allow for an easy way to show the vertical separation between the chemistry and French variable sets, hence the use of subscripts.

Because the students are a repeated variable set, "R" appears multiple times in the game, and the only way to track the different appearances of R is to use a subscript for each variable set (in this case, "C" for chemistry and "F" for French).

Internal Diagram Spacing

When creating diagrams for games that have two or more stacks, you *must* leave extra vertical space between the rows in case there is a need to place individual Not Laws under a space within a variable set. For example, consider the following diagram:

If you have diagrammed your variable sets vertically in columns, then leave extra horizontal space between each column.

Trans: ___ ___ ___ ___ ___

Int Color: ___ ___ ___ ___ ___

Ext Color: ___ ___ ___ ___ ___
Cars: 1   2   3   4   5

Now consider the problem presented by a rule such as the following:

The third car cannot have a red interior.

This rule can only be diagrammed as a Not Law, yet there is no space under the interior color row to place that Not Law. Thus, the Not Law would have to appear under the diagram, along with every other Not Law in the game. This would quickly become confusing because every Not Law for every variable set would appear under the diagram, and they would all be mixed together. However, if you provide sufficient vertical space, this rule can be diagrammed immediately under the interior color row:

Trans: ___ ___ ___ ___ ___

Int Color: ___ ___ ___ ___ ___
                         R̸

Ext Color: ___ ___ ___ ___ ___
Cars: 1   2   3   4   5

Leave extra space between each stack in case any Not Laws need to be placed below the spaces.

With this diagram, each Not Law can be efficiently connected to the proper variable set (any Not Laws that appear underneath the diagram would be connected to the exterior color variable set).

Side Not Laws

Not Laws do not always have to go directly below the space—they can be represented on the side of the diagram where appropriate.

4

The choice of placing the morning inspections as the bottom row is an arbitrary one. You could just as easily place the afternoon inspections as the bottom row (with the morning inspections then as the top row). Once you have chosen a base, unless the game specifically dictates that variable set should be in a specific row, you can order or stack the sets as you choose.

In certain situations, Not Laws can be placed to the side of the setup to indicate that a variable cannot be placed in the row. For example, after referring to the setup for the game in the middle of page 220, imagine that a rule was added to that game that stated the following:

Amity cannot be inspected in the morning.

This rule could be represented on the diagram as follows:

Afternoon Inspections: ___ ___ ___

Morning Inspections: ___ ___ ___ A̸
                M   T   W

This representation can save time and help to avoid confusion. Time is saved because the Not Law is written only once, not three times. Confusion is avoided since placing the Not Law under each space might give the false impression that A could not appear on either the morning or afternoon of that day (and under the pressure of the test, this confusion could occur).

Note that Side Not Laws typically only appear when one or more of the variable sets is used to fill in spaces created by other variable sets (as the banks and brokerages are in this game).

This type of rule diagramming also applies to vertical setups, although appropriate adjustments must be made for the change in perspective, namely that these Not Laws then appear at the top or bottom of the diagram (the "side" positions on a vertical diagram are simply regular Not Laws on individual spaces).

Advanced Linear Setup Practice Drill

Each of the following items presents an Advanced Linear game scenario. Using the space provided, diagram the game. Occasionally, a problem will contain a corresponding rule. Use your knowledge of rule representation to properly display each rule. *Answers on page 229*

1. Seven doctors—F, G, H, J, K, L, and M—are scheduled to interview for a position with a local hospital. The seven interviews are conducted on seven different days, Monday through Sunday. Each doctor is assigned to one of seven different interviewers—P, Q, R, S, T, V, and W.

2. Six runners—R, S, T, V, X, and Z—are assigned to six lanes on a track numbered 1 though 6. Exactly one runner is assigned to each lane, and each runner wears one of six letters—A, B, C, D, E, and F.

3. Three apartment buildings—the Highlander, the Ivy, and the Jacaranda—each have exactly five floors, numbered 1 through 5. Each floor of each building is decorated in exactly one of three styles—Colonial, Federal, or Georgian. Each style is used at least once in each building.

   In the Jacaranda, the only floor decorated in the Colonial style is immediately above the only floor decorated in the Georgian style.

   The fourth floor of the Highlander is not decorated in the Federal style.

Advanced Linear Setup Practice Drill

4. Eight librarians—C, D, E, F, G, H, J, and K—are assigned to eight work shifts at the local library. Each librarian is assigned exactly one shift, and only one librarian is assigned to each shift. The shifts are on Monday, Tuesday, Wednesday, and Friday, with one shift in the morning and one shift in the afternoon of each day. The assignments must be made according to the following conditions:

    Librarian C does not work in the morning of any day.

    Librarian F works an earlier shift than librarian G.

    Librarians D and E work in the morning on consecutive calendar days.

5. There are exactly ten houses and no others on Magnolia Street. On the west side of the street, from north to south, are houses 1, 3, 5, 7, and 9; on the east side of the street, from north to south, are houses 2, 4, 6, 8, and 10. The houses on the west side are located directly across the street from the houses on the east side, and the following pairs of houses face each other: 1 and 2; 3 and 4; 5 and 6; 7 and 8; 9 and 10. Each house is painted in exactly one of the following colors: blue, green, white, and yellow. The houses are painted according to the following rules:

    No house is painted in the same color as the house directly across the street.

    House 4 is painted green.

    No house on the west side of the street is painted white.

Advanced Linear Setup Practice Drill Answer Key

1. Seven doctors—F, G, H, J, K, L, and M—are
    scheduled to interview for a position with a local
    hospital. The seven interviews are conducted on seven
    different days, Monday through Sunday. Each doctor
    is assigned to one of seven different interviewers—P,
    Q, R, S, T, V, and W.

There are three variable sets in this problem: the seven interview positions (days), the seven doctors, and the seven interviewers. Because the days of the week have the greatest sense of inherent order, they should be chosen as the base. Consequently, the diagram should appear as follows:

Doc: F G H J K L M ^{7}
Int: P Q R S T V W ^{7}

Doc:	___	___	___	___	___	___	___
Int:	___	___	___	___	___	___	___
	M	Tu	W	Th	F	Sa	Su

2. Six runners—R, S, T, V, X, and Z—are assigned to
    six lanes on a track numbered 1 though 6. Exactly one
    runner is assigned to each lane, and each runner wears
    one of six letters—A, B, C, D, E, and F.

There are three variable sets in this problem: the six lanes, the six runners, and the six letters. Choosing the base in this problem requires a bit more thought because two variable sets—the lanes and the letters—appear to have inherent order. However, the letters do not have a fixed order; instead each can be assigned randomly to any runner. On the other hand, the lanes do have a fixed order, and they should be chosen as the base, leading to the following setup:

Run: R S T V X Z ^{6}
Lett: A B C D E F ^{6}

Letter:	___	___	___	___	___	___
Runner:	___	___	___	___	___	___
	1	2	3	4	5	6

3. Three apartment buildings—the Highlander, the Ivy, and the Jacaranda—each have exactly five floors, numbered 1 through 5. Each floor of each building is decorated in exactly one of three styles—Colonial, Federal, or Georgian. Each style is used at least once in each building.

> In the Jacaranda, the only floor decorated in the Colonial style is immediately above the only floor decorated in the Georgian style.
>
> The fourth floor of the Highlander is not decorated in the Federal style.

There are three variable sets in this problem: the three apartment buildings, the five floors, and the three styles. The best setup for buildings with floors is vertical, and thus the buildings should be the base, and the floors should number 1-5 from the bottom to the top, as the floors of a building appear in the real world:

```
5    ___        ___        ___

4    ___        ___        ___

3    ___        ___        ___

2    ___        ___        ___

1    ___        ___        ___
      H          I          J
```

The styles are a repeating variable set, and thus all three styles will appear in each building. However, if any given floor cannot be decorated in one of the styles, that will leave a dual-option of the other two styles.

The first rule establishes a vertical block:

Further, this rule indicates that C and G are each used exactly once in the Jacaranda, and thus we can infer that F must appear three times in the Jacaranda. We also know that in the Jacaranda, C cannot be on the first floor, and G cannot be on the fifth floor. These two Not Laws are written off to the side of the J column, and lead to dual-options. The second rule creates an F Not Law on floor 4 of the Highlander. This Not Law is written off to the side of the H column next to floor 4. and also creates a dual-option. Combining the information above leads to the following setup:

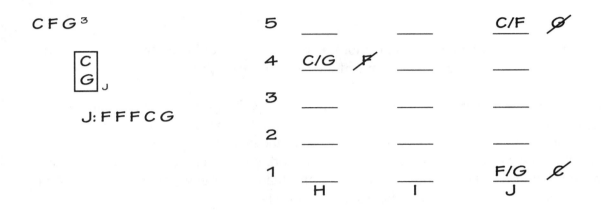

---

4. Eight librarians—C, D, E, F, G, H, J, and K—are assigned to eight work shifts at the local library. Each librarian is assigned exactly one shift, and only one librarian is assigned to each shift. The shifts are on Monday, Tuesday, Wednesday, and Friday, with one shift in the morning and one shift in the afternoon of each day. The assignments must be made according to the following conditions:

    Librarian C does not work in the morning of any day.

    Librarian F works an earlier shift than librarian G.

    Librarians D and E work in the morning on consecutive calendar days.

There are four variable sets in this problem: the four days, the four morning shifts, the four afternoon shifts, and the eight librarians. However, the librarians should be used to fill the morning and afternoon shifts, and thus only two stacks are necessary. The days of the week should, as usual, be chosen as the base. Also, note that although Thursday has been skipped in the list of days, you should still show Thursday but then "X" it out, as follows:

Advanced Linear Setup Practice Drill Answer Key

CDEFGHJK ^{8}

Aft:
XX
Morn:
XX
M
Tu
W
Th
F

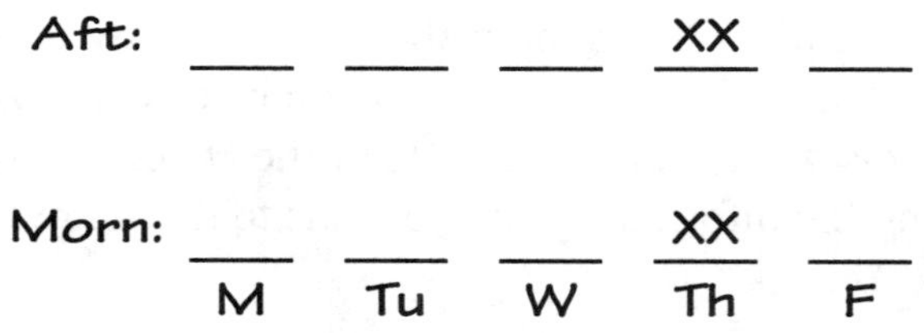

The first rule, "Librarian C does not work in the morning of any day," should be shown as a Side Not Law on the morning shift, thus relegating C to one of the four afternoon shifts.

The second rule, "Librarian F works an earlier shift than librarian G," can be very tricky. This rule, which is diagrammed as F —— G, does not automatically create Not Laws for G on Monday and for F on Friday. This is because "earlier" allows for F to work the morning shift and G to work the afternoon shift of the same day. Thus, G can be assigned to work on Monday, and, separately, F can be assigned to work on Friday. However, G cannot work on Monday morning, and F cannot work on Friday afternoon, and hence Not Laws must be placed on those positions.

The last rule, "Librarians D and E work in the morning on consecutive calendar days," creates a rotating block:

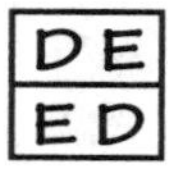

DE
ED

Because the rule references consecutive calendar days, this block must be assigned to Monday-Tuesday or Tuesday-Wednesday (remember, since Thursday is unavailable, Friday will not be consecutive with any other day). Accordingly, either D or E must be assigned to Tuesday morning.

Combining the information above leads to the following diagram:

CDEFGHJK ^{8}

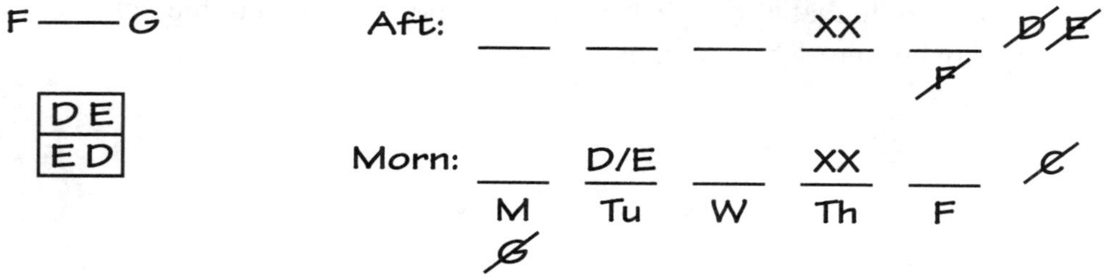

F —— G
DE
ED
Aft:
XX
D E
F
Morn:
D/E
XX
C
M
Tu
W
Th
F
G

There are further inferences to be made, such as the chain reaction that occurs when G is assigned to Monday afternoon: F must be assigned to Monday morning, and then the DE block must be assigned in some order to Tuesday and Wednesday mornings.

---

5. There are exactly ten houses and no others on Magnolia Street. On the west side of the street, from north to south, are houses 1, 3, 5, 7, and 9; on the east side of the street, from north to south, are houses 2, 4, 6, 8, and 10. The houses on the west side are located directly across the street from the houses on the east side, and the following pairs of houses face each other: 1 and 2; 3 and 4; 5 and 6; 7 and 8; 9 and 10. Each house is painted in exactly one of the following colors: blue, green, white, and yellow. The houses are painted according to the following rules:

    No house is painted in the same color as the house directly across the street.

    House 4 is painted green.

    No house on the west side of the street is painted white.

There are three variable sets in this problem: the five houses on the west side, the five houses on the east side, and the four house colors. Because of the geographic specifications of the problems, the houses should be used as the base, and the game should be diagrammed vertically.

The first rule creates a horizontal not-block. In order to save time, instead of writing out a not-block for each individual color, we will simply use the following designation:

"C" stands for color, and thus block means that the same color cannot appear at houses that are across from each other.

The second rule is diagrammed directly on the diagram, and the application of the first rule leads to the inference that house 3 is not green, and this inference is shown by a G Not Law.

The last rule is shown by a W Not Law at the bottom of the west side of houses. This is technically a Side Not Law, but since the diagram is presented vertically, it appears to be another basic Not Law. However, in vertical diagrams the "Side" is actually at the bottom.

Note that the combination of Not Laws on house 3 leads to a B/Y dual option.

Combining the information above, the diagram appears as follows:

B G W Y [4]

1	___	2	___
3	B/Y ~~G~~	4	G
5	___	6	___
7	___	8	___
9	___	10	___

~~W~~

Two Linear Inference Principles ▆▆▆▆

The Separation Principle™

The Separation Principle appears in both Basic Linear and Advanced
Linear games. The Separation Principle applies when variables involved
in not-blocks are placed into a limited number of spaces. For example,
suppose that two boys are being seated in three chairs, with the rule that
the two boys cannot sit next to one another. The minimum amount of room
needed to accommodate the not-block rule is:

Since the minimum requirement happens to be the same as the number of
available spaces, the boys are forced into spaces 1 and 3:

$$\frac{B}{1} \quad \frac{}{2} \quad \frac{B}{3}$$

Now suppose we expand the scenario to three boys being seated in five
chairs, still with the rule that no boy can sit next to another boy. The
minimum space required when the not-block rule is applied to the three
boys is:

$$\boxed{B \underline{} B \underline{} B}$$

Again, the minimum requirement happens to be identical to the number of
available spaces, and the boys are forced into spaces 1, 3, and 5:

$$\frac{B}{1} \quad \frac{}{2} \quad \frac{B}{3} \quad \frac{}{4} \quad \frac{B}{5}$$

Now suppose we expand the scenario to four boys being seated into
seven chairs, still with the rule that no boys can sit next to each other. The
minimum space required by the not-block rule is:

$$\boxed{B \underline{} B \underline{} B \underline{} B}$$

Again, the minimum space requirement happens to be identical to the number of available spaces, and the boys are forced into spaces 1, 3, 5, and 7:

$$\underset{1}{\underline{B}} \quad \underset{2}{\underline{\hphantom{B}}} \quad \underset{3}{\underline{B}} \quad \underset{4}{\underline{\hphantom{B}}} \quad \underset{5}{\underline{B}} \quad \underset{6}{\underline{\hphantom{B}}} \quad \underset{7}{\underline{B}}$$

Now, consider the following sample game scenario:

The Metro Zoo exhibits exactly seven animals—one bear, two lions, two tigers, and two zebras—in seven consecutive cages according to the following restrictions:

Each animal is exhibited exactly once, in one cage only. No cage is reused.

Two animals of the same type are never exhibited consecutively.

A lion is never exhibited immediately before or immediately after a tiger.

Here, instead of a universal AA not-block (A for animals) like the one we use at the bottom of page 233, we use separate not-blocks, because there are different types of animals.

The second rule creates three not-blocks:

The third rule creates two more not-blocks:

In the next chapter we will examine Grouping games, which tend to feature a greater number of "negative" rules, like not-blocks.

In a game with so many not-blocks, there are enormous restrictions facing the variables. Most games contain only one or two not-blocks, and those not-blocks typically do not place any variables on their own; they usually come into play only after the other rules have been applied. Not-block rules are also easy to forget, and thus you often see questions where the last inferential step involves a not-block. In some cases, games have contained not-block rules that were only used once, in the last question, probably based on the theory that some students will have forgotten that the not-block rule exists by that point.

The most important not-blocks in this game involve the lions and tigers. Essentially, the two lions and the two tigers form a group of four variables, none of which can be placed next to any other. This means that these four variables must be spread out over the seven spaces, with at least one space separating each variable. Because of the Separation Principle, this can only be accomplished by placing the four variables in spaces 1, 3, 5, and 7 (just like our example with four boys spread over seven spaces). Obviously the arrangement in this game is a bit harder to discern because the group of four variables contains two subgroups, the lions and tigers.

Because the lions and tigers represent four variables involved in not-blocks being placed into seven spaces, the following inference is made:

$$\frac{\text{L/T}}{1} \quad \frac{}{2} \quad \frac{\text{L/T}}{3} \quad \frac{}{4} \quad \frac{\text{L/T}}{5} \quad \frac{}{6} \quad \frac{\text{L/T}}{7}$$

The bear and the two zebras would then be exhibited in cages 2, 4, and 6 in some order. Obviously, a setup containing this much information would make answering the questions quite easy.

The point to derive from this discussion is that not-blocks can be quite powerful, especially when there are several of them and they are inter-related.

The Overlap Principle™

The Overlap Principle states:

> When members of two separate variable sets are both assigned into a fixed number of spaces, there will be an overlap between the groups if the sum of the two groups is greater than the total number of spaces.

If this Principle sounds a bit daunting, do not worry! To help make the definition make sense, we will use a simple example. Consider the following scenario:

> There are three chairs in a classroom. Two of the chairs are green and two boys sit in the chairs.
>
> Given the above information, what can be inferred?

The variable sets can be represented as follows:

Boys:	B B
Chair Color:	G G
Chairs:	1 2 3

In this case the three chairs would be the base and the other two variable sets would be stacked on top of the chairs in the usual fashion:

Boys:	___	___	___
Chair Color:	___	___	___
Chairs:	1	2	3

No matter how you place the two boys and the two green chairs, *at least one of the boys must sit in a green chair*. For example, if the boys sit in chairs 1 and 2, you could make chair 3 green, but then either chair 1 or 2 would have to be green. In this case the sum of boys (2) plus the sum of the green chairs (2) equals 4, but there are only 3 spaces available to hold all those elements. Thus, there must be an overlap between the boys and the chair color. This is not a principle that the test makers use frequently, but it is useful to be acquainted with the idea because the test makers will test to see if you recognize it when it appears.

The Overlap Principle can apply to a wide variety of group sizes, e.g., two groups of three being placed into a group of five, or a group of three and a group of two being placed into four spaces. Consider the following scenario:

A mechanic repairs seven cars in consecutive order. Four of the cars are red, two of the cars are blue, and one car is green. Each car is also either a convertible or hardtop, and four of the cars are convertible and three are hardtops.

From this scenario alone, prior to the consideration of any rules, you should be able to see that at least one of the red cars is a convertible car. Why? Because of the Overlap Principle:

The total number of red cars (4) plus the total number of convertibles (4) equals 8, which is greater than the total number of available spaces (7).

To better see this principle in action, imagine that the four red cars are the first four cars that the mechanic repairs. At least one of those first four red cars must have been a convertible, because at this point there are only three cars left to repair but we know there are four total convertibles.

From an occurrence standpoint, unlike the Separation Principle, which can occur in any Linear game, the Overlap Principle occurs only in Advanced Linear games. This is because the Overlap Principle appears with multiple variable sets. Like the Separation Principle, however, when the Overlap Principle is in play, the test makers always check to see whether you recognized its occurrence.

Final Pregame Note

Remember, Advanced Linear games are an extension of the Basic Linear games discussed in the previous chapter, and thus all of the rule representations and inference-making patterns discussed in that chapter still apply. The concept of linearity is a critical one on the LSAT, and so in addition to the games in Chapters Three and Four, you will also be seeing linearity in the games in Chapters Six, Seven, Eight, and Nine.

As always, please read the explanations to each game carefully, as they will give you a true sense of how to best attack each game. Plus, the explanations always include points that expand the discussion given above.

If you would like to test yourself under timed conditions, you should give yourself 8 minutes and 45 seconds for each game. Good luck on the games!

> In doing these games, **use scratch paper instead of writing directly on the game!** This will prepare you for the Digital LSAT format where you cannot write directly on the screen.

Eight physics students—four majors: Frank, Gwen, Henry, and Joan; and four nonmajors: Victor, Wanda, Xavier, and Yvette—are being assigned to four laboratory benches, numbered 1 through 4. Each student is assigned to exactly one bench, and exactly two students are assigned to each bench. Assignments of students to benches must conform to the following conditions:

> Exactly one major is assigned to each bench.
> Frank and Joan are assigned to consecutively numbered benches, with Frank assigned to the lower-numbered bench.
> Frank is assigned to the same bench as Victor.
> Gwen is not assigned to the same bench as Wanda.

1. Which one of the following could be the assignment of students to benches?

(A)   1: Frank, Victor; 2: Joan, Gwen; 3: Henry, Wanda; 4: Xavier, Yvette

(B)   1: Gwen, Yvette; 2: Frank, Xavier; 3: Joan, Wanda; 4: Henry, Victor

(C)   1: Henry, Wanda; 2: Gwen, Xavier; 3: Frank, Victor; 4: Joan, Yvette

(D)   1: Henry, Xavier; 2: Joan, Wanda; 3: Frank, Victor; 4: Gwen, Yvette

(E)   1: Henry, Yvette; 2: Gwen, Wanda; 3: Frank, Victor; 4: Joan, Xavier

GO ON TO THE NEXT PAGE.

2. If Victor is assigned to bench 2 and Wanda is assigned to bench 4, which one of the following must be true?

(A) Frank is assigned to bench 1.
(B) Gwen is assigned to bench 1.
(C) Henry is assigned to bench 3.
(D) Xavier is assigned to bench 1.
(E) Yvette is assigned to bench 3.

3. If Gwen and Henry are not assigned to consecutively numbered benches, which one of the following must be true?

(A) Victor is assigned to bench 2.
(B) Victor is assigned to bench 3.
(C) Wanda is assigned to bench 1.
(D) Wanda is assigned to bench 3.
(E) Wanda is assigned to bench 4.

4. If Henry and Yvette are both assigned to bench 1, which one of the following could be true?

(A) Gwen is assigned to bench 3.
(B) Joan is assigned to bench 2.
(C) Wanda is assigned to bench 2.
(D) Wanda is assigned to bench 3.
(E) Xavier is assigned to bench 3.

5. If Gwen is assigned to bench 4 and Xavier is assigned to bench 3, then any one of the following could be true EXCEPT:

(A) Gwen is assigned to the same bench as Yvette.
(B) Henry is assigned to the same bench as Wanda.
(C) Henry is assigned to the same bench as Xavier.
(D) Joan is assigned to the same bench as Xavier.
(E) Joan is assigned to the same bench as Yvette.

6. If Wanda is assigned to a lower-numbered bench than is Joan, then Henry must be assigned to a

(A) lower-numbered bench than is Frank
(B) lower-numbered bench than is Gwen
(C) lower-numbered bench than is Xavier
(D) higher-numbered bench than is Victor
(E) higher-numbered bench than is Yvette

7. Which one of the following could be the assignments for bench 2 and bench 4 ?

(A) 2: Gwen, Xavier
    4: Henry, Yvette
(B) 2: Henry, Yvette
    4: Joan, Xavier
(C) 2: Joan, Victor
    4: Gwen, Xavier
(D) 2: Joan, Wanda
    4: Gwen, Xavier
(E) 2: Joan, Xavier
    4: Henry, Yvette

GO ON TO THE NEXT PAGE.

In this Defined, Balanced game there are three variable sets: the four majors, the four nonmajors, and the four laboratory benches. Since the laboratory benches have an inherent sense of order, they should be selected as the base. A diagram similar to the following should be created:

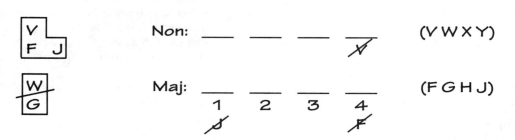

Nonmajors: V W X Y ⁴
Majors: F G H J ⁴

Non: ___ ___ ___ ___   (V W X Y)

Maj: ___ ___ ___ ___   (F G H J)
       1 2 3 4

The second rule can be somewhat confusing. "Lower-numbered" means that one number is less than another; for example, 2 is less than 3. Do not confuse the meaning of this rule with ranking-type games where 1 is ranked higher than 2, etc. (games like this *do* occur on the LSAT). When the rule discusses "lower-numbered" or "higher-numbered" elements, it means actual numerical value and 1 is always lower than 2, 2 is always lower than 3, 3 is always lower than 4, and so on. Thus the rule is properly diagrammed as an FJ block. Applying the basic principle of linkage to the second and third rules produces the VFJ super-block. This super block is clearly one of the keys to the game since it has a limited number of placement options. In fact, the game is made somewhat easier by the fact that there are only two "active" rules to track: the VFJ super-block and the GW not-block. The first rule is essentially dead since it is incorporated into the main setup. With only two active rules to consider, you should always be looking to apply them as you attack the questions.

The active rules also allow you to identify two helpful limitations, one involving W and the other involving G:

> Because W cannot be assigned with G, and because F is already assigned to V, either H or J *must* be assigned with W.

> Because G cannot be assigned with W or V, G must be assigned with X or Y.

Question #1: Global, Could Be True, List. The correct answer choice is (C)

As usual, apply the List question technique. Answer choice (A) can be eliminated since bench 2 contains two majors, a violation of the rules (and, of course, bench 4 contains two nonmajors). This question is rather irritating because of the layout chosen by the test makers. It would have been much easier had they separated the benches with some space instead of lining them up. Answer choice (C) is correct.

Question #2: Local, Must Be True. The correct answer choice is (B)

If V is assigned to bench 2, then, by application of the super-block, F must be assigned to bench 2, and J must be assigned to bench 3. Then, when W is assigned to bench 4, this affects G, who can no longer be assigned to bench 4, or benches 2 and 3 since they are taken by F and J. Therefore, G must be assigned to bench 1:

Non: ___ V ___ W

Maj: G F J H
      1 2 3 4̸

Since G must be assigned to bench 1, answer choice (B) is proven correct. Additionally, when G is assigned to bench 1, H is forced into bench 4. The last two variables, X and Y, create a dual option that rotates between benches 1 and 3.

Question #3: Local, Must Be True. The correct answer choice is (A)

The question stem contains the unusual condition that majors G and H cannot be consecutive, creating a GH not-block. The key to the question is realizing that since G and H are majors, their placement will have a direct effect on the other two majors, F and J, who happen to be in a block configuration. Since the VFJ super-block can only be assigned to three positions—benches 1 and 2, benches 2 and 3, or benches 3 and 4—it makes sense to quickly examine the effect these placements have on G and H. If F and J are assigned to benches 1 and 2, this would force G and H to be consecutive, and if F and J are assigned to benches 3 and 4, this would also force G and H to be consecutive, so the VFJ super-block must be assigned to benches 2 and 3:

Non: ___ V ___ ___

Maj: G/H F J H/G
       1   2 3   4

Consequently answer choice (A) is proven correct.

Should you find yourself having difficulty with this question, it is interesting to note that the hypothetical produced in question #2 (where G and H were not consecutive) can be used to eliminate answer choices (B), (C), and (D), leaving just answer choices (A) and (E) to attack. This a great example of how using applicable prior work can get you out of difficulty.

Question #4: Local, Could Be True. The correct answer choice is (D)

When H and Y are assigned to bench 1, the VFJ super block has only two options: benches 2 and 3 or benches 3 and 4. Since that much information could be tough to juggle in your mind, why not make two quick hypotheticals showing both possibilities?

Possibility #1: VFJ assigned to benches 2 and 3

Non: Y   V   W   X / ~~W~~

Maj: H   F   J   G
        1   2   3   4

Possibility #2: VFJ assigned to benches 3 and 4

Non: Y   X / ~~W~~   V   W

Maj: H   G   F   J
        1   2   3   4

In both possibilities the key to assigning the remaining variables is in the GW not-block. In possibility #1, when G is assigned to bench 4, W cannot be assigned to bench 4 and must instead be assigned to bench 3. In possibility #2, when G is assigned to bench 2, W cannot be assigned to bench 2 and must instead be assigned to bench 4. Possibility #1 proves that answer choice (D) is correct.

Question #5: Local, Could Be True, Except. The correct answer choice is (E)

Since this is an Except question, four of the answer choices Could Be True, and the one correct answer choice Cannot Be True. The question states that G is assigned to bench 4, and X to bench 3. From the global conditions, we know that W cannot be assigned to the same bench as G, so she cannot be at bench 4. From the super-block, we know that V cannot be at bench 4. Since X is at bench 3, he cannot be at bench 4. This leaves Y as the only possible non-major to sit at bench 4, so she must be seated there, and we now know that bench 4 seats only G and Y. Thus, answer choice (E) is correct because J cannot be assigned to the same bench as Y.

If you do not see the inference pattern above, remember that you can make hypotheticals based on the limited positions of the VFJ super-block. In this case, the VFJ super-block has only two possible assignments: benches 1 and 2 or benches 2 and 3:

Possibility #1: VFJ assigned to benches 1 and 2

Non:	V	W	X	Y
				W̶

Maj:	F	J	H	G
	1	2	3	4

Possibility #2: VFJ assigned to benches 2 and 3

Non:	W	V	X	Y
				W̶

Maj:	H	F	J	G
	1	2	3	4

Again, after the VFJ super-block is placed, the application of the GW not-block allows all the variables to be assigned. By comparing each answer choice against the two hypotheticals, you could still determine that answer choice (E) is correct.

The question stem sets up the following sequence:

$$W \text{——} J$$

Although this rule interrelates the majors and nonmajors, more importantly it ties in the VFJ super-block. If W is assigned to a lower-number bench than J, it follows that W is assigned to a lower-numbered bench than V and F as well:

$$W \text{——} \boxed{\begin{array}{l} V \\ F \ J \end{array}}$$

At this point, you can actually determine that answer choice (A) is correct because since W is assigned to a lower-numbered bench than J, only H remains to be assigned to the same bench as W, meaning that H must be assigned to a lower-numbered bench than F. However, if you do not see that inference immediately, move on to making hypotheticals.

Because the VFJ super-block is again forced into only two possible positions: benches 2 and 3 or benches 3 and 4, as in the previous two questions, you can quickly make the two applicable hypotheticals:

Possibility #1: VFJ assigned to benches 2 and 3

Non:	W	V	X/Y	Y/X
Maj:	H	F	J	G
	1	2	3	4

Possibility #2: VFJ assigned to benches 3 and 4

Non:	W/	/W	V	___
Maj:	H/G	G/H	F	J
	1	2	3	4

When the above hypotheticals are applied to the answer choices, it is apparent that answer choice (A) is correct. Answer choices (B), (C), and (E) could be true but do not have to be true. Answer choice (D) can never be true.

Question #7: Global, Could Be True, List. The correct answer choice is (D)

This is an unusual List question since it addresses only two of the four benches, and those benches are not sequential. An application of the VFJ super-block and the WG not-block eliminates only answer choice (C) (V is with J instead of F). That is a frustrating result, because in normal List questions the application of the rules knocks off several, if not all, of the incorrect answers. Since the rule application has only eliminated one answer choice, the key must be in the two benches that are not listed, benches 1 and 3. And this general way of thinking is a powerful tool in many other games as well: if the variables that you are working with do not seem to solve the problem, consider the other variables yet to be placed, or as in this situation, the other spaces that are unlisted and have yet to be considered.

Answer choice (A) can be eliminated because the assignment of the given variables leaves no room for the VFJ super-block. If you are uncertain of this, take a moment to make a hypothetical with G and X assigned to bench 2 and H and Y assigned to bench 4. It immediately becomes apparent that F and J will have to be assigned to benches 1 and 3, a violation of the rules.

Answer choices (B) and (E) can both be eliminated for the same reason: the assignment of the respective variables ultimately forces W and G together on one of the benches, a violation of the rules. For answer choice (B), W and G would be assigned together to bench 1, and for answer choice (E), W and G would be assigned together to bench 3.

Since answer choices (A), (B), (C), and (E) have been eliminated, answer choice (D) must be correct.

Overall, this is a tough question to face at the end of the game. Unless you focus on mentally placing the VFJ block and WG not-block into benches 1 and 3, none of the remaining answers appears incorrect. For many students the only solution is to try each answer choice and work out a hypothetical that proves or disproves the answer. Of course this is very time consuming. If you are having time difficulties with the games section, it might be useful to skip this question once you realize how long it is going to take. You could simply guess among answer choices (A), (B), (D), and (E).

Parts of this game—especially questions #4, #6, and #7—can take a considerable amount of work. But by focusing on the two active and powerful rules, you should be able to do this work at a fairly high rate of speed. Plus, the two rules are so potent that their application consistently yields the placement of other variables, and this tends to give most test takers a high degree of confidence with their answer choices. Even if it takes a little extra time to work with the hypotheticals, knowing that you have definitively reached the correct answer is a worthwhile reward.

A tour group plans to visit exactly five archaeological sites. Each site was discovered by exactly one of the following archaeologists—Ferrara, Gallagher, Oliphant—and each dates from the eighth, ninth, or tenth century (A.D.). The tour must satisfy the following conditions:

The site visited second dates from the ninth century.

Neither the site visited fourth nor the site visited fifth was discovered by Oliphant.

Exactly one of the sites was discovered by Gallagher, and it dates from the tenth century.

If a site dates from the eighth century, it was discovered by Oliphant.

The site visited third dates from a more recent century than does either the site visited first or that visited fourth.

13. Which one of the following could be an accurate list of the discoverers of the five sites, listed in the order in which the sites are visited?

(A) Oliphant, Oliphant, Gallagher, Oliphant, Ferrara

(B) Gallagher, Oliphant, Ferrara, Ferrara, Ferrara

(C) Oliphant, Gallagher, Oliphant, Ferrara, Ferrara

(D) Oliphant, Oliphant, Gallagher, Ferrara, Gallagher

(E) Ferrara, Oliphant, Gallagher, Ferrara, Ferrara

GO ON TO THE NEXT PAGE.

4

14. If exactly one of the five sites the tour group visits dates from the tenth century, then which one of the following CANNOT be a site that was discovered by Ferrara?

    (A)   the site visited first
    (B)   the site visited second
    (C)   the site visited third
    (D)   the site visited fourth
    (E)   the site visited fifth

15. Which one of the following could be a site that dates from the eighth century?

    (A)   the site visited first
    (B)   the site visited second
    (C)   the site visited third
    (D)   the site visited fourth
    (E)   the site visited fifth

16. Which one of the following is a complete and accurate list of the sites each of which CANNOT be the site discovered by Gallagher?

    (A)   third, fourth, fifth
    (B)   second, third, fourth
    (C)   first, fourth, fifth
    (D)   first, second, fifth
    (E)   first, second, fourth

17. The tour group could visit at most how many sites that were discovered by Ferrara?

    (A)   one
    (B)   two
    (C)   three
    (D)   four
    (E)   five

GO ON TO THE NEXT PAGE.

4

Analysis of Advanced Linear Game #2: October 2004 Questions 13-17

The setup of this Advanced Linear game is more challenging than the setup of the first game of this section, primarily because although this game appears to have only a few initial inferences, the relationship of the rules is such that most of the diagram can be filled in. With the proper diagram, the questions are relatively easy.

From the game scenario, we know that there are three variable sets: the five archaeological sites, the three archaeologists, and the three centuries. The five archaeological sites and the three centuries each have numerical order, but the archaeological sites are the better choice for the base since each site has a single archaeologist and a single date. This choice creates a linear setup with two stacks, one for the archaeologists and one for the centuries (remember to leave ample vertical space between the two stacks since each row will likely have its own Not Laws):

Centuries: 8 9 10 ^{3}
Archaeologists: F G O ^{3}
          *

Cent: ___ ___ ___ ___ ___

Arch: ___ ___ ___ ___ ___
       1   2   3   4   5

Because the rules have so many consequences, let's examine each rule individually.

Rule #1. This rule is the most straightforward rule of the game, and it can be represented by placing a "9" in second site space of the Century row:

Cent: ___ 9 ___ ___ ___

Arch: ___ ___ ___ ___ ___
       1   2   3   4   5

Rule #2. If neither the fourth nor fifth site was discovered by O, we can place O Not Laws on each space. And, because there are only three archaeologists, with O eliminated from discovering the fourth and fifth sites we can infer that either F or G discovered those sites. This fact can be represented by individual F/G dual-options on each site:

Cent: ___ 9 ___ ___ ___

Arch: ___ ___ ___ F/G F/G
       1   2   3   4   5
                    Ø̸   Ø̸

Rule #3. While the first two rules can be represented directly on the diagram, this rule must be diagrammed separately. The rule is a bit challenging to represent because it contains two separate pieces of information. The first piece of information is that G discovered exactly one site, and the second piece of information is that the site discovered by G dates from the 10th century. There are different ways to represent this rule, but we will use the following diagram:

$$G_{Once} \longrightarrow 10$$

From the contrapositive of this rule we can infer that any site that dates from the 8th or 9th century was not discovered by G, and must therefore have been discovered by F or O. Also, be careful not to make a Mistaken Reversal and assume that any site that dates from the 10th century was discovered by G; that is not necessarily the case.

Using the information above, we can infer that since the second site dates from the 9th century it was not discovered by G, and must therefore have been discovered by F or O:

Cent: ___ 9 ___ ___ ___

Arch: ___ F/O ___ F/G F/G
       1   2   3   4   5
            Ø̸   Ø̸   Ø̸

Rule #4. This is another important conditional rule, which can be diagrammed as follows:

$$8 \longrightarrow O$$

Operationally, this rule indicates that every time a site dates from the 8th century, it must have been discovered by O. The contrapositive of this rule reveals that if a site was not discovered by O, then it cannot date from the 8th century and must instead date from the 9th or 10th century. Thus, the fourth and fifth sites, which were not discovered by O, cannot date from the 8th century, and they must date from the 9th or 10th century. We can add this to our diagram with dual-options:

Cent: ___   9   ___   9/10   9/10
                             ~~8~~   ~~8~~

Arch: ___   F/O   ___   F/G   F/G
         1   2   3   4   5
            ~~8~~   ~~8~~   ~~8~~

Rule #5. Although we have already gained a fair amount of information from the first four rules, the final rule will allow us to fill in most of the remaining spaces in the diagram. First, however, a note about the language used in this rule. In most cases, "either…or" on the LSAT means "at least one of the two, possibly both." For example, if we see the rule "either A or B must attend," this means that at least one of the two must be there; they are not *both* required to attend, but they both *could* attend. In this particular rule, however, we should note that the word "either" is preceded by the conjunction "than" and is used at the end of a comparison. When this is the case, "either" actually means "both." For example, "He is taller than either of the other two boys on the team" means that he is the tallest of the three, and, "She likes History better than either Biology or Physics" means that History is her favorite of the three classes mentioned. So, the proper interpretation of this rule is that the third site is more recent than both the first and fourth sites.

Thus, when this rule states that the third site dates from a *more recent* century than either the first or fourth site, the third site cannot date from the 8th century, and the first and fourth sites cannot date from the 10th century. By itself, this information only seems to result in a series of dual-options for the dates of these sites. However, because we have already concluded that the fourth site must date from the 9th or 10th century (this inference was produced by combining the second and fourth rules), and this rule indicates that the fourth site cannot date from the 10th century, we can conclude that the fourth site dates from the 9th century. And, because the fourth site must date from the 9th century, we can use this rule to determine that the third site must date from the 10th century. Consequently, we can fill in the entire century row with either the exact site dates or with dual-options:

Cent: 8/9   9   10   9   9/10
       1   2   3   4   5
     ~~10~~   ~~8~~ ~~8~~
                       ~~10~~

Further, because the fourth site cannot date from the 10th century, from the third rule we can infer G cannot discover the fourth site, and so the fourth site must be discovered by F. We can also use the third rule to determine that the first site was not discovered by G, and must have been discovered by F or O. These inferences allow us to arrive at our final diagram:

Cent: 8/9   9   10   9   9/10
       1̶0̶   8̶   8̶
                        1̶0̶

Arch: F/O   F/O   ___   F   F/G
        1   2   3   4   5
        Ø̶   Ø̶   Ø̶   Ø̶
                            Ø̶

Note that not all of the dual-options are independent. For example, if the first site dates from the 8th century, then according to the fourth rule it must have been discovered by O. The third rule is also active, and during the game you must keep track of the placement of G. Regardless, you now have a powerful setup with which to attack the game.

Final Note: the language used by the test makers here only states that each site dates from a particular century, not that every century must be used (the same situation applies to the archaeologists). Thus, it is possible that some variables may not be used in the game. Each game is different, so always track the language used in a game carefully to ascertain the situation.

Question #13: Global, Could Be True, List. The correct answer choice is (E)

In this List question, if you use just the given rules, only rules #2 and #3 provide useful information. Thus, the easiest approach is to use the archaeologist row from the diagram to attack the answer choices.

Answer choice (A): According to the second rule, O cannot have discovered the fourth site, and thus this answer choice is incorrect.

Answer choice (B): From our discussion of the setup to this game, we know that G cannot discover the first site, and hence this answer choice is incorrect.

Answer choice (C): From the combination of the first and third rules of the game, we know that G cannot have discovered the second site, and so this answer choice is incorrect.

Answer choice (D): The second rule stipulates that G discovered exactly one of the sites. Because this answer choice shows G discovering two of the sites, it is incorrect.

With the first four answer choices eliminated, answer choice (E) is proven correct.

Question #14: Local, Cannot Be True. The correct answer choice is (C)

The question stem asserts that only one of the five sites dates from the 10th century, and because we have already established that the third site dates from the 10th century, we know that the third site is the only site from the 10th century. In addition, from the third rule we know that G must discover a site from the 10th century, and so we can conclude that G must discover the third site. In this Cannot Be True question, then, F cannot discover the third site and answer choice (C) is correct.

Note that although other deductions could be made (such as that the fifth site dates from the 9th century), and an entire diagram could be drawn out for this question, there is no point in doing so since our initial diagram already determined that the third site was from the 10th century, and that provides the starting point for a fast and clear path to the correct answer.

Answer choices (A), (B), (D), and (E) are each incorrect because F could discover any of the sites listed in these answer choices.

Question #15: Global, Could Be True. The correct answer choice is (A)

Although creating the setup to this game takes a fair amount of time, Global questions such as this one allow us to make up time. Our setup indicates that only one site—the first—could date from the 8th century, and thus answer choice (A) is correct.

Answer choices (B), (C), (D), and (E): Each of these sites must be from either the 9th or 10th century.

Question #16: Global, Cannot Be True, List. The correct answer choice is (E)

Again, our initial setup easily answers this question. The setup indicates that G cannot discover the first, second, and fourth sites. The only answer choice that contains these three sites is answer choice (E).

Answer choices (A), (B), (C), and (D): Because G could have discovered the third or fifth site, any answer choice that contains the third or fifth site is incorrect.

Question #17: Global, Must Be True, Maximum. The correct answer choice is (D)

From the diagram, we know that F discovered the fourth site, and the dual-options and Not Laws indicate that F could have discovered each of the other sites as well. Thus, it might appear that F could have discovered all five sites. However, this would be an incorrect conclusion because the third rule states that G must have discovered *exactly* one site. Thus, F cannot have discovered all five sites and answer choice (E) can be eliminated from contention.

Because F is a random in this game, four appears to be a very likely correct answer. Before simply choosing four as the correct answer, however, the rules regarding O should be examined to ensure that O does not have to discover one or more of the sites. A quick review of the rules and the diagram indicates that O does not have to discover any of the sites, and thus answer choice (D) is correct.

Answer choices (A), (B), and (C): Because the question stem asks for the *maximum* number of sites discovered by F, and each one of these answer choices is less than the maximum, these answers are incorrect.

Answer choice (E): Because G must have discovered exactly one site, F cannot discover all five sites and this answer choice is incorrect.

A locally known guitarist's demo CD contains exactly seven different songs—S, T, V, W, X, Y, and Z. Each song occupies exactly one of the CD's seven tracks. Some of the songs are rock classics; the others are new compositions. The following conditions must hold:

>S occupies the fourth track of the CD.
>Both W and Y precede S on the CD.
>T precedes W on the CD.
>A rock classic occupies the sixth track of the CD.
>Each rock classic is immediately preceded on the CD by a new composition.
>Z is a rock classic.

11. Which one of the following could be the order of the songs on the CD, from the first track through the seventh?

(A)   T, W, V, S, Y, X, Z
(B)   V, Y, T, S, W, Z, X
(C)   X, Y, W, S, T, Z, S
(D)   Y, T, W, S, X, Z, V
(E)   Z, T, X, W, V, Y, S

GO ON TO THE NEXT PAGE.

12. Which one of the following is a pair of songs that must occupy consecutive tracks on the CD?

(A) S and V
(B) S and W
(C) T and Z
(D) T and Y
(E) V and Z

13. Which one of the following songs must be a new composition?

(A) S
(B) T
(C) W
(D) X
(E) Y

14. If W precedes Y on the CD, then which one of the following must be true?

(A) S is a rock classic.
(B) V is a rock classic.
(C) Y is a rock classic.
(D) T is a new composition.
(E) W is a new composition.

15. If there are exactly two songs on the CD that both precede V and are preceded by Y, then which one of the following could be true?

(A) V occupies the seventh track of the CD.
(B) X occupies the fifth track of the CD.
(C) Y occupies the third track of the CD.
(D) T is a rock classic.
(E) W is a rock classic.

4

GO ON TO THE NEXT PAGE.

The diagram to this game is quite powerful since most of the spaces can be filled in.

From the game scenario, we know that there are three variable sets: the seven tracks, the seven songs, and the two types (new and rock classic). Because the seven tracks have a numerical order, they are the better choice for the base. This choice creates a linear setup with two stacks, one for the songs and one for the types (remember to leave ample vertical space between the two stacks since each row will likely have its own Not Laws):

4

Types: N R^2
Songs: S T V W X Y Z^7

Type: ___ ___ ___ ___ ___ ___ ___

Song: ___ ___ ___ ___ ___ ___ ___
       1   2   3   4   5   6   7

Because the rules have so many consequences, let's examine each rule:

Rule #1. This is the most straightforward rule of the game, and it can be represented by placing an "S" in fourth space of the Song row:

Type: ___ ___ ___ ___ ___ ___ ___

Song: ___ ___ ___ S   ___ ___ ___
       1   2   3   4   5   6   7

Rule #2. This rule states that both W and Y precede S on the CD, and this rule can be diagrammed as:

By itself, this rule means that W and Y cannot be tracks 5, 6, or 7 on the CD (because the first rule establishes that S is 4th)

Rule #3. This rule can be diagrammed as:

$$T \text{---} W$$

When combined with rule #2, we can create the following sequence:

This sequence indicates that T, W, and Y must all precede S on the CD. Of course, if T, W, and Y precede S, they occupy the first three spaces, and that leaves only spaces 5, 6, and 7 for V, X, and Z:

Thus, although all songs have not been specifically placed, we do know how they are divided on either side of S. Also, because T must precede W, we can ascertain that W cannot be first and T cannot be third.

Rule #4. This rule specifies that the sixth track is a rock classic. This information can be added directly to the diagram:

<u>Rule #5.</u> This rule can be diagrammed as:

$$R \longrightarrow \boxed{N \, R}$$

Note that this rule only applies to rock classics. A new song does not have to be followed by a rock classic.

The appearance of this rule creates several inferences. First, because a rock classic must be preceded by a new song, the first song on the CD must be a new song (a rock classic cannot be first because then it would not be preceded by a new song). Second, because the sixth song is a rock classic, we can automatically determine that the fifth song must be a new song. Third, because the sixth song is a rock classic, the seventh song must be a new song (if the seventh song was a rock classic, then the sixth song would have to be a new song). Adding this information creates the following setup:

Type: N ___ ___ ___ N R N

Song: (T —— W, Y) S (V, X, Z)
      1   2   3   4   5   6   7
     W̸   X̸

<u>Rule #6.</u> This rule states that Z is a rock classic. When considered with the fifth rule, this rule can be diagrammed as follows:

$$\boxed{\begin{array}{c} N \; R \\ \underline{} \; Z \end{array}}$$

However, we already know from the analysis in rule #3 that Z must be the fifth, sixth, or seventh song on the CD. And, since the analysis in rule #5 indicated that, of those three tracks, only the sixth track could be a rock classic, we can determine that Z must be the sixth track on the CD. Accordingly, V and X must occupy the fifth and seventh tracks, not necessarily in that order:

Type: N ___ ___ ___ N R N

Song: (T —— W, Y) S V/X Z X/V
      1   2   3   4   5   6   7
     W̸   X̸

Compiling all of the information above, we arrive at the final setup for this game:

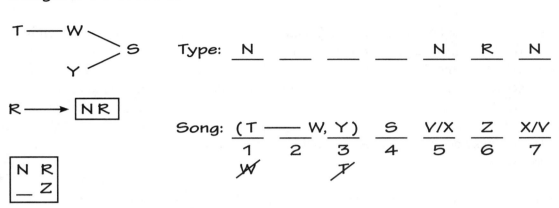

Types: N R²
Songs: S T V W X Y Z⁷

Type: N __ __ __ N R N

Song: (T —— W, Y) S V/X Z X/V
        1   2   3   4   5   6   7

Question #11: Global, Could Be True, List. The correct answer choice is (D)

To attack this List question in a foolproof manner, simply apply the first three rules. For an even faster approach, apply the rules and inferences together (for example, first apply the rule that states that S is fourth, then apply the inference that indicates that Z is sixth, etc).

Answer choice (A): This answer choice is incorrect because Y does not precede S, and Z is not sixth.

Answer choice (B): This answer choice can be eliminated because W does not precede S.

Answer choice (C): This answer choice is incorrect because V does not appear (and therefore S appears twice), and T does not precede W.

Answer choice (D): This is the correct answer choice.

Answer choice (E): This answer choice can be eliminated because S is not fourth and Z is not sixth.

Question #12: Global, Must Be True. The correct answer choice is (E)

Use the final diagram to quickly and easily solve this question. Examine each answer choice and determine whether the two songs *must* be consecutive, or whether they can be separated in a valid hypothetical.

Answer choice (A): This answer choice is incorrect because S and V can be the fourth and seventh tracks, respectively. While S and V can be consecutive in certain configurations of the game, they do not have to be consecutive, and thus S and V fail to meet the requirements of the question stem (other pairs of variables among the answer choices have the same relationship, such as the pairs in answer choices (B) and (D)).

Answer choice (B): This answer choice can be eliminated because S and W can be the second and fourth tracks, respectively.

Answer choice (C): This answer choice is incorrect because T is always first or second, and Z is always sixth.

Answer choice (D): This answer choice can be eliminated because T and Y can be the first and third tracks, respectively.

Answer choice (E): This is the correct answer choice. V must be fifth or seventh, and Z must be sixth, so V and Z are always consecutive, whether as VZ or ZV.

Question #13: Global, Must Be True. The correct answer choice is (D)

With Global questions in this game, simply refer to the main diagram. In this case, we know that the first, fifth and seventh songs must be new songs. With the first song, either T or Y must be first, but there is no way to determine which must be first. With the fifth and seventh songs, those two tracks are occupied by V and X, so both V and X must be new songs. A quick scan of the answer choices reveals that X is present, and thus answer choice (D) is correct.

Answer choices (A), (B), (C), and (E): These answer choices are incorrect because each of the listed songs could be rock classics.

Answer choice (D): This is the correct answer choice. X must be fifth or seventh, and both the fifth and seventh songs are new songs.

Question #14: Local, Must Be True. The correct answer choice is (D)

The question stem indicates that W precedes Y on the CD. That sets up the following chain relationship:

$$T \text{---} W \text{---} Y \text{---} S$$

Since S must be the fourth track on the CD, the diagram appears as follows:

Type: N   __   __   __   N   R   N

Song: T   W   Y   S   V/X   Z   X/V
       1   2   3   4   5   6   7

Answer choice (A): This answer is incorrect because S could be a new song or a rock classic.

Answer choice (B): This answer choice is incorrect because V is a new song.

Answer choice (C): This answer is incorrect because Y could be a new song or a rock classic.

Answer choice (D): This is the correct answer choice. T must be first, and the first track is a new song as discussed in the setup to the game.

Answer choice (E): This answer choice is incorrect because W could be a new song or a rock classic.

Question #15: Local, Could Be True. The correct answer choice is (E)

The condition in the question stem is worded in a clumsy fashion. Let's examine the statement piece by piece to derive what the test makers meant to say.

The question stem states that "there are exactly two songs on the CD that both precede V and are preceded by Y." The portion that states that "there are exactly two songs on the CD that both precede V," means that there are exactly two tracks in front of V, which would be diagrammed as follows:

The portion that states that "there are exactly two songs on the CD that...are preceded by Y," means that there are exactly two tracks behind Y, which would be diagrammed as follows:

Combing those two statements (they are combined by the "and" in the question stem) yields the following diagram:

Y	___	___	V

The challenge is now to place that split-block on the main diagram. Because V is restricted to fifth or seventh, V is a logical starting point. If V is seventh, then Y would have to be fourth, which is impossible since S must be fourth. Thus, V must be fifth, and therefore Y must be second under the conditions in this question:

Type:	N	___	___	___	N	R	N
Song:	T	Y	W	S	V	Z	X
	1	2	3	4	5	6	7

Of course, when Y is second, T must be first and W must be third (because T ——— W). Also, when V is fifth, X must be seventh, and thus the entire song order is established.

Answer choice (A): This answer choice is incorrect because V must be fifth.

Answer choice (B): This answer choice is incorrect because X must be seventh.

Answer choice (C): This answer choice is incorrect because Y must be second.

Answer choice (D): This answer choice is incorrect because T must be a new song.

Answer choice (E): This is the correct answer choice. W could be either a new song or a rock classic.

4

Doctor Yamata works only on Mondays, Tuesdays, Wednesdays, Fridays, and Saturdays. She performs four different activities—lecturing, operating, treating patients, and conducting research. Each working day she performs exactly one activity in the morning and exactly one activity in the afternoon. During each week her work schedule must satisfy the following restrictions:

> She performs operations on exactly three mornings.
> If she operates on Monday, she does not operate on Tuesday.
> She lectures in the afternoon on exactly two consecutive calendar days.
> She treats patients on exactly one morning and exactly three afternoons.
> She conducts research on exactly one morning.
> On Saturday she neither lectures nor performs operations.

8. Which one of the following must be a day on which Doctor Yamata lectures?

(A)   Monday
(B)   Tuesday
(C)   Wednesday
(D)   Friday
(E)   Saturday

GO ON TO THE NEXT PAGE.

9. On Wednesday Doctor Yamata could be scheduled to

    (A) conduct research in the morning and operate in the afternoon
    (B) lecture in the morning and treat patients in the afternoon
    (C) operate in the morning and lecture in the afternoon
    (D) operate in the morning and conduct research in the afternoon
    (E) treat patients in the morning and treat patients in the afternoon

10. Which one of the following statements must be true?

    (A) There is one day on which the doctor treats patients both in the morning and in the afternoon.
    (B) The doctor conducts research on one of the days on which she lectures.
    (C) The doctor conducts research on one of the days on which she treats patients.
    (D) The doctor lectures on one of the days on which she treats patients.
    (E) The doctor lectures on one of the days on which she operates.

11. If Doctor Yamata operates on Tuesday, then her schedule for treating patients could be

    (A) Monday morning, Monday afternoon, Friday morning, Friday afternoon
    (B) Monday morning, Friday afternoon, Saturday morning, Saturday afternoon
    (C) Monday afternoon, Wednesday morning, Wednesday afternoon, Saturday afternoon
    (D) Wednesday morning, Wednesday afternoon, Friday afternoon, Saturday afternoon
    (E) Wednesday afternoon, Friday afternoon, Saturday morning, Saturday afternoon

12. Which one of the following is a pair of days on both of which Doctor Yamata must treat patients?

    (A) Monday and Tuesday
    (B) Monday and Saturday
    (C) Tuesday and Friday
    (D) Tuesday and Saturday
    (E) Friday and Saturday

4

GO ON TO THE NEXT PAGE.

Analysis of Advanced Linear Game #4: February 1993 Questions 8-12

This Defined, Balanced game is one of our favorites of all time. The game contains four variable sets: days of the week, morning time slots, afternoon time slots, and the four different activities. In setting up the game most students make a crucial mistake: they fail to show Thursday on the diagram. At first, this would not seem to be a big issue since the game scenario does not identify Thursday as a day on which Doctor Yamata works. But, because of the rule that states that "she lectures on exactly *two consecutive calendar days*," the issue of consecutive days is critical, and a diagram without Thursday gives the false impression that Wednesday and Friday are consecutive. Once this mistake is made, the options for the LL block appear more numerous than they actually are, and making inferences becomes difficult. Fortunately, the first question of the game reveals that there is a major inference involving one of the lectures. Answering this question is critical to your success on the game (just as with question #20 of game #6 of the last chapter). Remember, if you are faced with a Global question that indicates that one (or more) of the variables *must* be placed in a certain position (as with questions #8 and #12 of this game), you must answer the question. If you do not, you will miss a critical piece of information that will likely affect your performance on all other questions. In the case of question #8, if you do not have the answer when you arrive at the question, it is a fairly clear signal that you have missed something big in the setup.

When representing Thursday, mark each slot with an "X" in order to indicate that no work is done:

Afternoon: ___ ___ ___ X ___ ___

Morning: ___ ___ ___ X ___ ___
     M Tu W Th F Sa

Note that you could also show Sunday, but it too would have an X in both slots and thus we have not shown it in the diagram. In a related note, we have placed the afternoon slots as the top row and the morning slots as the bottom row but the game works identically if you place the morning slots as the top row. The choice of which to use as the top row is a personal one, and neither approach is superior. Choose the representation that works best for you!

With this basic diagram in place, the rules can now be applied:

L O T R⁴

| L L | Afternoon: ___ ___ ___ X ___ ___ ← T T T LL

| O_M / O_Tu | Morning: ___ ___ ___ X ___ ___ ← O O O T R
        M Tu W Th F Sa
                 S̶a̶
                 ∅

Listing which activities occur in the morning and which take place in the afternoon takes a considerable amount of time, and these activities have been placed on the right side of the diagram. The rules indicate that in the afternoon there will be three Ts and two Ls, and in the morning there will be three Os, one R, and one T. This is extremely valuable information since it defines the composition of each row. Now that the rules have been added, we can begin to make inferences.

The first inference involves Saturday afternoon. According to the rules, Doctor Yamata can only lecture or treat patients in the afternoon. But on Saturday she cannot lecture, so it follows that she must treat patients, and a "T" can be placed on Saturday afternoon:

Afternoon:	___	___	___	X	___	T	T T T L L
Morning:	___	___	___	X	___	___	O O O T R
	M	Tu	W	Th	F	Sa	

Once T is established on Saturday afternoon, it becomes apparent that the LL block can only be placed on Monday-Tuesday or Tuesday-Wednesday:

Afternoon:	L/	L	/L	X	___	T	T T T L L
Morning:	___	___	___	X	___	___	O O O T R
	M	Tu	W	Th	F	Sa	

Note that Tuesday must always have a lecture and the other lecture will be placed on Monday or Wednesday, as shown by the split-option. Thus, in the afternoon, only two treatments remain to be assigned. One treatment will be placed on Friday afternoon (since it cannot be a lecture it must be a treatment), and the other treatment will fill in the Monday-Wednesday option:

Afternoon:	L/T	L	T/L	X	T	T	T T T L L
Morning:	___	___	___	X	___	___	O O O T R
	M	Tu	W	Th	F	Sa	

Consequently the afternoon spaces are filled, and it is revealed that only two solutions to the afternoon set exist:

	M	Tu	W	Th	F	Sa
Afternoon option #1:	L	L	T	X	T	T
Afternoon option #2:	T	L	L	X	T	T

When seen in this light, it becomes obvious that the answer to question #8 is (B).

With the afternoon completed, we can now turn to an analysis of the morning row. Since Doctor Yamata cannot operate on Saturdays, on Saturday morning she is left with the choice of either treating patients or conducting research. This is shown with a dual-option on Saturday morning:

	M	Tu	W	Th	F	Sa	
Afternoon:	L/T	L	T/L	X	T	T	T T T L L
Morning:				X		R/T	O O O T R

(Sa — X crossed out / ∅)

This leaves four morning spaces to be filled by three Os and the remainder of the T/R dual-option. At first glance it may seem that no inferences can be drawn regarding the placement of these variables. However, the rule involving operations on Monday and Tuesday has a powerful effect on the possible placement of the three Os: because only one operation can be performed on the Monday-Tuesday pair, this forces the other two operations to be performed on Wednesday and Friday:

	M	Tu	W	Th	F	Sa	
Afternoon:	L/T	L	T/L	X	T	T	T T T L L
Morning:			O	X	O	R/T	O O O T R

(Sa — X crossed out / ∅)

In summary, when an operation is performed on Monday, the operations rule prevents Doctor Yamata from operating on Tuesday; therefore, the remaining two operations must be performed on Wednesday and Friday. When an operation is performed on Tuesday, Doctor Yamata cannot operate on Monday, and the remaining two operations must again be performed on Wednesday and Friday. Hence, we can infer that operations are always performed on Wednesday and Friday.

The diagram is not yet complete. The final operation must be performed on Monday or Tuesday morning, next to the remainder of the T/R dual-option. This can be somewhat difficult to diagram, and we use a special parenthetical notation:

$$\underset{\text{M} \quad \text{Tu}}{(\,O\,,\ T/R\,)}$$

Morning:

The parentheses indicate that one of the two enclosed spaces must be an operation, and the other space must be a treatment or research; it also indicates that the order is unknown. In this way the notation efficiently captures the four possibilities for Monday and Tuesday morning: OT, OR, TO, and RO. With this final piece, the diagram for the game is complete:

LOTR⁴

	Afternoon:	T/L	L	L/T	X	T	T	←—TTT LL
LL								
O_M/O_Tu	Morning:	(O , T/R)	O	X	O	R/T	←—OOOT
		M	Tu	W	Th	F	Sa

Question #8: Global, Must Be True. The correct answer choice is (B)

As discussed in the setup to the game, the inference regarding the placement of the LL block in the afternoons proves answer choice (B) correct.

Question #9: Global, Could Be True. The correct answer choice is (C)

According to the final diagram, on Wednesday morning Doctor Yamata can only be scheduled to perform an operation. Thus, answer choices (A), (B), and (E) can be eliminated. On Wednesday afternoon she can only treat patients or lecture, and so answer choice (D) can be eliminated. Thus, answer choice (C) must be correct.

Question #10: Global, Must Be True. The correct answer choice is (E)

This is the most difficult question of the game. Each of the answers seems vague—in direct contrast to the final diagram, which is quite specific. The correct answer choice, (E), uses the Overlap Principle.

In answer choice (E) the Overlap Principle applies to the lectures and operations on Monday, Tuesday and Wednesday. Two operations and two lectures must be assigned within this three day period and consequently there must be an overlap between the two groups. Consider all the possible permutations of the lectures and operations for those days:

Afternoon:	L	L			Afternoon:		L	L
Morning:		O	O		Morning:		O	O
	M	Tu	W			M	Tu	W

Afternoon:	L	L			Afternoon:		L	L
Morning:	O		O		Morning:	O		O
	M	Tu	W			M	Tu	W

In each case at least one lecture is given on a day the doctor operates, and sometimes it occurs twice.

Question #11: Local, Could Be True. The correct answer choice is (E)

According to the rules, Doctor Yamata must treat patients once in the mornings and three times in the afternoons. Answer choices (A) and (B) are both incorrect because they feature two mornings and two afternoons. We have also determined that Doctor Yamata must operate on Wednesday morning, and therefore she cannot treat patients in that slot. Since answer choices (C) and (D) both include Wednesday morning, they are incorrect. Accordingly, answer choice (E) is correct. Note that there are a number of ways to attack this question. For example, it is known that Doctor Yamata must treat patients on both Friday and Saturday afternoon. That fact eliminates answer choices (A) and (C).

Question #12: Global, Must Be True. The correct answer choice is (E)

The first set of inferences proved that Doctor Yamata must treat patients on both Friday afternoon and Saturday afternoon. It follows that answer choice (E) is correct. In a sense, both question #8 and #12 are part of a pair: if you get one correct, you will likely get the other correct. That shows the powerful nature of the inferences, and the necessity of identifying those inferences.

It is also interesting to note that in this game, four of the five questions are Global. When a game has mostly Global questions, that often indicates that the game contains deep and challenging inferences. That is certainly the case here.

THE POWERSCORE LSAT LOGIC GAMES BIBLE

Chapter Five:
Grouping Games

Chapter Five: Grouping Games

POWERSCORE
BY BARBRI

The Principle of Grouping

Grouping games require you to analyze the variables in terms of which ones can and cannot be together. The emphasis on ordering—the basis of Linear games—is usually *not* present in Grouping games. Consider the following example:

> A four-member panel is selected from seven applicants—G, H, J, P, Q, R, and S. The panel is selected according to the following restrictions:
>> If J is selected, then R is selected.
>> If R is selected, then H is not selected.

In this game, the concept of order or linearity does not appear; instead, the focus is on placing the variables into a workable group. Let us first discuss some of the basics of identifying groups and diagramming them, and then discuss the elements that differentiate each type of Grouping game.

The Number of Groups

The first step when attacking a Grouping game is a simple one, and that is to identify the number of selection groups created in the game. Selection groups are created when variables are chosen for the activity at the center of the game (for instance, using the example above, when an applicant is chosen to be a member on the panel). There will be either a single selection group, or multiple selection groups (usually two, three, or four).

Games that feature a single group being selected—such as the game presented at the top of the page—will *always* have more variables available than spaces available. Thus, these games always feature some variables "in" the group and some variables "out" of the group (more on this point shortly).

Games with more than one selection group are not necessarily harder than single selection group games, they are just different. Here is an example of a multiple selection group game scenario:

> Exactly eight parents—M, O, P, R, S, T, U, and Z—serve on two four-person committees, the Athletic committee and the Scholastic committee. Each parent serves on exactly one of the two committees.

Grouping games involve a fundamentally different principle than Linear games.

Because in certain instances some variables are "in" and "others" are out, these games are sometimes called "In and Out" games.

In this game, two separate groups of four exist, and all eight parents are "in" the game. However, it is possible to construct multiple selection group games with an excess of variables. More on both single selection group games and multiple selection group games shortly.

Diagramming the Groups

In a diagram, the number of groups being created affects how the groups are shown. For example, if there is only one group to be selected, as in "There are nine candidates for a five-person group," the group should be displayed horizontally, as follows:

— — — — —
5-person group

Please note that the spaces are *not* numbered because being "first" or "second" in the group has no meaning.

Of course, this 5-person group only represents the variables that will be selected for the game (the "in" group). The variables that will *not* be selected can be shown underneath the group with Not Laws, or they can be shown as a second "out" group, in the following manner:

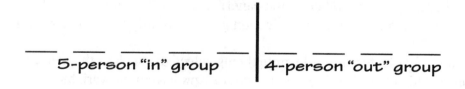

— — — — — | — — — —
5-person "in" group | 4-person "out" group

Note that the black vertical bar separating the two groups is there to emphasize the difference between the nature of the two groups.

Could a single selection group game be diagrammed vertically instead of horizontally? Yes, of course. If you prefer a vertical diagram, by all means diagram these games in that fashion. Operationally, there is no difference. For the purposes of this book, however, we will diagram single selection group games horizontally, and we will diagram multiple selection group games vertically.

When there are two or more "in" groups, the diagram will contain both horizontal and vertical elements. For example, if the game states, "There are two groups—group 1 and group 2—of four children each," the two groups will be displayed as follows:

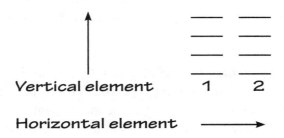

The numbering represents the group identifiers, and is not meant as a numerical ordering element.

If there is an "out" group in a game with multiple "in" groups, we would simply add that group to the side, again separated by a black bar. In this case, let's assume that the "out" group consists of just one variable:

The use of the vertical component will also affect the representation of certain rules, especially negative grouping rules. More on this point in the Diagramming the Rules section starting on page 288. First, however, let us examine the elements that distinguish the different types of Grouping games.

Unified Grouping Theory™ ▮▮▮▮▮▮

Along the Grouping Games spectrum, there are several different types of Grouping games. Because the unique features of each type require different approaches, identifying their characteristics will be helpful in properly attacking each game. Thus, in this section we will discuss the important features of each type, as well as some of the differences between them.

When analyzing these games, we use a system that is similar to the one for Linear games briefly discussed on page 102. This system can be used to classify every type of Grouping game that appears on the LSAT. However, because there are many elements to identify and classify, the Grouping games system might seem somewhat complex. **In an effort to keep all of the items clearly identified, our classification system features a number of different terms. Does that mean that you need to memorize every term? No. Although doing so would likely strengthen your grasp on each concept, the most important thing to draw from the forthcoming discussion is a basic understanding of the elements themselves, not their names.** You will not need to reference a Subdivided Game by name, but you should be able to recognize the concept when it appears in a game.

Group Definition

Correctly classifying each Grouping game will assist you in setting up the game.

As just stated, every Grouping game references a group or groups to be selected, and these groups are always used as the base for the game. We use the term "Definition" to describe whether the *exact* number of variables being selected is clearly stated, and the first step in attacking a Grouping game is to identify whether the game is Defined, Undefined, or Partially Defined.

One way to view this principle is to realize that to fully understand something, you must be able to identify and classify its component parts.

> **Defined**: In these games the exact number of variables to be selected is fixed in the scenario or the rules. For example, "Exactly six people will be selected to attend a dinner party," specifies that there are six spaces to be filled, and "there are three subcommittees, each having three members" indicates that there are nine spaces to be filled (three spaces in each of three subcommittees). Because the total number of variables to be selected is always constant, and thus the number of places remaining to be filled is always known, many students find these games preferable to Undefined or Partially Defined games.

Undefined: The number of variables to be selected in an Undefined game is not fixed, and is only limited by the total number of variables. For example, "A clothing store carries exactly ten clothing lines. The store is having a sale on some of these clothing lines" is more challenging because "a sale on *some* of these clothing lines" doesn't tell you how many spaces are to be filled. It could be one space, or five spaces, or nine spaces (or another total).

The lack of definition in Undefined games makes them more difficult because you never know with certainty how many variables are being selected until you process all of the rules and take into account any conditions in the question stem.

Undefined games are generally the most difficult type of Grouping game.

Partially Defined: In these games there is a minimum and/or maximum number of variables to be selected, but the *exact* number of variables selected in the game cannot be determined. For example, a game might state, "a committee of at least four members is formed from among nine candidates." Or, as stated in another game, "each teacher oversees at least two but no more than four students."

Partially Defined grouping games are generally preferable to Undefined games because although the exact numbers in each group are not specified, there is a more narrow range of possibilities.

When these games appear, you are typically forced to juggle several structural solutions, but this is not necessarily as difficult as it sounds. The key to handling these games is to make sure you account for the "loose" nature of the numbers when you create the setup. That accounting could involve something as simple as noting that there can be more members in a group, or it could be as complex as creating extra diagrams. The nature of the game will dictate the proper approach to use.

Regardless of the type of Grouping game you encounter, you *must* always track the selection group size (and if the game is not Defined, the various possibilities for the group size). There is no chance of success in a game if you do not focus on the group to be selected.

Multiple Group Characteristics

There is one additional subclassification that applies to Defined games only. This classification relates to the composition of a Defined grouping game with multiple groups (for example, the groups might be two groups of lawmakers or children assigned to three different canoes). The categories are:

Moving: In some games the test makers will indicate that an exact number of variables are to be selected (the Defined component) but there are still sub-groups within that set that are undefined, or "Moving." For example, consider this partial game scenario:

> In a debate tournament, seven students are assigned to three teams—teams 1, 2, and 3—with each student assigned to exactly one team. Each team has at least two members.

In this case there are seven positions—this is the Defined aspect—but the exact assignment of students to teams is uncertain, or "moving" inside the Defined group. Two of the teams will have two members and one of the teams will have three members (a 3-2-2 numerical distribution) but it cannot be ascertained exactly which team has the three members. Thus, this game would be classified as Defined-Moving.

Here is another example:

> Each of six people—C, D, F, G, H and K—plays exactly one of two sports—basketball or football.

Again, the game is defined as having six total slots, but the spread of the slots can vary from three in basketball and three in football (a 3-3 numerical distribution), to six in basketball and none in football (a 6-0 numerical distribution), etc. The number of people playing each sport "moves" depending on the constraints imposed by each question.

The Moving vs. Fixed classification does not apply to Undefined games because by definition they are always Moving.

Note also that the "moving" designation is often associated with a numerical distribution, which is a concept we will discuss in more detail in a later chapter.

Fixed: Games of this type are more straightforward. The selection groups are set (or "fixed") and there is no movement within the group or any existing sub-group. Here is an example:

> A track coach must select exactly two teams of four runners each to participate in a relay race. The coach must select the two teams from a group of ten runners—C, D, F, J, K, M, L, O, P, and S. No runner can be selected for more than one team.

In this game, the two teams of four selections each are Fixed and there is no uncertainty about the size of each group. The game would be classified as Defined-Fixed.

As a reminder, it's helpful but not essential to know all these specific names. The key is to understand that the ideas reflect what is happening with the groups and numbers in each Grouping game. As long as you recognize those aspects, you will do fine. The names do help us discuss each idea in compact form, however, and so you will see them frequently.

5

The Selection Pool

Another trackable grouping element involves the variables available to be placed (also known as the "selection pool"). Virtually all games have an exactly-defined number of available variables, but those variables do not always have the same characteristics.

Selection pool characteristics are a good example of an element within Unified Grouping Theory that looks ominous, but is fairly straightforward.

Do you need to know the exact names of each type of variable? No, you simply need to know that some selection pools are different from others, and then track those differences when they appear.

Uniform Variables: If the variables in the selection pool all have the same basic characteristics, the selection pool is known as Uniform. Here is an example of a Uniform selection group:

> There are exactly five instruments in storage: a clarinet, a flute, a saxophone, a trumpet, and a violin. Each instrument can be played by exactly one of three band members: Edwin, Jorge, or Marshall.

In this example, the five instruments are distributed to the three band members. Within this grouping and without respect to the rules, the five instruments are functionally identical and no one instrument has any special distinguishing marks aside from the name of each instrument.

Subdivided Variables: If the selection pool is divided into specific sub-groups and each sub-group has a unique characteristic, the selection pool is called Subdivided. Here is an example:

> The members of a six-person school honor board will be selected from among three parents—A, B, and C—three students—F, G, and H—and four teachers—R, S, T, and V.

In this game, you must track the differences between variables because, for example, B, a parent, has a differentiating characteristic from G, a student. As you might expect, the test makers then use these different groups in the rules and the questions. To track these groups, often the best approach is the use of subscripts, such as:

$$B_P \qquad G_S \qquad R_T$$

Subdivided selection pools make a game more difficult because there are more elements to track and remember.

Subdivided selection pools make a game more difficult because there are more elements to track.

The Relationship of the Selection Pool to the Group Size

Identifying the relationship of the number of available variables to the number of available spaces is critical. This relationship is known as Balance. Just as with Linear games, understanding the element of Balance will help you spot problems in a game and suggest certain areas that require your attention.

Balance applies to all Defined games (and some Partially Defined games). Undefined games, because of their lack of certainty, do not have a Balance element. Balance, as it relates to Grouping, can be analyzed as follows:

The issue of Balance involves the number of variables available to fill the given spaces.

Balanced: The number of variables to be selected is equal to the overall number of available spaces. For example, "eight students are divided into two four-person study groups."

Unbalanced: The number of variables to be selected is *not* equal to the overall number of available spaces. Unbalanced games are either Overloaded or Underfunded:

Overloaded: There are extra candidates for the available spaces. For example, "nine candidates for a five-person research panel." In Overloaded games, each valid solution contains some unused or unselected variables.

Underfunded: There are not enough candidates for the available spaces. This lack is almost always solved by reusing one or more of the candidates. For example, "seven television advertisements must be aired during two weeks, five advertisements per week." In this example, some of the advertisements would be repeated until all ten slots are filled.

As a technical aside, please note that the issue of Balance is one that relates only to the number of variables available for the number of selections to be made. If a game has 9 candidates for 5 spaces, it could be viewed as 9 variables being placed into 2 groups: a group of 5 "selected" or "in" variables and a group of 4 "unselected" or "out" variables. From this perspective the game could be called Balanced (9 into 9). But in the

Grouping games will be classified in different ways according to the game. For example, an Undefined game cannot have a Balance component, since there is not a set number of spaces to be filled. On the other hand, Defined games always have a Balance component.

classification above, we have chosen to use Balance as an indicator of the relative number of variables to selected positions. If there are fewer or greater variables than selected positions, the game will be classified as Unbalanced. Thus, a game of 9 candidates for 5 spaces will be classified as Defined (exactly 5 spaces are available), Unbalanced (there are 9 candidates for the 5 spaces), and Overloaded (there are a greater number of candidates than selection spaces).

This classification decision can also affect the way certain Grouping games are diagrammed. For example, when diagramming an Overloaded game, we will not diagram the "unselected" variable group. Note that this is a decision based on preference and efficiency. For most students it is easier to work with just the spaces for the selected variables and then mentally consider the remaining variables. However, it may be that for some students, it helps to show the "unselected" group. There is no right or wrong here—just what works best for you. In our diagrams, when a game has 9 candidates for 5 spaces, we will show just the 5 spaces for the selected candidates, and we will *not* show the 4 spaces for the unselected candidates.

Now that the entire Unified Grouping Theory has been delineated, you may wonder why there are so many classifications and subclassifications for the games. The Theory is complex because the LSAT is complex; to accurately characterize the variety of Grouping game elements used by the test makers requires a system that is comprehensive and detailed. Fortunately, in the discussion of each game at the end of a chapter, there will be an opportunity to revisit the classification system and observe its application and utility. In the meantime, review the discussion to make certain that you understand the kind of elements that must be tracked when you encounter a Grouping game, and then try the drill on the next page.

Some games have complex classifications, such as Defined-Moving, Unbalanced: Overloaded. Some have very simple classifications such as Undefined. The classification depends on the elements presented by the test makers.

Grouping Games—Unified Grouping Theory Classification Drill

Each of the following items provides a Grouping game scenario. In the space provided, supply the most accurate classification of the game using the categories defined by the Unified Grouping Theory (Defined/Partially Defined/Undefined, Fixed/Moving, Balanced/Unbalanced, Overloaded/Underfunded). Note: all selection pools in this drill are Uniform. *Answers on page 286*

1. Nine realtors are divided among exactly three offices—office 1, office 2, and office 3. Each office will be assigned exactly three realtors, and each realtor will be assigned to only one office.

    Classification: _____

    _____

2. Exactly eight of ten rowers are each assigned to two rowing teams of four persons each.

    Classification: _____

    _____

3. Ten candidates are being considered for some positions at a law firm. Only applicants who are interviewed will be hired.

    Classification: _____

    _____

4. A dinner reservation for at least five people will be made at a local restaurant. The diners will be selected from a group of eleven friends.

    Classification: _____

    _____

5. Exactly six of nine book editors are selected to edit exactly four books, with each selected editor editing exactly one book and each book being edited by at least one editor.

    Classification: _____

    _____

6. Exactly eight students are assigned to two buses, bus 1 and bus 2. Each student is assigned to exactly one bus.

    Classification: _____

    _____

7. The members of three committees will be selected from among seven applicants. Each committee must have exactly three members. Each applicant must be assigned to at least one committee, and applicants can be assigned to more than one committee.

    Classification: _____

    _____

Grouping Games—Unified Grouping Theory Classification Drill Answer Key

1. Nine realtors are divided among exactly three offices—office 1, office 2, and office 3. Each office will be assigned exactly three realtors, and each realtor will be assigned to only one office.

   ### Classification: Defined-Fixed, Balanced

   Because exactly nine realtors are assigned, and each office contains exactly three realtors, the game is Defined-Fixed. Since there are nine realtors for exactly nine positions, the game is Balanced.

2. Exactly eight of ten rowers are each assigned to two rowing teams of four persons each.

   ### Classification: Defined-Fixed, Unbalanced: Overloaded

   Because each rowing team contains exactly four rowers, the game is Defined-Fixed. Since there are ten rowers for exactly eight positions, the game is Unbalanced: Overloaded.

3. Ten candidates are being considered for some positions at a law firm. Only applicants who are interviewed will be hired.

   ### Classification: Undefined

   Since the number of candidates to be hired at the law firm is unknown, the game is Undefined. Since the game is Undefined there is no Moving/Fixed element, nor is there a Balance element.

4. A dinner reservation for at least five people will be made at a local restaurant. The diners will be selected from a group of eleven friends.

   ### Classification: Partially Defined

   Since the number of diners is at least five, but it is uncertain exactly how many diners there will be, the game is Partially Defined. Since the game is Partially Defined, there is no Moving/Fixed element, nor is there a Balance element.

5. Exactly six of nine book editors are selected to edit exactly four books, with each selected editor editing exactly one book and each book being edited by at least one editor.

Classification: Defined-Moving, Unbalanced: Overloaded

Since exactly six editors will be assigned to the four books, but it is unknown how many editors will edit each book (it is either a 3-1-1-1 numerical distribution or a 2-2-1-1 numerical distribution of editors-to-books), the game is Defined-Moving. Since there are nine editors for the six positions, the game is Unbalanced: Overloaded.

6. Exactly eight students are assigned to two buses, bus 1 and bus 2. Each student is assigned to exactly one bus.

Classification: Defined-Moving, Balanced

Since each of the eight students is assigned to a bus, but it is unknown exactly how many students are assigned to each bus, the game is Defined-Moving. Since all eight students are assigned to the two buses, the game is Balanced.

7. The members of three committees will be selected from among seven applicants. Each committee must have exactly three members. Each applicant must be assigned to at least one committee, and applicants can be assigned to more than one committee.

Classification: Defined-Fixed, Unbalanced: Underfunded

Because exactly nine spaces will be filled, and each committee contains exactly three members, the game is Defined-Fixed. Since there are only seven applicants for the nine positions, the game is Unbalanced: Underfunded. The seven-into-nine scenario creates a numerical distribution of 3-1-1-1-1-1-1 or 2-2-1-1-1-1-1. Remember, each of the seven applicants must be assigned to at least one committee. That means that seven of the nine committee spaces are automatically filled. The remaining two spaces go to either one applicant who is then assigned to all three committees—the 3-1-1-1-1-1-1 distribution—or to two applicants who are each assigned to two committees—the 2-2-1-1-1-1-1 distribution. Numerical Distributions will be revisited in a later chapter.

Diagramming the Rules ▬▬▬

Many grouping
rules can be
displayed using
the "arrows" from
the conditional
reasoning section
in Chapter Three.

Many of the rules in Grouping games can be diagrammed in the same way as those in Linear games. Nevertheless, since the emphasis in Grouping games is on the assemblage of the variables, more of the rules involve conditional reasoning. Fortunately, you can use the same symbology introduced in the conditional rules section on page 61 of Chapter Three. To revisit those principles, consider the following example:

If J is selected, then R is selected.

<u>Diagram:</u>

J ⟶ R

In a Grouping game, this rule indicates then when J is chosen for a group, R must also be chosen for that group. Via the contrapositive, if R is not chosen for a group, then J cannot be chosen for that group.

A second example:

If R is selected, then H is not selected.

<u>Diagram:</u>

R ⟶ H̸

This rule indicates that when R is chosen for a group, H cannot also be chosen for that group. Via the contrapositive, if H is chosen for a group, then R cannot be chosen for that group.

With the basics of conditional diagramming refreshed, let us examine some more advanced conditional reasoning concepts.

Advanced Conditional Reasoning ▮

Conditional reasoning in LSAT Logic Games often goes beyond simple two-variable statements like the ones on the previous page. In this section, we will examine conditional chains, advanced symbology, and statements containing multiple sufficient or necessary conditions.

Conditional Chains

In an effort to create complexity, the test makers often link two or more conditional statements. If an identical condition is sufficient in one rule and necessary in another, the two can be linked to create a chain, as follows:

Rule 1:   A ⟶ B

Rule 2:   B ⟶ C

Chain: A ⟶ B ⟶ C

Inference: A ⟶ C

The "B" condition is common to both Rule 1 and 2, and serves as the linking point. In this instance, because every A is a B, and every B is a C, we can make the inference that all As are Cs: A ⟶ C. Of course, the contrapositive, C̸ ⟶ A̸, would then follow from this inference.

Not all linkage is the same. The above example is one of the most frequently used constructions, but the test makers can also link two sufficient conditions, or two necessary conditions. These linkages yield different inferences (or none at all), and we will explore them in more detail in the drill and games at the end of the chapter.

The Double-Not Arrow™

While many of the statements you encounter on the LSAT involve conditions that are positive (that is, no negative occurs in the condition), not every conditional statement contains two positive conditions. With that in mind, let us further evaluate a statement from earlier in this section:

If R is selected, then H is not selected.

<u>Diagram:</u>

As stated, when R is selected, then H is not selected, and, via the contrapositive, when H is selected, then R is not selected. Thus, if R or H is selected, then the other cannot be selected, and we can infer that R and H can *never* be selected together. To represent this relationship accurately, we use the following symbol, known as the *double-not arrow*:

R ⟵—⟶ H

In this symbolization, the two terms at the ends of the sign cannot be selected together. In this sense the double-not arrow is a "super-symbol," one that captures all meanings of the negative relationship. Using this symbol can increase your efficiency and speed in Grouping games.

Note: if you diagram statements with the single arrow and slash as in the first diagram, you will not be making a mistake, but you will be using a less effective representation.

To review, the double-not arrow only prohibits one scenario—that where the two terms occur together. Using the R/H example above, several possible scenarios can occur:

1. R is selected, H is not selected.　　(R and H̸)

2. H is selected, R is not selected.　　(R̸ and H)

3. Neither R nor H is selected.　　(R̸ and H̸)

The double-not arrow is similar to a "not equal" sign; the two terms at the end of the sign cannot be selected at the same time.

Why use the double not-arrow? Because it allows for better linkage with other arrow statements, and it has the "super" element of rule display: it fully displays all aspects of the rule.

The only outcome that cannot occur is that both R and H are selected.

Let us now add in another rule to this example:

If J is selected, then R is selected.

Diagram:

If we link the very first arrow relationship with the double-not arrow relationship, the following diagram results:

Since J must be selected with R, and R cannot be selected with H, it can be inferred that J and H can never be selected together:

J ←——|——→ H

This particular rule combination and resulting inference appears frequently in Grouping games and you should familiarize yourself with it.

The Double Arrow

The double arrow indicates that the two terms must always occur together.

Many of the conditional statements in the Logic Games section feature arrows that point in only one direction. But, as you saw in the discussion of the double-not arrow, there are some statements that produce arrows that point in both directions. These arrows, also known as biconditionals, indicate that each term is both sufficient and necessary for the other. As such, they create a very limited set of possibilities. Consider the following example:

Arun will be selected if and only if Bai is selected.

As you can see, this sentence contains the conditional indicators "if" and "only if" connected by the term "and." This effectively creates two separate conditional statements:

1. "A   if   B"

and

2. "A   only if   B"

Be careful with statement 1: do not forget that "if" introduces a sufficient condition!

The "A if B" portion creates the following diagram:

$$B \longrightarrow A$$

The "A only if B" portion creates the following diagram:

$$A \longrightarrow B$$

Combined, the two statements create the double arrow:

$$A \longleftrightarrow B$$

Only two scenarios are possible under this double arrow:

Terms in a double arrow relationship always occur together

    1. A and B both selected   (A and B)

    2. Neither A nor B are selected   (A̶ and B̶)

Any scenario where one of the two is selected but the other is not selected is impossible.

The double arrow is typically introduced in any of the following three ways:

1. Use of the phrase "if and only if" (as in the example above), or a similar variant, such as "if but only if" or "if yet only if."

2. Use of the phrase "vice versa" (as in "If A is selected then B is selected, and vice versa.").

3. By repeating and reversing the terms (as in "If A is selected then B is selected, and if B is selected then A is selected.").

If you encounter a double-arrow statement in the rules, simply treat it as you would a regular block.

The Contrapositive in Grouping Games

Because arrows will still be used to display a number of the rules in Grouping games, you must be familiar with the inferences that result from conditional rules. As discussed previously, the contrapositive is an important tool for gaining insight into a game. For any complex or tricky conditional rule, always take the contrapositive:

S is not selected if R is not selected.

Diagram:

The rule can be interpreted as, "If R is not selected then S is not selected." Please note that the diagram above is correct since the "if" in the middle of the rule introduces the sufficient condition. But, in this form, the diagram is somewhat difficult to negotiate. Let us take the contrapositive of the diagram and observe how much easier it is to interpret (remember, reverse the terms and negate both):

$$S \longrightarrow R$$

The rule now reads, "If S is selected then R must be selected," and the elimination of the negatives makes the rule easier to grasp.

Consider another example:

If J is selected then exactly four variables total are selected.

Diagram:

$$J \longrightarrow 4$$

Contrapositive:

$$\cancel{4} \longrightarrow \cancel{J}$$

Always take the contrapositive of any unusual conditional rule.

5

The contrapositive can be interpreted as, "If exactly 4 variables are not selected then J is not selected." In other words, a group of any size besides 4 cannot contain J.

Remember, there is a contrapositive for any conditional statement, and if the initial statement is true, then the contrapositive is also true. The contrapositive is simply a different way of expressing the initial statement. To analogize, it is like examining a penny: each side looks different but intrinsically the value is the same.

Now, let us take a moment to examine conditional statements that are a bit more complex, and to also observe how the contrapositive operates in such statements.

Multiple Sufficient and Necessary Conditions

So far, all of the conditional statements we have examined have contained only one sufficient condition and one necessary condition. However, there are many statements on the LSAT that contain either multiple sufficient conditions or multiple necessary conditions. Consider the following statement:

If R is selected, then both S and T must be selected.

In this statement there are two necessary conditions that must be satisfied in order for R to be selected: 1. S must be selected and 2. T must be selected. Thus, the proper diagram for this statement is:

$$R \longrightarrow \begin{array}{c} S \\ \text{and} \\ T \end{array}$$

A "+" sign can be substituted for the "and" in the diagram to the left, as in:

$$R \longrightarrow \begin{array}{c} S \\ + \\ T \end{array}$$

The difficulty in handling multiple sufficient or necessary conditions is with the contrapositive. But, as we know from the prior page, the contrapositive is a critical tool in Logic Games, and so we must understand how to handle the contrapositive with these statements.

In the example above, if *either one* of the two necessary conditions is not met, then R cannot be selected. It is *not* required that both necessary conditions *fail* to be met in order to prevent the sufficient condition from occurring. Thus, the proper diagram of the contrapositive of the statement is:

Whenever you take a contrapositive of a statement with multiple terms in the sufficient or necessary condition, "and" turns into "or," and "or" turns into "and."

Note that in taking the contrapositive, the "and" in the necessary condition is changed to "or." The reverse would be true if the necessary conditions had originally been linked by the term "or." Consider the following statement:

If R is selected, then S or T must be selected.

The proper diagram for this statement is:

$$R \longrightarrow \begin{array}{c} S \\ \text{or} \\ T \end{array}$$

In this case, for R to be selected, only one of the two necessary conditions needs to be satisfied. This does not preclude the possibility of satisfying both conditions, but it is not necessary to do so. Now let's take the contrapositive of this statement:

$$\begin{array}{c} \cancel{S} \\ \text{and} \\ \cancel{T} \end{array} \longrightarrow \cancel{R}$$

This diagram indicates that if neither S nor T is selected (that is, both are not selected), then R cannot be selected. Again, note that as the contrapositive occurred, the "or" joining the original necessary conditions changed to "and."

Now, let us examine a statement with two sufficient conditions. Consider the following statement:

If C and D are selected, then E must be selected.

The proper diagram for this statement is:

Note that *both* C and D must be selected in order to meet the sufficient condition, and when both C and D are selected then E must be selected as well. Now, let us take the contrapositive:

$$\cancel{E} \longrightarrow \cancel{C} \text{ or } \cancel{D}$$

The contrapositive indicates that if E is not selected, then either C or D is not selected. Thus, if E is not selected, then C is not selected, or D is not selected, or both are not selected. Note that once again the "and" has become "or."

Of course, just as with the statement with two necessary conditions, if a statement with two sufficient conditions were to appear and those conditions were linked by "or," then the contrapositive of that statement would change the "or" to "and."

Note that any compound sufficient condition that uses "or" can be turned into two separate arrow diagrams (because "or" in the sufficient implies that each condition individually is sufficient to produce the necessary condition).

Similarly, any compound necessary condition that uses "and" can be turned into two separate arrow diagrams (because "and" in the necessary implies that each condition is individually produced by the sufficient condition).

Please see the book site for more information on these concepts.

Linear versus Grouping Symbolizations

Symbolizations in the two major game types generally indicate different concepts. Although they can be substituted at times, it is important to understand the underlying intent of each symbolization. Consider the aforementioned inference:

J and H cannot be selected together.

Linear Game Diagram: Grouping Game Diagram:

 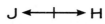

In Grouping games both arrows and blocks are used, depending on the specific components of the game.

The block diagram used in Linear games typically indicates adjacency. The arrow diagram used in Grouping games typically indicates association.

In Grouping games we use blocks in three specific situations:

1. When working with diagrams that have vertical components. Blocks represent the relationship between the variables in a visually powerful way, and are therefore the best diagramming choice. For example, "In a game involving two groups—group 1 and group 2—of four children each, A must be in the same group as B," the diagram is as follows:

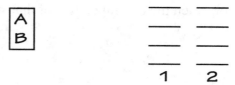

2. When diagramming rules that contain three or more variables in a positive or negative grouping relationship, such as "D, F, and G cannot all be selected together." This is diagrammed as:

3. To represent groups that must occupy a specified number of spaces, such as "In a game where four horses are selected, exactly two horses from the group H, J, K must be selected." The diagram is:

2 *of* H, J, K

$$\boxed{\text{H \quad J \quad K}} \ \underline{\quad} \ \underline{\quad}$$
4 Horses

Of course, this automatically implies that one of H, J, and K is not selected, and thus that could be shown in an "out" group diagram:

2 *of* H, J, K

$$\boxed{\text{H \quad J \quad K}} \ \underline{\quad} \ \underline{\quad} \quad \Big| \quad \text{H/J/K}$$
4 In   1 Out

While there may be more than one horse in the "out" group, that information would be contained elsewhere in the game scenario.

Grouping Games Rule Diagramming Drill

In the space provided, supply the best symbolic representation (if any) of each of the following rules. If applicable, show any corresponding implications on the diagram provided. *Answers on page 302*

Answers on page 302

1. Of the four applicants R, S, T, and V, exactly three are hired.

Group of 5 Hirees | Non-hiree

2. W, X, and Y cannot all be selected together.

Group of 5 Selections | Non-selections

3. D and E cannot be selected for the same team, and every player is assigned to exactly one of the teams.

1   2

Grouping Games Rule Diagramming Drill

4. If either M or N is assigned, then O must be assigned.

5. R and X cannot be selected together.

6. Either F or G, but not both, must be selected.

1. Of the four applicants R, S, T, and V, exactly three are hired.

    Because 3 of R, S, T, and V are selected, a block of space can be carved out for those four variables on the "in" diagram. Also, because one of the variables is always "out," that can be noted on that group with the R/S/T/V notation.

    3 of R, S, T, and V

2. W, X, and Y cannot all be selected together.

    No representation can be made on the "in" diagram because it is uncertain as to whether any of W, X, or Y will be "in." However, because all three cannot be "in," we can infer that at least one must be "out," leading to the triple option W/X/Y on one of the non-selection spaces (although, of course, more than one of W, X, and Y could be "out").

3. D and E cannot be selected for the same team, and every player is assigned to exactly one of the teams.

    Remember to show the D/E dual-option on the diagram. D and E are represented in a block to the side since there is a vertical element in the setup.

4. If either M or N is assigned, then O must be assigned.

    The diagram of the rule itself is straightforward:

    Diagram:

    Contrapositive:

    Because O, M, and N can all be simultaneously assigned or unassigned, no "in" or "out" representation can be made on the diagram:

    ___ ___ ___ ___ ___ | ___ ___ ___
    Group of 5 Selections | **Non-selections**

5. R and X cannot be selected together.

    R ◄———┼———► X

    The rule is shown with the double-not arrow since there is no vertical element in the setup. Although we cannot be certain that either of R or X is always selected, at least one can never be selected, and thus an R/X dual-option appears on the "out" group.

    ___ ___ ___ ___ ___ | **R/X** ___
    Group of 5 Selections | **Non-selections**

6. Either F or G, but not both, must be selected.

    F ◄———┼———► G

    Reserve one space in each group for the choice of F or G since exactly one must be selected, and exactly one cannot be selected.

    F/G ___ ___ ___ ___ | **F/G**
    Group of 5 Selections | **Non-selection**

Making Inferences ▌

Making inferences is one of the keys to attacking the Logic Games section. In Grouping games, there are always multiple areas to examine in order to make inferences, and this section explores those areas.

Linkage

When looking for inferences always start by linking the rules together.

As discussed in Chapter Three, the first step in making inferences is to find a variable that appears in at least two rules, combine the two rules, and then evaluate the implications.

In addition, combine any sub-groups that appear in the game, as in the following example:

> Nine people—five adults and four children—take a trip in two cars, car 1 and car 2. The adults are A, B, C, D, and E; the children are V, W, X, and Y. The following conditions apply:
>   Three adults ride in Car 1.
>   If A rides in car 2 then B also rides in car 2, and if B rides in car 2 then
>   A must also ride in car 2.

The second rule in the example to the right features a double-arrow, which means that A and B are always together. Thus, even though the second rule mentions just Car 2, A and B are either both in Car 2, or they are both in Car 1.

The cars are the two "main" groups, and the adults and children are each a "sub-group." At first the two rules above may not appear to be connected, but since A and B are both members of the adult sub-group, the two rules can be combined in the following way:

> Because the first rule states that three adults must ride in car 1, it follows that the remaining two adults must ride in car 2. According to the second rule, A and B must always ride together: they are either together in car 2 or they are together in car 1. Thus, if A or B ride in car 2, they both ride in car 2, and the other three adults—C, D, and E—would have to ride in car 1. Conversely, if A and B ride in car 1, then one of C, D, and E must ride in car 1, and the remaining two would have to ride in car 2.

Thus, by focusing on the presence of the Adult sub-group and the role it plays in the two rules, we have discovered a controlling inference in the game, and one that we could display within our diagram. This is one more example of why you should always begin your inference search by linking the rules together.

Negative Grouping Rules

Negative grouping rules state that two or more variables *cannot* be selected together. As previously discussed, negative grouping rules can be displayed either with not-blocks or with the double-not arrow. In Grouping games, negative rules are as equally important as positive rules (rules that state two or more variables must be selected together). This is in contrast to Linear games, where blocks are typically far more useful than not-blocks.

Negative and positive rules are of equal importance because both equally affect the selection of variables, albeit in opposite ways. Just as a set of positive grouping rules can yield powerful inferences, a collection of negative grouping rules can do the same. Thus, you should always carefully consider any collection of negative grouping rules to see if some powerful relationship is revealed. In addition, always consider the combinations of positive and negative grouping rules, especially when a common variable is present—those relationships often yield inferences (as discussed previously in this chapter).

In Grouping games, negative rules appear as frequently as positive rules.

5

Restrictions

Restrictions are areas in a game where the number of options are limited. Restrictions can occur with almost any game element, but most notably with variables and available spaces. Because points of restriction almost always yield useful inferences, they are one of the first areas to search for when seeking to make inferences. Here are several areas of restriction to check within games:

Examining restrictions can sometimes lead to dramatic, game-changing inferences.

Limited variable placement options

When a variable can only be placed into a limited number of places—such as with a split-option—the situation is inherently restricted and inferences often result when other rules are considered. For example, rules such as the following must be constantly kept in mind:

> "Janara must be assigned to either Group 1 or Group 2."

> "C is performed either second or fifth."

These rules will often come into play as other variables are placed, and spaces are thereby occupied.

Restrictions can be so powerful that they sometimes lead to identifying the Possibilities, a technique that will be discussed in a later chapter.

Restrictions on a space or spaces

When a single space or set of spaces has a limited number of variables available for placement, the situation is restricted. Here are several rules featuring this concept:

> "Either the Q or R must be third."

> "There must be exactly one student on the committee."

> "Exactly two teachers from the group of F, G, and H must teach."

Space restrictions can also result from a combination of rules. For example, a large number of restrictions for a single space can leave only one or two variables available to fill that space.

Structural Limitations

In certain games there are structural limitations that automatically spawn inferences. Here are two situations in which this occurs:

1. Small Group Size

   In a game with multiple groups, when one of the groups is relatively small there is the potential for inferences. For example, a game with a group of two members and a group of five members would likely have limitations created by the fact that the group with two spaces would tend to fill up very quickly.

   Also, keep in mind that group size can be affected by the rules. For example, a game with three groups of three members each would at first seem like infertile ground for a structural analysis based on group size. However, if one of the rules permanently placed a variable in one of the groups, then that group would only have two remaining spaces, and you would be well advised to always analyze those two spaces as you attacked the questions.

2. Two-Value Systems

   A two-value system occurs in Defined, Balanced games that feature two groups (that is, there are two groups and all of the variables are assigned to one of the two groups). When a two-value system is present, there are often rules that create powerful inferences. Consider the following example:

Exactly eight products—H, K, L, M, P, Q, R, and S—will be
divided into exactly two 4-product testing groups—group 1
and group 2. Each product is assigned to exactly one of the two
groups according to the following condition:
    If H is in group 1, then L must be in group 1.

This Defined-Fixed, Balanced game would be diagrammed as
follows:

H K L M P Q R S[8]

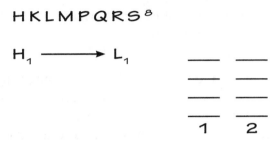

Because all eight variables must be assigned to exactly one of the
two groups, the game uses a "two-value system," which means that
if a variable is not assigned to one group, it must automatically be
assigned to the other group. Because of this feature, an unusual
contrapositive arises from the rule:

Rule: $H_1 \longrightarrow L_1$

Contrapositive: $\cancel{L}_1 \longrightarrow \cancel{H}_1$

Applying the two-value system, we can infer that if L is not
assigned to group 1 then L must be assigned to group 2, and if H
is not assigned to group 1 then H must be assigned to group 2.
Consequently, the contrapositive is properly diagrammed as:

$$L_2 \longrightarrow H_2$$

The proper representation of the rule allows for much greater
insight into the game and is thus significantly more valuable.
Always take the contrapositive in a two-value system game!

In short, although structural limitations do not occur in every game, you
should always check to see if they exist, and if so, consider the implications
as they may have a dramatic effect on your ability to complete the game
quickly.

Hurdle the Uncertainty™

Hurdle the
Uncertainty
appears at some
point in virtually
every Grouping
game.

This powerful technique can be used in many different games, and it attacks a concept frequently used by the test makers. In games, during the placement of variables, situations occur where even though you cannot determine the exact variables being selected, you can "leap" that uncertainty to determine that other variables must be selected. Here is the simplest example:

Three variables—A, B, and C—are available to fill two spaces.
Rule: A and B cannot be selected together.

Because A and B cannot be selected together, it follows that they can only "fill" one of the two spaces. And, although we cannot be certain whether A or B is selected, we can "hurdle" that uncertainty and determine that C must fill the remaining space. Note how the choice of A or B is shown as a dual-option, as in Linear games:

$$\underline{A/B} \quad \underline{C}$$

This situation can also occur with more than three variables:

Four variables—A, B, C, and D—are available to fill three spaces.
Rule: A, B, and C cannot be selected together.

Hurdling the
Uncertainty
often occurs in
"end-of-question"
scenarios where
some of the
variables have
been placed and
only a few remain
unplaced.

In this scenario, A, B, and C can "fill" only two of the spaces, and thus we can determine that D must fill the remaining space. So, even though we are uncertain about which two variables—A, B, or C—are selected, we can still use the knowledge that they can occupy only two of the three spaces in order to conclude that D must be selected, resulting in the following diagram:

$$\boxed{\underline{A/B/C}} \quad \underline{D}$$

Here is a more complex situation that uses the same idea:

Five variables—A, B, C, D, and E—are divided into two groups:
a group of three and a group of two.
Rules: A and B cannot be in the same group.
        C and D must be in the same group.

Because A and B cannot be in the same group, we know that one of A or B must be in the group of three and the remainder must be in the group of two. But, we cannot be certain exactly which group contains A or B. The best way to handle this uncertainty is to reserve a space in each group for the choice of A or B. This should be shown as an A/B dual-option:

$$
\frac{\underline{\qquad}}{\substack{\underline{A/B} \quad \underline{B/A} \\ 3 \qquad 2}}
$$

This leaves only one remaining space in the group of two, and it follows that the CD block must then be placed into the group of three. Since this fills all the available spaces in the group of three, E must then fill the remaining space in the group of two:

$$
\frac{D}{\underline{\dfrac{C}{\underline{A/B}}} \quad \underline{\dfrac{E}{B/A}}} \\
\quad 3 \qquad 2
$$

Again, although it cannot be determined exactly in which group A or B is placed, the fact that a space must be reserved in each group affects the other variables; and in spite of the A/B uncertainty we can conclude that C and D must be in the group of three and E must be in the group of two.

Here is another variation on the same theme:

Five variables—A, B, C, D, and E—are available to fill three spaces.
Rules: A and B cannot be selected together.
C and D cannot be selected together.

Since A and B can only fill one space, and C and D can only fill one space, it follows that E must fill the remaining space:

$$
\underline{A/B} \quad \underline{C/D} \quad \underline{E}
$$

At this point you may have noticed that every example is built around a fairly tight numerical scenario: in each case there are exactly the right amount of variables to fill the spaces, or there are only one or two extra variables available. From this perspective, Hurdle the Uncertainty situations often arise when there are a limited number of variables available to fill the given positions.

Recycling Inferences

Recycling inferences is especially useful when one or more variables appears in several different rules.

Once you have made an inference in a game, do not forget to consider the implications of that inference on rules that you have already processed. New inferences sometimes appear as a result of combining a previously discovered inference with the original rules. For example, consider the following three rules:

> Rules: If F is selected, then G is selected.
> G and H cannot be selected together.
> If F is not selected, then I is not selected.

Most students successfully combine the first two rules in the following fashion:

Based on this relationship, they correctly infer that F and H cannot be selected together:

The reasoning behind this inference is that if F requires G, and G and H cannot be selected together, then F cannot be selected with H.

Fewer students recycle the F ←—→ H inference and combine it with the third rule. This oversight occurs because the third rule is presented with negatives, and some students make the mistake of believing that the first and third rules are unrelated, and that consequently there is no further reason to assess the relationship between the first and third rules, or the relationship between the third rule and any inference related to the first rule.

In order to better understand this phenomenon, let us examine the third rule more closely. The third rule is diagrammed as:

The contrapositive of this rule eliminates the negatives:

$$I \longrightarrow F$$

With the negatives removed, the relationship between the first rule and the previously-made inference should be clearer.

$$I \longrightarrow F \longleftrightarrow\!\!\!| \longrightarrow H$$

The relationship yields a powerful new inference:

$$I \longleftarrow\!\!\!| \longrightarrow H$$

Of course, we could have used a different recycling path to arrive at the same inference. By linking the first and third rules, we can deduce that:

$$I \longrightarrow F \longrightarrow G$$

This relationship yields the new inference that:

$$I \longrightarrow G$$

Recycling this inference with the second rule yields:

$$I \longrightarrow G \longleftarrow\!\!\!| \longrightarrow H$$

This relationship allows us to arrive at the same inference we previously deduced:

$$I \longleftarrow\!\!\!| \longrightarrow H$$

Even after you have made an inference, do not forget that the inference might be reusable, and actively search *all* of the rules to see if you can make a further connection.

Avoiding False Inferences

Correctly interpreting the rules is crucial to success in the Games section. As you know, some rules and situations more frequently lead to misinterpretation. Here are several mistakes that students often make:

Conditional Rule Reversal

Because conditional rules play such a large role in Grouping games, you must guard against making a Mistaken Reversal.

As previously discussed, a conditional rule is triggered when the sufficient condition occurs. For example, consider the following rule:

> When P is selected, then Q is selected.

This rule would be diagrammed as:

$$P \longrightarrow Q$$

When P is selected, then Q *must* also be selected. However, many test takers make the mistake of reversing the relationship, and when faced with Q being selected, they assume that P must also be selected. This error is known as a Mistaken Reversal.

Mistaken Reversals are one of the most frequent errors made by students.

Negative Grouping Rule Misinterpretation

Negative grouping rules can be tricky to work with in practice, and students often make one of the following two errors when working with the double-not arrows that these statements produce.

1. Mistaking the Possibilities

    Consider the following relationship:

    $$A \longleftarrow\!\!\!|\!\!\!\longrightarrow B$$

Some students make the error of believing that the statement implies that one and only one of A and B must be selected. While it is the case that A and B cannot be selected together, some students also mistakenly believe that it is impossible for A and B to both be absent. This is incorrect because the statement merely indicates that when one of A or B is present, then the other cannot be present. Thus, it is possible for both to be absent. Remember, under the double-not arrow, the following three results can occur:

- A is selected, and B is not selected.
- B is selected, and A is not selected.
- Neither A nor B is selected.

The only result that cannot occur is both A and B being selected.

2. Mistaking the Connections

Linking related statements is a powerful method for producing inferences. With the double-not arrow, we have already reviewed the following inference-producing relationship:

$$F \longrightarrow G \longleftarrow\!\!\!|\!\!\!\longrightarrow H$$

Based on this relationship, the correct inference is that F and H cannot be selected together:

$$F \longleftarrow\!\!\!|\!\!\!\longrightarrow H$$

The nature of the relationships given above is critical, and changing just a small portion can lead to a different result. Consider the following two rules:

M and N cannot be selected together.
When N is selected, then O is selected.

These two rules can be combined to produce the following diagram:

The relationship
to the right yields
the inference,
"Some Os are
not Ms," but
that inference is
largely useless
in Logic Games.
That inference is
tested in Logical
Reasoning,
however, and so
we cover that
concept in far
more detail in the
Logical Reasoning
Bible.

Compare this relationship with the one above. Both contain a double-not arrow and a single arrow, but the relationships are different in that the single arrow in the bottom diagram "leads away" from the double-not arrow relationship. This seemingly insignificant difference has a large effect. While a powerful Games inference was possible in the first relationship, *no usable inference can be drawn in the second relationship*. Here is the reasoning behind this fact:

Although M and N cannot be selected together, it is possible for M and O to be selected together. If O is selected, N does not have to be selected, and thus, if M and O are selected together, there is no violation.

You must be very alert for the relationship discussed in this item because when the test makers present it in a game, they expect that a large number of students will misinterpret the relationship and draw a mistaken deduction.

Negative Sufficient Condition Confusion

Conditional statements with a negative sufficient condition often cause a large number of mistakes. Consider the following rule:

When A is not selected, then B is selected.

This rule would be diagrammed as:

There have been a
number of games
in recent years
that featured
rules like the one
to the right.

Although this rule appears the same as any other single arrow relationship, the negative on the sufficient condition has a dramatic effect. In essence, the sufficient condition in this statement is one where something does not occur; in this case, A is not selected. The fact that an act of omission then indicates that something must occur is confusing for most people. Let us examine the contrapositive:

The two diagrams, when combined, indicate that when one of the variables is *not* selected, then the other must be selected. Thus, one of the two must always be in the selection group. Many students understand this point, but then they make the mistake of assuming that this rule relationship precludes the possibility of both A and B being selected together. The rule, as stated, above does not prohibit both A and B from appearing in the selection group. Here is why:

All that is indicated from the rule and its contrapositive is that A and B will never both be unselected, because as soon as one is not selected then the other must be selected. They could, however, both be selected at the same time because the rules never address what happens when either A or B is selected, only what happens when A or B is not selected. Thus, when A is selected, B could be selected or B might not be selected. When B is selected, A could be selected or A might not be selected.

Thus, there are three possible outcomes under the rule given above:

- A is not selected and B is selected.
- B is not selected and A is selected.
- Both A and B are selected.

Ultimately, this rule means that A and B cannot both be absent.

When you encounter a rule such as the one under discussion, remember that it is possible for the two variables to occur together.

One final note on diagramming this relationship. Because the one outcome that is prohibited by this rule involves both variables being unselected, we could represent this relationship with a double-not arrow, as follows:

However, in the diagrams in this book we usually will not represent this relationship with the double-not arrow since so many people find it too difficult to work with. Regardless, the diagram simply indicates that A and B cannot be left unselected.

Overall, the rule discussed in this section is a tricky one because the negative is on the sufficient condition, and that has a powerful effect on how the rule operates. Fortunately, this type of statement appears less frequently on the test than statements where the negative is on the necessary condition.

Warning! Always pay close attention to rules that feature a negative sufficient condition. These rules can be quite confusing, and they are among the most dangerous rules on the LSAT.

As discussed previously, when you encounter statements with multiple sufficient or multiple necessary conditions, you must be careful when taking the contrapositive.

Whenever you take a contrapositive of a statement with multiple terms in the sufficient or necessary condition, remember that "and" turns into "or," and "or" turns into "and." This is true regardless of whether the term is in the sufficient or necessary condition.

Two-value System Errors

Two-value systems can allow for powerful inferences, but there is one false inference that you must avoid. Let us take a moment to revisit the game scenario we used when we first discussed this concept:

> Exactly eight products—H, K, L, M, P, Q, R, and S—will be divided into exactly two 4-product testing groups—group 1 and group 2. Each product is assigned to exactly one of the two groups according to the following condition:

Now, let us discard the rule used previously and instead add a new rule:

> If K is in group 1, then M must be in group 2.

This Defined-Fixed, Balanced game would be diagrammed as follows:

H K L M P Q R S^8

$K_1 \longrightarrow M_2$

$$\begin{array}{cc} \underline{} & \underline{} \\ \underline{} & \underline{} \\ \underline{} & \underline{} \\ \underline{} & \underline{} \\ 1 & 2 \end{array}$$

Most students, upon encountering this rule, take the contrapositive:

Of course, because this is a two-value system, when M is not in group 2 then M must be in group 1, and when K is not in group 1 then K must be in group 2. This insight allows the rule to be represented in more efficient fashion:

$$M_1 \longrightarrow K_2$$

So far, every step we have taken is correct. However, at this point some students, after observing that K and M *seem* to be in different groups, assume that K and M can never be in the same group together. This is not the case. The rule and its contrapositive both reference what occurs when one of the variables is assigned to group 1. When one of the variables is assigned to group 1, then the other must be assigned to group 2. However, both variables can be assigned to group 2 because the rule does not address what occurs when either K or M is assigned to group 2. If K is assigned to group 2, then M could be assigned to group 1 or group 2. If M is assigned to group 2, then K could be assigned to group 1 or group 2.

Here is a similar error that also occurs in two-value systems. Using the same setup as before, let us discard the previous rule and consider an entirely new, unrelated rule:

If P is in group 2, then Q must be in group 2.

This rule is properly diagrammed as:

$$P_2 \longrightarrow Q_2$$

The contrapositive, after accounting for the effect of the two-value system, is diagrammed as:

$$Q_1 \longrightarrow P_1$$

Again, each step taken thus far is correct. However, some students, after observing that P and Q *seem* to be in the same group, assume that P and Q are a block that must be assigned to the same group together. This is not the case.

The rule references what occurs when P is assigned to group 2, and the contrapositive references what occurs when Q is assigned to group 1. The statements do not address what occurs when Q is assigned to group 2 or when P is assigned to group 1. When P is assigned to group 1, Q could be assigned to group 1 or group 2 (no sufficient condition addresses P in group 1, so anything could occur). When Q is assigned to group 2, P could be assigned to group 1 or group 2 (again, no sufficient condition addresses Q in group 2, so anything could occur). Thus, P and Q are not a block, and it can occur that P is assigned to group 1 while Q is assigned to group 2 (note that P being assigned to group 2 while Q is assigned to group 1 cannot occur because that would violate the rule).

Remember, when you encounter two-value systems and conditional rules, focus on the sufficient condition in each rule, the meaning of the conditional relationship created by the rule, and the contrapositive of the rule. Avoid making assumptions based on surface appearances or a cursory glance at the rule.

Note

Grouping is a challenging concept, and many students find these games to be among the most difficult on the LSAT. If you have the opportunity, go back and review the discussions of rule representation, inference making, and avoiding false inferences. Then, try your hand at the drill on the next page, and eventually on the five games that follow the drill.

As always, please read the explanations to each drill and game carefully, as they will give you a true sense of how to best attack Grouping games.

Grouping Setup Practice Drill

Each of the following items presents a scenario and corresponding rules similar to those found in actual Logic Games sections. Using the space provided, diagram the setup and include a representation of all rules and inferences. Each problem contains a corresponding question or questions. Use your knowledge of the rules and the setup to answer the question(s). After you complete *each* item, check your work against the diagram in the answer key, and carefully read the comments concerning each diagram. *Answers on page 325*

1. A hiring committee must select three people from a group of five applicants—A, B, C, D, and E—in accordance with the following conditions:

    If C is not selected, then B is not selected.
    D and E cannot both be selected.
    In order for A to be selected, B must be selected.

Question 1.1. Which one of the following must be true?

(A)   A is selected for the committee.
(B)   B is selected for the committee.
(C)   C is not selected for the committee.
(D)   D is not selected for the committee.
(E)   E is not selected for the committee.

5

Grouping Setup Practice Drill

2. A business school offers at least one of the following seven courses during the winter term: accounting, economics, finance, law, marketing, operations, and sales. The following restrictions apply:

> If accounting is offered, then finance is also offered but economics is not.
>
> If law is offered, then economics is also offered but marketing is not.
>
> If operations or sales is offered, then accounting is also offered.

Question 2.1. If law is offered, then each of the following must be false EXCEPT:

    (A)   Accounting is offered.
    (B)   Finance is offered.
    (C)   Marketing is offered.
    (D)   Operations is offered.
    (E)   Sales is offered.

Grouping Setup Practice Drill

3. Seven senators—P, Q, R, S, T, V, and X—serve on two subcommittees. Each subcommittee has at least three members. The following is known about the two subcommittees:

> Every senator serves on at least one subcommittee, and no senator serves on both subcommittees.
> If P serves on a subcommittee, then Q does not serve on that subcommittee.
> R and S do not serve on the same subcommittee.
> T serves on a subcommittee only if V serves on the same subcommittee.

<u>Question 3.1</u>. Which one of the following must be true?

(A) P must serve on the subcommittee that has three members.

(B) Q must serve on the subcommittee that has three members.

(C) R must serve on the subcommittee that has four members.

(D) S must serve on the subcommittee that has four members.

(E) T must serve on the subcommittee that has four members.

<u>Question 3.2</u>. Which one of the following CANNOT be true?

(A) P and R serve on the same subcommittee.
(B) Q and S serve on the same subcommittee.
(C) T and R serve on the same subcommittee.
(D) V and X serve on the same subcommittee.
(E) X and Q serve on the same subcommittee.

5

Grouping Setup Practice Drill

4. A set of five products—D, E, F, G, and H—is
    assigned to two product testers—tester 1 and tester 2.
    Each product must be tested at least once, and each
    tester conducts three tests. Once a tester has tested a
    product she cannot test that product again. The testing
    meets the following conditions:

    If D is assigned to tester 1, then E is assigned to
      tester 2.
    F and G cannot be assigned to the same tester.
    D is tested twice.

Question 4.1. Each of the following could be true
EXCEPT:

(A)   D and E are each tested by the same tester.
(B)   D and F are each tested by the same tester.
(C)   E and G are each tested by the same tester.
(D)   E and H are each tested by the same tester.
(E)   G and H are each tested by the same tester.

5

Grouping Setup Practice Drill

5. The members of a six-person panel will be selected from among four parents—J, K, L, and M—and four students—W, X, Y, and Z. The selection of panel members will meet the following conditions:

The panel will include exactly three parents and exactly three students.

W and X cannot both be selected.

J cannot be selected unless W is selected.

K cannot be selected unless X is selected.

Question 5.1. Which one of the following could be a complete and accurate list of the people NOT selected for the panel?

(A) J, Y
(B) K, X
(C) L, Z
(D) M, Y
(E) W, X

Grouping Setup Practice Drill

6. Chris is choosing flowers for his garden from among the following choices: B, C, D, F, G, H, L, and M. The flowers are chosen in a manner consistent with the following conditions:

    If he chooses B, he does not choose D.

    If he chooses B, then he chooses G.

    If he chooses C, then he chooses D.

    If he chooses G, then he chooses B.

    If he does not choose H, then he chooses L.

    If he chooses M, he does not choose L.

Question 6.1. If Chris chooses G but not H, then it could be true that he also chooses

    (A)   B and C

    (B)   B and F

    (C)   B and M

    (D)   C and L

    (E)   C and M

1. A hiring committee must select three people from
    a group of five applicants—A, B, C, D, and E—in
    accordance with the following conditions:
    If C is not selected, then B is not selected.
    D and E cannot both be selected.
    In order for A to be selected, B must be selected.

The scenario states that there are five applicants for three positions, and thus the grouping
classification of this drill is Defined-Fixed, Unbalanced: Overloaded.

A B C D E [5]

___ ___ ___ | ___ ___
3 Selections   Out

The first rule states that if C is not selected, then B is not selected. This conditional rule should be
diagrammed as follows:

C̸ ———→ B̸

When you see a conditional rule or inference where both the sufficient condition and the necessary
condition are negative, always take the contrapositive, which, in this case is:

B ———→ C

The second rule indicates that both D and E cannot be selected, and this rule can be represented as:

D ←—|—→ E

And, at least one of D/E is is always in the "out" group (and possibly both, as this rule does not
preclude that outcome.

The third rule is diagrammed as:

$$A \longrightarrow B$$

Using linkage, the first and third rules can be connected to create a chain relationship:

$$A \longrightarrow B \longrightarrow C$$

Thus, we have the following situation:

A B C D E[5]

A ——→ B ——→ C

D ◄——┼——► E

___ ___ ___   D/E ___

3 Selections   Out

At this point, many students choose to move on to the question. This is a premature move. We have one powerful conditional chain and one powerful negative grouping rule. Just considering the second rule, our selection pool is down to the choice of A, B, C, or D/E:

A	B	C	D/E

Of course, we still have our conditional chain to consider. The selection of A would automatically force the selection of B and C, and so if A is selected then there is only one solution. But, what would occur if one of the variables in the chain was not selected? Remember, when a necessary condition does not occur in a conditional chain, then all of the sufficient conditions also cannot occur. Thus, in Grouping games, *always* examine the necessary conditions of any chain relationship to see if the non-occurrence of those variables will have a significant effect. In this drill, we must always have three variables selected, but the second rule has already removed at least one of the five candidates from the pool (either D or E, or both, cannot be selected). This leaves only four variables for three spaces, and therefore problems would result if one of the necessary conditions were not selected.

Grouping Setup Practice Drill Answer Key

For example, if C were not selected, the following contrapositive would occur:

$$\cancel{C} \longrightarrow \cancel{B} \longrightarrow \cancel{A}$$

The removal of C would thus eliminate three variables (A, B, and C), leaving only D or E to fill the selection group. Because this would violate the scenario, this cannot occur, and we can conclude that C must always be selected.

This is a powerful inference, but do not stop there. What about the other necessary condition within the chain, B? If B is removed, the following contrapositive occurs:

$$\cancel{B} \longrightarrow \cancel{A}$$

With both A and B removed from the selection pool, only C and the choice of D/E would be available to fill the selection group. Because this would also violate the scenario, this cannot occur, and we can conclude that B must also always be selected.

Thus, both B and C must always be selected, and the only remaining choice is whether A, D, or E is the final applicant selected:

$$\underline{B} \quad \underline{C} \quad \underline{A/D/E} \quad \bigg| \quad \underline{D/E} \quad \underline{A/D/E}$$
$$\text{3 Selections} \qquad\qquad \text{Out}$$

Consequently, the game has only three solutions:

    Solution 1: A, B, C
    Solution 2: B, C, D
    Solution 3: B, C, E

With the setup to the game in hand, we can now turn to the question.

Question 1.1. Which one of the following must be true?

    (A)   A is selected for the committee.
    (B)   B is selected for the committee.
    (C)   C is not selected for the committee.
    (D)   D is not selected for the committee.
    (E)   E is not selected for the committee.

Grouping Setup Practice Drill Answer Key

Question 1.1. The correct answer is (B). As discussed previously, no viable solution can be created without the presence of B, and thus B must be selected to the committee.

Answer choice (A) is incorrect because A does not have to be selected to the committee.

Answer choice (C) is incorrect because C must be selected to the committee.

Answer choice (D) is incorrect because D could be selected to the committee.

Answer choice (E) is incorrect because E could be selected to the committee.

2. A business school offers at least one of the following seven courses during the winter term: accounting, economics, finance, law, marketing, operations, and sales. The following restrictions apply:
    If accounting is offered, then finance is also offered but economics is not.
    If law is offered, then economics is also offered but marketing is not.
    If operations or sales is offered, then accounting is also offered.

Although the scenario states that there are seven courses in the selection pool, the exact number of courses offered by the school is never defined. Thus, the grouping classification of this drill is Undefined.

The first two rules each have two necessary conditions. The first rule is diagrammed as:

The second rule is diagrammed as:

THE POWERSCORE LSAT LOGIC GAMES BIBLE

At first, these two rules may not appear to be capable of being linked, but they can be, through the presence of E. Because the first rule requires E to not be offered and the second rule requires E to be offered, the necessary conditions are opposite, and we can infer that the two sufficient conditions—A and L—cannot both be offered together. In short, if A is offered then E is not offered, but when L is offered E must be offered. Thus, there is no way to offer both A and L because they have needs that are exactly opposite, and we can draw the following inference:

$$A \longleftarrow\!\!\!\!|\!\!\!\!\longrightarrow L$$

Thus, one of A or L is always "out" in this game (a fact that can be shown separately in an "out" group).

Consider an analogy to help make the relationship between A and L clearer:

Statement 1: To get into Harvard you must be rich.

Statement 2: To get into Harvard you must be poor.

If the two statements above are true, is it possible for anyone to attend Harvard? No, because no one can be both rich and poor at the same time (and yes, for the purposes of discussion let's assume that rich and poor in this context refer to monetary wealth, and not spiritual wealth, etc.). Our situation here is slightly different, but the underlying principle is the same.

If the above discussion still does not make sense, take the contrapositive of one of the two rules and then link them together. The result will be the same.

The third rule has two sufficient conditions:

$$\begin{matrix} O \\ or \\ S \end{matrix} \longrightarrow A$$

Because the necessary condition of the third rule is identical to the sufficient condition in the first rule, the two can be combined to create a super-rule:

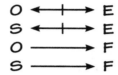

Note that this relationship leads to host of sub-inferences, including the following:

$$O \longleftrightarrow E$$
$$S \longleftrightarrow E$$
$$O \longrightarrow F$$
$$S \longrightarrow F$$

However, because the super-rule contains those inferences inherently as part of the chain, we will not draw them on the final diagram. This final diagram thus appears as:

A E F L M O S [7]

O
or ⟶ A ⟶ and
S   E̸

Inf

A ⟷ L

E
L ⟶ and
       M̸

O
or ⟷ L
S

Remember, Undefined games do not allow you to specify the number of variables being selected.

Note: the contrapositive for each of the three rules can also be diagrammed; the choice is yours. If you think they will help you better understand and control the variables, show them.

Question 2.1. If law is offered, then each of the following must be false EXCEPT:

    (A)   Accounting is offered.
    (B)   Finance is offered.
    (C)   Marketing is offered.
    (D)   Operations is offered.
    (E)   Sales is offered.

Question 2.1. The correct answer is (B). When L is offered, according to the second rule E is offered and M is not offered. This information eliminates answer choice (C). We also know from the inference that when L is offered then A is not offered. This eliminates answer choice (A). When A is not offered, via the contrapositive of the third rule, both O and S are not offered. This inference eliminates answer choices (D) and (E).

Also, always remember to convert false into true in question stems. Applying that process, the "must be false" portion of this question asks for what "cannot be true," and then the "except" portion turns that around so that this question actually asks for which one of the following Could Be True.

---

3. Seven senators—P, Q, R, S, T, V, and X—serve on two subcommittees. Each subcommittee has at least three members. The following is known about the two subcommittees:

    Every senator serves on at least one subcommittee, and no senator serves on both subcommittees.
    If P serves on a subcommittee, then Q does not serve on that subcommittee.
    R and S do not serve on the same subcommittee.
    T serves on a subcommittee only if V serves on the same subcommittee.

The scenario states that there are seven senators serving on two subcommittees of at least three members each. This makes the game appear Partially Defined, but then the first rule specifies that no senator serves on both subcommittees but that all senators must serve. This means that one of the subcommittees must have three members and the other subcommittee must have four members. This makes the game Defined, and although the game appears to be moving, no subcommittee names are ever specified, and so we simply have the "subcommittee of three" and the "subcommittee of four," leading this game to be Fixed. The final classification is Defined-Fixed, Balanced.

The initial numerical scenario appears as follows:

$$P\ Q\ R\ S\ T\ V\ X^7$$
*

$$\underline{\quad} \quad \underline{\quad}$$
$$\underline{\quad} \quad \underline{\quad}$$
$$\underline{\quad} \quad \underline{\quad}$$
$$\quad\ \ \underline{\quad}$$
$$3 \qquad 4$$

The first two rules are fairly easy to diagram as they are both negative grouping rules.

First rule:

Second rule:

The third rule can be a bit more challenging, but remember that "only if" introduces a necessary condition. The proper diagram is thus:

$$T \longrightarrow V$$

Note that, since all senators in this game serve on a subcommittee (and thus T must serve), this rule could also be shown as a block.

Applying the first two rules to the diagram, although we cannot ascertain where each variable serves, we do know that one of P or Q serves on each subcommittee, and one of R or S must serve on each subcommittee. These relationships can be shown as split dual-options:

$$
\begin{array}{cc}
\overline{} & \overline{} \\
R/S & S/R \\
P/Q & Q/P \\
\hline
3 & 4
\end{array}
$$

With so many spaces on the diagram occupied, the situation is restricted, and we can now examine the effects of that restriction on the third rule. Because when T serves on a subcommittee then V must also serve on that same subcommittee, we can infer that T cannot serve in the group of three (because then there would be no space for V). Thus, T must serve on the subcommittee with four members, and by applying the third rule we can conclude that V must serve on that subcommittee as well. The only remaining variable is X, the random, and the only remaining space is in the group of three, and so X must serve on the subcommittee with three members. The complete diagram is:

Grouping Setup Practice Drill Answer Key

$$\frac{V}{T}$$

X	V/T
R/S	S/R
P/Q	Q/P
3	4

With this information, the question should be relatively easy.

Question 3.1. Which one of the following must be true?

- (A) P must serve on the subcommittee that has three members.
- (B) Q must serve on the subcommittee that has three members.
- (C) R must serve on the subcommittee that has four members.
- (D) S must serve on the subcommittee that has four members.
- (E) T must serve on the subcommittee that has four members.

Question 3.1. The correct answer is (E). As explained above, the actions of the two pairs of variables involved in the negative grouping rules—P and Q, and R and S—force T to serve on the subcommittee of four. Each of the variables cited in the first four answers (not surprisingly, P, Q, R, and S) could serve on either subcommittee. In a Must Be True question such as this one, you should immediately avoid answers that contain moving variables such as P, Q, R, or S.

Question 3.2. Which one of the following CANNOT be true?

- (A) P and R serve on the same subcommittee.
- (B) Q and S serve on the same subcommittee.
- (C) T and R serve on the same subcommittee.
- (D) V and X serve on the same subcommittee.
- (E) X and Q serve on the same subcommittee.

Question 3.2. The correct answer is (D). The answer choices present pairs of variables, and you are asked to identify the pair that cannot serve together. As discussed in the explanation to the first question, we know that P, Q, R, and S could serve on either subcommittee. Thus, answers that contain any of those four variables would be a poor choice (unless it was two variables known to be locked in a negative grouping rule, such as P and Q. But, the test makers would never make it that easy.). Answer choices (A), (B), (C), and (E) all contain one or more of those variables, and in each instance, the cited pairs can serve together.

Answer choice (D) is correct because we determined that V serves on the subcommittee of four and X must serve on the subcommittee of three. Consequently, V and X cannot serve on the same subcommittee.

4. A set of five products—D, E, F, G, and H—is
assigned to two product testers—tester 1 and tester 2.
Each product must be tested at least once, and each
tester conducts three tests. Once a tester has tested a
product she cannot test that product again. The testing
meets the following conditions:

    If D is assigned to tester 1, then E is assigned to
      tester 2.

    F and G cannot be assigned to the same tester.

    D is tested twice.

The scenario states that there are two testers who each test three products. Thus, the selection group is Defined-Fixed. There are five products assigned to the two tests, and thus the variable pool is Unbalanced: Underfunded. Fortunately, the final rule specifies that D is tested twice, and this balances out the scenario, and creates the following 2-1-1-1-1 numerical distribution:

Six tests =	2	-	1	-	1	-	1	-	1
"Six" products =	D		E		F		G		H

The quote marks appear on the "six" with products because there are really five products, but because one is tested twice, those products are used six times.

The initial scenario appears as follows:

$DDEFGH^6$

$$
\begin{array}{cc}
\underline{\hspace{1.5em}} & \underline{\hspace{1.5em}} \\
\underline{\hspace{1.5em}} & \underline{\hspace{1.5em}} \\
\underline{\hspace{1.5em}} & \underline{\hspace{1.5em}} \\
1 & 2
\end{array}
$$

The first rule can be diagrammed as follows:

$$D_1 \longrightarrow E_2$$

The second rule is a negative grouping rule:

Grouping Setup Practice Drill Answer Key

We have already discussed the numerical impact of third rule in our discussion above, but functionally, if D is tested twice and no product is tested twice by the same tester, then D must be assigned to both testers:

$$\frac{\overline{\hspace{1cm}} \quad \overline{\hspace{1cm}}}{\underset{1}{\underline{D}} \quad \underset{2}{\underline{D}}}$$

The second rule also has an impact on the diagram because F and G cannot be tested by the same tester:

$$\frac{\underline{F/G} \quad \underline{G/F}}{\underset{1}{\underline{D}} \quad \underset{2}{\underline{D}}}$$

The situation is now quite restricted because there is only one space left in each group. However, we have yet to consider the impact of the first rule on the two remaining products—E and H. When D is tested by tester 1, as is the case in this scenario, the E must be tested by tester 2:

$$\frac{\overline{\hspace{1cm}} \quad \underline{E}}{\underline{F/G} \quad \underline{G/F}} \\ \underset{1}{\underline{D}} \quad \underset{2}{\underline{D}}$$

The remaining unused product—H—must then be assigned to the only remaining space, and we arrive at the final diagram:

$$\frac{\underline{H} \quad \underline{E}}{\underline{F/G} \quad \underline{G/F}} \\ \underset{1}{\underline{D}} \quad \underset{2}{\underline{D}}$$

Grouping Setup Practice Drill Answer Key

Note that reading all of the rules before diagramming makes this game easier to handle, because you can place both Ds, and then the remaining variables fall into place. Students who start diagramming immediately will operate less efficiently and will possibly be forced to rework their diagram when they encounter the third rule.

<u>Question 4.1</u>. Each of the following could be true EXCEPT:

    (A)   D and E are each tested by the same tester.
    (B)   D and F are each tested by the same tester.
    (C)   E and G are each tested by the same tester.
    (D)   E and H are each tested by the same tester.
    (E)   G and H are each tested by the same tester.

Question 4.1. The correct answer is (D). As explained above, E must be assigned to tester 2 and H must be assigned to tester 1.

Answer choices (A) and (B) both contain D, and we know that because D is assigned to both testers, then every variable is, at some point, assigned to the same tester as D.

Answer choices (B), (C) and (E) each contain F or G, and we know that F and G rotate between the two testers. Thus, F and G could, depending on the scenario, be assigned to the same tester as every other product. These answer choices are thus incorrect. Note again how the uncertainty of placement of variables involved in a negative grouping rule plays a role in a question with a strong Could Be True element (in this Could Be True Except question, the correct answer choice Cannot Be True and the four incorrect answer choices Could Be True). In this sense, this question is similar to questions 3.1 and 3.2.

---

5.   The members of a six-person panel will be selected from among four parents—J, K, L, and M—and four students—W, X, Y, and Z. The selection of panel members will meet the following conditions:
        The panel will include exactly three parents and exactly three students.
        W and X cannot both be selected.
        J cannot be selected unless W is selected.
        K cannot be selected unless X is selected.

The scenario states that a six-person panel will be selected, so the group is Defined-Fixed. There are eight candidates for the panel, so the selection pool is Unbalanced, Overloaded. The candidates are also divided into two groups—parents and students—and so the pool is Subdivided.

Grouping Setup Practice Drill Answer Key

Note that an 8 into 6 scenario such as this one is quite restricted because when any two variables are eliminated then the remaining six variables must be selected. The first rule further limits the game by establishing that exactly three members from each group must be selected:

Par: J K L M ^{4}
Stu: W X Y Z ^{4}

$$\boxed{\underline{J} \quad \underline{K} \quad \underline{L} \quad \underline{M} \quad | \quad \underline{W} \quad \underline{X} \quad \underline{Y} \quad \underline{Z}}$$

Panel of 6 $\underline{J/K/L/M} \quad \underline{W/X/Y/Z}$

Out

The second rule reveals that W and X cannot be selected together, creating further restrictions on the student group. In fact, because the student group only has one "extra" member, the second rule leads to the inference that both Y and Z must be selected:

$$W \longleftarrow\!\!\!|\!\!\!\longrightarrow X \quad \boxed{\underline{J} \quad \underline{K} \quad \underline{L} \quad \underline{M} \quad | \quad \underline{W/X} \quad \underline{Y} \quad \underline{Z}}$$

Panel of 6 $\underline{J/K/L/M} \quad \underline{W/X}$

Out

The third and fourth rules are conditional, and can be diagrammed as follows:

$$J_P \longrightarrow W_S$$

$$K_P \longrightarrow X_S$$

The "P" and "S" subscripts designate the parent and student groups, respectively.

Interestingly, these rules can both be connected to the second rule. The second rule and third rules combine to form the following chain:

$$J_P \longrightarrow W_S \longleftarrow\!\!\!|\!\!\!\longrightarrow X_S$$

From this relationship we can infer that:

$$J_P \longleftarrow\!\!\!|\!\!\!\longrightarrow X_S$$

Of course, we can also recycle this inference with the fourth rule to create the following relationship:

$$K_P \longrightarrow X_S \longleftarrow\mid\longrightarrow J_P$$

From this relationship we can infer that:

$$K_P \longleftarrow\mid\longrightarrow J_P$$

This is a powerful inference because it removes one of the parents from consideration. Note that we could have also drawn this inference by starting with the second and fourth rules:

$$K_P \longrightarrow X_S \longleftarrow\mid\longrightarrow W_S$$

This relationship yields the following inference:

$$K_P \longleftarrow\mid\longrightarrow W_S$$

When this inference is recycled and combined with the third rule, the following relationship results:

$$J_P \longrightarrow W_S \longleftarrow\mid\longrightarrow K_P$$

This relationship produces the same inference drawn at the top of this page:

$$J_P \longleftarrow\mid\longrightarrow K_P$$

Thus, on the parent side, there is also a limitation. Because J and K cannot both be selected, and the parent group originally had only one "extra" member, we can infer that both L and M must be selected, leading to our final setup:

Grouping Setup Practice Drill Answer Key

Par: J K L M ^{4}
Stu: W X Y Z ^{4}

J/K	L	M		W/X	Y	Z		J/K		W/X

Panel of 6   Out

W ◄———► X

J$_P$ ————► W$_S$

K$_P$ ————► X$_S$

J$_P$ ◄———► X$_S$

K$_P$ ◄———► W$_S$

J$_P$ ◄———► K$_P$

This final setup leaves us in a strong position to answer the question.

Question 5.1. Which one of the following could be a complete and accurate list of the people NOT selected for the panel?

    (A)   J, Y
    (B)   K, X
    (C)   L, Z
    (D)   M, Y
    (E)   W, X

Question 5.1. The correct answer is (B). As previously determined, the two unselected variables in this game must be exactly one of J and K, and exactly one of W and X. Only answer choice (B) contains a pair of variables that meets these criteria, and thus answer choice (B) is correct.

Answer choice (A) is incorrect because Y must always be selected for the panel.

Answer choice (C) is incorrect because L and Z must always be selected for the panel.

Answer choice (D) is incorrect because M and Y must always be selected for the panel.

Answer choice (E) is incorrect because at least one of W and X must be selected to the panel in order to meet the criterion that three of the panel members are students.

6. Chris is choosing flowers for his garden from among
   the following choices: B, C, D, F, G, H, L, and M.
   The flowers are chosen in a manner consistent with
   the following conditions:
   > If he chooses B, he does not choose D.
   > If he chooses B, then he chooses G.
   > If he chooses C, then he chooses D.
   > If he chooses G, then he chooses B.
   > If he does not choose H, then he chooses L.
   > If he chooses M, he does not choose L.

This game is classified as Undefined because no specification is made as to how many flowers will be selected.

Because there are six rules, we will number them for easy reference. The six rules, as stated, can be diagrammed as follows:

$$1. \quad B \longleftrightarrow\!\!\!| \quad D$$

$$2. \quad B \longrightarrow G$$

$$3. \quad C \longrightarrow D$$

$$4. \quad G \longrightarrow B$$

$$5. \quad \cancel{H} \longrightarrow L$$

$$6. \quad M \longleftarrow\!\!|\longrightarrow L$$

The second and fourth rules should immediately be combined to create a single super-rule:

$$2 + 4. \quad B \longleftrightarrow G$$

This rule combination forces B and G to act as a block.

With these rules in place, we can begin to make inferences. The first four rules can be combined to create the following inferences:

$$\text{Combination of 1 + 3.} \quad C \longleftarrow\!\!|\longrightarrow B$$

$$\text{Combination of 1 + 4.} \quad G \longleftarrow\!\!|\longrightarrow D$$

The first inference can be combined with our super-rule to create the following inference:

$$C \longleftrightarrow G$$

The fifth and sixth rules can also be combined:

$$\cancel{H} \longrightarrow L \longleftrightarrow M$$

This relationship yields the following inference:

$$\cancel{H} \longrightarrow \cancel{M}$$

The contrapositive of this inference is:

$$M \longrightarrow H$$

Thus, we can collect all of the rules and inferences into one main diagram:

B C D F G H L M⁸
        *

	Rules		Inferences	
1.	B $\longleftrightarrow$ D		C $\longleftrightarrow$ B	
2 + 4.	B $\longrightarrow$ G		G $\longleftrightarrow$ D	
3.	C $\longrightarrow$ D		C $\longleftrightarrow$ G	
5.	$\cancel{H}$ $\longrightarrow$ L		M $\longrightarrow$ H	
6.	M $\longleftrightarrow$ L			

<u>Question 6.1</u>. If Chris chooses G but not H, then it could
be true that he also chooses

    (A)   B and C
    (B)   B and F
    (C)   B and M
    (D)   C and L
    (E)   C and M

Question 6.1. The correct answer is (B).

When G is chosen, from the rules we know that B must also be chosen. From the inferences, we know that when G is chosen that C and D cannot be chosen. This information eliminates answer choices (A), (D), and (E), each of which contain C.

When H is not chosen, the L must be chosen, and when L is chosen then M cannot be chosen. This information eliminates answer choices (C) and (E), both of which contain M. Consequently, the only remaining answer choice is (B).

Note that once you ascertain that variable B is chosen, you could select answer choice (B) immediately because F, the other flower in that answer choice, is a random that does not appear in any rule, and thus can always be chosen regardless of what other variables are chosen or not chosen.

Final Pregame Note ▬▬▬▬▬▬

Grouping is a tricky concept, but one that appears on the LSAT frequently. If you feel any uncertainty on any of the concepts in this chapter—especially conditional reasoning—take a few minutes to review those concepts.

As always, please read the explanations to each game carefully, as they will give you a true sense of how to best attack each game. Plus, the explanations always include points that expand the discussions given previously.

If you would like to test yourself under timed conditions, you should give yourself 8 minutes and 45 seconds for each game. Good luck on the games!

> In doing these games, **use scratch paper instead of writing directly on the game!** This will prepare you for the Digital LSAT format where you cannot write directly on the screen.

A university library budget committee must reduce exactly five of eight areas of expenditure—G, L, M, N, P, R, S, and W—in accordance with the following conditions:

    If both G and S are reduced, W is also reduced.

    If N is reduced, neither R nor S is reduced.

    If P is reduced, L is not reduced.

    Of the three areas L, M, and R, exactly two are reduced.

6.   Which one of the following could be a complete and accurate list of the areas of expenditure reduced by the committee?

(A)   G, L, M, N, W

(B)   G, L, M, P, W

(C)   G, M, N, R, W

(D)   G, M, P, R, S

(E)   L, M, R, S, W

GO ON TO THE NEXT PAGE.

7. If W is reduced, which one of the following could be a complete and accurate list of the four other areas of expenditure to be reduced?

(A)   G, M, P, S
(B)   L, M, N, R
(C)   L, M, P, S
(D)   M, N, P, S
(E)   M, P, R, S

8. If P is reduced, which one of the following is a pair of areas of expenditure both of which must be reduced?

(A)   G, M
(B)   M, R
(C)   N, R
(D)   R, S
(E)   S, W

9. If both L and S are reduced, which one of the following could be a pair of areas of expenditure both of which are reduced?

(A)   G, M
(B)   G, P
(C)   N, R
(D)   N, W
(E)   P, S

10. If R is not reduced, which one of the following must be true?

(A)   G is reduced.
(B)   N is not reduced.
(C)   P is reduced.
(D)   S is reduced.
(E)   W is not reduced.

11. If both M and R are reduced, which one of the following is a pair of areas neither of which could be reduced?

(A)   G, L
(B)   G, N
(C)   L, N
(D)   L, P
(E)   P, S

12. Which one of the following areas must be reduced?

(A)   G
(B)   L
(C)   N
(D)   P
(E)   W

GO ON TO THE NEXT PAGE.

5

The game should be set up as follows:

GLMNPRSW[8]

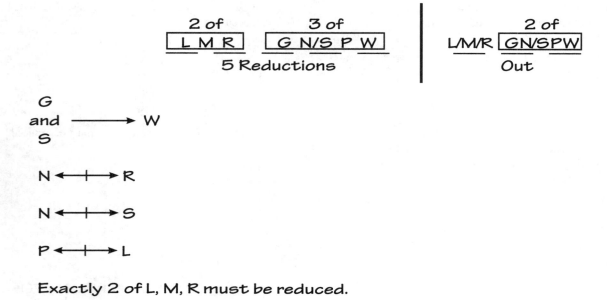

Exactly 2 of L, M, R must be reduced.

The selection of exactly five variables means the game is Defined-Fixed. Since there are eight variables from which to select, the game is Unbalanced: Overloaded.

The second rule bears further analysis. When N is reduced, neither R nor S is reduced, and it can be inferred from the contrapositive that when R or S is reduced, N cannot be reduced. Thus, N and R cannot be reduced together, and N and S cannot be reduced together. Consequently, we have written the rule in two separate parts to fully capture this powerful information.

Because the last rule reserves two of the five spaces, it is the most important one. Any rule that controls the numbers in a game is always important, and this rule is no exception. If two of L, M, and R are reduced, then of the remaining five areas of expenditure—G, N, S, P, and W—exactly three must be reduced. And since N and S cannot be reduced together, the choice is further limited. On the diagram this has been represented with the two blocks to represent these sub-groups. This separation of the variables into two groups is the key to making several powerful inferences:

1. Because two of the group of L, M, and R must be reduced:

   When L is not reduced, M and R must be reduced.
   When M is not reduced, L and R must be reduced.
   When R is not reduced, L and M must be reduced.

2. Because three of the group of G, P, W, N/S must be reduced:

   If G is not reduced, then P, W, and N/S must be reduced.
   If P is not reduced, then G, W, and N/S must be reduced.
   If W is not reduced, then G, P, and N/S must be reduced.
       (Later it will be discovered that W must always be reduced so this final inference will
       not be applicable.)

3. If G and S are reduced, then W is reduced. Since these three variables fill the reduction allotment of G, N, S, P, and W, it follows that when G and S are reduced, N and P are not reduced:

$$
\begin{array}{c} G \\ \text{and} \\ S \end{array} \longrightarrow W, \cancel{N}, \cancel{P}
$$

4. When N is reduced, R and S are not reduced. When R is not reduced, L and M must be reduced. When L and M are reduced, P is not reduced. Thus, when N is reduced, R, S, and P are not reduced. Since there are only eight variables for five slots, when R, S, and P are not reduced, it follows that all five of the remaining variables must be reduced. Thus, when N is reduced, G, L, M, and W must also be reduced.

5. When L is not reduced, M and R must be reduced, and when R is reduced, N is not reduced. Thus, when L is not reduced, N is not reduced. By the same reasoning, when M is not reduced, N is not reduced.

6. When P is reduced, L is not reduced. When L is not reduced, M and R must be reduced. Thus, when P is reduced, M and R must also be reduced. This inference is tested directly on question #8.

Understanding how the two sub-groups work—both separately and together—is clearly a powerful weapon against the questions. In this instance the groups are generated by the final rule, a rule concerning numbers. Always be on the lookout for rules that address the numbers in a game!

Question #6: Global, Could Be True, List. The correct answer choice is (A)

The application of proper List question technique (take a single rule and apply it to all five answer choices consecutively; take another rule and apply it to the remaining answer choices, etc.) eliminates every answer except for answer choice (A). Answer choice (B) is incorrect since both P and L are reduced. Answer choice (C) is incorrect since both N and R are reduced. Answer choice (D) is incorrect since G and S are reduced and W is not reduced. Answer choice (E) is incorrect because all three of L, M, and R are reduced. Consequently, answer choice (A) is correct. Of course, one of the most valuable results of answering a List question correctly is that we now know that the hypothetical G-L-M-N-W is a valid solution to the game.

Question #7: Local, Could Be True, List. The correct answer choice is (E)

Another List question, this time a Local question with the stipulation that W is selected. Do not make the mistake of thinking that because W is reduced that G and S are both reduced! This is a mistaken reversal of the rule. Answer choice (A) is incorrect since two of L, M, and R must be reduced and only M is reduced. Answer choice (B) is incorrect since both N and R are reduced, or alternately, because all three of L, M, and R are reduced. Answer choice (C) is incorrect because both P and L are reduced. Answer choice (D) is incorrect since both N and S are reduced. Consequently, answer choice (E) is correct, and we now know that the hypothetical W-M-P-R-S is a valid solution to the game.

Question #8: Local, Must Be True. The correct answer choice is (B)

As described earlier, when P is reduced, L cannot be reduced. When L is not reduced, M and R must be reduced, and hence answer choice (B) is correct.

Question #9: Local, Could Be True. The correct answer choice is (A)

When L is reduced, P cannot be reduced. Consequently, any answer choice that contains P can be eliminated, and answer choices (B) and (E) can be discarded. When S is reduced, N cannot be reduced and it follows that answer choices (C) and (D) are incorrect. Thus, answer choice (A) is correct.

5

Question #10: Local, Must Be True. The correct answer choice is (A)

This is one of the key questions of the game. The initial approach taken by most students is to consider the implications of R not being reduced. When R is not reduced, L and M must be reduced, and when L is reduced, P is not reduced. This provides sufficient information to eliminate answer choice (C). At this point the diagram next to the question looks like this:

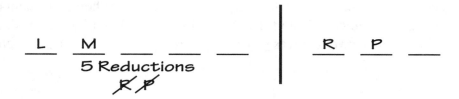

But this leaves four answer choices in contention with no obvious path towards the correct solution. However, there are several approaches to finding the correct answer:

1. Based on our discussion of the reduction of three of the five expenditures G, N, S, P, and W, when P is not reduced then G, W, and N or S must be reduced:

   Consequently, only answer choice (A) must be true.

2. Another approach is to make a few hypotheticals based on L and M being selected. The various hypotheticals can then be used to eliminate answer choices.

3. Since making new hypotheticals is useful, checking the hypotheticals created in questions #6 and #7 to see if they apply to question #10 might be even better. Although the W-M-P-R-S hypothetical in question #7 answer choice (E) is inapplicable since R is reduced, the hypothetical in question #6 answer choice (A) meets the criteria in question #10. By applying the G-L-M-N-W solution, we can eliminate answer choices (B), (C), (D), and (E), leaving only answer choice (A).

   Remember, always check back to earlier problems to see if you already have enough information to solve the current problem. Of course, only applicable work can be used. Do not forget that you should only use work that you are fully confident is correct. That is why answering List questions correctly is so important!

Question #11: Local, Cannot Be True. The correct answer choice is (C)

When R is reduced, N cannot be reduced. When both M and R are reduced, L cannot be reduced. Answer choice (C), which contains both L and N, is therefore correct.

Question #12: Global, Must Be True. The correct answer choice is (E)

This global question may come as somewhat of a surprise: apparently there is an area of expenditure that is always reduced. Yet this inference did not appear in our initial diagram! To have had this inference would have made the game easier, but it goes to show that there are times where you can miss an inference and still complete the game successfully.

The best way to attack this question is to use previous work. As in question #10, start with the hypotheticals created by questions #6 and #7. G-L-M-N-W, the hypothetical from question #6, shows that P does not have to be reduced, and therefore answer choice (D) can eliminated. W-M-P-R-S, the hypothetical from question #7, shows that G, L, and N do not have to be reduced, and therefore answer choices (A), (B), and (C) can be eliminated. Thus, with little or no work, it can be determined that answer choice (E) is correct. Consider how much faster and easier using this mode of attack is than the alternative of working out several independent solutions.

Abstractly, answer choice (E) is correct because ultimately no valid solution to the game can be created unless that solution contains W. If W is not reduced, then G, P and N must be reduced (see the GSW rule and the group of 3), but when G, P, and N are reduced you cannot reduce R or L (see the second and third rules), and thus the maximum number of reductions that could be made would be four: G, P, N, and M. Because there must be exactly five reductions and eliminating W does not allow for five reductions, it follows that W must be reduced.

One final point must be made about the restriction inherent in the L, M, and R rule. Since only three basic scenarios result under that rule—LM, LR, and MR—one entirely different approach to this game involves creating three templates based on each of those options. Although we feel this approach can be quite effective, its usefulness is dependent on making the inference regarding the three reductions from G, N, S, P, and W. As many students fail to make this inference, the value of the template approach is diminished here. In a later section the Identify the Templates approach will be revisited, and we will see that at times there is no better way to attack a game.

At a benefit dinner, a community theater's seven sponsors—K, L, M, P, Q, V, and Z—will be seated at three tables—1, 2, and 3. Of the sponsors, only K, L, and M will receive honors, and only M, P, and Q will give a speech. The sponsors' seating assignments must conform to the following conditions:

> Each table has at least two sponsors seated at it, and each sponsor is seated at exactly one table.
> Any sponsor receiving honors is seated at table 1 or table 2.
> L is seated at the same table as V.

1. Which one of the following is an acceptable assignment of sponsors to tables?

(A) Table 1: K, P; Table 2: M, Q; Table 3: L, V, Z
(B) Table 1: K, Q, Z; Table 2: L, V; Table 3: M, P
(C) Table 1: L, P; Table 2: K, M; Table 3: Q, V, Z
(D) Table 1: L, Q, V; Table 2: K, M; Table 3: P, Z
(E) Table 1: L, V, Z; Table 2: K, M, P; Table 3: Q

GO ON TO THE NEXT PAGE.

2. Which one of the following is a list of all and only those sponsors any one of whom could be among the sponsors assigned to table 3 ?

   (A) P, Q
   (B) Q, Z
   (C) P, Q, Z
   (D) Q, V, Z
   (E) P, Q, V, Z

3. If K is assigned to a different table than M, which one of the following must be true of the seating assignment?

   (A) K is seated at the same table as L.
   (B) L is seated at the same table as Q.
   (C) M is seated at the same table as V.
   (D) Exactly two sponsors are seated at table 1.
   (E) Exactly two sponsors are seated at table 3.

4. If Q is assigned to table 1 along with two other sponsors, which one of the following could be true of the seating assignment?

   (A) K is seated at the same table as L.
   (B) K is seated at the same table as Q.
   (C) M is seated at the same table as V.
   (D) M is seated at the same table as Z.
   (E) P is seated at the same table as Q.

5. If the sponsors assigned to table 3 include exactly one of the sponsors who will give a speech, then the sponsors assigned to table 1 could include any of the following EXCEPT:

   (A) K
   (B) M
   (C) P
   (D) Q
   (E) Z

6. If three sponsors, exactly two of whom are receiving honors, are assigned to table 2, which one of the following could be the list of sponsors assigned to table 1 ?

   (A) K, M
   (B) K, Z
   (C) P, V
   (D) P, Z
   (E) Q, Z

7. Which one of the following conditions, if added to the existing conditions, results in a set of conditions to which no seating assignment for the sponsors can conform?

   (A) At most two sponsors are seated at table 1.
   (B) Any sponsor giving a speech is seated at table 1 or else table 2.
   (C) Any sponsor giving a speech is seated at table 2 or else table 3.
   (D) Exactly three of the sponsors are seated at table 1.
   (E) Any table at which both L and V are seated also has a third sponsor seated at it.

5

GO ON TO THE NEXT PAGE.

It is immediately apparent that this game differs from the previous game in that the groups are not fixed. Although the number of variables—sponsors in this case—being placed is Defined at seven, the number of spaces per table is not precisely defined, and therefore the game is Moving. This type of uncertainty almost always increases the difficulty of a game because it introduces another element that must be tracked during the game. In addition, each of the seven sponsors will be seated at one of the three tables and thus the game is Balanced. Therefore, the game is Defined-Moving, Balanced.

The first rule establishes that each table must have at least two sponsors seated at it, and since there are a total of seven sponsors, it can be deduced that one of the three tables will have three sponsors seated at it and the other two tables will each seat two sponsors. This is a 3-2-2 numerical distribution. In this case, the 3-2-2 distribution is considered "unfixed," since the three sponsors could be seated at either table 1, table 2, or table 3. In some games "fixed" distributions occur, and these fixed distributions are generally a benefit since they limit the possibilities within a game.

The other rules of the game are relatively straightforward, and the initial setup should appear similar to the following:

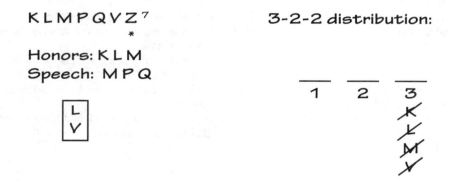

Since K, L, and M must sit at either table 1 or table 2, they cannot sit at table 3. Since V must sit at the same table as L, it follows that V cannot sit at table 3. Since K, L, M, and V cannot sit at table 3, only P, Q, and Z can possibly sit at table 3. Clearly then, table 3 is extremely restricted. As in any game, always examine the points of restriction since they often yield powerful inferences. In this case, since table 3 must have at least two sponsors, and only P, Q, and Z can possibly sit at table 3, at least two of the P, Q, Z group must always sit at table 3. Therefore, if a question states that one of the P, Q, Z group is seated at table 1 or table 2, then the remaining two sponsors must *automatically* be seated at table 3. Furthermore, any arrangement that attempts to seat two of the P, Q, or Z group at table 1 or table 2 will violate the rules and thus cannot occur. Ultimately, this simple analysis has uncovered the most important inference of the game. To reiterate, since table 3 has only three available sponsors to fill at least two seats, if any one of the sponsors is seated elsewhere, the remaining two sponsors must be seated at table 3. This is a variation of the type of inferences common when a dual-option is present, and you can expect at least one or two of the questions to directly test your knowledge of this inference.

Question #1: Global, Could Be True, List. The correct answer choice is (D)

As in many games, the first question in this game is a List question. The optimal attack for List questions is as always to apply one rule at a time to each of the five answer choices, eliminating answer choices from consideration until only one answer choice remains. In choosing the first rule to apply, try to choose a rule that can be easily applied from a visual standpoint. In this game, the LV block and the Not Laws on table 3 are the easiest to apply. The 3-2-2 distribution, although not difficult to apply, is more time consuming than the other two rules and thus should be applied last.

Applying the LV block rule eliminates answer choice (C). Applying the Not Laws on table 3 eliminates answer choices (A) and (B), as well as (C) again. Finally, applying the 3-2-2 numerical distribution rule eliminates answer choice (E). Answer choice (D) is thus proven correct by process of elimination.

Question #2: Global, Could Be True, List. The correct answer choice is (C)

From our earlier analysis of table 3 we know that answer choice (C) is correct.

Question #3: Local, Must Be True. The correct answer choice is (E)

If K and M are assigned to different tables, one must be assigned to table 1 and the other must be assigned to table 2. Since we cannot be certain which is assigned to table 1 or table 2, it is best to display this situation as a dual option and then Hurdle the Uncertainty:

$$\frac{\overline{\quad}\ \ \overline{\quad}\ \ \overline{\quad}}{\text{K/M}\ \ \text{M/K}}$$
$$\ \ 1\quad\ \ 2\quad\ \ 3$$

Since the LV block must be seated at either table 1 or table 2, it follows that table 1 or table 2 must have three sponsors seated at it. Therefore, table 3 can only have two sponsors seated at it and answer choice (E) is proven correct. Answer choice (D) is incorrect since it is possible for three sponsors to sit at table 1. Answer choices (A) and (C) are both incorrect since the LV block can sit at either table 1 or table 2, as can K or M. Thus, although many combinations of K, M, and the LV block are possible, none must occur. Answer choice (B) is incorrect since L and Q can never sit together given the condition in the question stem.

Question #4: Local, Could Be True. The correct answer choice is (B)

If Q is assigned to table 1, P and Z must be assigned to table 3:

$$
\begin{array}{ccc}
 & & Z \\
\overline{} & \overline{} & \overline{P} \\
\overline{Q} & \overline{} & \overline{P} \\
1 & 2 & 3
\end{array}
$$

Since the question stem also states that table 1 has three sponsors, the numerical distribution is now fixed at 3-2-2:

$$
\begin{array}{ccc}
 & & Z \\
\overline{} & \overline{} & \overline{P} \\
\overline{Q} & \overline{} & \overline{P} \\
1 & 2 & 3
\end{array}
$$

Since the four remaining unseated sponsors are K, M, L, and V, two of that group must sit at table 1 and the other two must sit at table 2. Because L and V must sit together as a block, it follows that K and M must also sit together as a block. Thus, the KM block and the LV block cannot sit together:

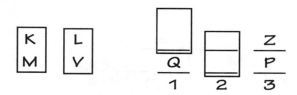

This information is sufficient to prove answer choice (B) correct.

Question #5: Local, Could Be True, Except. The correct answer choice is (E)

Remember, a Could Be True EXCEPT question asks for what Cannot Be True. This is the first question to address the "speech" subgroup established in the initial conditions of the game. Since M, P, and Q form the speech subgroup, and M cannot be seated at table 3, it follows that the one sponsor seated at table 3 who gives a speech must be either P or Q. Additionally, since at least two sponsors from the group P, Q, and Z must be seated at table 3, we can Hurdle the Uncertainty and infer that Z must be seated at table 3:

$$
\begin{array}{ccc}
 & & Z \\
\underline{} & \underline{} & \underline{P/Q} \\
1 & 2 & 3
\end{array}
$$

Thus, answer choice (E) is correct.

Question #6: Local, Could Be True, List. The correct answer choice is (B)

This is the first question to address the "honors" subgroup established in the initial conditions of the game. The conditions in the question stem establish the following 2-3-2 fixed numerical distribution setup:

Fixed Numerical Distribution 2-3-2:

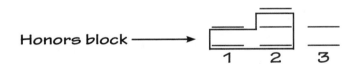

Since table 1 can only have one sponsor from the honors subgroup, answer choice (A) can be eliminated. Conversely, answer choices (C), (D), and (E) can be eliminated since table 1 must have exactly one sponsor from the honors subgroup, and none of these answer choices meet that criterion. Alternately, answer choices (D) and (E) can be eliminated since they contain two sponsors from the P, Q, and Z group that must supply table 3 with two sponsors. By process of elimination, answer choice (B) is proven correct.

Question #7: Global, Cannot Be True, Justify. The correct answer choice is (B)

Justify questions, which appear infrequently in the Logic Games section, require you to select an answer choice that, when added to the initial rules of the game, forces the condition requested in the question stem to occur. In this case, the answer choice must force a situation in which no possible hypothetical can meet all of the conditions of the game. Since we know table 3 is the most restricted point in the game, it is a good bet that the answer choice will in some way affect the sponsors available to meet the table 3 requirements. This occurs in answer choice (B), which places P and Q at tables 1 or 2, leaving only Z to fulfill the requirement that two sponsors sit at table 3.

This question also provides an excellent example of the technique of using hypotheticals from other questions to eliminate incorrect answer choices. For example, answer choice (A) states that "At most two sponsors are seated at table 1." From question #6 we know that this scenario produces several workable hypotheticals. Since any workable hypothetical would conflict with the desired result of question #7, answer choice (A) must be wrong. Answer choice (D) can be eliminated by the same process. Answer choice (D) states, "Exactly three of the sponsors are seated at table 1." The information in the stem from question #4 and also answer choice (D) in question #1 shows that this occurrence also allows several workable hypotheticals. Thus, answer choice (D) is incorrect. Answer choice (E) can be eliminated by examining the hypotheticals from question #3 as well as answer choice (D) in question #1. Remember, when a working hypothetical from another question meets the required conditions of a particular question, that hypothetical can be used to eliminate wrong answers or confirm the correct answer.

5

This game, from the June 1997 LSAT, is representative of the type of Grouping games that frequently appear on the LSAT. There are two powerful lessons to learn from this game. First, always examine the restricted points in a game. In a Grouping game this often means examining the available variables for a particular group, or examining the variables that cannot be placed together. Second, always examine any rule that deals with numbers. Often these numerical rules introduce a controlling factor into a game, such as a numerical distribution. Numerical Distributions will be discussed in more detail in Chapter Eight.

5

An album contains photographs picturing seven friends: Raimundo, Selma, Ty, Umiko, Wendy, Yakira, Zack. The friends appear either alone or in groups with one another, in accordance with the following:

Wendy appears in every photograph that Selma appears in.

Selma appears in every photograph that Umiko appears in.

Raimundo appears in every photograph that Yakira does not appear in.

Neither Ty nor Raimundo appears in any photograph that Wendy appears in.

13. Which one of the following could be a complete and accurate list of the friends who appear together in a photograph?

(A)   Raimundo, Selma, Ty, Wendy
(B)   Raimundo, Ty, Yakira, Zack
(C)   Raimundo, Wendy, Yakira, Zack
(D)   Selma, Ty, Umiko, Yakira
(E)   Selma, Ty, Umiko, Zack

GO ON TO THE NEXT PAGE.

5

14. If Ty and Zack appear together in a photograph, then which one of the following must be true?

   (A)   Selma also appears in the photograph.
   (B)   Yakira also appears in the photograph.
   (C)   Wendy also appears in the photograph.
   (D)   Raimundo does not appear in the photograph.
   (E)   Umiko does not appear in the photograph.

15. What is the maximum number of friends who could appear in a photograph that Yakira does not appear in?

   (A)   six
   (B)   five
   (C)   four
   (D)   three
   (E)   two

16. If Umiko and Zack appear together in a photograph, then exactly how many of the other friends must also appear in that photograph?

   (A)   four
   (B)   three
   (C)   two
   (D)   one
   (E)   zero

17. If exactly three friends appear together in a photograph, then each of the following could be true EXCEPT:

   (A)   Selma and Zack both appear in the photograph.
   (B)   Ty and Yakira both appear in the photograph.
   (C)   Wendy and Selma both appear in the photograph.
   (D)   Yakira and Zack both appear in the photograph.
   (E)   Zack and Raimundo both appear in the photograph.

GO ON TO THE NEXT PAGE.

5

Analysis of Grouping Game #3: December 2004 Questions 13-17

This is an Undefined Grouping game. The game is Undefined because we do not know how many photographs are displayed in the album, nor do we know exactly how many people are in a photograph. With these elements unspecified, we cannot create a diagram in the traditional sense; that is, we cannot create a group of say, five spaces and then place variables in those spaces. Instead, we must diagram the rules and make inferences, and then proceed to the questions without a defined group in place. Although this task sounds difficult, it is not, and games of this nature are not unusual on the LSAT. Some similar games are: October 2005 #2 (Light Switches), December 2005 #1 (Electrical Appliances), and June 2006 #3 (Summer Courses).

Instead of showing an initial diagram, we will begin by examining each rule and then at the end of the rule analysis and inference we will present the completed setup.

The Rules

Rule #1. One of the easiest mistakes to make in this game is to misinterpret the wording in each of the rules. This rule indicates that whenever S appears in a photograph, then W appears in that same photograph. The correct diagram for that relationship is:

Many students mistakenly reverse the above diagram. To avoid doing so, consider the rule for a moment: does the rule say that every time W appears in a photograph that S also appears? No. Although the difference is subtle, the wording in the rule is that W appears in every photograph *that S appears in*. Thus, S is the sufficient condition, and the appearance of S indicates that W will appear in that same photograph.

Rule #2. The wording in this rule is identical to the wording in rule #1, and so it is just as easy to make an error when diagramming this rule. The correct diagram is:

When we get to the "Inference" section we will discuss how the first and second rules can be linked. Also, note that since both of the first two rules are "positive" (no negative terms involved) we are not diagramming contrapositives since you should know those as an automatic result of seeing any conditional statement.

Rule #3. This is also a tricky rule, not only because of the wording, but also because the conditional relationship between R and Y is easy to misunderstand. First, let us diagram the rule:

$$\cancel{Y} \longrightarrow R$$

Since this rule contains a negative, let us also diagram the contrapositive:

$$\cancel{R} \longrightarrow Y$$

Many students will interpret these two diagrams as reduced to a simple double-not arrow relationship: $Y \longleftarrow\!\!\!|\!\!\!\longrightarrow R$. This is *not* the meaning of the rule! Instead, consider the exact relationship between Y and R: when Y is not in the photograph, then R must be in the photograph; and, via the contrapositive, when R is not in the photograph, then Y must be in the photograph. Thus, when one of the two is *not* in the photograph, the other *must* be in the photograph, and that relationship can best be expressed by stating that both cannot be absent from the photograph. The correct double-not arrow diagram, then, is:

$$\cancel{R} \longleftarrow\!\!\!|\!\!\!\longrightarrow \cancel{Y}$$

The operating result of this rule is that *either Y or R, or both, must appear in each photograph* (note that R and Y *can* appear in a photograph together; the rule does not prohibit this occurrence).

Rule #4. This rule is actually two rules in one: one rule states that T and W do not appear in the same photograph, and the other states that R and W do not appear in the same photograph. Let's consider each part separately.

As stated directly, when W is in a photograph, T is not in that same photograph:

$$W \longrightarrow \cancel{T}$$

This rule can be turned into the a double-not arrow indicating that T and W are never in the same photograph:

$$W \longleftarrow\!\!\!|\!\!\!\longrightarrow T$$

The other part of the rule states that when W is in a photograph, R is not in that same photograph:

$$W \longrightarrow \cancel{R}$$

This rule can be turned into the a double-not arrow indicating that R and W are never in the same photograph:

$$W \longleftarrow\!\!\!|\!\!\!\longrightarrow R$$

One note about the rules: every variable is mentioned in the rules except Z. Thus, Z is a random in this game, and since there is not a specified number of spaces, Z is largely powerless in this game. If a question stem includes Z as part of a local condition, there *must* be other information included in the question stem, and you should focus on the other information first.

In review, the four rules contain five basic grouping relationships that create many different inferences. When you consider the four rules, you can see that the test makers placed a trap for the unwary student. A student who quickly reads through the rules and does not read for meaning can easily mis-diagram one or more of the rules, and of course mis-diagramming during the setup is almost always costly.

After correctly negotiating each of the rule diagrams, the next step is to make inferences by connecting the rules. In this game, there are many inferences, and so the challenge becomes managing the information.

The Inferences

Inference #1. By connecting the first and second rules, we can create the following chain:

$$U \longrightarrow S \longrightarrow W$$

This connection is important because it shows that if U appears in a photograph then two other friends must also appear in that same photograph. Via the contrapositive, the relationship also indicates that if W does not appear in a photograph, then neither S nor U can appear in that photograph.

Inferences #2 and #3. The first and fourth rules can be connected through W:

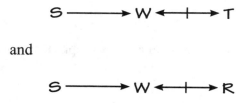

and

$$S \longrightarrow W \longleftarrow\!\!\!|\!\!\!\longrightarrow R$$

These two relationships yield the following inferences:

$$S \longleftarrow\!\!\!|\!\!\!\longrightarrow T$$

and

$$S \longleftarrow\!\!\!|\!\!\!\longrightarrow R$$

Inferences #4 and #5. The two previous inferences connected S to T and R through S's relationship with W. Since U also has a relationship with S from the second rule, we can connect the second rule to inferences we just made:

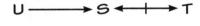

and

$$U \longrightarrow S \longleftarrow\!\!\!|\!\!\!\longrightarrow R$$

These two relationships yield the following inferences:

$$U \longleftarrow\!\!\!|\!\!\!\longrightarrow T$$

and

$$U \longleftarrow\!\!\!|\!\!\!\longrightarrow R$$

Inference #6. Because R appears in the third and fourth rules, we can make a connection using R:

$$\cancel{X} \longrightarrow R \longrightarrow \cancel{W}$$

This relationship results in the unique inference that:

$$\cancel{X} \longrightarrow \cancel{W}$$

Because both conditions are negative, take the contrapositive:

Thus, if W appears in a photograph, then Y must appear in that photograph as well.

Inferences #7 and #8. From the inference we just made we know that when W is in a photograph, then Y must also be in that photograph. We can add this to the chain that appeared in inference #1 (which was the combination of the first two rules):

$$U \longrightarrow S \longrightarrow W \longrightarrow Y$$

These relationships yield the following two inferences:

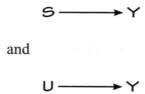

and

Thus, the appearance of either S or U will ultimately force Y to appear. This makes U a powerful variable: when U appears in a photograph, then S, W, and Y must also appear, and R and T cannot appear. Thus, the appearance of U allows for only two solutions, depending on whether Z is in the photograph.

There are other ways to arrive at some of these inferences (for example, when S has a relationship with a variable, U has the same relationship because of the second rule), but each inference above is a product of combining the rules or of combining the rules and inferences (do not forget to recycle your inferences!).

Compiling all of the information above, we arrive at the final setup for this game:

R or Y must appear in each picture: R̲/̲Y̲

Rules

S ⟶ W

U ⟶ S

X̷ ⟶ R

R̷ ⟶ Y

W ⟵—⟶ T

W ⟵—⟶ R

Inferences

U ⟶ S ⟶ W ⟶ Y

S ⟵—⟶ T

S ⟵—⟶ R

U ⟵—⟶ T

U ⟵—⟶ R

X̷ ⟶ W̷

W ⟶ Y

S ⟶ Y

U ⟶ Y

As long as you focus on connecting the variables in the rules and inferences, you can attack the questions and complete each problem with relative ease. Remember, this game is not logically difficult; it is simply an information management game, so do not be intimidated!

Question #13: Global, Could Be True, List. The correct answer choice is (B)

Because there is no lack of rules or inferences to apply to this List question, this should be a relatively easy question.

Answer choice (A): This answer choice is incorrect because W cannot appear in a photograph with R or T. Alternately, this answer could be eliminated because when W is in a photograph then Y must be in that photograph.

Answer choice (B): This is the correct answer choice.

Answer choice (C): This answer choice is incorrect because W cannot appear in a photograph with R.

Answer choice (D): This answer choice can be eliminated because when S appears in a photograph, W must also appear in that photograph. Alternately, this answer can be eliminated because T cannot appear in a photograph with S or U.

Answer choice (E): This answer choice can be eliminated because when S appears in a photograph, W must also appear in that photograph. Alternately, this answer can be eliminated because either Y or R must appear in the photograph, or because T cannot appear in a photograph with S or U.

Question #14: Local, Must Be True. The correct answer choice is (E)

The question stem indicates that T and Z appear in a photograph. As discussed before, because Z is a random you should ignore Z in your consideration of who can and cannot appear together in a photograph. Consequently, let's revisit what we know about T:

From the fourth rule:	W ←⟊→ T
From the second inference:	S ←⟊→ T
From the fourth inference:	U ←⟊→ T

Thus, when T is in a photograph, then W, S, and U cannot appear in that photograph. Consequently, answer choice (E) must be correct.

Another way of thinking about this question would be to apply the fourth rule and conclude that when T is in a photograph then W is not in that photograph. Then, using the contrapositive of the first two rules, we can conclude that when W is not in a photograph, then S is not in that photograph, and U is not in that photograph.

Answer choice (A): This answer is incorrect because S cannot appear in any photograph that T appears in.

Answer choice (B): This answer choice is incorrect because although Y could appear in a photograph with T, Y does not have to appear in a photograph when T is in that photograph.

Answer choice (C): This answer is incorrect because W cannot appear in any photograph that T appears in.

Answer choice (D): This answer choice is incorrect because although R does not have to appear in a photograph with T, R could appear in a photograph when T is in that photograph.

Note also the language used in the five answer choices: the first three answer choices specify variables that must appear with T (positive relationships), whereas the last two answers specify variables that *cannot* appear with T (negative relationships). Always make sure to read each answer choice closely, because the addition of "not" changes the entire meaning of the answer choice!

Question #15: Local, Must Be True, Maximum. The correct answer choice is (D)

In this question you are asked to find the maximum number of friends that can appear in a photograph when Y does not appear in the photograph. This requires two steps: first you must establish what must be true and what cannot be true when Y does not appear, and second you must then arrange the other variables in a way that allows for the most number of friends to appear in the picture. Let's examine both steps:

Step 1: From the third rule, when Y does not appear in a photograph, then R must appear in that photograph:

$$\cancel{Y} \longrightarrow R$$

From the fourth rule, when R appears in a photograph, then W cannot appear in that photograph:

$$R \longrightarrow \cancel{W}$$

Via the contrapositive of the first and second rules, when W does not appear in a photograph, then S and U cannot appear in that photograph:

$$\cancel{W} \longrightarrow \cancel{S} \longrightarrow \cancel{U}$$

Thus, when Y does not appear in a photograph, then R must appear in the photograph, and W, S, and U cannot appear in the photograph.

Step 2: The remaining two variables that have not yet been addressed are T and Z. Because Z is a random, Z can automatically be included in the photograph. So, the final question is whether T is compatible with R, and the answer is yes. Although R and T both figure in the fourth rule, that rule individually relates R and T to W, and it does not make a direct connection between R and T. Thus, R and T can appear in a photograph together, and the maximum number of friends that can appear is three—R, T, and Z. Answer choice (D) is correct.

Answer choices (A), (B), (C): Each of these answer choices is incorrect because more than three friends cannot appear in the photograph when Y does not appear.

Answer choice (D): This is the correct answer choice.

Answer choice (E): This answer choice is incorrect because the question asks for the *maximum* number friends who can appear in the photograph when Y does not appear, and this answer is not the maximum.

Question #16: Local, Must Be True. The correct answer choice is (B)

The question stem asks for the number of *other* friends who must appear when U and Z appear together in a photograph.

As we have already established, Z is irrelevant in this type of question because Z is a random. Thus, the question revolves around U. From the first two rules, we know that when U appears in a photograph then S and W must also appear in that photograph. The appearance of W in the photograph (and S and U), forces Y to appear in the photograph. None of the other friends must appear, and thus the correct answer is three: S, W, and Y.

Answer choices (A), (C), (D), and (E): These answer choices are incorrect because they do not contain a number that equals the number of other friends who *must* appear in the photograph.

Question #17: Local, Could Be True Except. The correct answer choice is (A)

This is the only question of the game to define the number of friends who can appear in a photograph; in this case, three. With only three spaces in the photograph, every variable becomes important, especially those that bring along other variables.

Because this is a Could Be True Except question, the correct answer choice Cannot Be True, and is one that provides a pair of friends that together result in four or more friends appearing in the photograph. Thus, you should immediately scan the answers for a variable such as U, who by itself brings S, W, and Y. Unfortunately, U does not appear in the answers (but it is worth taking the time to see if the question could be solved that easily).

Answer choice (A): This is the correct answer choice. When S appears in a photograph, then W and Y must also appear in that photograph. Since the answer choice also establishes that Z is in this photograph, that totals four friends (S, W, Y, and Z), and thus this answer cannot be true and is correct.

Answer choice (B): This answer choice is incorrect. T and Y could appear in a photograph of exactly three friends, as proven by the following hypothetical: T-Y-Z.

Answer choice (C): This answer choice is incorrect. W and S could appear in a photograph of exactly three friends, as proven by the following hypothetical: W-S-Y.

Answer choice (D): This answer choice is incorrect. Y and Z could appear in a photograph of exactly three friends, as proven by the following hypothetical: T-Y-Z.

Answer choice (E): This answer choice is incorrect. Z and R could appear in a photograph of exactly three friends, as proven by the following hypothetical: R-T-Z.

Remember, if you do not see a quick solution to a problem such as this one, you should immediately make hypotheticals from the answer choices to see what is possible. Never waste time on the LSAT simply staring at a problem!

5

To prepare for fieldwork, exactly four different researchers—a geologist, a historian, a linguist, and a paleontologist—will learn at least one and at most three of four languages—Rundi, Swahili, Tigrinya, and Yoruba. They must learn the languages according to the following specifications:

> Exactly one researcher learns Rundi.
> Exactly two researchers learn Swahili.
> Exactly two researchers learn Tigrinya.
> Exactly three researchers learn Yoruba.
> Any language learned by the linguist or paleontologist is not learned by the geologist.
> Any language learned by the geologist is learned by the historian.

6. Which one of the following could be true?

(A)   The linguist learns three languages—Rundi, Swahili, and Tigrinya.

(B)   The linguist learns three languages—Swahili, Tigrinya, and Yoruba.

(C)   The historian learns three languages—Rundi, Swahili, and Tigrinya.

(D)   The historian learns three languages—Swahili, Tigrinya, and Yoruba.

(E)   The paleontologist learns three languages—Rundi, Swahili, and Tigrinya.

GO ON TO THE NEXT PAGE.

7. If the linguist learns three of the languages, then which one of the following must be true?

   (A)   The linguist learns Tigrinya.
   (B)   The linguist learns Rundi.
   (C)   The linguist learns Swahili.
   (D)   The paleontologist learns Rundi.
   (E)   The paleontologist learns Swahili.

8. Each of the following could be true of the researcher who learns Rundi EXCEPT:

   (A)   The researcher also learns Tigrinya but not Swahili.
   (B)   The researcher learns neither Tigrinya nor Swahili.
   (C)   The researcher also learns Tigrinya but not Yoruba.
   (D)   The researcher also learns both Tigrinya and Yoruba.
   (E)   The researcher also learns Yoruba but not Tigrinya.

9. Each of the following could be a complete and accurate list of the researchers who learn both Swahili and Yoruba EXCEPT:

   (A)   the historian
   (B)   the paleontologist
   (C)   the historian, the linguist
   (D)   the historian, the paleontologist
   (E)   the linguist, the paleontologist

10. If the geologist learns exactly two of the languages, then which one of the following could be true?

   (A)   The paleontologist learns Rundi.
   (B)   The paleontologist learns Swahili.
   (C)   The historian learns Rundi.
   (D)   The paleontologist learns exactly three of the languages.
   (E)   The historian learns exactly two of the languages.

11. Which one of the following must be true?

   (A)   Fewer of the languages are learned by the historian than are learned by the paleontologist.
   (B)   Fewer of the languages are learned by the geologist than are learned by the historian.
   (C)   Fewer of the languages are learned by the geologist than are learned by the linguist.
   (D)   Fewer of the languages are learned by the paleontologist than are learned by the linguist.
   (E)   Fewer of the languages are learned by the paleontologist than are learned by the historian.

12. If exactly two of the languages are learned by the historian, then which one of the following must be true?

   (A)   The paleontologist does not learn Rundi.
   (B)   The geologist does not learn Swahili.
   (C)   The linguist does not learn Rundi.
   (D)   The historian does not learn Rundi.
   (E)   The paleontologist does not learn Swahili.

GO ON TO THE NEXT PAGE.

5

Similar to game #2 in this section, and in contrast to games #1 and #3, the variables in this game are separated into different selection groups. Unlike the last game, the size of each group is fixed. Thus, the game is Defined-Fixed. And unlike either of the two previous games, there are fewer variables (four researchers) than spaces available (eight language slots) and so the game can be classified as Unbalanced: Underfunded. The complete classification is Defined-Fixed, Unbalanced: Underfunded.

When you create the setup, it is critical that the correct base be selected. There are two choices: the four researchers or the four languages. Since the researchers can learn one to three languages but it is uncertain exactly how many languages each researcher learns, the researchers seem a poor choice for the base. On the other hand, the number of researchers learning each language is clearly specified in the rules and as such the languages are the best choice for the base:

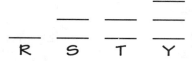

The distribution of researchers to languages is thus fixed at 1-2-2-3, and since there are only four researchers, it is clear that at least two researchers will have to learn more than one language (in fact, at least two researchers and at most three researchers will learn more than one language). Using the above base, we can set up the game as follows:

G H L P⁴

G ⟶ H

3 ≥ R ≥ 1

Because G appears in both the non-numerical rules, it is clear that G is a power variable. The key inference involving G comes with Yoruba. Because Yoruba must be learned by exactly three researchers, and G cannot be selected with either L or P, it can be inferred that G cannot learn Yoruba, and the other three researchers must learn Yoruba. Additionally, since when G is selected H must also be selected, it is not possible for G to learn Rundi, as there is no room for H to be selected. Consequently, since G must learn at least one language, G (in the form of a GH block) must learn either Swahili or Tigrinya or both. From this inference it follows that neither L nor P can learn *both* Swahili and Tigrinya.

Question #6: Global, Could Be True. The correct answer choice is (D)

Since it has already been established that H, L, and P must each learn Yoruba, answer choices (A), (C), and (E) can be eliminated. Since we have established that G must at a minimum learn either Swahili or Tigrinya, and it is therefore known that neither L or P can learn *both* Swahili and Tigrinya, answer choice (B) (as well as answer choices (A) and (E)) can be eliminated. Thus, answer choice (D) is proven correct by process of elimination.

Question #7: Local, Must Be True. The correct answer choice is (B)

Keeping in mind the inference that L cannot learn both Swahili and Tigrinya, when L learns three languages, we can Hurdle the Uncertainty to determine those languages must be Yoruba, Rundi, and either Swahili or Tigrinya. Consequently, answer choice (B) is correct.

Question #8: Global, Cannot Be True. The correct answer choice is (C)

Since G cannot learn Rundi, it can automatically be deduced that either H, L, or P must learn Rundi. Since H, L, and P each learn Yoruba, it must be the case that the researcher who learns Rundi also learns Yoruba. It follows that answer choice (C) cannot occur and is therefore correct.

Question #9: Global, Cannot Be True, List. The correct answer choice is (B)

The incorrect answers in this question list researchers who could learn both language in a valid solution to the game. The correct answer lists a researcher or researchers who cannot learn both languages in *any* solution to the game.

In a question requiring a complete list of researchers who cannot learn both Swahili and Yoruba, the first researcher to check is G, because G cannot learn Yoruba. Unfortunately, G does not appear in any answer choice. The next step is to consider the implications of learning both Swahili and Yoruba. Since H, L, and P each learn Yoruba, it seems likely that any combination of two of those three researchers could learn Swahili. Since answer choices (C), (D), and (E) each list two of H, L, or P, it seems unlikely that any of those answer choices are correct. Thus, let us focus on answer choices (A) and (B). Answer choice (A) lists just H, but under the following hypothetical H can be the only researcher who learns both Swahili and Yoruba:

$$
\begin{array}{cccc}
 & & & P \\
 & H & & L \\
 & G & & H \\
\hline
R & S & T & Y
\end{array}
$$

Let us check answer choice (B):

$$
\begin{array}{cccc}
 & & & P \\
 & & & L \\
 & P & & H \\
\underline{} & \underline{} & \underline{} & \underline{} \\
R & S & T & Y
\end{array}
$$

In this instance the second researcher who learns Swahili cannot be H or L since neither is listed in the answer choice. G also cannot learn Swahili since there is no room for H. Thus P cannot be the only person who learns both Swahili and Yoruba and answer choice (B) is correct.

With answer choice (B), when P is the sole researcher learning both Swahili and Yoruba, a problem arises because a second researcher is needed to learn Swahili, but according to the conditions of the question it must be one who does not also learn Yoruba. In this situation, who could you choose? You cannot choose L or H because they already learn Yoruba. That leaves only G, but if you select G for the second researcher slot in Swahili, you immediately violate the last rule because there is no room for H (and H could not be chosen anyway because that would be a violation as H learns Yoruba already). Hence, answer choice (B) cannot be a complete and accurate list of researchers who learn both Swahili and Yoruba.

When you are trying to figure out a situation such as the one above, always remember to try to work out the solution by creating hypotheticals. In this instance you can create viable hypotheticals for (A), (C), (D), and (E), but you cannot create one for (B).

Question #10: Local, Could Be True. The correct answer choice is (A)

If G learns exactly two languages, those languages must be Swahili and Tigrinya:

$$
\begin{array}{cccc}
 & & & P \\
 & H & H & L \\
P/L & G & G & H \\
\underline{} & \underline{} & \underline{} & \underline{} \\
R & S & T & Y \\
\cancel{G} & & & \\
\cancel{H} & & &
\end{array}
$$

Since H will then learn Swahili, Tigrinya, and Yoruba, due to the rule that limits a researcher to learning at most three languages, it follows that H cannot learn Rundi, and only P or L can learn Rundi. Answer choice (A) is thus correct.

Question #11: Global, Must Be True. The correct answer choice is (B)

The correct answer choice, answer choice (B), partially tests your understanding of the conditional relationship between G and H. According to the rule, every time G learns a language then H must also learn that same language. Consequently, H must learn at least as many languages as G. And since H also learns Yoruba and G cannot learn Yoruba, it must be that G learns fewer languages than H. The hypothetical from question #10 can be used to disprove answer choices (A), (C), and (D).

Question #12: Local, Must Be True. The correct answer choice is (D)

Since it has already been established that H learns Yoruba, the second language that H learns must come in conjunction with G, since G must learn at least one language. Since G must learn either Swahili or Tigrinya, it follows that H cannot learn Rundi and thus answer choice (D) is correct.

Like game #1, one possible approach to this game is to create three basic templates based on the position of G: G learning Swahili only, G learning Tigrinya only, and G learning both Swahili and Tigrinya. As with the first game, we believe this approach is less efficient than using the diagram and inferences described earlier, in part because the templates still leave a large number of possibilities unrealized.

5

Bird-watchers explore a forest to see which of the following six kinds of birds—grosbeak, harrier, jay, martin, shrike, wren—it contains. The findings are consistent with the following conditions:

If harriers are in the forest, then grosbeaks are not.

If jays, martins, or both are in the forest, then so are harriers.

If wrens are in the forest, then so are grosbeaks.

If jays are not in the forest, then shrikes are.

6. Which one of the following could be a complete and accurate list of the birds NOT in the forest?

(A) jays, shrikes
(B) harriers, grosbeaks
(C) grosbeaks, jays, martins
(D) grosbeaks, martins, shrikes, wrens
(E) martins, shrikes

GO ON TO THE NEXT PAGE.

7. If both martins and harriers are in the forest, then which one of the following must be true?

    (A) Shrikes are the only other birds in the forest.
    (B) Jays are the only other birds in the forest.
    (C) The forest contains neither jays nor shrikes.
    (D) There are at least two other kinds of birds in the forest.
    (E) There are at most two other kinds of birds in the forest.

8. If jays are not in the forest, then which one of the following must be false?

    (A) Martins are in the forest.
    (B) Harriers are in the forest.
    (C) Neither martins nor harriers are in the forest.
    (D) Neither martins nor shrikes are in the forest.
    (E) Harriers and shrikes are the only birds in the forest.

9. Which one of the following is the maximum number of the six kinds of birds the forest could contain?

    (A) two
    (B) three
    (C) four
    (D) five
    (E) six

10. Which one of the following pairs of birds CANNOT be among those birds contained in the forest?

    (A) jays, wrens
    (B) jays, shrikes
    (C) shrikes, wrens
    (D) jays, martins
    (E) shrikes, martins

11. If grosbeaks are in the forest, then which one of the following must be true?

    (A) Shrikes are in the forest.
    (B) Wrens are in the forest.
    (C) The forest contains both wrens and shrikes.
    (D) At most two kinds of birds are in the forest.
    (E) At least three kinds of birds are in the forest.

12. Suppose the condition is added that if shrikes are in the forest, then harriers are not. If all other conditions remain in effect, then which one of the following could be true?

    (A) The forest contains both jays and shrikes.
    (B) The forest contains both wrens and shrikes.
    (C) The forest contains both martins and shrikes.
    (D) Jays are not in the forest, whereas martins are.
    (E) Only two of the six kinds of birds are not in the forest.

GO ON TO THE NEXT PAGE.

Analysis of Grouping Game #5: December 2000 Questions 6-12

Similar to the third game, the number of variables being selected—birds in this case—is left open, and so the game is classified as Undefined. Although a maximum of six birds can be in the forest (remember, there are only six birds total), prior to consideration of the rules there could be anywhere from zero to six birds in the forest. This uncertainty increases the difficulty of the game and is an element that must be tracked throughout the game. Of course, since it cannot be determined how many birds are in the forest, there is no pre-set group of selections as in a Defined game:

G H J M S W ^{6}

Inferences:

Like many Undefined Grouping games, this one contains a large number of conditional rules. By using basic linkage, we can draw a slew of inferences. Let us examine these in greater detail:

1. J ◄—┼—► G. This inference results from linking the first two rules.

2. M ◄—┼—► G. This inference results from linking the first two rules.

3. W ◄—┼—► H. This inference results from linking the first and third rules.

4. J ◄—┼—► W. This inference results from linking the first inference and the third rule. Note how the first inference has been recombined or "recycled" with the original rules.

5. M ◄—┼—► W. This inference results from linking the second inference and the third rule. The third rule here refers to the rules as listed in the game.

6. $\cancel{S}$ ——► J ——► H ——► $\cancel{G}$, $\cancel{W}$. The final rule is tricky and bears further analysis. When J is not in the forest, then S must be in the forest. Via the contrapositive, when S is not in the forest, then J must be in the forest. In each case, the absence of one of the birds forces the other bird to appear in the forest. This type of "omission" rule appears infrequently on LSAT games, but when it does, it tends to cause problems. It is easy to forget that the absence of a variable forces other variables to be present. In this case, when S is not in the forest, then J must be in the forest, and from the second rule, when J is in the forest, it follows that H must be in the forest. Of course, from the first rule and third inference, when H is in the forest, then G cannot be in the forest and W cannot be in the forest.

7. W ——► $\cancel{J}$ ——► S. From the fourth inference it is known that W and J cannot be in the forest together. Thus, when W is in the forest, then J cannot be in the forest, and from the last rule it follows that S must be in the forest (W ——► S). This is another classic example of recycling an inference.

8. G ——► $\cancel{J}$ ——► S. Similar to the previous inference, when G is in the forest, then J cannot be in the forest, and from the last rule it follows that S must be in the forest (G ——► S).

In light of all these inferences, the bigger question becomes, "When do you know you have made all of the inferences?" In this case the application of basic Linkage creates a large number of inferences, and then the recycling of those inferences leads to even more inferences. At some point the time pressure of this section demands that you move on to the questions. Although in our diagram we could continue to make inferences (for example, if H is not in the forest, then J is not in the forest and S must be in the forest), there comes a point when you must ask yourself, "Do I have enough information to effectively attack the questions?" The answer here is undeniably "yes." It may be that you do not discover every inference in the game (as with the first game in this section), but when you feel you have exhausted all the obvious routes of inference-making, it is time to move on to the questions. The challenge in the questions then becomes keeping track of all the information at your disposal.

Question #6: Global, Cannot Be True, List. The correct answer choice is (D).

In attacking this question, keep in mind that since each answer choice is supposed to be a complete and accurate list of the birds not in the forest, all of the birds not named on each list will be in the forest. Given the number of negative grouping rules in play, that is an important consideration. For example, in answer choice (B), when only H and G are not in the forest, J, M, S, and W are in the forest. But, according to the fourth inference, J and W cannot both be in the forest and therefore answer choice (B) is incorrect. Answer choice (E) can be eliminated by identical reasoning. Answer choice (C) can be eliminated because, via the third inference, H and W cannot both be in the forest. Answer choice (A) can be eliminated by applying the last rule. Answer choice (D) is therefore proven correct by process of elimination.

Question #7: Local, Must Be True. The correct answer choice is (E)

If H is in the forest, then G cannot be in the forest. If G cannot be in the forest, then W cannot be in the forest. At this point it has been established that H and M are in the forest and G and W are not in the forest. The only unaddressed birds are S and J, and at least one of them, possibly both, must be in the forest. Answer choices (A) and (B) are therefore incorrect because it is possible that both S and J can be in the forest. Answer choice (C) is incorrect because, due to the final rule, the forest always contains at least S or J. Answer choice (D) is incorrect because it is possible there is only one other kind of bird in the forest (S or J). Answer choice (E) is thus correct since at most S and J can be in the forest in addition to M and H.

Question #8: Local, Cannot Be True. The correct answer choice is (D)

This question has been phrased in terms of falsity. Remember, always convert "false" questions into terms of "true." As discussed earlier, "Must Be False" is identical to "Cannot Be True," and so this question simply asks which one of the following Cannot Be True. If J is not in the forest, then according to the last rule, S must be in the forest, and answer choice (D) cannot be true and is therefore correct.

Question #9: Global, Must Be True, Maximum. The correct answer choice is (C)

In this question you must select the variables in such a way as to maximize the number of birds in the forest. This means that birds that tend to knock out several other birds must be removed. An examination of the list of inferences indicates that W must be removed since, when W is in the forest, then H, J, and M cannot be in the forest. The other bird that must be removed is G since, when G is in the forest, then H cannot be in the forest, and when H is not in the forest, then neither J nor M can be in the forest. If G and W are removed from consideration, then the remaining four birds are J, H, M, and S. Ultimately, four is the maximum number of birds in the forest, and answer choice (C) is correct.

Another approach to this question involves referring to work done on other questions. When this approach is used, hypotheticals are examined to eliminate certain answer choices. For example, in question #7 we were able to determine that four birds could be in the forest: M, H, S, and J. This hypothetical eliminates answer choices (A) and (B). To effectively use this approach, however, it would be best to skip this question and return after completing all other questions in order to have as many hypotheticals as possible.

A third approach involves considering the negative grouping rules in the setup. For example, since the first rule establishes that H and G cannot both be in the forest, answer choice (E) can be rejected. And since at least one of H and G cannot be in the forest and at least one of W and H (or W and J for that matter) cannot be in the forest, a case can also be made against answer choice (D). When you examine these rules, it is important to consider negative grouping rules that contain entirely different sets of variables. You cannot simply count all the negative rules and arrive at an answer because some of the rules will revolve around the same variable, and when that variable is removed the other variables can be selected.

Finally, let's take a moment to examine a mistake that is made by a number of test takers. Some students, upon encountering the final rule, make the classic error of assuming that the jays and the shrikes cannot be in the forest together. As discussed in the Avoiding False Inferences section of this chapter, on page 312, this is a false inference, and thus it is possible for J and S to be in the forest together. Let us take a moment to review:

Most LSAT Logic Game conditional rules place the "not" on the necessary condition, but in this rule, the "not" is on the sufficient condition. While that difference may seem minor, in effect it completely changes the meaning of the rule.

According to the rule, if J is not in the forest, then S must be in the forest, and via the contrapositive if S is not in the forest, then J must be in the forest. Essentially, this means that if either bird (S or J) is absent (not in the forest), then the other bird cannot also be absent (they cannot both be out of the forest at the same time; at least one must always be in the forest). In other words, all we know from the fourth rule is that they will never both be *out* of the forest, because as soon as one is out the other must be in. They could, however, both be in the forest at the same time. The rules never tell us anything about what happens when either J or S is *in* the forest, only what happens when J or S is not in the forest.

Since it is possible for both J and S to be in the forest at the same time, that possibility impacts the choices you have in questions #9 and #10. In #9, most people assume that one of J or S is always out of the forest. Obviously, that is not the case, and when arriving at the maximum number of birds in the forest you should include both J and S. In question #10, many people select answer choice (B) because they misinterpret the fourth rule. As explained above, J and S—the pair in answer choice (B) of question #10—can both be in the forest at the same time.

Question #10: Global, Cannot Be True. The correct answer choice is (A)

With Global Must Be True or Global Cannot Be True questions always make sure to check your inferences as the first step in attacking the question. Per inference #4 answer choice (A) is correct.

Note that this possibility is also discussed in the solution to question #9.

Question #11: Local, Must Be True. The correct answer choice is (A)

Per the final inference, when G is in the forest, then S must be in the forest, and answer choice (A) is proven correct. A review of the entire inference chain shows that, when G is in the forest, then H is not in the forest (from rule #1), and when H is not in the forest, then neither J nor M is in the forest (from rule #2). When J is not in the forest, then S must be in the forest (from rule #4).

In this question, be sure to avoid making a Mistaken Reversal: although from the third rule we know that when W is in the forest then G must be in the forest, this does not mean that when G in the forest that W must also be in the forest.

Question #12: Local, Could Be True. The correct answer choice is (B)

This is not a Suspension question because the rule is simply added to the given information. In this way it acts like a normal Local question. The extra condition stipulates that S and H cannot both be in the forest. This affects both J and M because, when either J or M is in the forest, then H is in the forest. Thus, neither J and S nor M and S can be in the forest at the same time. This information is sufficient to reject answer choices (A) and (C). Answer choice (D) can also be rejected since, when J is not in the forest, then S must be in the forest, and when S is in the forest, then H is not in the forest, and when H is not in the forest, then neither J nor M is in the forest. Finally, answer choice (E) can be disproven since if H, for example, is in the forest, then G, S, and W are not in the forest. It follows that answer choice (B) is correct.

Despite the large number of inferences in this particular game, the typical student eventually comes to find this type of game completely reasonable, and certainly doable in the allotted time. As you develop the ability to make inferences more quickly, you will begin to see a game like this one as an opportunity to make up time, especially if you know how to handle the last rule.

Chapter Six: Grouping/Linear Combinations Games

Chapter Six: Grouping/Linear Combinations Games

Working with the Combination of Major Principles

Grouping and Linearity are the two fundamental principles test makers use to form the Logic Games section, and typically over 90% of the games in each section feature at least one of these concepts. It is not surprising, therefore, to see a number of games that combine these principles.

Because Chapters Three, Four, and Five covered the basic principles of linearity and grouping, an extensive review of those ideas is unnecessary. However, when attacking games that combine these principles, keep in mind this basic Hierarchy of Game Power™:

The diagram above indicates that the higher term dominates the lower term. When you set up a game, always consider the dominant term first. Because a group must be established before the members of that group can be lined up, always examine the grouping elements first, and then examine the linear elements. Although this may seem like a logical recommendation, students often tend to gravitate towards examining linearity first because they typically feel most comfortable with that concept. Naturally, this hierarchy can also be seen in real life:

> Suppose that you are offered six free Super Bowl tickets. Your first reaction wouldn't be to start putting people in the first seat, or second seat, or sixth seat, etc. Instead, you would first select the group of six people to attend the game and then, once at the game, consider how to line up the individuals in the seats.

Typically, in Grouping/Linear combination games an Unbalanced: Overloaded set of variables must be narrowed down and then the remaining variables must be placed into a diagram that has a linear element. For example, consider the following:

> A theater director must select exactly seven of nine plays to be presented over seven consecutive months, January through July.

The Hierarchy of Game Power will be revisited in Chapter Nine in the Numerical Distribution section. At that time the Hierarchy will be expanded to include numerical ideas.

This example will also be expanded in Chapter Nine.

6

The first point of emphasis will be to watch the grouping rules, especially since the nine-into-seven relationship leaves only two "extra" plays that won't be presented. This is a very small margin, and if any two plays are knocked out by the rules, then each of the remaining seven plays must be presented. Thus, in these games, negative grouping rules take on a heightened importance. When a play is known to be presented—whether from the rules or from a question—first examine how that affects the plays still under consideration to be selected, and whether any other plays are eliminated from contention.

After you examine the grouping aspect of the game, the second point of emphasis will be to consider how the linear rules affect the plays being presented. Although in each case it may be impossible to determine every play presented, the rules will undoubtedly allow for linear inferences irrespective of the grouping element.

Thus, we can distill the correct approach to these games into two steps:

1. Focus on the Grouping aspect of the game and determine if any variables must be selected and which variables are the most powerful. In any question, first attempt to determine the group of variables that must be selected.

2. In each question, once you have isolated as many of the variables in use as possible, next focus on the ordering rules and use your knowledge of Linear games to manipulate the variables, make inferences, and solve the questions.

With this in mind, let's look at one more example:

A hospital administrator must schedule a supervising physician for the morning and evening shifts at a hospital over a single two-day weekend. Exactly one physician serves as the supervising physician each shift, and no physician can serve as supervising physician more than once. The administrator must select from the following list: Gomez, Han, Jackson, Klein, Linden, Martinez, and Otan. The following conditions must apply:
   Han must be one of the supervising physicians on Saturday.
   Either Jackson or Klein must work as a supervising physician during the weekend, but both cannot work during the weekend.
   Either Martinez or Otan must work as a supervising physician during the weekend, but both cannot work during the weekend.
   If Linden works as supervising physician during the weekend, then she must work earlier than Han.

In this example, the first step is to establish the Grouping parameters, namely that there are seven candidates for four ordered positions:

G H J K L M O⁷

PM ___ ___
AM ___ ___ | ___ ___ ___
    Sa   Su | Out

Because exactly four of the seven physicians will be selected, three physicians will always be "out" in this game, and that fact has been shown as a separate "out" group. On the selection side of the diagram, Saturday and Sunday have been chosen as the base, with AM and PM used to delineate the morning and evening shifts (AM or PM can appear as the bottom row depending on your diagramming preference).

With the basic diagram established, next turn your attention to the rules about grouping, namely the first three rules. In those three rules, H is included in the selection group, with the stipulation that H works on Saturday. The other two rules establish that J and K do not work together, and M and O do not work together. This effectively eliminates two physicians from consideration, and greatly limits the number of available physicians to fill the available positions. Let us consider the general "in" and "out" groups for a moment:

From the first rule, H must be in the "in" group, and from the second and third rules, exactly one of J and K, and exactly one of M and O must be in the "in" group, and the other must be in the "out" group:

___ ___ ___ ___ | ___ ___ ___
 H   J/K M/O | K/J O/M
       In | Out
                           H̶

Note that this scenario leaves a limited set of variables available for the remaining space in each group: only G and L remain unaddressed, and although both are randoms, the restrictions created by the scenario and other rules result in the inference that exactly one of G and L must be in the "in" group, and the other must be in the "out" group:

$$\underline{H} \quad \underline{J/K} \quad \underline{M/O} \quad \underline{G/L} \quad \Big| \quad \underline{K/J} \quad \underline{O/M} \quad \underline{L/G}$$

$$\text{In} \qquad\qquad\qquad\qquad \text{Out}$$

At this point, the fourth and final rule should be considered, which is a Linear rule that ultimately forces L into the Saturday AM slot and H into the Saturday PM slot when L is selected as a supervising physician.

After careful consideration of the Grouping aspect and then the Linear aspect, your approach to these games should then be the same as any other Grouping or Linear game.

Grouping/Linear Combination Setup Practice Drill

Each of the following items presents a scenario and corresponding rules similar to those found in actual Logic Games. Using the space provided, diagram the setup and include a representation of all rules and inferences. Each problem contains a corresponding question or questions. Use your knowledge of the rules and the setup to answer the question(s). After you complete *each* item, check your work against the diagram in the answer key, and carefully read the comments concerning each diagram. *Answers on page 396*

1. A television executive must schedule exactly three of six television programs—Priceless, Quest, Reckoning, SingOff, Trauma, and Unspeakable for Saturday evening programming that runs consecutively from 8 P.M. until 11 P.M. Each program is exactly one hour in length, and no program is shown more than once. The following conditions must apply:

    Singoff must be scheduled earlier than Unspeakable if both are scheduled.

    If Reckoning is scheduled, then Trauma is scheduled.

    Either Priceless or Quest is scheduled for 8 P.M., but both cannot be scheduled for the evening programming.

Question 1.1. Which one of the following could be the three programs scheduled for Saturday evening, in order from earliest to latest?

  (A)   Priceless, Reckoning, Unspeakable
  (B)   Priceless, SingOff, Quest
  (C)   Quest, Unspeakable, Trauma
  (D)   Quest, Unspeakable, SingOff
  (E)   SingOff, Trauma, Reckoning

Question 1.2. If Trauma is not scheduled for the evening's programming, then which one of the following must be true?

  (A)   Priceless is scheduled for 8 P.M.
  (B)   Quest is scheduled for 8 P.M.
  (C)   Reckoning is scheduled for 9 P.M.
  (D)   SingOff is scheduled for 10 P.M.
  (E)   Unspeakable is scheduled for 10 P.M.

6

Grouping/Linear Combination Setup Practice Drill

2. A zoo will schedule exactly six different tours over three days—days 1, 2, and 3. Each day there will be exactly two tours given, one in the morning and one in the afternoon. The six tours are drawn from a group of nine tours—Amphibians, Birds, Continents, Fish, Habitats, Insects, Mammals, Plants, and Reptiles. The schedule is bound by the following constraints:

    Amphibians and Reptiles can only be scheduled for the afternoon.

    If Birds is scheduled, then Mammals must the very next tour scheduled.

    Continents is scheduled for day 1 if and only if Plants is scheduled for day 3, and Plants is scheduled for day 1 if and only if Continents is scheduled for day 3.

    Neither Fish nor Habitats can be scheduled for the same day as Insects.

Question 2.1. Which one of the following could be the schedule of tours?

- (A)   Day 1 morning: Birds; Day 1 afternoon: Continents
      Day 2 morning: Mammals; Day 2 afternoon: Fish
      Day 3 morning: Plants; Day 3 afternoon: Insects
- (B)   Day 1 morning: Fish; Day 1 afternoon: Habitats
      Day 2 morning: Continents; Day 2 afternoon: Insects
      Day 3 morning: Reptiles; Day 3 afternoon: Amphibians
- (C)   Day 1 morning: Habitats; Day 1 afternoon: Insects
      Day 2 morning: Birds; Day 2 afternoon: Mammals
      Day 3 morning: Fish; Day 3 afternoon: Amphibians
- (D)   Day 1 morning: Insects; Day 1 afternoon: Plants
      Day 2 morning: Continents; Day 2 afternoon: Birds
      Day 3 morning: Mammals; Day 3 afternoon: Fish
- (E)   Day 1 morning: Mammals; Day 1 afternoon: Amphibians
      Day 2 morning: Plants; Day 2 afternoon: Habitats
      Day 3 morning: Insects; Day 3 afternoon: Reptiles

Question 2.2. If Insects and Birds are scheduled for the afternoons of day 1 and day 2, respectively, which one of the following CANNOT be true?

- (A)   Continents is scheduled for day 1.
- (B)   Fish is scheduled for day 2.
- (C)   Habitats is scheduled for day 3.
- (D)   Mammals is scheduled for day 3.
- (E)   Plants is scheduled for day 3.

Grouping/Linear Combination Setup Practice Drill

3. A human resources manager reviewing a group of seven applicants—D, G, I, K, M, Q, and R—must select exactly five of the applicants for interviews. The interviews will be conducted during a single afternoon, one at a time, with each applicant being interviewed exactly once, consistent with the following conditions:

> If D is interviewed, then G is interviewed.
>
> If G is interviewed, then M is interviewed.
>
> Q is interviewed, and must be interviewed earlier than K and R if either are interviewed.
>
> If I is not interviewed then R must be interviewed.

Question 3.1. Which one of the following applicants must be interviewed?

    (A)   D
    (B)   G
    (C)   K
    (D)   M
    (E)   R

Question 3.2. If G is not interviewed, which one of the following CANNOT be true?

    (A)   I is interviewed first.
    (B)   K is interviewed second.
    (C)   M is interviewed first.
    (D)   Q is interviewed fourth.
    (E)   R is interviewed third.

6

Grouping/Linear Combination Setup Practice Drill

4. From ten comics—Arkan, Chen, Davide, Fine, Gutierrez, Hancock, Jensen, Klatt, Liu, and Nassif—exactly eight will be scheduled for individual performances on four consecutive days—Thursday, Friday, Saturday, and Sunday. Each day, exactly two comics perform—one on an east stage and one on a west stage. The performances are subject to the following constraints:

> Liu performs on the day immediately before the day Nassif performs.
> Arkan and Chen cannot perform on Thursday.
> Gutierrez, Hancock, and Jensen cannot perform on the east stage.
> Davide and Klatt cannot perform on the same day.
> Fine cannot perform on Saturday unless Hancock perform on Saturday.

Question 4.1. If Davide performs Thursday on the west stage, and Nassif performs on Saturday, then which one of the following must be true?

    (A)   Arkan performs Friday on the east stage.
    (B)   Fine performs Thursday on the east stage.
    (C)   Gutierrez performs Saturday on the west stage.
    (D)   Hancock performs Sunday on the west stage.
    (E)   Liu performs Friday on the east stage.

Question 4.2. If the comics performing on the west stage are Davide, Fine, Jensen, and Klatt, not necessarily in that order, which one of the following could be true?

    (A)   Chen performs Sunday.
    (B)   Fine performs Saturday.
    (C)   Gutierrez performs Friday.
    (D)   Hancock performs Thursday.
    (E)   Nassif performs Saturday.

Grouping/Linear Combination Setup Practice Drill

5. From the seven remaining finalists at a biennial dog show—Lawrence, Monty, Nora, Opey, Ponch, Quirks, and Rusty—only the top five are ranked by number and awarded trophies, consistent with the following conditions:

If Nora is awarded a trophy, Opey does not win a trophy.

If Monty wins a trophy, Ponch must also win a trophy, and Ponch's rank must be exactly three spots lower than Monty's rank.

Rusty does not win the fourth place trophy.

Question 5.1. Which one of the following CANNOT be True?

(A) Monty is not awarded a trophy, and Opey is awarded a trophy.

(B) Rusty is not awarded a trophy, and Nora is awarded a trophy.

(C) Monty wins the second place trophy, and Quirks is not awarded a trophy.

(D) Opey wins the first place trophy, and Ponch wins the second place trophy.

(E) Nora is awarded a trophy, and Ponch is not awarded a trophy.

Question 5.2. Which one of the following, if true, would determine the ranks of all five trophy winners?

(A) Ponch's rank is above Opey's, and directly below Quirk's.

(B) Quirk's rank is below Monty's, and directly above Ponch's

(C) Lawrence wins the first place trophy, and Nora wins the third place trophy

(D) Monty's rank is below Nora's, and directly above Lawrence's

(E) Monty wins the first place trophy, and Quirks wins the second place trophy

6

1. A television executive must schedule exactly three of
   six television programs—Priceless, Quest, Reckoning,
   SingOff, Trauma, and Unspeakable for Saturday
   evening programming that runs consecutively from 8
   P.M. until 11 P.M. Each program is exactly one hour
   in length, and no program is shown more than once.
   The following conditions must apply:

   Singoff must be scheduled earlier than
   Unspeakable if both are scheduled.

   If Reckoning is scheduled, then Trauma is
   scheduled.

   Either Priceless or Quest is scheduled for 8 P.M.,
   but both cannot be scheduled for the evening
   programming.

The scenario states that there are six programs for three scheduling positions, and that the programs
are scheduled in a Linear fashion. The "six into three" relationship means that three programs are
always selected and three are not selected, and with that many "extra" variables, the Grouping aspect
is not overly restricted in the game.

The initial scenario appears as follows:

P Q R S T U⁶

$$\underline{\quad}\ \underline{\quad}\ \underline{\quad}\ \bigg|\ \underline{\quad}\ \underline{\quad}\ \underline{\quad}$$
$$8\quad 9\quad 10\qquad\qquad Out$$

The first rule is a conditional sequencing rule, meaning that the sequencing relationship is forced to
occur if the sufficient condition is met, which in this case is when S and U are both scheduled:

$$\begin{matrix} S \\ + \\ U \end{matrix} \longrightarrow (S \text{——} U)$$

Thus, if both S and U are scheduled, S cannot be scheduled for 10 P.M., and U cannot be scheduled
for 8 P.M. But, if one of the two is not scheduled, then there are no restrictions on the scheduling of
the other program.

The second rule is also conditional, and indicates that if R is scheduled then T is scheduled:

$$R \longrightarrow T$$

This rule is important because it has a significant effect on the group of programs that can be scheduled at this point:

> If R is scheduled, then every scheduling group must consist of R and T, and the choice of P, Q, S, or U.

> If T is *not* scheduled, then via the contrapositive R is not scheduled, and only P, Q, S, and U are available to be scheduled for the three programming positions.

Both groups becomes further limited when the third rule is considered.

The third rule is really two rules in one. First, the rule establishes that P or Q must be scheduled for 8 P.M., and then it establishes that both P and Q cannot be scheduled. Thus, one is always scheduled for 8 P.M., and the other is always out of the scheduling group:

$$\underset{8}{\underline{P/Q}} \quad \underset{9}{\underline{}} \quad \underset{10}{\underline{}} \quad \Big| \quad \underset{}{\underline{Q/P}} \quad \underset{Out}{\underline{}} \quad \underline{}$$

Because this third rule automatically eliminates one of the six programs from consideration, take a moment to consider its effects, especially in regard to the second rule which already limited the selection of programs. Specifically, when R is selected, then the selection group is P or Q, R, and T:

$$\underset{8}{\underline{P/Q}} \quad \underset{9}{\underline{R/T}} \quad \underset{10}{\underline{T/R}} \quad \Big| \quad \underset{}{\underline{Q/P}} \quad \underset{Out}{\underline{S}} \quad \underline{U}$$

6

Grouping/Linear Combination Setup Practice Drill Answer Key

When T is not selected, the following must occur:

If T is *not* scheduled, then via the contrapositive R is not scheduled, and only P, Q, S, and U are available to be scheduled for the three programming positions. However, because P and Q cannot both be selected, only one can be scheduled, and that program must be scheduled for 8 P.M. thus, the other two programs that must be scheduled are S and U, and due to the effects of the first rule, S and U must be scheduled for 9 P.M. and 10 P.M. respectively:

$$\underset{8}{\underline{P/Q}} \quad \underset{9}{\underline{S}} \quad \underset{10}{\underline{U}} \quad \Big| \quad \underset{}{\underline{Q/P}} \quad \underset{Out}{\underline{R}} \quad \underline{T}$$

Note that other solutions to the game do exist (namely when R is not selected). With the rules analyzed and their interaction considered, you should now move to the questions.

Question 1.1. Which one of the following could be the three programs scheduled for Saturday evening, in order from earliest to latest?

(A)   Priceless, Reckoning, Unspeakable
(B)   Priceless, SingOff, Quest
(C)   Quest, Unspeakable, Trauma
(D)   Quest, Unspeakable, SingOff
(E)   SingOff, Trauma, Reckoning

Question 1.1. This is a standard List question, so apply the rules to each of the answer choices, eliminating incorrect answer choices along the way.

Answer choice (A) is incorrect because from the second rule, when R is scheduled then T must also be scheduled.

Answer choice (B) is incorrect because from the third rule, both P and Q cannot be scheduled for the evening programming.

Answer choice (C) is the correct answer.

Answer choice (D) is incorrect because from the first rule, when both S and U are scheduled, S must be scheduled earlier than U.

Answer choice (E) is incorrect because from the third rule, either P or Q must be scheduled for 8 P.M.

Grouping/Linear Combination Setup Practice Drill Answer Key

<u>Question 1.2</u>. If Trauma is not scheduled for the evening's programming, then which one of the following must be true?

    (A)   Priceless is scheduled for 8 P.M.
    (B)   Quest is scheduled for 8 P.M.
    (C)   Reckoning is scheduled for 9 P.M.
    (D)   SingOff is scheduled for 10 P.M.
    (E)   Unspeakable is scheduled for 10 P.M.

Question 1.2. As discussed during the setup, from the second rule when T is not scheduled then via the contrapositive R cannot be scheduled, leaving only P, Q, S, and U available to be scheduled for the three programming positions. However, because P and Q cannot both be selected due to the third rule, S and U must both be scheduled, resulting in the final setup for this question:

$$\frac{P/Q}{8} \quad \frac{S}{9} \quad \frac{U}{10} \quad \bigg| \quad \frac{Q/P}{} \quad \frac{R}{Out} \quad \frac{T}{}$$

Accordingly, answer choice (E) must be true and is therefore correct.

2. A zoo will schedule exactly six different tours over three days—days 1, 2, and 3. Each day there will be exactly two tours given, one in the morning and one in the afternoon. The six tours are drawn from a group of nine tours—Amphibians, Birds, Continents, Fish, Habitats, Insects, Mammals, Plants, and Reptiles. The schedule is bound by the following constraints:

    Amphibians and Reptiles can only be scheduled for the afternoon.

    If Birds is scheduled, then Mammals must the very next tour scheduled.

    Continents is scheduled for day 1 if and only if Plants is scheduled for day 3, and Plants is scheduled for day 1 if and only if Continents is scheduled for day 3.

    Neither Fish nor Habitats can be scheduled for the same day as Insects.

The scenario states that there are exactly nine available tours for six schedule positions, and indicates the scheduling conforms to an Advanced Linear setup. The "nine into six" Grouping aspect means that exactly three of the applicants are always "out," and thus there is a reasonable margin to work with to form the group. This makes the Grouping aspect less important than in a more restricted game, but still something that should always be considered. The initial setup appears as follows:

A B C F H I M P R⁹

The first rule is easily displayed using side Not Laws on the morning row:

The second rule is more complicated than the first, and creates an unusual block that is triggered by the presence of B. This block is vertical if B is scheduled for the morning (and thus M is scheduled for the afternoon of the same day), but if B is scheduled for the afternoon, then M must be scheduled for the next tour, which would be the morning of the following day (creating a sort of diagonal block within the diagram):

Note that because the rule is conditional, B can never be scheduled without M, but M can be scheduled without B. Thus, if B is scheduled, it can never be scheduled for the afternoon of day 3:

The third rule creates an interesting double-arrow relationship between C and P when either is scheduled for day 1 or 3:

$$C_{1/3} \longleftrightarrow P_{3/1}$$

Under this rule, if either C or P is scheduled for day 1, the other is scheduled for day 3, and if either C or P is scheduled for day 3, the other is scheduled for day 1. The rule does not mention morning or afternoon, and thus any placement on day 1 or day 3 activates the rule. When this rule is combined with the second rule, a set of interesting inferences results. For example, if B is scheduled for the morning of day 1 or day 3, that forces M into the afternoon of that same day. With day 1 or day 3 fully occupied by B and M, the conditions of the third rule cannot be met, and thus C or P, if they were scheduled, could only be scheduled for day 2.

The fourth rule creates two vertical not-blocks that rotate (hence the circle representation), thus occurring irrespective of morning or evening scheduling:

With each of the rules analyzed, it is time to attack the questions.

    (A)   Day 1 morning: Birds; Day 1 afternoon: Continents
                Day 2 morning: Mammals; Day 2 afternoon: Fish
                Day 3 morning: Plants; Day 3 afternoon: Insects
    (B)   Day 1 morning: Fish; Day 1 afternoon: Habitats
                Day 2 morning: Continents; Day 2 afternoon: Insects
                Day 3 morning: Reptiles; Day 3 afternoon: Amphibians
    (C)   Day 1 morning: Habitats; Day 1 afternoon: Insects
                Day 2 morning: Birds; Day 2 afternoon: Mammals
                Day 3 morning: Fish; Day 3 afternoon: Amphibians
    (D)   Day 1 morning: Insects; Day 1 afternoon: Plants
                Day 2 morning: Continents; Day 2 afternoon: Birds
                Day 3 morning: Mammals; Day 3 afternoon: Fish
    (E)   Day 1 morning: Mammals; Day 1 afternoon: Amphibians
                Day 2 morning: Plants; Day 2 afternoon: Habitats
                Day 3 morning: Insects; Day 3 afternoon: Reptiles

6

Question 2.1. This is a standard List question, so apply the rules to each of the answer choices, eliminating incorrect answer choices as you encounter them.

Answer choice (A) is incorrect because it violates the second rule. While B and M are scheduled for consecutive days, the rule is clear about M being in the *tour* that immediately follows B, which in this case would be the afternoon of day 1 afternoon.

Answer choice (B) is incorrect because R is scheduled for the morning, a violation of the first rule.

Answer choice (C) is incorrect because H and I are scheduled for the same day (day 1), a violation of the fourth rule.

Answer choice (D) is incorrect because P is scheduled for day 1, but C is not scheduled for day 3, a violation of the third rule.

Answer choice (E) is the correct answer. Note that M is scheduled for the morning of day 1, which is acceptable since B is not scheduled at all. Thus, the second rule is not violated.

Question 2.2. If Insects and Birds are scheduled for the afternoons of day 1 and day 2, respectively, which one of the following CANNOT be true?

    (A)   Continents is scheduled for day 1.
    (B)   Fish is scheduled for day 2.
    (C)   Habitats is scheduled for day 3.
    (D)   Mammals is scheduled for day 3.
    (E)   Plants is scheduled for day 3.

Grouping/Linear Combination Setup Practice Drill Answer Key

Question 2.2. The placement of I and B in the afternoons of day 1 and day 2 immediately activates the second rule, forcing M to be scheduled for the morning of day 3:

```
PM    I     B    ___              |
                                  |
AM   ___   ___    M               |   ___   ___   ___
      1     2     3               |          Out
```

From the fourth rule, neither F nor H can be scheduled for the morning of day 1, leaving that slot with a limited number of options:

> I, B, and M are already scheduled elsewhere, and thus they cannot be scheduled for the morning of day 1. From the fourth rule, F and H cannot be scheduled for the morning of day 1, and from the first rule A and R cannot be scheduled for the morning. Thus, seven of the nine tours are eliminated from consideration, leaving only C or P to be scheduled for the morning of day 1.

With C or P scheduled for day 1, the other must be scheduled for day 3. And since the only available position on day 3 is the afternoon, the following setup results:

```
PM    I     B    P/C              |
                                  |
AM   C/P   ___    M               |    A     R    ___
      1     2     3               |         Out
```

With I, B, M, C, and P scheduled, and A and R unavailable due to the first rule, only F and H remain to be scheduled for the morning of day 2:

```
PM    I     B    P/C              |
                                  |
AM   C/P   F/H    M               |    A     R    H/F
      1     2     3               |         Out
```

Accordingly, answer choice (C) cannot be true and is correct.

3. A human resources manager reviewing a group of
   seven applicants—D, G, I, K, M, Q, and R—must
   select exactly five of the applicants for interviews.
   The interviews will be conducted during a single
   afternoon, one at a time, with each applicant being
   interviewed exactly once, consistent with the
   following conditions:

   If D is interviewed, then G is interviewed.
   If G is interviewed, then M is interviewed.
   Q is interviewed, and must be interviewed earlier
     than K and R if either are interviewed.
   If I is not interviewed then R must be interviewed.

The scenario states that there are seven applicants for five interview positions, and that the interviews are conducted in Linear fashion. The "seven into five" Grouping aspect means that just two of the applicants are always "out," and thus there is a small margin to work with to form the group. This fact plays a role in both questions.

Each of the rules has a Grouping element. The first two rules can be combined into a chain relationship:

This chain is exceedingly important, because it establishes that M is a necessary condition for two other applicants, D and G. Thus, via the contrapositive, if M were not interviewed, then D and G could not be interviewed, resulting in three applicants not interviewed. This would violate the game scenario as only two applicants are not interviewed, and thus we can infer that M must always be interviewed:

$$\underline{\text{M}} \quad \underline{\quad} \quad \underline{\quad} \quad \underline{\quad} \quad \underline{\quad}$$
5 Interviewees

The third rule is actually two rules in one. The first part of the rules establishes that Q is interviewed, and thus Q can be added to the interview selection group:

$$\underline{\text{M}} \quad \underline{\text{Q}} \quad \underline{\quad} \quad \underline{\quad} \quad \underline{\quad}$$
5 Interviewees

The second part of the rule is a conditional sequencing rule, meaning that the rule only comes into play once the sufficient condition is enacted. In this case, the sufficient condition is that K or R, or both, are selected to be interviewed. When that occurs, then Q must be interviewed earlier than any of K and R. This is not the easiest rule to diagram, but it should appear as follows:

$$
\begin{matrix}
K & & & & & K \\
or & \longrightarrow & Q & & \diagup & \\
R & & & & & \diagdown & R \\
\end{matrix}
$$

The fourth rule contains a negative sufficient condition, and can be diagrammed as:

$$
\cancel{I} \longrightarrow R
$$
$$
\cancel{R} \longrightarrow I
$$

Because the absence of either I or R forces the other to be interviewed, the operational effect of this rule is that at the minimum, I or R is *always* interviewed (and possibly both are interviewed). Thus, the interview pool can be can be narrowed further:

$$
\underline{\text{M}} \quad \underline{\text{Q}} \quad \underline{\text{I/R}} \quad \underline{\quad} \quad \underline{\quad}
$$
$$
\text{5 Interviewees}
$$

6

This information can be combined to produce the final setup for the game:

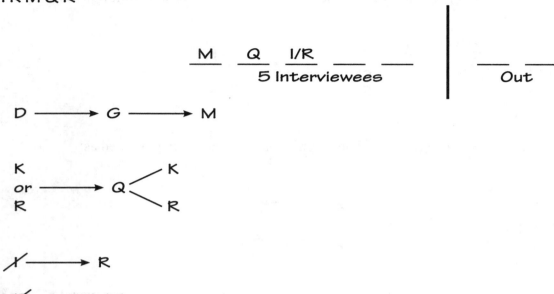

With the setup to the game in hand, we can now turn to the two questions.

Question 3.1. Which one of the following applicants must be interviewed?

    (A)   D
    (B)   G
    (C)   K
    (D)   M
    (E)   R

Question 3.1. As discussed during the setup, because M is a necessary condition for two variables (D and G), removing M from the interview group would not allow five interviews to be scheduled. Thus, M must always be interviewed, and answer choice (D) is correct.

Question 3.2. If G is not interviewed, which one of the following CANNOT be true?

    (A)   I is interviewed first.
    (B)   K is interviewed second.
    (C)   M is interviewed first.
    (D)   Q is interviewed fourth.
    (E)   R is interviewed third.

Question 3.2. If G is not interviewed, then from the contrapositive of the first rule D also can not be interviewed. Thus, the other five applicants— I, K, M, Q, and R—must be interviewed. With K and R interviewed, the second portion of the third rule is enacted, and Q must be interviewed earlier than K and R, creating the following setup:

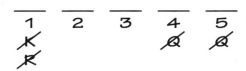

The question asks for what cannot be true, and thus the four incorrect answers could be true. As shown by the Not Laws above, Q cannot be interviewed fourth, and thus answer choice (D) is correct.

4. From ten comics—Arkan, Chen, Davide, Fine, Gutierrez, Hancock, Jensen, Klatt, Liu, and Nassif— exactly eight will be scheduled for individual performances on four consecutive days—Thursday, Friday, Saturday, and Sunday. Each day, exactly two comics perform—one on an east stage and one on a west stage. The performances are subject to the following constraints:

    Liu performs on the day immediately before the day Nassif performs.

    Arkan and Chen cannot perform on Thursday.

    Gutierrez, Hancock, and Jensen cannot perform on the east stage.

    Davide and Klatt cannot perform on the same day.

    Fine cannot perform on Saturday unless Hancock perform on Saturday.

Although games that feature the days of the week almost always have the days as a horizontal base, in this instance the geographic aspect of west and east makes the most sense to use as the horizontal base, and then the days are used as a vertical element, as follows:

ACDFGHJKLN[10]

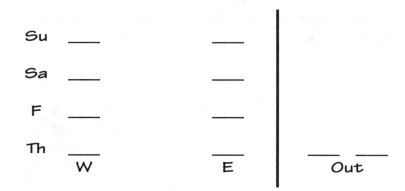

Thursday can be the lowest row of spaces on the diagram (as shown above) or the highest row—the choice is personal and has no operational effect on the game.

The rules are relatively reasonable to diagram, starting with the first rule:

The "day" notation allows the block to be shown without regard for the exact stage each comic performs on each day. This rule also spawns Not Laws on Thursday and Sunday:

Note that this rule is not conditional because the language states that L and N both perform (and will each perform once); if there had been conditional language included (such as "*If* Liu performs..." or "on *any* day immediately before"), then the block representation would need to be presented as the necessary portion of a conditional relationship.

The second and third rules can be shown with Not Laws:

Su   ___ X̸   ___ X̸

Sa   ___   ___

F   ___   ___

Th   ___ N̸Ḱ̸C̸   ___ N̸Ḱ̸C̸
     W   E
                  G̸
                  H̸
                  J̸

Note that at this juncture, Thursday's east stage performance is very restricted, with only D, F, L, and K available as performers.

The fourth rule yields a rotating horizontal not-block:

The fifth rule initially appears as follows:

$$F_{SA} \longrightarrow H_{SA}$$

But, after considering the third rule, which states that H cannot perform on the east stage, this rule can be amended to include the information that if F performs on Saturday, it must be on the east stage (with H on the west stage):

$$F_{SAE} \longrightarrow H_{SAW}$$

This also results in the Not Law that F cannot perform on the west stage on Saturday, and the final main diagram for the game:

```
Su  ___  K̸           ___  K̸

Sa  ___  F̸           ___

F   ___               ___

Th  ___  N̸Ȧ̸Ċ̸   D/F/K/L  N̸Ȧ̸Ċ̸
     W                    E
                          G̸
                          H̸
                          J̸
```

6

With this information, and with the focus firmly on the options for Thursday's east stage performance, we can move to the questions.

Question 4.1. If Davide performs Thursday on the west stage, and Nassif performs on Saturday, then which one of the following must be true?

(A) Arkan performs Friday on the east stage.
(B) Fine performs Thursday on the east stage.
(C) Gutierrez performs Saturday on the west stage.
(D) Hancock performs Sunday on the west stage.
(E) Liu performs Friday on the east stage.

Question 4.1. The question stem results in the following initial setup:

```
Su  ___           ___

Sa  N/            /N

F   L/            /L

Th  D             ___
     W             E
```

Note that N and L cannot be specifically placed because neither is tied to a specific stage, just specific days. However, because D, L, and N can no longer perform on Thursday on the east stage, only F remains to perform in that slot. Thus, answer choice (B) must be true and is correct.

Question 4.2. If the comics performing on the west stage are Davide, Fine, Jensen, and Klatt, not necessarily in that order, which one of the following could be true?

   (A)   Chen performs Sunday.
   (B)   Fine performs Saturday.
   (C)   Gutierrez performs Friday.
   (D)   Hancock performs Thursday.
   (E)   Nassif performs Saturday.

Question 4.2. If the comics performing on the west stage are D, F, J, and K, and G and H cannot perform on the east stage, then the east stage comics can only be A, C, L, and N. From that lineup, only L can perform on Thursday, forcing N to perform on Friday. A and C then rotate between Saturday and Sunday:

```
Su    ___              C/A

Sa    ___    F̶        A/C

F     ___              N

Th    ___              L
       W                E
```

Accordingly, answer choice (A) could be true and is correct.

Answer choice (B) is incorrect because, due to the fifth rule, F cannot perform on Saturday unless H performs on Saturday.

Answer choice (C) is incorrect because G cannot perform under the conditions in the question stem.

Answer choice (D) is incorrect because H cannot perform under the conditions in the question stem.

Answer choice (E) is incorrect because N must perform on Friday.

5. From the seven remaining finalists at a biennial dog
    show—Lawrence, Monty, Nora, Opey, Ponch, Quirks,
    and Rusty—only the top five are ranked by number
    and awarded trophies, consistent with the following
    conditions:
    > If Nora is awarded a trophy, Opey does not win a
    > trophy.
    > If Monty wins a trophy, Ponch must also win a
    > trophy, and Ponch's rank must be exactly three
    > spots lower than Monty's rank.
    > Rusty does not win the fourth place trophy

In this scenario, there are seven dogs competing for only five available trophies in the dog show.
There are more finalists than trophies, and this seven-into-five relationship creates an In Group of
exactly five, and an Out Group of exactly two, as follows:

L M N O P Q R⁷

$$\underline{\quad}\ \underline{\quad}\ \underline{\quad}\ \underline{\quad}\ \underline{\quad} \Big| \underline{\quad}\ \underline{\quad}$$
$$\ \ 1\quad 2\quad 3\quad 4\quad 5\qquad Out$$

The first rule specifies that if N wins a trophy O does not win a trophy. This can be diagrammed as a
simple conditional statement:

N ⟶ Ø

The contrapositive would then be diagrammed as follows:

O ⟶ N̸

The entire rule can also be shown as a double-not arrow, as we will show it in this fashion later. This
conditional relationship indicates that *at least* one space in the Out Group must always be reserved
for either N or O, because there cannot be a scenario in which both N and O are awarded trophies (so
one must always be Out). This dual option thus belongs in the Out Group and would be diagrammed
as follows:

L M N O P Q R⁷

$$\underline{\quad}\ \underline{\quad}\ \underline{\quad}\ \underline{\quad}\ \underline{\quad} \Big| \underline{\underset{N/O}{\quad}}\ \underline{\quad}$$
$$\ \ 1\quad 2\quad 3\quad 4\quad 5\qquad Out$$

Note that while the N and O duo must claim at least one spot in the Out Group, they are not limited to just that one position; while the rule requires that at least one of those two be unranked, the rule allows for the prospect that both N and O go home without trophies.

The next rule specifies that if M is ranked among the trophy winners (which will simply be noted as "M" without a subscript for position), P must be ranked exactly three spots lower than M. This conditional rule can be diagrammed as follows:

$$M \longrightarrow \boxed{M \; \_\_ \; \_\_ \; P}$$

Note that if P is three spaces below M's rank, that means that there are exactly *two* spaces between M and P in the block, and thus if M wins a trophy, M must win the first or second place trophy (and P would then win the fourth or fifth place trophy, respectively).

The contrapositive of the rule above would be diagrammed as follows:

$$\boxed{\cancel{M \; \_\_ \; \_\_ \; P}} \longrightarrow \cancel{M}$$

In other words, if there is no room for the $\boxed{M \; \_\_ \; \_\_ \; P}$ block, then M cannot win a trophy. Consequently, if P is neither fourth nor fifth (the only places it can occupy in the $\boxed{M \; \_\_ \; \_\_ \; P}$ block configuration), then M must be unranked:

$$\cancel{P}_{4/5} \longrightarrow \cancel{M}$$

Looking at this rule further, note that it puts M in a position of needing P. When M wins a trophy, then P must also win a trophy. But what if P wasn't ranked (which is a variation on the contrapositive here)? That would knock M out of the trophy rankings as well, which would create an issue: M, P, and either N or O would all be unranked, which is too many dogs in the Out Group (3 for just 2 places). Thus, because of the limitation on the number of unranked dogs, we can infer that P *always* wins a trophy, which we can show with Not Laws on both unranked spots. Does that then mean that P must always be fourth or fifth? No, because M does not have to win a trophy, and if M is unranked, P is free to occupy any position. However, if M wins a trophy, it must be first or second, meaning that it can never be third, fourth, or fifth, leading to the following setup through the first two rules:

L M N O P Q R[7]

CHAPTER SIX: GROUPING/LINEAR COMBINATION GAMES

The third rule states that R cannot win the fourth place trophy, rounding out the global game diagram as follows:

L M N O P Q R⁷

L and Q do not appear in any rule and are thus are noted as randoms.

Question 5.1. Which one of the following CANNOT be True?

(A) Monty is not awarded a trophy, and Opey is awarded a trophy.

(B) Rusty is not awarded a trophy, and Nora is awarded a trophy.

(C) Monty wins the second place trophy, and Quirks is not awarded a trophy.

(D) Opey wins the first place trophy, and Ponch wins the second place trophy.

(E) Nora is awarded a trophy, and Ponch is not awarded a trophy.

Question 5.1. This is a global Cannot Be True question, which means that the correct answer choice will be the only one that is prohibited by the game's basic setup. The four incorrect answer choices, then, will all fall under the category of "could be true" (including the possibility that an incorrect answer choice *must* be true).

If you scan the answer choices, you can pick out that answer choice (E) must be the correct answer since it contains P not being awarded a trophy, which is impossible as discussed previously. But let's go through each answer since many people miss that inference about P in the setup.

Answer choice (A) is incorrect because it could be true. If M is ranked, it has a much greater impact on the overall setup than if M is unranked, as here. In other words, there is nothing prohibiting M's presence in the Out Group, and O's ranking among the top five is not problematic either; this would simply dictate that N be a member of the Out Group with M.

Answer choice (B) is incorrect because it could be true. R never wins fourth place, but nothing in the rules precludes its placing among the two unranked spots in the Out Group. When O takes the other position in the Out Group (due to N winning a trophy), this leads to the inference that M is among the top five, meaning that the M ___ ___ P block is present, either in spaces 1 - 4 or spaces 2 - 5:

1. M _____ P   R   O

2. ___ M _____ P | R   O
    1   2   3   4   5   ‾‾Out‾‾
                R̶

Answer choice (C) is incorrect because it could be true. M placing second would require that P place fifth. No rule, or convergence of rules, dictates that Q must win a trophy, so that requirement would present no issues, presuming that a space is reserved in the Out Group for either O or N, and R goes first or third:

    ___ M ___ ___ P | O/N Q
    1   2   3   4   5   ‾‾Out‾‾
                R̶

Answer choice (D) is incorrect because it could be true. If O wins the first place trophy, that dictates that N is part of the Out Group. Note that P's second place finish means that M cannot possibly win a trophy, considering the contrapositive of the M ___ ___ P block conditional rule:

    O   P   R/ L/Q /R | N   M
    1   2   3   4   5   ‾‾Out‾‾
                R̶

Answer choice (E) is the correct answer choice, because it is the only choice that cannot be true under any circumstances. If N is awarded a trophy, that means that O must be a member of the Out Group. If, as this choice provides, P is also a member of the Out Group, that means M must win a trophy (as there are no more Out Group spaces available), conflicting with the conditional M ___ ___ P block rule.

Question 5.2. Which one of the following, if true, would determine the ranks of all five trophy winners?

- (A) Ponch's rank is above Opey's, and directly below Quirk's.
- (B) Quirk's rank is below Monty's, and directly above Ponch's
- (C) Lawrence wins the first place trophy, and Nora wins the third place trophy
- (D) Monty's rank is below Nora's, and directly above Lawrence's
- (E) Monty wins the first place trophy, and Quirks wins the second place trophy

Question 5.2. Although this is technically a Global question since it does not introduce a new condition or restraint, it is a bit like a "5 if" question, in that you are forced to consider five separate local scenarios. If you are running low on time these are often good questions to skip and come back to later.

Your initial thought here should be to evaluate which variables are most powerful and which need to be addressed in some way. First, placing M would be extremely helpful since it places P. Addressing N or O would also be useful since if one of them wins a trophy the other does not. Last, both L and Q are randoms, and somehow they need to be placed. Only one answer (which is D) addresses all three of those elements, and ultimately (D) turns out to be correct. But let's look at each answer and see what occurs.

Answer choice (A): This choice introduces several new conditions, but it is incorrect because it fails to establish all five trophy-winning dogs.

First, P is ranked in a spot above O's rank (P ——— O), and second, P is ranked directly below Q (QP). These two new conditions can be expressed as the following QP ——— O. Since this rule requires that O is ranked, that means that N must take one spot in the Out Group. This choice is incorrect, however, because the new conditions introduced still leave many placement options alive in the diagram.

Answer choice (B): This choice provides that Q's rank is in some spot below M's rank (M ——— Q), and that Q is ranked directly above P (QP). Together, these could be diagrammed as M ——— QP .

Further, since this choice establishes that M is ranked, this brings the M __ __ P block into play, combining with the new conditions from this choice as follows:

M _ Q P

6

Although this choice provides some additional information, it still leaves a significant degree of flexibility and can thus be ruled out of contention.

Answer choice (C): This choice allows us to fill in the blanks for both the first and third trophies, and, since N wins a trophy, it means that O must join the unranked Out Group. Since this choice leaves much of the diagram unestablished, however, it cannot be the correct answer and should be eliminated.

Answer choice (D): This is the correct answer choice. Since this choice provides that N is ranked, that leads to the inference that O must be among the unranked in the Out Group. Since M is ranked, the large $\boxed{\text{M \_\_\_ P}}$ block is in effect.

Further, this choice provides that M is directly above L. This new ML block combines with the global $\boxed{\text{M \_\_\_ P}}$ block to create a new block: $\boxed{\text{ML \_ P}}$.

Since this choice also provides that M is below N in the rankings, that pushes the new $\boxed{\text{ML \_ P}}$ block to the right, in spaces 2-5:

The only two variables that remain to be placed are Q and R, and the only remaining space available is 4th place. Since R is prohibited from winning the fourth place trophy, that leaves Q as the only possible contender, completing the diagram as follows:

Answer choice (E): This choice establishes M's placement in the first place position, which also means that P must take the fourth place position. Q's placement is also dictated, but since this choice fails to establish the entire top-five line-up, it should be eliminated.

6

Final Pregame Note

Because these games are a combination of the Grouping and Linear games discussed in the previous chapters, there are only two examples provided.

More games featuring Grouping will appear in Chapter Nine.

Please make sure to read the explanations carefully as they will give you a true sense of how to best attack each game, and the explanations always include points that expand the discussion given above.

If you would like to test yourself under timed conditions, you should give yourself 8 minutes and 45 seconds for each game. Good luck on the games!

> In doing these games, **use scratch paper instead of writing directly on the game!** This will prepare you for the Digital LSAT format where you cannot write directly on the screen.

6

A soloist will play six different guitar concertos, exactly one each Sunday for six consecutive weeks. Two concertos will be selected from among three concertos by Giuliani—H, J, and K; two from among four concertos by Rodrigo—M, N, O, and P; and two from among three concertos by Vivaldi—X, Y, and Z. The following conditions apply without exception:

    If N is selected, then J is also selected.

    If M is selected, then neither J nor O can be selected.

    If X is selected, then neither Z nor P can be selected.

    If both J and O are selected, then J is played at some time before O.

    X cannot be played on the fifth Sunday unless one of Rodrigo's concertos is played on the first Sunday.

19. Which one of the following is an acceptable selection of concertos that the soloist could play on the first through the sixth Sunday?

	1	2	3	4	5	6
(A)	H	Z	M	N	Y	K
(B)	K	J	Y	O	Z	N
(C)	K	Y	P	J	Z	M
(D)	P	Y	J	H	X	O
(E)	X	N	K	O	J	Z

GO ON TO THE NEXT PAGE.

20. If the six concertos to be played are J, K, N, O, Y, and Z and if N is to be played on the first Sunday, then which one of the following concertos CANNOT be played on the second Sunday?

(A) J
(B) K
(C) O
(D) Y
(E) Z

21. If J, O, and Y are the first three concertos to be played, not necessarily in the order given, which one of the following is a concerto that CANNOT be played on the fifth Sunday?

(A) H
(B) K
(C) N
(D) P
(E) X

22. If O is selected for the first Sunday, which one of the following is a concerto that must also be selected?

(A) J
(B) K
(C) M
(D) N
(E) X

23. Which one of the following is a concerto that must be selected?

(A) J
(B) K
(C) O
(D) Y
(E) Z

24. Which one of the following is a concerto that CANNOT be selected together with N?

(A) M
(B) O
(C) P
(D) X
(E) Z

GO ON TO THE NEXT PAGE.

6

Since the concertos from each composer produce the variables that are used in the linear setup, they are the logical starting point for our analysis. Each composer supplies two concertos, and the groups are as follows:

Giuliani: H, J, K ———→ ____ ____

Rodrigo: M, N, O, P ———→ ____ ____

Vivaldi: X, Y, Z ———→ ____ ____

Of the three groups, Giuliani and Vivaldi are the most restricted, since they only have three concertos to fill the required two selections per composer. Thus, if any one concerto is unavailable from either the Giuliani or Vivaldi group, then the other two concertos must be selected. In a situation such as this, it is always best to immediately check the rules for any negative grouping rules among the members of the restricted groups. The third rule contains such a relationship:

$$X \longleftrightarrow Z$$

Since X and Z can never be selected together, we can Hurdle the Uncertainty and infer that Y must be selected from Vivaldi's group:

$$\underline{\quad Y \quad} \quad \underline{\quad X\backslash Z \quad}$$

The scenario above, three variables for two spaces, is perhaps the most common inference scenario that appears in Grouping games. Any negative grouping rule or any question stem that knocks out one of the three variables leads to the inference that some other variable must be selected. In the above scenario, the rule involving X and Z effectively knocks one of those two variables out of the selection pool, forcing Y to be selected. One of the best examples of this type of inference occurred in a game from the 1980s. In that game, seven basketball players were selected for five starting spots. Clearly, this leaves only two "extra" variables in the selection pool. However, as the rules unfold it turns out that two separate pairs of variables cannot be selected together, in each case effectively reducing the candidate pool by one player. Since this occurred twice, it had to be that the three players not involved in the negative grouping rules were selected, a classic Hurdle the Uncertainties situation:

R S T U V W X⁷

U ⟵——⟶ S

W ⟵——⟶ V

$$\underline{\quad R \quad} \ \underline{\quad T \quad} \ \underline{\quad X \quad} \ \underline{\ U/S\ } \ \underline{\ W/V\ }$$
5 Players

Of course, a similar scenario can be produced with a wide variety of numerical combinations, four candidates for three spaces (one negative grouping rule means the other two candidates must be selected), eight candidates for six spaces (two negative grouping rules mean the other four candidates must be selected), etc. It is also important to note that many questions introduce "if" statements that ultimately result in limited scenarios, such as three candidates for two spaces or four candidates for three spaces. The point is that any selection group that is limited in size relative to the number of members that must be selected will probably yield an important inference, and you must always watch for situations such as these in games. In the guitar concerto game under consideration, in Question #23 we benefit directly from our inference that Y must always be selected.

Continuing with the setup of the game, we arrive at the following representation of the rules:

N ———⟶ J

M ⟵——⟶ J

M ⟵——⟶ O

X ⟵——⟶ Z

X ⟵——⟶ P

J, O ———⟶ (J —— O)

X_5 ———⟶ M, N, or O_1 (P is not included due to the third rule)

$$\underline{\quad} \ \underline{\quad} \ \underline{\quad} \ \underline{\quad} \ \underline{\quad} \ \underline{\quad}$$
1   2   3   4   5   6

$$\underline{\quad} \ \underline{\quad} \ \underline{\quad} \ \underline{\quad}$$
Out

A combination of the first and second rules produces the following additional deduction:

N ⟵——⟶ M

This deduction provides the answer to Question #24. There are also several other, less important inferences that can be made. For example, according to the second rule, when M is selected, J and O cannot be selected. Via the contrapositive, when J is not selected then N cannot be selected. From Rodrigo's group then, when M is selected, P is also selected:

$$M \longrightarrow P$$

And since J is not selected, H and K must be selected from Giuliani's group:

$$M \longrightarrow P, H, K$$

However, when P is selected, then X is not selected, and thus from Vivaldi's group Y and Z must be selected:

$$M \longrightarrow P, H, K, Y, Z$$

So, if M is selected, the other five positions are automatically filled. A similar situation arises with X. When X is selected, Z and P are not selected. Since P is not selected, M cannot be selected (see the inference above). Since both M and P are not selected, N and O must be selected from Rodrigo's group. Of course, Y is always selected:

$$X \longrightarrow Y, N, O$$

According to the first rule, if N is selected, then J must be selected:

$$X \longrightarrow Y, N, O, J$$

These last two major inferences involving M and X are helpful, but they are not essential to answering the questions in the game. We discuss them here simply to indicate the type of inferences that can follow from restricted situations. The only other rule of note is the last rule, which states that if X is played on the fifth Sunday then one of Rodrigo's concertos must be played on the first Sunday. This rule is noteworthy because it is so specific. It should be easy to track while answering the questions, because it relies so heavily on two designated spaces.

Question #19: Global, Could Be True, List. The correct answer choice is (B)

This List question is easily answered by a systematic application of the rules.

Answer choice (A) is incorrect because N is selected but J is not selected, a violation of the first rule.

Answer choice (B) is the correct answer.

Answer choice (C) is incorrect because both M and J are selected, a violation of the second rule.

Answer choice (D) is incorrect because both X and P are selected, a violation of the third rule.

Answer choice (E) is incorrect because J and O are both selected yet O is played before J (a violation of the fourth rule), and also because both X and Z are selected (a violation of the third rule).

Question #20: Local, Cannot Be True. The correct answer choice is (C)

This question provides a nice test of your linkage ability. Since the six variables are selected by the question stem, only the last two rules are applicable (both deal with the ordering of the variables). Since N (a concerto by Rodrigo) is to be played on the first Sunday, the conditions for the last rule (X on the fifth Sunday) are satisfied and this rule is not likely to play a role in answering the questions. However, since both J and O have been selected, the rule that states that J must be played before O is still in force. Since N will be played on the first Sunday, the sequencing relationship between J and O yields the Not Laws that J cannot be played on the sixth Sunday and O cannot be played on the second Sunday. Accordingly, answer choice (C) is correct.

Question #21: Local, Cannot Be True. The correct answer choice is (E)

The linkage chain in this question should be obvious. The question stem specifically refers to the fifth Sunday, a reference that also appears in the last rule. For X to play on the fifth Sunday, one of Rodrigo's concertos must be played on the first Sunday. According to the question stem, the only Rodrigo concerto that could be played on the first Sunday is O, but since J and O have both been selected, their sequencing relationship precludes O from being played on the first Sunday. It follows that X cannot be played on the fifth Sunday and thus answer choice (E) is correct.

Question #22: Local, Must Be True. The correct answer choice is (B)

If O is selected for the first Sunday, according to the sequencing rule involving J, J cannot be selected, and answer choice (A) is incorrect. Since J cannot be selected, the grouping restrictions come into play and H and K must be selected to represent Giuliani. Answer choice (B) is thus correct.

Question #23: Global, Must Be True. The correct answer choice is (D)

As previously discussed, answer choice (D) is correct.

Question #24: Global, Cannot Be True. The correct answer choice is (A)

As previously discussed, by combining the first two rules, we can infer that answer choice (A) is correct.

Perhaps the most important lesson of this game is to be mindful of the candidate restrictions in Grouping games. When some variables must be selected from a limited pool of candidates, invariably some powerful inferences will arise during the game, whether at the outset or during the questions.

An art teacher will schedule exactly six of eight lectures—
fresco, history, lithography, naturalism, oils, pastels,
sculpture, and watercolors—for three days—1, 2, and 3.
There will be exactly two lectures each day—morning
and afternoon. Scheduling is governed by the following
conditions:

> Day 2 is the only day for which oils can be scheduled.
> Neither sculpture nor watercolors can be scheduled
> for the afternoon.
> Neither oils nor pastels can be scheduled for the same
> day as lithography.
> If pastels is scheduled for day 1 or day 2, then the
> lectures scheduled for the day immediately following
> pastels must be fresco and history, not necessarily in
> that order.

12. Which one of the following is an acceptable schedule
of lectures for days 1, 2, and 3, respectively?

(A) Morning: lithography, history, sculpture
      Afternoon: pastels, fresco, naturalism

(B) Morning: naturalism, oils, fresco
      Afternoon: lithography, pastels, history

(C) Morning: oils, history, naturalism
      Afternoon: pastels, fresco, lithography

(D) Morning: sculpture, lithography, naturalism
      Afternoon: watercolors, fresco, pastels

(E) Morning: sculpture, pastels, fresco
      Afternoon: lithography, history, naturalism

GO ON TO THE NEXT PAGE.

13. If lithography and fresco are scheduled for the afternoons of day 2 and day 3, respectively, which one of the following is a lecture that could be scheduled for the afternoon of day 1?

   (A) history
   (B) oils
   (C) pastels
   (D) sculpture
   (E) watercolors

14. If lithography and history are scheduled for the mornings of day 2 and day 3, respectively, which one of the following lectures could be scheduled for the morning of day 1?

   (A) fresco
   (B) naturalism
   (C) oils
   (D) pastels
   (E) sculpture

15. If oils and lithography are scheduled for the mornings of day 2 and day 3, respectively, which one of the following CANNOT be scheduled for any day?

   (A) fresco
   (B) history
   (C) naturalism
   (D) pastels
   (E) sculpture

16. If neither fresco nor naturalism is scheduled for any day, which one of the following must be scheduled for day 1?

   (A) history
   (B) lithography
   (C) oils
   (D) pastels
   (E) sculpture

17. If the lectures scheduled for the mornings are fresco, history, and lithography, not necessarily in that order, which one of the following could be true?

   (A) Lithography is scheduled for day 3.
   (B) Naturalism is scheduled for day 2.
   (C) Fresco is scheduled for the same day as naturalism.
   (D) History is scheduled for the same day as naturalism.
   (E) History is scheduled for the same day as oils.

GO ON TO THE NEXT PAGE.

6

This Grouping/Linear combination game features eight lectures filling six spaces, and thus whenever two lectures are eliminated from the scheduling, the remaining six lectures *must* be scheduled. Questions #16 and #17 are excellent examples of this principle in action. The morning and afternoon variable sets also add an advanced linear element to the game, and consequently the game is more difficult than game #1 in this section. The setup to the game is as follows:

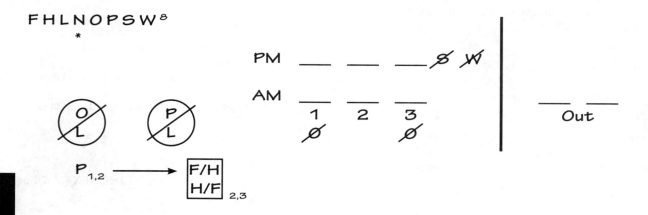

Since the three days contain an inherent sense of order, they are chosen as the base and the morning and afternoon variable sets are stacked on top. "Morning" and "Afternoon" have been abbreviated as AM and PM because they are too time-consuming to write out. It makes no difference whether your diagram has the AM set as the top row or as the bottom row.

Because of the vertical component, the OL and PL rules are written in block form. For convenience L has been placed on the bottom in both rules, but it is essential to understand that O and L (and P and L) can never be scheduled for the same day, regardless of which one is in the AM or PM (and hence the circle representation to indicate that the variables can rotate):

If you find this confusing at all, each rule can be written out both ways for clarity:

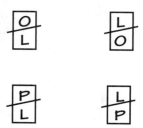

Note also that the first rule has not been written out. Instead of showing that O *could* go on day 2 (note: O should *not* be placed on day 2 on the diagram because we cannot be sure O is one of the six scheduled lectures), it is preferable to show that O cannot go on day 1 and day 3. Superior representations always reflect the absolutes—what must occur and what cannot occur. In examining the diagram it is also important to note that the O Not Laws on day 1 and day 3 apply to both the AM and PM. They can be placed beneath the slots in each row for each day if you feel that is helpful.

The last rule is difficult to diagram concisely. There are two scenarios under the rule: when P is scheduled for day 1, then F and H are scheduled for day 2, and when P is scheduled for day 2 then F and H are scheduled for day 3. In the form we have chosen, we have combined the two possibilities and represented them through the "1, 2" and "2, 3" subscripts. If you find this confusing, write out each scenario separately. This rule is especially important because it needs a lot of space. Also, do not forget to take the contrapositive of the rule: if any variable other than F or H is scheduled for day 2, then P cannot be scheduled for day 1, and if any variable other than F or H is scheduled for day 3, then P cannot be scheduled for day 2. This important inference is tested.

Because each appears in two rules, O and P are the key variables in the game and you must always be aware of them. In contrast to O and P, N is a random and relatively weak variable. Remember that in games with a large number of variables—say 9 or 10—randoms are relatively weak, and that in games with few variables—5 or 6—randoms are stronger and need to be given more consideration.

Finally, it is notable that this game does not contain any extremely deep inferences. There are some obvious inferences—for example, if L is scheduled for day 2, then O cannot be scheduled at all— but nothing truly challenging. This may in part explain why five of the six questions are Local: to create challenging situations the test makers had to supply local conditions to create limitation. Some games with deep inferences or limited possibilities have a large number of Global questions to test your knowledge of the inferences.

Question #12: Global, Could Be True, List. The correct answer choice is (B)

Remember to apply the simplest and most visually powerful rules first. In this case that conveniently happens to be the order in which the rules are presented:

The first rule eliminates answer choice (C).

The second rule eliminates answer choice (D).

The third rule eliminates answer choice (A).

And the fourth rule eliminates answer choice (E).

Thus, answer choice (B) is the correct answer.

Question #13: Local, Could Be True. The correct answer choice is (A)

Irrespective of the Local conditions, answer choices (B), (D), and (E) can be eliminated by the PM and day 1 Not Laws. With the answers narrowed to (A) and (C), we can consider the Local condition in the question stem. The stem produces the following mini-diagram next to the question:

PM   ___   L   F

AM   ___   ___   ___
        1   2   3

Note that in doing the question on the test, we would not take the time to write out AM, PM, 1, 2, and 3.

This setup automatically rules out P being scheduled on day 1, since if P is scheduled for day 1, then both F and H have to be scheduled for day 2. Since F is already scheduled for day 3, answer choice (C) can be eliminated. Answer choice (A) is therefore correct.

Question #14: Local, Could Be True. The correct answer choice is (E)

Irrespective of the Local conditions, answer choice (C) can be eliminated by applying the Not Laws. The conditions produce the following diagram:

___   ___   ___
      L   H
1   2   3
Ø   Ø   Ø

Once L is scheduled for day 2, O cannot be scheduled for day 2, and, consequently O cannot be scheduled for any of the days. The other lecture affected by the local conditions is P. As in question #2, P cannot be scheduled on day 1, since if P is scheduled for day 1 then both F and H have to be scheduled for day 2. Since H is already scheduled for day 3, answer choice (D) can be eliminated.

There are now three answer choices remaining: F, N, and S. Forced to guess with just the information at hand, you might suspect that S could be scheduled for the morning of day 1 because S is a variable already confined to the morning spaces. Although answer choice (E) is correct, it is important to understand why both answer choices (A) and (B) are incorrect. Consider that for the three afternoon spaces there are initially eight lectures: F, H, L, N, O, P, S, and W. From the second rule both S and W cannot lecture in the afternoon, so the pool is now down to six: F, H, L, N, O, and P. The conditions in the question place L and H in the morning and eliminate O from scheduling, and so the candidate pool is now three: F, N, and P. Thus, F, N, and P must be the three afternoon lectures in this question. If any of the three is placed in a morning space then there would not be enough lectures for the afternoon. **This illustrates a critical grouping concept: it is as important to evaluate the variables left for consideration as it is to evaluate the variables already placed.**

Question #15: Local, Cannot Be True. The correct answer choice is (D)

The question stem specifically places L and O, so consider the rules that relate to both variables, and the effects of each rule:

L: L appears directly in the third rule. Because the question stem specifies that L is scheduled for day 3, from the third rule P cannot be scheduled for day 3 (O also appears in the third rule, but that is moot since O is already scheduled for day 2 according to the question stem).

Although L is not directly named in the fourth rule, the fourth rule specifies that an entire day is devoted to F and H. Thus, once L is scheduled for the day 3, that enacts a contrapositive of the fourth rule, resulting in the inference that P cannot be scheduled for day 2. Thus, from the analysis of L, it can be inferred that P cannot scheduled for day 2 or day 3.

O: O appears directly in the first and third rules. Because O is scheduled for day 2, the condition in the first rule is met. And, because O and L are scheduled for different days, the condition in the third rule is met.

Similar to the case with L, although O is not directly named in the fourth rule, the fourth rule specifies that an entire day is devoted to F and H. Thus, once O is scheduled for day 2, that enacts a contrapositive of the fourth rule, resulting in the inference that P cannot be scheduled for day 1.

From the analysis of the placement of L and O in the question stem, it can be inferred that P cannot be scheduled for day 1, day 2 or day 3. Hence, P cannot be scheduled as a lecture, and it follows that answer choice (D) is correct.

6

Question #16: Local, Must Be True. The correct answer choice is (B)

Irrespective of the Local conditions, answer choice (C) can be eliminated by applying the Not Laws.

Since neither F nor N is scheduled, it follows that H, L, O, P, S, and W must be scheduled. And since F is not scheduled, P cannot be scheduled for day 1 or day 2 (the contrapositive of the final rule). Consequently P must be scheduled for day 3 and thus answer choice (D) is incorrect. Since O is scheduled for day 2 and P is scheduled for day 3, the third rule can be applied, and it follows that since L cannot be scheduled with O or P, then L must be scheduled for day 1. Thus, answer choice (B) is correct.

Question #17: Local, Could Be True. The correct answer choice is (E)

Since F, H, and L are scheduled for the three morning slots, the pool of afternoon lectures is S, W, N, O, and P. However, because S and W cannot be scheduled in the afternoon, only N, O, and P can be scheduled for the afternoon slots. Accordingly, O must be scheduled for day 2, P must be scheduled for day 3 (apply the last rule!), and thus N is scheduled for day 1. Since O and P are scheduled for days 2 and 3 respectively, L must be scheduled for day 1. F and H represent a dual-option on the mornings of days 2 and 3:

PM	N	O	P
AM	L	H/F	F/H
	1	2	3

Answer choice (E) is therefore correct.

Chapter Seven:
Pure Sequencing
Games

Chapter Seven: Pure Sequencing Games

Pure Sequencing Games ■■■■■■■

Pure Sequencing games use the sequencing principles introduced in Chapter Three. Although the sequences always overlay a linear scenario, the games are called *Pure Sequencing* because all of the rules are sequential in nature, and thus your primary task is tracking the relative positions of the variables.

Linear games with sequencing rules appear very frequently, so you must have the ability to handle these types of rules. Games based solely on sequencing rules, such as the ones in this chapter, have appeared less frequently over the years, but at times the test makers have presented these games with high frequency. Consider the history of Pure Sequencing games thus far on the modern LSAT (June 1991 to the present):

1. Between June 1991 and February 1994, five different LSATs contained a Pure Sequencing game.

2. Between June 1994 and December 1998, no released LSAT contained a Sequencing game (This time lapse between the appearances of Pure Sequencing games is not unprecedented: there was a three-year gap in the appearance of Pure Sequencing between the October 1983 LSAT and the June 1986 LSAT).

3. From February 1999 to October 2008, Pure Sequencing games appeared twelve times. The September 2007 LSAT actually contained two Pure Sequencing games, meaning that games of this type comprised 50% of the Logic Games section of that exam.

4. From December 2008 to October 2013, Pure Sequencing games appeared just one time.

5. From December 2013 to the present, Pure Sequencing games have appeared three times already.

Thus, although Pure Sequencing games go in and out of favor with the test makers, you should fully master the principles presented on the following pages because there is an extremely high probability that a future LSAT will contain a Pure Sequencing game, and it is *certain* that future Linear games will contain sequencing elements.

7

Pure Sequencing Diagramming Guidelines

Linear games contain rules that fix the position of variables, such as "P must be third."

Sequencing games contain rules that place variables in relative positions.

Pure Sequencing games involve the ranking or ordering of variables. The key to understanding a Pure Sequencing game is recognizing that all of the relationships among the variables are relative and not precisely fixed. For example, a rule might state, "Lopez's salary is greater than Nassar's salary." From this rule, it is known only that Lopez makes more than Nassar, but not how much more. Lopez could make just a dollar more than Nassar, or thousands of dollars more than Nassar. There is also no indication of where they stand on the salary scale: Lopez could be making $100,000 a year or $100 a year. This uncertainty about the specifics of each relationship is inherent in Sequencing games and is the focus of the questions. In each game you must attempt to determine what must be true, and at the same time avoid making any unwarranted assumptions. Use the following guidelines to create ideal Pure Sequencing setups:

1. Use lines (——) to represent relative relationships.

    Example:

    Petra is faster than Tai and slower than Sara.

    $$S —— P —— T$$

    In the context of sequencing, the lines simply mean "to the left of" and "to the right of." Thus, "S —— P" indicates that S is to the left of P on the diagram, and P is to the right of S on the diagram.

2. Keep in mind that unless ties are ruled out by the game scenario (which is normally the case), variables can be equal. If equality is part of a relationship in a sequencing game, expect to be tested on that relationship at least once during the course of the game. Possible equality between variables is represented with two parallel lines.

    Example:

    Jahru is not faster than Miles.

    $$M == J$$

    If the two variables were always equal, then they would be in a block formation (a vertical block for a horizontal setup).

3. Search for variables that appear in more than one rule, and link them together in order to build the most complete chain sequence.

Example:

> Jahru is not faster than Miles.
> Miles is slower than Noguchi.

$$N \longrightarrow M = J$$

4. Always test the limits of the game by checking the first and last positions.

Example:

> Who could be fastest, and who could be slowest?

This process is critical because it helps you establish the range of possibilities at the endpoints, and thus within the game as a whole.

5. Use Multi-Branched Verticals to represent variables whose relationship is uncertain.

Double Branched Vertical Example:

> Tai is faster than both Vernon and Wendy.

Visually, the two lines separate V and W into two independent "branches." Beyond the fact that V and W are both slower than T, the variables in each branch are completely unrelated to each other. Thus, V or W could be slowest, or both could be equally slow. If the rules stipulate that there can be no ties, then the possibility of V and W being equally slow would be eliminated.

Branched Verticals were introduced in Chapter Three during the Linear games discussion.

Double Branched Vertical Example:

Vernon and Wendy are both faster than Tai.

V and W are both faster than T, but no relationship can be inferred between V and W. V could be fastest, W could be fastest, or they could be equally fast.

Triple Branched Vertical Example:

Vernon, Wendy, and Zazi are all faster than Tai.

V, W, and Z are each faster than T, but again the variables in each branch are completely unrelated to each other. Thus, V could be fastest, W could be fastest, or Z could be fastest. Or, if ties are allowed, all three could be equally fast.

6. Branches can be added from any point, and the length of the line does not indicate anything about the nature of the relationship. Thus, if you need to add variables to a pre-existing chain, do not be concerned if the addition "looks" unbalanced.

Example:

> Paula is faster than Tai and slower than Sara.
> Noguchi is slower than Tai.
> Jahru is not faster than Miles.
> Miles is slower than Noguchi.

$$S \text{---} P \text{---} T \text{---} N \text{---} M \text{===} J$$

If Fuad is faster than Tai, you can diagram the new rule as:

$$S \text{---} P \text{---} T \text{---} N \text{---} M \text{===} J$$
$$\diagup$$
$$F$$

F is now in a second branch, and no assumption can be made about the relationship between F and S, or between F and P. Further, in the diagram above, the length of the branch between F and T is notably longer than the other lines in the diagram. This has no meaning, and is simply done for the sake of convenience and clarity.

Let us take a look at another example.

Example:

> A is heavier than B and lighter than C.
> B is heavier than D, and D is heavier than E.
> F is heavier than B.
> G is lighter than F.

Most students handle the first two rules fairly easily, and create a diagram that appears as follows:

$$C \text{---} A \text{---} B \text{---} D \text{---} E$$

The third and fourth rules may appear to present a problem because they connect to B, which is in the middle of the chain sequence. However, you can easily connect F to B with an extra line, and then do the same to connect F to G. Thus, handling both rules with extra lines is easy:

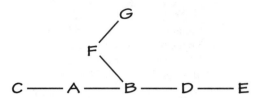

Pure Sequencing
games are
designed in part
to test whether
you will make
unwarranted
assumptions.

The diagram above indicates that F "floats" relative to B, and that G "floats" relative to F. Yes, this is a tougher diagram form to handle, but the test makers typically construct games with the intention of making the setup challenging. How you handle the rules will have a direct effect on your success on the game.

Note also that in the first diagram of this item F was placed below the main chain, whereas in the diagram above F is placed above the main chain. This has no significance, and can be done based on what works best for the game at hand.

Mutually
exclusive chains
will be discussed
in more detail in
just a few pages.

7. Watch for rules that create two separate, mutually exclusive possibilities. If you encounter such a rule, you must diagram both chain possibilities.

Example (assumes no ties allowed):

B is faster than D, or else C is faster than D, but not both.

This rule allows for only two outcomes, each of which excludes the other:

B ——— D ——— C

or

C ——— D ——— B

Unless one of the other rules in the game eliminates one of the two possibilities, you must proceed as if the game itself has two branches, and create a separate diagram for each branch—one built around B ——— D ——— C, and one built around C ——— D ——— B.

8. Track the appearance of outside restrictions or occurrences by circling the affected variable.

Example:

Vernon, Wendy, and Zazi are all faster than Tai.
Wendy cannot be fastest, and there are no ties.

If the variables above are the only four in the game, then the only possibilities for Wendy are to be second or third (which could be shown within the diagram with a "2/3" next to W. In order to help remember that W has a special restriction, place a circle around W as indicated on the diagram above.

9. The key to superior performance on sequencing games is to avoid making unwarranted assumptions. Physical proximity within the diagram does not necessarily indicate an actual relationship; for example, R may be ahead of W on the diagram, but do not assume that R must be ahead of W in terms of the game. Consider the following example:

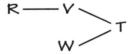

In this diagram, R appears to be physically ahead of W, but in fact W could be ahead of R. Since R and W are part of two separate branches, their relationship is unknown; R could be faster than W, R and W could be equally fast, or W could be faster than R. The same possibilities hold true for V and W.

In determining relationships between variables, do not let physical proximity on the diagram influence your evaluation. Use only the rules of the game and your own diagram to establish the truth of each relationship.

Pure Sequencing Diagramming Drill

Use the Pure Sequencing Diagramming Guidelines to set up sequencing chains for each of the following items. The rules may yield more than one chain per item, and ties are possible for the purposes of this drill. *Answers on page 444*

1. Rules: E is taller than F.
                     E is shorter than D.
                     D is shorter than B and C.
                     A is taller than B.

A. Which of the variables in the chain could be tallest?

B. Which of the variables in the chain could be shortest?

2. Rules: R and S are heavier than T.
                     V is heavier than W and X.
                     U is lighter than X.

A. Which of the variables could be heaviest?

B. Which of the variables could be lightest?

3. Rules: F is larger than G and H.
                     G is larger than I.
                     I is larger than J and K.
                     K is not the smallest.

A. Which of the variables in the chain could be largest?

B. Which of the variables in the chain could be smallest?

7

Pure Sequencing Diagramming Drill

4.   Rules: E is heavier than A.
                            A and B are heavier than C.
                            D and H are lighter than C.
                            F is lighter than D, and G is lighter
                              than H.

A.   Which of the variables in the chain could be heaviest?

B.   Which of the variables in the chain could be lightest?

5.   Rules: Q and R are both larger than S.
                            R and T are both larger than V.

A.   Which of the variables in the chain could be largest?

B.   Which of the variables in the chain could be smallest?

6.   Rules: A is taller than B and C.
                            D is not taller than C.
                            G and H are taller than A.
                            H is shorter than I and J.

A.   Which of the variables in the chain could be tallest?

B.   Which of the variables in the chain could be shortest?

Pure Sequencing Diagramming Drill Answer Key

1. Rules: E is taller than F.
                    E is shorter than D.
                    D is shorter than B and C.
                    A is taller than B.

A. Which of the variables in the chain could be tallest?

B. Which of the variables in the chain could be shortest?

Tallest: A, C

Shortest: F

---

2. Rules: R and S are heavier than T.
                    V is heavier than W and X.
                    U is lighter than X.

A. Which of the variables could be heaviest?

B. Which of the variables could be lightest?

Heaviest: R, S, V

Lightest: T, U, W

3. Rules: F is larger than G and H.
                       G is larger than I.
                       I is larger than J and K.
                       K is not the smallest.

A. Which of the variables in the chain could be largest?

B. Which of the variables in the chain could be smallest?

Largest: F

Smallest: H, J

K is circled because K is not the smallest.

4. Rules: E is heavier than A.
                       A and B are heavier than C.
                       D and H are lighter than C.
                       F is lighter than D, and G is lighter than H.

A. Which of the variables in the chain could be heaviest?

B. Which of the variables in the chain could be lightest?

Heaviest: B, E

Lightest: F, G

5. Rules: Q and R are both larger than S.
                    R and T are both larger than V.

A. Which of the variables in the chain could be largest?

B. Which of the variables in the chain could be smallest?

Largest: Q, R, T

Smallest: S, V

Circling R is optional; R can circled because R is uniquely connected by the rules to both S and V.

___

6. Rules: A is taller than B and C.
                    D is not taller than C.
                    G and H are taller than A.
                    H is shorter than I and J.

A. Which of the variables in the chain could be tallest?

B. Which of the variables in the chain could be shortest?

Tallest: G, I, J

Shortest: B, C*, D

*C could only tie for shortest.

7

Conditional Sequencing

Conditional
Sequencing rules
can occur in both
Pure Sequencing
and Basic or
Advanced Linear
games.

In certain Logic Games, some of the sequencing rules are stated in conditional fashion, meaning that certain sequential relationships are triggered by other events. These rules tend to come in two types: standard conditional relationships, and relationships that trigger two mutually exclusive possibilities. Let's examine both.

Standard Conditional Relationships

Sequencing elements can be added to any conditional relationship, in the sufficient or necessary condition (or both). Consider the following example:

If D is taller than F, then X is taller than Y.

This rule is only enacted if D is taller than F, and most students diagram the rule as follows:

$$(D——F) \longrightarrow (X——Y)$$

The contrapositive of the rule is a bit more interesting. Diagramming simply with negatives, the contrapositive appears as:

$$(X\not——Y) \longrightarrow (D\not——F)$$

Linear games
often include
Conditional
Sequencing rules,
and typically
the sequence is
tied to a specific
occurrence,
such as in the
following example:
"If L is third,
then P must be
scheduled earlier
than S." Such
a rule would be
diagrammed as:

$$L_3 \longrightarrow P——S$$

Thus, whenever
L is third, the
sequence is
forced to occur.

However, if this game includes no ties—and most Logic Games explicitly eliminate the possibility of ties—then when X is *not* taller than Y, it must be that Y is taller than X, and when D is *not* taller than F, it must be that F is taller than D. When this information is taken into account, the rule can be redisplayed as follows:

$$(Y——X) \longrightarrow (F——D)$$

Thus, one of the most important considerations when you encounter a conditional sequencing rule is to examine the contrapositive, and if there are no ties, redisplay the relationships in a way that removes any negatives.

Mutually Exclusive Outcomes

In some cases, conditional sequencing rules can create two separate, mutually exclusive possibilities that then dictate the direction of the game. Consider the following example:

Either R is taller than S, or else R is taller than T, but not both.

Most students diagram the rule as follows:

$$R \text{—} S$$
or
$$R \text{—} T$$

While this representation is factually accurate, it does not capture the full truth of what is occurring with R, S, and T. Note that the rule uses the phrase "but not both," which means that one or the other occurs, but that both cannot occur. So, when R —— S, it cannot also be the case that R —— T, and vice versa. But, in games in which no ties are possible (and most games fall into that category), if R is not taller than T, then T must be taller than R (T —— R). When this relationship is added to the existing R —— S, relationship, we can infer that T —— R —— S.

A similar case exists when R —— T. Because R —— S *cannot* also be true, we can infer that S —— R, creating a chain of S —— R —— T.

Therefore, under this rule, only two arrangements of R, S, and T are possible:

1. T —— R —— S

or

2. S —— R —— T

Thus, every solution to the game will conform to either the T —— R —— S sequence or to the S —— R —— T sequence. This is an incredibly powerful inference, and one that divides the game into two fundamentally different pathways. If you encounter a game that contains a similar rule, you should immediately recognize that two distinct possibilities exist, and explore both options in terms of how they interact with the remaining rules.

Note also that the initial rule, while conditional in nature, does not use one of the most common indicators (such as "if" or "only") to create conditionality. Instead, the conditional phrase "either/or, but not both" is used. Interestingly, in many of the conditional sequencing rules that create just two possible directions for the game, the phrase "but not both" is present.

Here is another example that also creates two separate, mutually exclusive possibilities, along with the two separate directions that result:

Example:

R sings at some time before S or at some time after L, but not both.

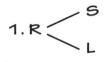

or

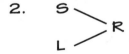

Rules that create two distinct pathways have become increasingly common on recent LSATs, and you must recognize these rules when they appear, and understand the implications created by such rules. Here are several games you can review that feature similar rules:

December 2006 LSAT, Game #2
September 2007 LSAT, Game #4
December 2007 LSAT, Game #2
October 2010 LSAT, Game #2
September 2014 LSAT, Game #1

However, when considering conditional rules involving sequencing, be careful not to assume that any sequencing rule stated in conditional fashion automatically creates two and only two directions for the game. Consider the following example:

If A's presentation is earlier than B's presentation, then B's presentation is earlier than C's presentation.

Most students diagram the prior rule in the following manner:

$$(A \longrightarrow B) \longrightarrow (B \longrightarrow C)$$

This is an accurate diagram, but it does not perfectly capture the fact that functionally the rule creates an A —— B —— C chain *when* A's presentation is known to be earlier than B's presentation. Take a moment to consider the contrapositive of the above rule, which can be drawn as:

$$(B \not\longrightarrow C) \longrightarrow (A \not\longrightarrow B)$$

In games where no ties are possible, if B's presentation is *not* earlier than C's presentation, then we can infer that C —— B, and if A's presentation is *not* earlier than B's presentation, then we know that B —— A. Thus, the contrapositive actually appears as:

$$(C \longrightarrow B) \longrightarrow (B \longrightarrow A)$$

From a functional standpoint, then, the contrapositive creates a C —— B —— A chain when C's presentation is known to be earlier than B's presentation.

Combining the original statement and its contrapositive, many students *improperly* infer there are only two possible relationship possibilities for A, B, and C in this game:

$$1.\ A \longrightarrow B \longrightarrow C$$

or

$$2.\ C \longrightarrow B \longrightarrow A$$

7

THE POWERSCORE LSAT LOGIC GAMES BIBLE

But, while both sequences are possible, two other possible sequences also exist:

3. B —— A —— C

4. B —— C —— A

Thus, even though a conditional rule involving sequencing is present, the game is *not* divided into two basic paths. The general principle is that when conditional indicators appear, you should immediately analyze the rule to see if two mutually exclusive chains are created, but be aware that not all conditional rules involving sequencing narrow the possibilities to only two chains.

Conditional Sequencing Diagramming Drill

Use the Pure Sequencing and Conditional Sequencing Diagramming Guidelines to set up diagrams for each of the following rules. The rules may yield more than one chain per item. Assume no ties are possible. *Answers on page 453*

1. If the earrings are more expensive than the necklace, then the ring must be more expensive than the brooch.

4. X is larger than Y, or else X is larger than W, but not both.

2. Either Sandoval is interviewed after both Kun and Newman, or both Kun and Newman are interviewed after Sandoval.

5. If Flores is hired before Hart, then Flores is also hired before Jun and Okonwo.

7

6. M is scheduled earlier than Q, or scheduled later than T, but not both.

3. If R is older than T, then neither C nor D is older than F.

Conditional Sequencing Diagramming Drill Answer Key

1. If the earrings are more expensive than the necklace, then the ring must be more expensive than the brooch.

    Diagram: (E ——— N) ——————→ (R ——— B)

    Contrapositive: (B ——— R) ——————→ (N ——— E)

---

2. Either Sandoval is interviewed after both Kun and Newman, or both Kun and Newman are interviewed after Sandoval.

    or

---

3. If R is older than T, then neither C nor D is older than F.

$$(R \text{———} T) \longrightarrow F \Big\langle \begin{matrix} C \\ D \end{matrix}$$

The contrapositive of this rule would be enacted if C or D (or both) were older than F. The result would be that T ——— R.

4. X is larger than Y, or else X is larger than W, but not
   both.

$$1.\ W \longrightarrow X \longrightarrow Y$$

or

$$2.\ Y \longrightarrow X \longrightarrow W$$

5. If Flores is hired before Hart, then Flores is also hired
   before Jun and Okonwo.

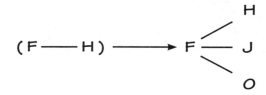

The contrapositive of this rule would be enacted if H, J, or O (or any two, or all three) were
hired before F. The result would be that H ——— F.

6. M is scheduled earlier than Q, or scheduled later than
   T, but not both.

or

7

Final Pregame Note

Because these games feature ideas that were discussed in previous chapters, and because these games are relatively rare, there are only two examples provided.

Please make sure to read the explanations carefully, as they will give you a true sense of how to best attack each game, and the explanations always include points that expand the discussion given above.

If you would like to test yourself under timed conditions, you should give yourself 8 minutes and 45 seconds for each game. Good luck on the games!

> In doing these games, **use scratch paper instead of writing directly on the game!** This will prepare you for the Digital LSAT format where you cannot write directly on the screen.

If you are looking for more Sequencing Games, consider one of our LSAT Logic Game Training Type book.

The Training Type book contains every Logic Game from 20 PrepTests (80 per book), all sorted according to game type so you can focus on the kinds of games causing you the most problems.

7

Each of seven television programs—H, J, L, P, Q, S, V—is assigned a different rank: from first through seventh (from most popular to least popular). The ranking is consistent with the following conditions:

    J and L are each less popular than H.
    J is more popular than Q.
    S and V are each less popular than L.
    P and S are each less popular than Q.
    S is not seventh.

1.   Which one of the following could be the order of the programs, from most popular to least popular?

    (A)   J, H, L, Q, V, S, P
    (B)   H, L, Q, J, S, P, V
    (C)   H, J, Q, L, S, V, P
    (D)   H, J, V, L, Q, S, P
    (E)   H, L, V, J, Q, P, S

GO ON TO THE NEXT PAGE.

2. If J is more popular than L, and S is more popular than P, then which one of the following must be true of the ranking?

    (A)   J is second.
    (B)   J is third.
    (C)   L is third.
    (D)   Q is third.
    (E)   P is seventh.

3. Which one of the following programs CANNOT be ranked third?

    (A)   L
    (B)   J
    (C)   Q
    (D)   V
    (E)   P

4. If V is more popular than Q and J is less popular than L, then which one of the following could be true of the ranking?

    (A)   P is more popular than S.
    (B)   S is more popular than V.
    (C)   P is more popular than L.
    (D)   J is more popular than V.
    (E)   Q is more popular than V.

5. If Q is more popular than L, then each of the following must be true of the ranking EXCEPT:

    (A)   H is first.
    (B)   L is fourth.
    (C)   V is not fourth.
    (D)   J is not third.
    (E)   Q is third.

GO ON TO THE NEXT PAGE.

Analysis of Pure Sequencing Game #1: December 2000 Questions 1-5

Because Pure Sequencing is generally favorable for most test takers, this was an excellent way to begin this particular LSAT.

Use the Pure Sequencing Diagramming Guidelines to create the following diagram:

H J L P Q S V [7]

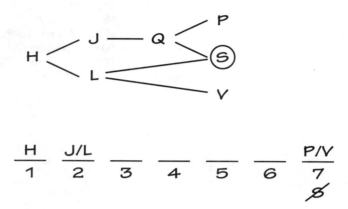

In creating the sequence diagram, the most problematic television program is S. S is less popular than both Q and L, but Q and L are in separate branches. We have solved this problem by placing S at the terminus of two lines (one from Q, and one from L), and then circling S.

As with most Pure Sequencing games, this one is built on top of a linear relationship. H must be the most popular television program and only J or L could be second. Since S cannot be seventh, P or V must be the least popular. With this information we can attack the questions, watching the following two areas:

1. In Pure Sequencing games the test makers always check to see whether you will make unwarranted assumptions about the relationships between the variables.

2. Via Local questions, the test makers typically introduce new relationships into the sequence to test your understanding of how the original relationships are affected.

Question #1: Global, Could Be True, List. The correct answer choice is (C)

Apply the rules and inferences in this order: inference that H must be first, fifth rule, second rule, and finally, the first, third, and fourth rules can be applied in any order since they are roughly equivalent in form.

Answer choice (A) is incorrect because H must be more popular than J.

Answer choice (B) is incorrect because J must be more popular than Q.

Answer choice (C) is the correct answer.

Answer choice (D) is incorrect because L must be more popular than V.

Answer choice (E) is incorrect because S cannot be seventh.

Question #2: Local, Must Be True. The correct answer choice is (A)

When examining the linear portion of the setup, take special note of the dual-options. A favorite trick of the test makers is to "take away" one of the variables in a dual-option to see if you recognize that the other variable is then forced into a position. Because either J or L must be second, and according to the question stem J is more popular than L, L cannot be second and J must be second. Answer choice (A) reflects that fact and is correct.

Question #3: Global, Cannot Be True. The correct answer choice is (E)

A program that cannot be ranked third is one that has either three or more variables ranked before it, or five or more variables ranked behind it (such as H). Applying the former criterion produces the following analysis:

> H   minimum of 0 variables ranked ahead, cannot be ranked third since must be ranked first
> J   minimum of 1 variable ranked ahead (H), can be ranked third
> L   minimum of 1 variable ranked ahead (H), can be ranked third
> P   minimum of 3 variables ranked ahead (H, J, Q), cannot be ranked third
> Q   minimum of 2 variables ranked ahead (H, J), can be ranked third
> S   minimum of 4 variables ranked ahead (H, J, Q, L), cannot be ranked third
> V   minimum of 2 variables ranked ahead (H, L), can be ranked third

Accordingly, H, P, and S cannot be ranked third. Since only P appears among the answer choices, answer choice (E) is correct.

Note that this question does not require any writing. The listing above has been provided for the purpose of clarity. Since speed is a factor during the test, the number of variables ranked ahead should be visually scanned and counted.

Question #4: Local, Could Be True. The correct answer choice is (D)

The condition in the question stem produces the following mini-diagram:

S must be ranked ahead of P because otherwise S would be ranked seventh, a violation of the rules.

In a Could Be True question the correct answer choice could actually have the characteristic of Must Be True, but that usually does not occur on the LSAT. Consequently, since the correct answer will contain a scenario that is possible but not certain to occur, the best strategy is to look immediately for the uncertainty in the diagram and attack that area. Since the only uncertainty in this question involves J and V (J could be ranked ahead of V or V could be ranked ahead of J), immediately scan the answer choices for one that contains both J and V. In this case only answer choice (D) contains J and V. After a brief examination, it is apparent that answer choice (D) could be true and is therefore correct.

If the diagram to this question had more areas of uncertainty, the strategy above would still have been successful but would have taken more time to apply.

Question #5: Local, Must Be True, Except. The correct answer choice is (B)

Remember, *Must Be True EXCEPT* is the same as *Not Necessarily True*. The condition in the question stem produces the following diagram:

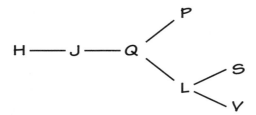

H, J, and Q must be ranked first, second, and third, respectively. Answer choices (A), (D), and (E) can thereby be eliminated. The highest V can be ranked is fifth and that eliminates answer choice (C). Since P could be fourth, it follows that L does not have to be fourth and answer choice (B) is correct.

For most test takers the appearance of a Pure Sequencing game is cause for celebration. Remember, Pure Sequencing games can be easily identified since the majority of rules are relative in nature. As you work through this book, keep in mind that part of your task is to learn how to quickly identify each game type.

Six hotel suites—F, G, H, J, K, L—are ranked from most expensive (first) to least expensive (sixth). There are no ties. The ranking must be consistent with the following conditions:

    H is more expensive than L.

    If G is more expensive than H, then neither K nor L is more expensive than J.

    If H is more expensive than G, then neither J nor L is more expensive than K.

    F is more expensive than G, or else F is more expensive than H, but not both.

6.   Which one of the following could be the ranking of the suites, from most expensive to least expensive?

    (A)   G, F, H, L, J, K
    (B)   H, K, F, J, G, L
    (C)   J, H, F, K, G, L
    (D)   J, K, G, H, L, F
    (E)   K, J, L, H, F, G

GO ON TO THE NEXT PAGE.

7. If G is the second most expensive suite, then which one of the following could be true?

   (A) H is more expensive than F.
   (B) H is more expensive than G.
   (C) K is more expensive than F.
   (D) K is more expensive than J.
   (E) L is more expensive than F.

8. Which one of the following CANNOT be the most expensive suite?

   (A) F
   (B) G
   (C) H
   (D) J
   (E) K

9. If L is more expensive than F, then which one of the following could be true?

   (A) F is more expensive than H.
   (B) F is more expensive than K.
   (C) G is more expensive than H.
   (D) G is more expensive than J.
   (E) G is more expensive than L.

10. If H is more expensive than J and less expensive than K, then which one of the following could be true?

   (A) F is more expensive than H.
   (B) G is more expensive than F.
   (C) G is more expensive than H.
   (D) J is more expensive than L.
   (E) L is more expensive than K.

GO ON TO THE NEXT PAGE.

The key to this game is to use the last rule to create the two mutually exclusive sequences that control this game.

From the game scenario, we know the following linear scenario underpins the sequences:

F G H J K L⁶

$$\underline{}\ \underline{}\ \underline{}\ \underline{}\ \underline{}\ \underline{}$$
$$\ \ 1\ \ \ \ \ 2\ \ \ \ \ 3\ \ \ \ \ 4\ \ \ \ \ 5\ \ \ \ \ 6$$

Because there are no ties, this is a balanced game, wherein each of the six hotel suites is assigned to a different space.

Ultimately, the final rule controls the game , and students who begin diagramming before reading all of the rules often find themselves scrambling to re-diagram. Remember, always read the entire scenario and accompanying rules prior to starting your diagram.

For the purpose of clarity, let's review each rule individually. At the conclusion of showing the diagram for each rule, we will combine the diagrams into two super-sequences.

    <u>Rule #1</u>. This is a basic sequential rule:

H —— L

    <u>Rule #2</u>. This is a conditional rule, and the sufficient condition is that G is more expensive than H. When that occurs, then J is more expensive than both K and L:

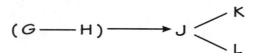

    <u>Rule #3</u>. This is another conditional rule, and the sufficient condition is that H is more expensive than G. When that occurs, then K is more expensive than both J and L:

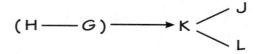

<u>Rule #4</u>. Initially this rule seems like a simple either/or rule, where F is either more expensive than G (diagrammed as F ——— G) or F is more expensive than H (diagrammed as F ——— H). However, the "but not both" portion of the rule means that F is more expensive than *only one* of G or H at a time, and since there are no ties, that means that the other variable must be more expensive than F. So, when F is more expensive than G, then H must be more expensive than F, producing the following sequence:

H ——— F ——— G

And, when F is more expensive than H, then G must be more expensive than F, producing the following sequence:

G ——— F ——— H

Every game solution must conform to one of the two sequences produced by rule #4, and thus you should take those two base sequences and create two templates for the game.

Sequence Template #1

This template is produced by the part of rule #4 that produces the H ——— F ——— G sequence. To build a super-sequence that captures the relationship between all six hotel suites, first add rule #1 to the sequence:

The next step is to add rule #3 to the sequence (rule #2 does not apply to this sequence, and can be ignored). This step is more difficult than the first step above, because adding the third rule creates an unwieldy diagram:

The relationship between K, J, and L is clear when isolated in rule #3, but when added to a sequence where L is already less expensive than another hotel suite, H, the relationship is a bit more difficult to diagram. In the above diagram, K and H have no relationship other than both being more expensive than L.

The tricky part comes in analyzing the relationship between H and J, and between K and F ——— G. In both instances, there is no relationship. That is, J can be more or less expensive than H, and K can be more or less expensive than both F or G. Of course, this difficulty in representation and analysis is exactly what the test makers intended.

To better understand the possibilities inherent in this sequence, consider the following hypotheticals, all of which are valid:

> Hypothetical 1: K - H - F - G - J - L
> Hypothetical 2: K - J - H - L - F - G
> Hypothetical 3: H - F - G - K - L - J
> Hypothetical 4: H - F - K - J - G - L
> Hypothetical 5: H - K - L - F - G - J

Also, remember to use the Sequencing Diagramming Guidelines, and consider which variables can be first and which can be last. In the sequence above, only K or H can be first, and only G, J, or L can be last.

This template is produced by the part of rule #4 that produces the G ——— F ——— H sequence. To build a super-sequence that captures the relationship between all six hotel suites, first add rule #1 to the sequence:

$$G \text{——} F \text{——} H \text{——} L$$

The next step is to add rule #2 to the sequence (rule #3 does not apply to this sequence, and can be ignored). This step is more difficult than the first step above because adding the second rule creates a slightly unwieldy diagram:

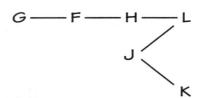

The relationship between K, J, and L is clear when isolated in rule #2, but when added to a sequence where L is already less expensive than three other hotel suites, the relationship is more difficult to diagram (although not as troubling as the first sequence template). The tricky part comes in analyzing the relationship between J and K and the other variables. J must be more expensive than K and L, but J has no relationship with G, F, or H. Similarly, K must be less expensive than J but otherwise K has no relationship with any other variable in the chain. Analyzing which variables can be first and which can be last in the sequence above, only G or J can be first, and only K or L can be last.

To better understand the possibilities inherent in this sequence, consider the following hypotheticals, each of which is valid:

      Hypothetical 1: G - F - H - J - L - K
      Hypothetical 2: J - K - G - F - H - L
      Hypothetical 3: J - G - F - H - L - K
      Hypothetical 4: G - J - F - K - H - L
      Hypothetical 5: G - F - J - H - K - L

Combining all of the information above leads to the following optimal setup for the game:

F G H J K L⁶

$$\overline{\quad} \ \overline{\quad} \ \overline{\quad} \ \overline{\quad} \ \overline{\quad} \ \overline{\quad}$$
1   2   3   4   5   6

H ——— L

(G ——— H) ———→ J ⟨ K
                           L

(H ——— G) ———→ K ⟨ J
                           L

     H ——— F ——— G
           or
     G ——— F ——— H

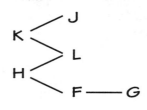

Sequence Template #1

K ⟨ J
    L
H ⟨
    F ——— G

Sequence Template #2

G ——— F ——— H ——— L
                       J ⟨
                             K

Use the two sequence templates to answer the questions.

7

Question #6: Global, List. The correct answer choice is (B)

As with any List question, simply apply the rules to the answer choices.

Answer choice (A): This answer choice is incorrect because it violates rule #2. Specifically, when G is more expensive than H, then L cannot be more expensive than J.

Answer choice (B): This is the correct answer choice.

Answer choice (C): This answer choice is incorrect because it violates rule #3. Specifically, when H is more expensive than G, then J cannot be more expensive than K.

Answer choice (D): This answer choice is incorrect because it violates rule #4: F is less expensive than both G and H.

Answer choice (E): This answer choice is incorrect because it violates rule #1.

Question #7: Local, Could Be True. The correct answer choice is (C)

The condition in the question stem specifies that G is the second most expensive suite. Reviewing the two sequence templates, template #1 does not allow for this possibility (at best, G can be the third most expensive suite), and thus template #2 is the only template that applies to this question. In template #2, when G is the second most expensive suite, then J must be the most expensive suite:

$$\frac{J}{1} \quad \frac{G}{2} \quad \frac{}{3} \quad \frac{}{4} \quad \frac{}{5} \quad \frac{}{6}$$

The remainder of the spaces are controlled by the following relationship:

$$F \longrightarrow H \longrightarrow L$$

and

$$K$$

Answer choice (A): This answer choice is incorrect because H cannot be more expensive than F in template #2.

Answer choice (B): This answer choice is incorrect because H cannot be more expensive than G in template #2.

Answer choice (C): This is the correct answer choice. Under template #2, K could be more expensive than F. The following hypothetical shows one possible way: J - G - K - F - H - L.

Answer choice (D): This answer choice is incorrect because K cannot be more expensive than J in template #2.

Answer choice (E): This answer choice is incorrect because L cannot be more expensive than F in template #2.

Question #8: Global, Cannot Be True. The correct answer choice is (A)

From our analysis of the two sequence templates, we know that in template #1 only H and K can be the most expensive. This information eliminates answer choices (C) and (E). In template #2 only G and J can be the most expensive, and that eliminates answer choice (B) and (D). Thus, answer choice (A) is proven correct by process of elimination.

Alternatively, answer choice (A) can be proven correct because in template #1, F must be less expensive than H, and in template #2, F must be less expensive than G.

Answer choice (A): This is the correct answer choice.

Answer choices (B) and (D): These two answer choices are incorrect because sequence template #2 allows for G or J to be the most expensive suite.

Answer choices (C) and (E): These two answer choices are incorrect because sequence template #1 allows for H or K to be the most expensive suite.

Question #9: Local, Could Be True. The correct answer choice is (D)

If L is more expensive than F (L ——— F), then only Template #1 can apply to this question. Let's revisit template #1 with the addition of L ——— F:

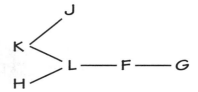

In the above diagram, both K and H are more expensive than the L ——— F ——— G chain, and J is simply less expensive than K.

Answer choice (A): This answer choice is incorrect because F cannot be more expensive than H according to the diagram above.

Answer choice (B): This answer choice is incorrect because F cannot be more expensive than K according to the diagram above.

Answer choice (C): This answer choice is incorrect because G cannot be more expensive than H according to the diagram above.

Answer choice (D): This is the correct answer choice. G can be more expensive than J.

Answer choice (E): This answer choice is incorrect because G cannot be more expensive than L according to the diagram above.

Question #10: Local, Could Be True. The correct answer choice is (D)

The question stem adds the following condition:

$$K \text{——} H \text{——} J$$

Because template #2 specifies that J ——— K, template #2 cannot apply, and only template #1 is applicable. Adding the question stem condition to template #1 produces the following diagram:

$$
\begin{array}{c}
\qquad\qquad J \\
\qquad\quad \diagup \\
K \text{——} H \text{——} L \\
\qquad\quad \diagdown \\
\qquad\qquad F \text{——} G
\end{array}
$$

Consequently, K is the most expensive suite and H is the second most expensive suite.

Answer choice (A): This answer choice is incorrect because F cannot be more expensive than H according to the diagram above.

Answer choice (B): This answer choice is incorrect because G cannot be more expensive than F according to the diagram above.

Answer choice (C): This answer choice is incorrect because G cannot be more expensive than H according to the diagram above.

Answer choice (D): This is the correct answer choice. J can be more expensive than L.

Answer choice (E): This answer choice is incorrect because L cannot be more expensive than K according to the diagram above.

Overall, this game is made easier *if* you use the last rule to create two super-sequence templates. If you do not recognize how the game is controlled by the templates, this game can be very tricky and time-consuming.

Chapter Eight: The Forgotten Few

Chapter Eight: The Forgotten Few

Three Rare Game Types

In this chapter, we will examine three types of games that have appeared infrequently on recent LSATs:

- Pattern games

- Circular Linearity games

- Mapping games

About 90% of all Logic Games are Grouping or Linear games, so it is unlikely that you would see more than one of the Forgotten Few on a current LSAT. However, even though each of these types appears rarely, each could appear on a future LSAT (and will at some point), and thus a working knowledge of their basic principles is critical if one appears on an LSAT that you take.

Before we discuss these three game types, take a moment to consider why the test makers use different kinds of games. As with the Logical Reasoning section, presenting different types of games helps the test makers keep you off balance as you move through the section. Imagine how much easier a Logical Reasoning section would be if it were composed of 25 Weaken questions or 25 Must Be True questions. You could establish a rhythm and pound out the questions quickly and efficiently. Not surprisingly, the test makers do not want that to occur, so they mix up different types of questions in the section. The same is true of the Logic Games section. By using different game types—especially rarely-seen game types—the test makers have a better chance of throwing you off and causing confusion. You can thwart this tactic by knowing the basics of every type of game that might appear on the LSAT.

Although the majority of your Logic Games section will be composed of Linear and Grouping games, it is worthwhile to prepare for any game type the test makers might use.

8

Pattern Games

The Linear Component

Because producing a pattern requires some orderly reference point, Pattern games are typically Linear in nature, and thus these games are a specific sub-type of the Linear games discussed in Chapters Three and Four. If the game is not strictly Linear, then there will be some numerical component that helps produce the arrangement of the variables.

Pattern games are a specific type of Linear game.

Non-Variable-Specific Rules and Setups

In a Pattern game, the rules typically govern the general action of all variables, as opposed to the variable-specific rules found in standard Linear games.

Variable-specific rules define the placement of individual variables, and encompass many of the rules we have already seen in this book, including rules such as "P must speak third" or "R sits next to Q."

On the other hand, Pattern game rules tend not to name specific variables, and instead generally affect the action of *all* variables equally. Thus, these rules are broader in nature, as in the following examples:

> Each singer must perform last at least one time.
>
> Every losing team drops exactly two places in the rankings.
>
> No professor lectures for three consecutive terms.

In each of the examples above, no variable is named specifically; instead the rules apply to every one of the variables in the same manner. This lack of variable-specific rules creates setups that do not contain much in the way of detailed information, and instead are often just basic representations of the spaces. Consider the following example:

> A tour operator schedules four tours—1, 2, 3, and 4—over a period of four days—Monday, Tuesday, Wednesday, and Thursday. Each day there are exactly two different tours scheduled, and each tour is scheduled exactly twice. The tours are scheduled according to the following conditions:
> No tour is given on consecutive days.

The initial setup to this game appears fairly simple:

$1\ 1\ 2\ 2\ 3\ 3\ 4\ 4^8$

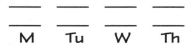

In this example, each tour is scheduled twice, hence each number appears twice on the variable list, for a total of eight variables. There are two tours per day, and thus two slots above each day, for a total of eight slots. The game is Balanced, with eight tours filling the eight spaces.

The sole rule in this game creates a series of not-blocks: each tour cannot appear on consecutive days, and thus, for example, tour 1 cannot appear on both Tuesday and Wednesday, tour 4 cannot appear on both Wednesday and Thursday, and so on. This rule could be captured by creating a set of not-blocks for each tour number, or by simply creating a TT not-block ("T" for tour, to reflect that no tour can appear on consecutive days). The scenario also stipulates that "two different tours" are scheduled each day, so the same tour cannot appear twice in one day. This limits the number of possible solutions.

Note that the rule in this game is directed equally at all four variables (1 2, 3, and 4), meaning that each variable is affected in exactly the same manner as the next variable. Tellingly, none of the variables are mentioned by name in the rule. When the rules fail to mention specific variables, the setup will often be devoid of solid information (because no variable can then be placed or ruled out of a space). In this case, most people would diagram the completed setup as follows:

$1\ 1\ 2\ 2\ 3\ 3\ 4\ 4^8$

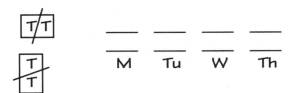

In Pattern games, the interaction of these broad rules often produces deep-seated patterns within the game but very little setup information. Unlike a typical Linear game, because none of the variables are placed into the diagram, there are no Not Laws, dual-options, etc. For this reason, most Pattern games have few Global questions, and instead have a majority of Local questions that provide the specific information lacking in the rules. Thus, we come to one of the rules of attack when you encounter a Pattern game that seems confusing:

> If you have difficulty understanding a Pattern game, try a few hypotheticals after reading the rules to help clarify the patterns that result from the interaction of the rules.
>
> Alternately, look for the Local questions containing the greatest amount of information. These questions allow you to attack the game by using a question with the greatest amount of initial information, and then the work done in the question produces a hypothetical that can help you understand the game.

8

Pattern Generation

The name *Pattern game* is a reference to the fact that patterns exist within the placement of variables. If you can identify any patterns present in a game, then you will have an advantage in attacking the questions. However, it is not essential for you to identify the patterns, and in some cases it is quite difficult. For example, in the game on the previous page, the two rules produce a set of four patterns that appear in every solution to the game:

Pattern A: Monday - Wednesday
Pattern B: Monday - Wednesday
Pattern C: Tuesday - Thursday
Pattern D: Tuesday - Thursday

The patterns are lettered for convenience; the patterns could be listed in any order. The days within each pattern—such as Monday - Wednesday—refer to the two days a tour must be scheduled if it follows that pattern. For example, the first pattern indicates that a tour must be scheduled for Monday and Wednesday. Every valid solution to the game contains one tour—it could be any one of the four—that fits this Monday - Wednesday pattern. The second pattern indicates that there is a second tour that fits this same pattern, and the final two patterns indicate that there are two other tours that each fit a Tuesday - Thursday pattern. To see this in action, consider what occurs when tours 1 and 2 are scheduled for Monday:

$$\begin{array}{c|c|c|c} 2 & \_\_\_ & \_\_\_ & \_\_\_ \\ \hline 1 & \_\_\_ & \_\_\_ & \_\_\_ \\ \hline M & Tu & W & Th \end{array}$$

Because the rule then eliminates tours 1 and 2 from being scheduled for Tuesday, tours 3 and 4 must be scheduled for Tuesday:

$$\begin{array}{c|c|c|c} 2 & 4 & \_\_\_ & \_\_\_ \\ \hline 1 & 3 & \_\_\_ & \_\_\_ \\ \hline M & Tu & W & Th \end{array}$$

1̶
2̶

Check the December 1994 Clan game or the February 1997 Train game for examples of more challenging numerical patterns.

Of course, when tours 3 and 4 are scheduled for Tuesday, then they cannot be scheduled for Wednesday, and tours 1 and 2 must be scheduled for Wednesday. And, consequently, again due to the first rule they cannot be scheduled for Thursday and tours 3 and 4 must be scheduled for Thursday:

$$\frac{2}{1} \quad \frac{4}{3} \quad \frac{2}{1} \quad \frac{4}{3}$$

$$\text{M} \quad \text{Tu} \quad \text{W} \quad \text{Th}$$

Thus, due to the nature of the game scenario and one rule, a controlling pattern emerges that can be applied to any variable, no matter which day it is scheduled. For example, if tour 3 is scheduled for Wednesday, then it must also be scheduled for Monday. Or if tour 2 is scheduled for Tuesday, it must also be scheduled for Thursday. One might wonder why the same tour cannot be scheduled for Monday and Thursday. While that schedule would not directly violate the rule, it would ultimately cause other tours to violate the rule, and thus a Monday-Thursday assignment for a tour is impossible.

Admittedly, this is a simplified example, but the point is that controlling patterns can emerge even from very basic variable and rule combinations, and thus complicated patterns can be created with the addition of more rules. Of course, not every pattern game is based on numbered sequences (such as the ones in the example), but the point is that certain signature occurrences are produced by the rules in these games, and focusing on those occurrences gives you an advantage when attacking the questions. If you did not see the patterns within the game during the setup, do not be concerned. While detecting the patterns when setting up a game would make the questions significantly easier, a game can still be attacked successfully without ever understanding the patterns if you identify strongly with each individual rule. This is the key to Pattern games: because the rules are the only real weapons available to attack the questions, you must use the rules as a hammer against the questions. Although this is true of all games, it is even more important in Pattern games where there is not a conventional, information-filled setup.

8

How to Identify Pattern Games

Pattern games can be difficult to identify at first glance. Here a few indicators that you may be facing a Pattern game:

1. The game is Linear. Often, Pattern games feature multiple stacks, but that is not a necessity.

2. The rules do not name specific variables and instead the rules govern the action of all variables equally. There can, of course, be rules that *do* name specific variables, so the presence of such a rule does not immediately mean the game is not a Pattern game.

3. The rules often involve numbers. Patterns are often numerically-based, but if not, there are usually numbers involved in helping to create the pattern.

4. The setup is entirely free of placed or fixed variables. For this reason, creating a Pattern game setup usually takes a minimal amount of time, and leaves you with the feeling that there should be more to the setup.

5. There are very few Global questions, and most of the questions are Local. Because the setup will have a minimal number of placed elements, it is more difficult (if not impossible) to make specific inferences about variable placement or what limitations exist. Thus, in order to ask specific questions, the test makers must supply additional information, which is done in the form of a Local question.

Remember, the very nature of a Pattern game is somewhat abstract, and thus there is usually no feature that obviously identifies the game or automatically makes it a Pattern game.

How to Attack Pattern Games

Once you recognize the presence of a Pattern game, there are several steps you can take to attack this unique game type:

1. Do not agonize over the fact that your setup seems "empty." The generalized nature of Pattern games usually leads to setups without a lot of information, so simply accept that fact and move on.

2. Because the setup will be minimal, focus on fully understanding the rules. The rules are all that you will have to rely upon, so you must make certain that you completely understand each rule.

3. Attack any List question first.

4. If the nature of the game is still causing you difficulty, create one or two hypotheticals to help you work with the rules and gain insight into how they interact with the variables.

5. If you continue to have difficulty, seek out the Local questions with the greatest amount of information and use those questions to create more hypotheticals. Remember to use those hypotheticals to attack other questions when applicable.

Final Pregame Note ▮▮▮▮▮▮▮▮

Please be sure to read the explanations carefully as they will give you a true sense of how to best attack each game. In addition, the explanations include points that expand the discussion given above.

If you would like to test yourself under timed conditions, you should give yourself 8 minutes and 45 seconds for each game.

After these two games, this chapter will continue on to the next game type, Circular Linearity games, and thereafter, Mapping games.

In doing these games, **use scratch paper instead of writing directly on the game!** This will prepare you for the Digital LSAT format where you cannot write directly on the screen.

Five candidates for mayor—Q, R, S, T, and U—will each speak exactly once at each of three town meetings—meetings 1, 2, and 3. At each meeting, each candidate will speak in one of five consecutive time slots. No two candidates will speak in the same time slot as each other at any meeting. The order in which the candidates will speak will meet the following conditions:

> Each candidate must speak either first or second at at least one of the meetings.
> Any candidate who speaks fifth at any of the meetings must speak first at at least one of the other meetings.
> No candidate can speak fourth at more than one of the meetings.

19. Which one of the following could be the order, from first to fifth, in which the candidates speak at the meetings?

(A)   meeting 1: Q, U, R, T, S
        meeting 2: S, T, R, U, Q
        meeting 3: T, U, Q, R, S
(B)   meeting 1: R, S, Q, T, U
        meeting 2: U, T, S, R, Q
        meeting 3: Q, R, T, U, S
(C)   meeting 1: S, Q, U, T, R
        meeting 2: U, T, Q, R, S
        meeting 3: R, Q, S, T, U
(D)   meeting 1: T, R, S, U, Q
        meeting 2: Q, R, S, T, U
        meeting 3: U, S, R, Q, T
(E)   meeting 1: U, T, R, S, Q
        meeting 2: Q, R, S, T, U
        meeting 3: S, T, U, Q, R

GO ON TO THE NEXT PAGE.

20. If R speaks second at meeting 2 and first at meeting 3, which one of the following is a complete and accurate list of those time slots any one of which could be the time slot in which R speaks at meeting 1?

(A)   fourth, fifth
(B)   first, second, fifth
(C)   second, third, fifth
(D)   third, fourth, fifth
(E)   second, third, fourth, fifth

21. If the order in which the candidates speak at meeting 1 is R, U, S, T, Q, and the order in which they speak at meeting 2 is Q, R, U, S, T, which one of the following could be true of meeting 3 ?

(A)   Q speaks first.
(B)   R speaks third.
(C)   S speaks first.
(D)   T speaks second.
(E)   U speaks fifth.

22. If R speaks first at meetings 1 and 2, and S speaks first at meeting 3, which one of the following must be true?

(A)   R speaks second at meeting 3.
(B)   R speaks fourth at meeting 3.
(C)   S speaks second at at least one of the meetings.
(D)   S speaks fifth at exactly one of the meetings.
(E)   S speaks fifth at exactly two of the meetings.

23. It could be true that at all three meetings T speaks

(A)   first
(B)   second
(C)   in some time slot after the time slot in which R speaks
(D)   in some time slot after the time slots in which S and U speak
(E)   in some time slot before the time slots in which R and U speak

24. If S, T, and U speak second at meetings 1, 2, and 3, respectively, which one of the following must be true?

(A)   The fifth speaker at at least one of the meetings is either Q or R.
(B)   Either Q speaks first at exactly two of the meetings or else R does so.
(C)   Neither S nor T speaks fifth at any of the meetings.
(D)   Q speaks third at one of the meetings, and R speaks third at another of the meetings.
(E)   Q speaks fourth at one of the meetings, and R speaks fourth at another of the meetings.

GO ON TO THE NEXT PAGE.

8

As with virtually all Pattern games, the setup contains little in the way of concrete information, as we will see shortly. The initial scenario appears as follows:

QRSTU[5]

Meeting 1: ____ ____ ____ ____ ____

Meeting 2: ____ ____ ____ ____ ____

Meeting 3: ____ ____ ____ ____ ____
          1   2   3   4   5

As is often the case in Pattern games, the rules are difficult to diagram. However, it is important to symbolize the rules in some way since the focus of the game will be on their application. Fortunately, in this game the rules are relatively simple and thus easy to remember.

The first rule states that "Each candidate must speak either first or second at at least one of the meetings." This rule can represented off to the side of the diagram, and also as a block around the first two positions, as follows:

QRSTU[5]

All = 1st or 2nd

Meeting 1: ____ ____ | ____ ____ ____

Meeting 2: ____ ____ | ____ ____ ____

Meeting 3: ____ ____ | ____ ____ ____
          1   2   3   4   5
        ALL 5

Because there are three meetings, it follows that there are six available slots for the candidates to meet this requirement. Since there are five candidates, each of whom must appear once in these six spaces, it can be inferred that exactly one candidate must appear twice within the first two speaking slots of all three meetings, and the rest of the candidates appear only once. This is an unfixed speakers-to-slots numerical distribution of 2-1-1-1-1 for the six spaces that represent the first and second speaking slots of the three meetings. Essentially, this rule means that if one speaker speaks within the first two slots at two of the meetings, then the remaining slots must be filled with the rest of the speakers. For example, if Q speaks first at meeting 1 and second at meeting 2, then R, S, T, and U each speak once in the remaining first or second positions of the meetings. This inference comes into play on all of the questions, particularly questions #20 and #21.

8

The second rule states that, "Any candidate who speaks fifth at any of the meetings must speak first at at least one of the other meetings." This rule can be diagrammed as follows,

$$5^{th} \longrightarrow 1^{st}$$

This is a powerful rule because it establishes a constant and very controlling connection between the first and fifth spaces. However, this can also be a very confusing rule. Let's go over the rule in more detail:

The rule means this: if a candidate speaks fifth at one of the meetings, then that candidate *must* speak first at one of the other meetings. So, if Q were to speak fifth at the first meeting, then Q must speak first at either the second meeting or third meeting, *or both*. So, any candidate who speaks fifth will also speak first at another meeting.

If the same candidate speaks fifth at more than one meeting (which is possible), then keep in mind that the candidate must then speak first at the other meeting. For example, if S speaks fifth at meetings 1 and 2, then S must speak first at meeting 3.

If a candidate speaks first at one of the meetings, this does *not* mean that the candidate must speak fifth at a different meeting (to make this assumption would be a Mistaken Reversal). For example, if the fifth speaker at each of the three meetings, is R, R, and T respectively, then the first speaker at each of the three meetings could be T, Q, and R respectively. In this instance, R and T speak fifth, and both speak first at another meeting, so the second rule is satisfied. Q speaks first at the second meeting, but does not speak fifth at any of the meetings. However, this is not a violation of the second rule, and thus this is acceptable.

Because the fifth slot cannot be filled by the same candidate at all three meetings (that candidate would have to speak first at at least one of the meetings, which would be impossible if the candidate was already speaking fifth at each meeting), it follows that there are always two or three different speakers in the fifth slot for all three meetings:

If there are three different candidates speaking in the fifth slot, then those same three candidates will also speak in the first slot at a meeting, in a different order.

If there are two different candidates speaking in the fifth slot, then those same two candidates will speak in the first slot, with either another candidate in the remaining first slot or with one of the two candidates doubling up.

Remember, if two different candidates fill all three of the fifth speaking slots, it is possible for a candidate to speak first at a meeting and not speak fifth.

The third rule establishes that the fourth slot must be filled by three different speakers. This rule can be shown off to the side, and by a box inside the diagram, producing the final diagram for the game:

QRSTU⁵

All = 1ˢᵗ or 2ⁿᵈ

5ᵗʰ ⟶ 1ˢᵗ

4ᵗʰ at most once

Meeting 1:

Meeting 2:

Meeting 3:

| 1 | 2 | 3 | 4 | 5 |

ALL 5   MAX 1

Thus, once a candidate speaks fourth, he or she cannot speak fourth again.

This is a complicated game, mainly because the nature of the second rule is confusing. And, when that rule is combined with the first and third rules, a complex interaction of the variables arises.

Question #19: Global, Could Be True, List. The correct answer choice is (D)

In Pattern games always be sure to attack List questions first, in order to establish a workable hypothetical. The easiest rule to apply from a visual standpoint is the last rule, "No candidate can speak fourth at more than one of the meetings." After that, the second rule should be applied, and then the first rule (the first rule should be last because it involves counting six positions).

Answer choice (A) violates the first rule (R does not appear among the first two speaking slots at any meeting) and is therefore incorrect.

Answer choice (B) violates the second rule, because S speaks fifth at the third meeting but does not speak first at any of the meetings.

Answer choice (C) violates the third rule because T speaks fourth at two meetings.

Answer choice (D) is the correct answer choice.

Answer choice (E) also violates the second rule. In this answer R speaks fifth at the third meeting but does not speak first at any of the meetings.

8

Question #20: Local, Could Be True, List. The correct answer choice is (D)

This is the first local question of the game. If R speaks second at meeting 2 and first at meeting 3, then according to our analysis of the first rule, R cannot speak first or second at meeting 1. Accordingly, answer choices (B), (C), and (E) can be eliminated.

The difference between the remaining two answer choices is whether R can speak third at meeting 1. Since there is no constraint on speaking third, and no violation caused by R speaking third, it follows that answer choice (D) is correct.

Note that answer choice (D) includes the fifth meeting as a possible speaking slot. This reflects the fact that a candidate can speak first without also having to speak fifth, as discussed in the analysis of the second rule.

Question #21: Local, Could Be True. The correct answer choice is (B)

The information in the question stem produces the following initial setup:

	1	2	3	4	5
Meeting 1:	R	U	S	T	Q
Meeting 2:	Q	R	U	S	T
Meeting 3:					

Because R, Q, and U speak first or second at meetings 1 and 2, T and S must speak in the first two slots of meeting 3. Because T speaks fifth at meeting 2, and fourth at meeting 1, from the second rule T must speak first at meeting 3, and it follows that S must then speak second at meeting 3:

	1	2	3	4	5
Meeting 1:	R	U	S	T	Q
Meeting 2:	Q	R	U	S	T
Meeting 3:	T	S			

Accordingly, answer choices (A), (C), and (D) can be eliminated. Answer choice (E) can also be eliminated since if U spoke fifth, from the second rule U would have to speak first at another meeting and that is not possible in this situation. Thus, answer choice (B) is correct.

In this question, the second rule often gives rise to a Mistaken Reversal. Remember, the second rule means that if a speaker speaks fifth at one of the meetings, then that speaker must speak first at one of the other meetings (**5ᵗʰ ⟶ 1ˢᵗ**). Many students wrongly interpret this rule to mean that if a speaker speaks first at one of the meetings then that speaker must speak fifth at another meeting (**1ˢᵗ ⟶ 5ᵗʰ**). While that interpretation may sound logical, that is not actually what the second rule states, and it does not have to be true. For example, the following hypothetical for meeting 3 in this question satisfies all the rules: T-S-R-U-Q. Note that, with this hypothetical in question #21, anyone who speaks fifth (Q and T) also speaks first (in meetings 2 and 3). R, who speaks first at meeting 1, does not speak fifth at any meeting, but this is acceptable under the wording of the second rule.

Question #22: Local, Must Be True. The correct answer choice is (E)

If R speaks first at meetings 1 and 2, and S speaks first at meeting 3, then, according to our analysis of the second rule, R must speak fifth at meeting 3 and S must speak fifth at meetings 1 and 2. It follows that answer choice (E) is correct.

Specifically, in question #22, we know that:

```
Meeting 1:    R    __   __   __   __

Meeting 2:    R    __   __   __   __

Meeting 3:    S    __   __   __   __
              1    2    3    4    5
```

So, from the question stem we already know which speakers are first at each meeting. That brings up an interesting situation for the other speakers. For example, could T speak fifth at one of the meetings, say meeting 1? No, because then there would be no meeting where T could speak first (those positions are already taken by R or S), and that would violate the second rule. The same situation would apply to Q and U, and so T, Q, and U can never speak fifth in the scenario presented in question #22. Hence, R and S must fill all of the fifth speaking spaces, and that means we can infer that S speaks fifth at meetings 1 and 2, R speaks fifth at meeting 3:

```
Meeting 1:    R    __   __   __   S

Meeting 2:    R    __   __   __   S

Meeting 3:    S    __   __   __   R
              1    2    3    4    5
```

This scenario proves answer choice (E) is correct.

Question #23: Global, Could Be True. The correct answer choice is (C)

From our discussion of the first rule, answer choices (A) and (B) can be eliminated.

Answer choice (D) can be eliminated because if T always speaks after both S and U, T can never speak first or second, a violation of the first rule.

Answer choice (E) can be eliminated since if T always speaks before R and U, then T would speak first at least twice, but could never speak fifth, which would ultimately cause a violation of the first rule.

Thus, answer choice (C) is proven correct by process of elimination. Here is a hypothetical that satisfies all of the rules of the game and the condition in answer choice (C):

Meeting 1:	R	T	U	S	Q
Meeting 2:	S	R	T	U	Q
Meeting 3:	Q	U	R	T	S
	1	2	3	4	5

Note that Q and S are the only candidates who speak fifth. Since they both speak first at some point, the second rule is satisfied.

Question #24: Local, Must Be True. The correct answer choice is (A)

If S, T, and U speak second, the following initial setup results:

Meeting 1:   ___   S   ___   ___   ___

Meeting 2:   ___   T   ___   ___   ___

Meeting 3:   ___   U   ___   ___   ___
          1   2   3   4   5

In order to accord with the first rule, we can deduce that Q and R must each appear in the first speaking slot at least once. Because of this, either Q or R must speak in the fifth slot at one of the meetings, and it follows that answer choice (A) is correct. For example, consider the following hypothetical:

Meeting 1:   R   S   ___   ___   ___

Meeting 2:   Q   T   ___   ___   ___

Meeting 3:   Q   U   ___   ___   ___
          1   2   3   4   5

In an example such as the one above, S, T, and U cannot be fifth because there's no room for them to speak first. Thus, Q and R have to be fifth. Of course, there's no necessity that Q (or R) speaks first twice, in which case that would open up the options for the fifth speaker. However, because Q and R occupy two of the first speaker positions, at least one of them must speak fifth, and hence answer choice (A) is correct.

Also, from a structural standpoint, answer choices (D) and (E) are very unlikely to be correct since they deal with the third and fourth slots, which are less affected in this question than the first, second, and fifth slots.

Remember, in Pattern games the setup is generally quick and easy to create, and therefore you have a greater amount of time to analyze the rules and ascertain their relationship to the pattern of the game (there are exceptions though!). And, armed with the knowledge that Pattern games produce few inferences, you should not be unduly concerned when your setup seems relatively empty. Also, when in doubt, do the List questions first or try a hypothetical to help gain an understanding of the nature of the game.

8

Three boys—Karl, Luis, and Miguel—and three girls—Rita, Sarah, and Tura—are giving a dance recital. Three dances—1, 2, and 3—are to be performed. Each dance involves three pairs of children, a boy and a girl partnering each other in each pair, according to the following conditions:

> Karl partners Sarah in either dance 1 or dance 2.
> Whoever partners Rita in dance 2 must partner Sarah in dance 3.
> No two children can partner each other in more than one dance.

14. If Sarah partners Luis in dance 3, which one of the following is a complete and accurate list of the girls any one of whom could partner Miguel in dance 1?

(A) Rita
(B) Sarah
(C) Tura
(D) Rita, Sarah
(E) Rita, Tura

GO ON TO THE NEXT PAGE.

15. If Miguel partners Rita in dance 2, which one of the following could be true?

   (A) Karl partners Tura in dance 1.
   (B) Luis partners Sarah in dance 2.
   (C) Luis partners Sarah in dance 3.
   (D) Miguel partners Sarah in dance 1.
   (E) Miguel partners Tura in dance 3.

16. If Miguel partners Sarah in dance 1, which one of the following is a pair of children who must partner each other in dance 3?

   (A) Karl and Rita
   (B) Karl and Tura
   (C) Luis and Rita
   (D) Luis and Tura
   (E) Miguel and Tura

17. If Luis partners Sarah in dance 2, which one of the following is a pair of children who must partner each other in dance 1?

   (A) Karl and Rita
   (B) Karl and Tura
   (C) Luis and Rita
   (D) Luis and Tura
   (E) Miguel and Rita

18. If Miguel partners Rita in dance 1, which one of the following must be true?

   (A) Karl partners Rita in dance 2.
   (B) Karl partners Sarah in dance 3.
   (C) Karl partners Tura in dance 1.
   (D) Luis partners Rita in dance 2.
   (E) Luis partners Tura in dance 3.

GO ON TO THE NEXT PAGE.

8

Analysis of Pattern Game #2: October 1993 Questions 14-18

Some games are difficult because they contain a large number of rules or variables; other games are difficult because they are built around complex concepts that lead to several deep inferences. This Pattern game is an example of the latter.

For a Pattern game it is somewhat unusual that the rules address specific variables, but this is not unprecedented. For example, the third game on the October 1996 LSAT contains similar rules. In this case the interaction of the partners helps establish the three patterns that exist in every game solution. Creating a setup that effectively captures this information is critical. The first important decision in this game is how to display the dancing couples for each dance. Many students attempt to use a basic setup similar to the following:

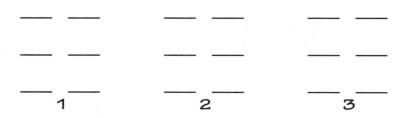

Unfortunately, this setup represents the information inefficiently. For each of the three dances, decisions must still be made for each of the six variables, eighteen total for all three dances. If at all possible, it would be preferable to fix some of the variables in the setup and thus reduce the number of variables to consider for each dance. By realizing that the individuals who dance with each girl are a single variable set, we can stack rows for R, S, and T above each of the three numbered dances:

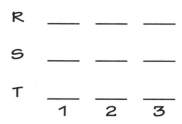

The stacking of R, S, and T in the diagram leaves only the placement of the three boys in each of the three dances. This effectively reduces the total number of variables to be placed to nine, down from eighteen in the previous setup. Choosing to display R, S, and T is superior to choosing K, L, and M because it allows the second rule to be displayed within the diagram:

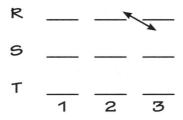

Note that the second rule is represented with a double arrow (if one occurs, then the other must occur). If we know who partners Rita in dance 2, that person must partner Sarah in dance 3, and if we know who partners Sarah in dance 3, that same person must partner Rita in dance 2.

According to the last rule, "No two children can partner each other in more than one dance." By combining this rule with the second rule, we can infer that the boy who partners Rita in dance 2 and Sarah in dance 3 must partner Tura in dance 1. This pattern holds true for every possible game configuration. This inference can also be added to the setup:

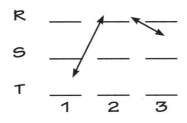

Since the game now has one established pattern, it is quite possible that other patterns exist. For example, examine the boy who dances with Rita in dance 1. In dance 2 this same boy can partner Sarah or Tura, and in dance 3 he can partner only Tura (remember, Sarah is already taken and he can't partner with Rita again). But wait—if he must partner Tura in dance 3, then he cannot partner her in dance 2, and thus he must partner Sarah in dance 2. It therefore follows that whomever partners Rita in dance 1 must partner Sarah in dance 2 and Tura in dance 3. Now that this second pattern exists, there can be only one possible pattern for the boy who partners Sarah in dance 1: Tura in dance 2 and Rita in dance 3 (remember each of the other two girls in dances 2 and 3 are involved in other patterns). Thus, by analyzing the interaction of the second and third rules, we have established that three patterns must exist in every game:

One boy must partner T in dance 1, R in dance 2, and S in dance 3. (T - R - S)

One boy must partner R in dance 1, S in dance 2, and T in dance 3. (R - S - T)

One boy must partner S in dance 1, T in dance 2, and R in dance 3. (S - T - R)

Obviously, uncovering this pattern within the rules makes the game easy to conquer. But, before beginning the questions, keep in mind that Karl must partner with Sarah in dance 1 or 2 (which means that he will be in either the STR pattern or the RST pattern).

Question #14: Local, Could Be True, List. The correct answer choice is (D)

If Luis partners Sarah in dance 3, he must partner Rita in dance 2 and Tura in dance 1. This leaves either Rita or Sarah for Miguel to partner in dance 1, and thus answer choice (D) is correct.

Question #15: Local, Could Be True. The correct answer choice is (B)

If Miguel partners Rita in dance 2, he must partner Sarah in dance 3 and Tura in dance 1. This information is sufficient to eliminate answer choices (A), (C), (D), and (E). It follows that answer choice (B) is correct.

Question #16: Local, Must Be True. The correct answer choice is (B)

If Miguel partners Sarah in dance 1, Karl must partner Sarah in dance 2. This being the case, Luis must partner Sarah in dance 3. Of course, if Luis partners Sarah in dance 3, he must partner Rita in dance 2 and Tura in dance 1. Adding this information to the patterns already established fills in the entire diagram:

$$
\begin{array}{cccc}
R & \underline{K} & \underline{L} & \underline{M} \\
S & \underline{M} & \underline{K} & \underline{L} \\
T & \underline{L} & \underline{M} & \underline{K} \\
 & 1 & 2 & 3
\end{array}
$$

It follows that answer choice (B) is correct.

Question #17: Local, Must Be True. The correct answer choice is (C)

Like the previous question, the information in the question stem fills in the entire diagram:

$$
\begin{array}{cccc}
R & \underline{L} & \underline{M} & \underline{K} \\
S & \underline{K} & \underline{L} & \underline{M} \\
T & \underline{M} & \underline{K} & \underline{L} \\
 & 1 & 2 & 3
\end{array}
$$

Thus answer choice (C) is correct.

Question #18: Local, Must Be True. The correct answer choice is (D)

While the four previous questions can be answered without an understanding of the three patterns that control this game, this generally difficult question is made easy by applying the patterns.

First, M must partner with R in dance 1, and then, according to the pattern, M must partner with S in dance 2, and with T in dance 3:

```
R    M    ___   ___

S    ___   M    ___

T    ___  ___    M
      1    2     3
```

Second, to comply with the first rule, K must partner with S in dance 1, and from the patterns, K must then partner with T in dance 2, and R in dance 3:

```
R    M    ___    K

S    K     M    ___

T    ___   K     M
      1    2     3
```

Finally, L fills the last pattern, partnering with T in dance 1, R in dance 2, and S in dance 3:

```
R    M     L     K

S    K     M     L

T    L     K     M
      1    2     3
```

The setup indicates that answer choice (D) is correct.

In retrospect, this game has a few unusual features for a Pattern game (deep inferences, variables mentioned in the rules), but it also displays features that are very patternistic, such as all five questions being Local. This game was universally considered by students to be the hardest game on the October 1993 LSAT, if not one of the hardest games of the modern era. However, an application of the basic rules allows any test taker to answer at least the first four questions, and those students who discovered the three patterns found the game quite easy. Remember, just because a game contains a few simple rules does not necessarily mean that the setup is also simple or uninformative. Always examine the interaction of the rules, even if there are only two or three.

Circular Linearity Games ▮▮▮▮▮

Circular Linearity games consist of a fixed number of variables assigned to spaces distributed around a circle. Usually the scenario involves people sitting around a table. Essentially these games are Linear games wrapped around a circular diagram, hence the name. As linearity is still the controlling principle, the Linear games approach discussed in earlier chapters still applies. However, there are several effects of the circularity:

1. In a normal Linear game, the base is written out horizontally or vertically in consecutive slots. Since Circular Linearity games feature a table, the diagramming is a bit different. Consider the following example:

   > Eight individuals sit around a circular conference table with eight chairs.
   > At most one individual sits in each chair.

   Most students attempt to diagram the game by drawing a circle with seats placed equidistantly around the circle:

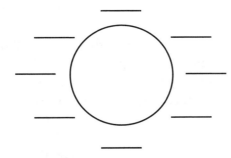

Do not waste your time by drawing out a table!

8

Although visually appealing, this diagram is too time-consuming to draw, too space inefficient, and can be confusing to use. The following diagram captures the seating and can be drawn more quickly:

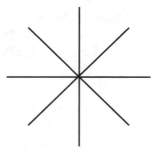

Each seat is represented by the end of a "spoke." Since there are eight seats, four spokes are needed.

2. In Circular Linearity games the number of variables affects how you attack the game. In games with an even number of variables, rules involving opposite variables (such as "A must sit opposite of B") are the most important rules. The "spoke" diagram above has the additional benefit of perfectly portraying opposites. In games without opposite rules, block rules are the most important.

In games with an odd number of variables, there can be no opposites (when seven people sit equidistantly around a table no person is directly opposite another). In these games, blocks are the most important rules and should be considered first.

3. Although most games do not have assigned seat numbers, when they do, remember that, since the linear diagram is wrapped around a circle, the person in the "first" seat and the person in the "last" seat are in fact seated next to each other. Knowledge of this fact is usually tested in List questions.

4. The phrases "to the left of" and "to the right of" refer to the left and right of the variable in question, not your left and right.

5. During the setup, some of the variables can usually be placed on the diagram in spite of the fact that you have to place them in an arbitrary fashion (you pick the spoke). If there are rules involving variables that are opposites, place those variables first. Opposites are powerful because they divide the table into two parts. If there are no opposites, then place any variables in a block. The following game will address this point.

Circular Linearity games have appeared infrequently in the released sections of the modern LSAT, most notably on the June 1991 and October 2003 tests (although also in an *unreleased* exam from July 2018). A Circularity Linearity Mini-Drill is presented on the next page, and then the June 1991 game is presented thereafter.

In spite of the fact that few Circular Linearity games have appeared on released LSATs, we do expect that a future LSAT will contain a similar game.

8

Circular Linearity Mini-Drill

Allow yourself approximately 5 minutes to complete all 4 questions. *Answers on page 506*

Eight students—A, B, C, D, E, F, G, and H—are each seated around a circular table with eight seats. Each student sits in exactly one seat, and each seat is filled by exactly one student. The seating arrangement must conform to the following limitations:

A and B are seated exactly opposite of one another.
C and D are seated next to each other.
F and G are not seated next to each other.

1. Which one of the following could be the order in which the students are seated around the table?

    (A)   A, C, D, H, B, G, F, E
    (B)   A, C, E, F, B, D, G, H
    (C)   A, D, C, G, B, E, H, F
    (D)   A, E, B, C, D, F, H, G
    (E)   A, F, D, C, B, G, H, F

2. If E and D are seated exactly opposite of one another, which one of the following cannot be true?

   (A)   A is seated next to H.
   (B)   C is seated next to H.
   (C)   F is seated next to H.
   (D)   E and F are not seated next to each other.
   (E)   G and H are not seated next to each other.

4. If E and F are seated next to each other, which one of the following could be true?

   (A)   C and E are seated next to each other.
   (B)   C and F are seated next to each other.
   (C)   D and F are seated next to each other.
   (D)   E and G are seated next to each other.
   (E)   G and H are seated next to each other.

3. If C and E are seated exactly opposite of one another, which one of the following must be true?

   (A)   A and E are not seated next to each other.
   (B)   B and C are not seated next to each other.
   (C)   C and H are not seated next to each other.
   (D)   D and E are not seated next to each other.
   (E)   D and F are not seated next to each other.

8

Circular Linearity Mini-Drill Answer Key

This drill sets up a table of eight students. The positions are not numbered, and thus your base diagram should appear as follows:

A B C D E F G H⁸

As far as rule diagrams, because the first rule contains a pair of variables that sit exactly opposite, we will choose to place them directly on the diagram, and since the seats are not numbered, we will arbitrarily choose to show the A and B variables at the "top" and "bottom" of the table diagram. The second and third rules are diagrammed to the side, and E and H are noted as randoms:

A B C D E F G H⁸
  *   *

CD or DC

F̶G̶ and G̶F̶

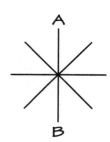

Perhaps the most notable aspect of this game scenario is how the AB rule divides the table into two halves, each with three open seats. This also shows how there's no "wrong" place to seat A and B at the table—as long as they are opposite, no matter where they are seated the table is divided into two equal parts.

Secondly, the CD rule must occupy two of the open spaces on one of the sides, which will affect what occurs in the other open spaces. For example, if E or H are seated on the same side of the table as C and D, then F and G will both be seated on the other side of the table, and neither could be in the "center" seat to keep them from sitting next to one another. Other effects follow from the

8

Circular Linearity Mini-Drill Answer Key

interplay of the rules, but since the second and third rules are the only two that are active at this point, you must pay particularly close attention to those variables.

Question #1: Global, Could Be True, List question. The correct answer is (C)

In this List question, start by applying each rule to all five answer choices. Start with the second rule (CD together) and then the third rule (FG apart) since those two are the easiest to visually identify within each answer. Last, apply the first rule (AB opposite), which is the most difficult to see within each list of eight variables:

Answer choice (A) can be eliminated since it violates the third rule (FG non-consecutive).

Answer choice (B) can be eliminated since it violates the second rule (CD consecutive).

Answer choice (C) conforms to all of the rules and is the correct answer.

Answer choice (D) can be eliminated since it violates the first rule (A and B opposite).

Answer choice (E) can be eliminated since F appears twice and E does not appear, violating the stipulation that each of the listed students is seated.

Question #2: Local, Cannot Be True question. The correct answer is (B)

This is the most difficult question of this mini-drill. The AB rule essentially divides the table into two halves, with three open seats on each "side." The CD block ends up on one side of the table, leaving just three possible "basic" positions for D. When D is seated in the middle of the three seats, C must be seated between D and then either A or B, and thus C cannot be seated next to H in this instance:

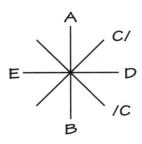

Note that the positions of A, B, D, and E aren't fixed as shown above; that's just an easy way to understand how C is "surrounded" when D is seated in a "middle" seat. In a diagram with two pairs of opposites, you typically show one as fixed and the other as rotating, as we will do in the next diagram.

When D is seated next to A or B (which we can show below as an A/B rotating option), then C is in a middle seat. There is one open seat next to C, and two open seats next to each other on the opposite side after E is placed opposite D:

The three remaining students to be seated are F, G, and H. Because of the third rule, F and G cannot both be on the same side in this arrangement since they would be in consecutive seats, and thus one of them *must* be seated next to C:

Thus, H and the other of F and G are seated next to each other on the opposite side of C.

Consequently, no matter what arrangement we choose for the CD block, C can never be seated next to H, and thus answer choice (B) can never occur and is correct.

If this problem is still confusing after you read the explanation above, one way to test the correct answer is to plug the scenario given in answer choice (B) into a hypothetical. From there, you will find that you cannot create a workable solution.

Circular Linearity Mini-Drill Answer Key

Question #3: Local, Must Be True question. The correct answer is (D)

There are different ways to solve this problem, but one way to see that answer choice (D) must occur is that since C and D are seated next to each other, and E is seated opposite of C, then there is no way for D and E to be near each other; they are always on opposite sides of the table separated by the A/B split:

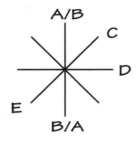

or

Question #4: Local, Could Be True question. The correct answer is (D)

The question stem adds an EF block to the original rules. When this occurs, you can immediately make several deductions. First, since the AB rule divides the table into two halves, the CD block must go on one of these sides, and the new EF block must go on the other side. Thus, the CD and EF blocks cannot be adjacent, which means that members of one block can never sit next to members of the other block. This means that answer choices (A), (B), and (C)—which each contain a single member of each pair— can never occur, and thus can be eliminated.

Because the CD and EF blocks each occupy two of the three open spaces on each side, there is only one space available on each side, leaving one of G and H to occupy each of these single spaces. Thus, G and H can never sit next to each other, and therefore answer choice (E) can be eliminated.

The remaining answer choice is (D), which can occur when E sits in the center seat on one of the sides, with F on one side of E, and G on the other side of E. The CD block and H sit on the opposite side of the table.

8

Exactly six trade representatives negotiate a treaty: Klosnik, Londi, Manley, Neri, Osata, Poirier. There are exactly six chairs evenly spaced around a circular table. The chairs are numbered 1 through 6, with successively numbered chairs next to each other and chair number 1 next to chair number 6. Each chair is occupied by exactly one of the representatives. The following conditions apply:

Poirier sits immediately next to Neri.

Londi sits immediately next to Manley, Neri, or both.

Klosnik does not sit immediately next to Manley.

If Osata sits immediately next to Poirier, Osata does not sit immediately next to Manley.

1. Which one of the following seating arrangements of the six representatives in chairs 1 through 6 would NOT violate the stated conditions?

(A)   Klosnik, Poirier, Neri, Manley, Osata, Londi
(B)   Klosnik, Londi, Manley, Poirier, Neri, Osata
(C)   Klosnik, Londi, Manley, Osata, Poirier, Neri
(D)   Klosnik, Osata, Poirier, Neri, Londi, Manley
(E)   Klosnik, Neri, Londi, Osata, Manley, Poirier

GO ON TO THE NEXT PAGE.

2. If Londi sits immediately next to Poirier, which one of the following is a pair of representatives who must sit immediately next to each other?

    (A)   Klosnik and Osata
    (B)   Londi and Neri
    (C)   Londi and Osata
    (D)   Manley and Neri
    (E)   Manley and Poirier

3. If Klosnik sits directly between Londi and Poirier, then Manley must sit directly between

    (A)   Londi and Neri
    (B)   Londi and Osata
    (C)   Neri and Osata
    (D)   Neri and Poirier
    (E)   Osata and Poirier

4. If Neri sits immediately next to Manley, then Klosnik can sit directly between

    (A)   Londi and Manley
    (B)   Londi and Poirier
    (C)   Neri and Osata
    (D)   Neri and Poirier
    (E)   Poirier and Osata

5. If Londi sits immediately next to Manley, then which one of the following is a complete and accurate list of representatives any one of whom could also sit immediately next to Londi?

    (A)   Klosnik
    (B)   Klosnik, Neri
    (C)   Neri, Poirier
    (D)   Klosnik, Osata, Poirier
    (E)   Klosnik, Neri, Osata, Poirier

6. If Londi sits immediately next to Neri, which one of the following statements must be false?

    (A)   Klosnik sits immediately next to Osata.
    (B)   Londi sits immediately next to Manley.
    (C)   Osata sits immediately next to Poirier.
    (D)   Neri sits directly between Londi and Poirier.
    (E)   Osata sits directly between Klosnik and Manley.

7. If Klosnik sits immediately next to Osata, then Londi CANNOT sit directly between

    (A)   Klosnik and Manley
    (B)   Klosnik and Neri
    (C)   Manley and Neri
    (D)   Manley and Poirier
    (E)   Neri and Osata

GO ON TO THE NEXT PAGE.

8

This is the very first game of the first LSAT of the modern era (marked by the introduction of the 120-180 scoring scale). It is also the last time a Circular Linearity game appeared in a released LSAT section before other Circular games appeared in February 1999 and October 2003. The setup is as follows:

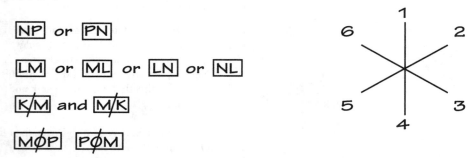

Since there are six chairs and six trade representatives, this is a Balanced game. The chair numbers prove to be relevant only on Question #1. Since the game contains no rules of opposition, the best defined block, PN, should be placed on the diagram:

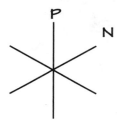

The placement of the PN block is arbitrary. They could be placed at the end of any pair of spokes, and could be in the order PN or NP. Do not assume that P and N are in chairs 1 and 2. Nevertheless, it is important to place the block on the diagram, as it will provide a starting point for adding other variables.

The final rule also bears further analysis. The rule states, "If O sits immediately next to P, O does not sit immediately next to M." Accordingly, every time O and P sit next to each other, then M cannot sit next to O and the configurations MOP and POM are impossible. Even though the rule can be written as a conditional, the representation we have provided is superior since it is easier to apply from a visual standpoint.

Question #1: Global, Cannot Be True, List. The correct answer choice is (B)

Employ the rules in order of ease of application: answer choice (E) can be eliminated since P and N are separated; an application of the KM rule eliminates answer choice (D) (Remember, chairs 1 and 6 are next to each on the circular table!); an application of the LM or LN rule eliminates answer choice (A); and finally, an application of the MOP rule eliminates answer choice (C). Answer choice (B) is correct.

Because none of the other questions include the chair numbers, the rest of the game can be treated as a Basic Linear exercise.

Question #2: Local, Must Be True. The correct answer choice is (A)

The Local condition in the question stem produces the following mini-diagram:

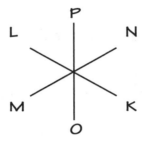

Since P and N are a block, when L sits next to P, either an LPN or NPL block is formed (the diagram above has LPN). Since L must sit next to N or M, and N is already occupied, it follows that M must sit next to L. There are now only two open spaces. Since K cannot sit next to M, K must sit next to N. O sits in the final chair, next to K and M. Answer choice (A) is correct.

8

Question #3: Local, Must Be True. The correct answer choice is (B)

The Local condition in the question stem produces the following mini-diagram:

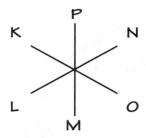

Adding the Local condition to the PN block produces a L-K-P-N sequence. Since L must sit next to M or N, M must sit next to L, and, again, O sits in the final chair. Answer choice (B) is correct.

Question #4: Local, Could Be True. The correct answer choice is (E)

Adding the Local condition to the PN block produces a P-N-M sequence. Since L must sit next to M or N, L must sit next to M. Since there are no restrictions on K or O, they form a dual-option:

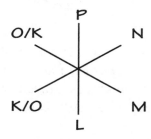

Consequently answer choice (E) is correct.

Question #5: Local, Could Be True, List. The correct answer choice is (E)

The question stem solidifies the second rule to establish that L is sitting next to M. Since this information does not allow a complete diagram to be created, the best approach is to quickly refer to previous questions to see whether any meet the criteria that L and M sit next to each other. If so, the work in those questions can be used to attack question #5.

In question #1 L and M are seated next to each other, so the hypothetical created by the correct answer in #1, K-L-M-P-N-O, can be used to prove that L can sit next to K. Accordingly, any answer choice in question #5 that does not contain K must be eliminated. Answer choice (C) can be discarded. Next, consider the work done in question #2. The solution meets the criterion that L and M sit next to each other, and reveals that L can sit next to P. Again, any answer choice that does not contain P must be rejected. Answer choices (A) and (B) can now be discarded. Only answer choices (D) and (E) remain. Question #3 also applies but only reveals that L can sit next to K, a fact established by the analysis of question #1. In question #4 it is shown that O can sit next to L, but since both answer choices (D) and (E) contain O, no progress is made. Since answer choices (D) and (E) are differentiated only by the presence of N, make a quick hypothetical to test N. The following hypothetical proves that N can sit next to L when L and M are seated next to each other:

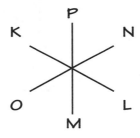

Answer choice (E) is therefore correct.

Question #6: Local, Cannot Be True. The correct answer choice is (C)

If L sits next to N, a P-N-L sequence is created:

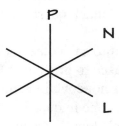

The three remaining variables are K, M, and O. Since K and M cannot sit next to each other, by Hurdling the Uncertainty we can infer that O must separate K and M:

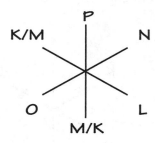

Since O is between K and M, answer choice (C) is correct.

Question #7: Local, Cannot Be True. The correct answer choice is (E)

The question stem creates a KO block. Since no obvious diagramming inferences can be made, reuse information, as was done in question #5.

The hypothetical from Question #1 applies since K and O are next to each other (remember, the first and last variables are next to each other); and this hypothetical proves that L can sit directly between K and M. That is sufficient to eliminate answer choice (A). The work from question #2 also applies and is sufficient to eliminate answer choice (D). Question #3 does not apply. Question #4 does apply and proves that L can sit between M and O (not in the answers) or M and K (already known from question #1). The hypothetical from question #6 must be examined closely. In spite of the fact that M and K rotate in the dual-option, K will always sit next to O, and thus the hypothetical reveals that L can sit between K and N as well as M and N. This information eliminates answer choices (B) and (C). Answer choice (E) is therefore correct via process of elimination.

This question again reveals the power of reusing previous work. With minimal effort all four incorrect answer choices are eliminated. And since the hypotheticals can be visually scanned at a high rate, the question takes less time than a question requiring a new diagram.

Circular Linearity games appear once in a blue moon, and it is not likely that one will appear on your test. Nevertheless, it is worthwhile to be acquainted with the basic principles in case such a game happens to appear.

8

Mapping Games ▐███████▌　　██████▌

In many games
the numerical
aspect is as
simple as the
one-to-one
relationships
described earlier.

Pure Mapping
games contain
no numerical
element.

All Logic Games can be classified as numerical or non-numerical. The vast majority of games are numerical in nature, where numbers play an important role in the game solution (Linear, Grouping, Pattern, etc.). The only non-numerical game type is Mapping, and even among Mapping games, some contain enough grouping to be numerical.

Mapping games appeared several times in the early 1990s on the LSAT, but recently they have been rare. Nevertheless, they can be quite troublesome to the unprepared student. There are three types of Mapping games:

1. <u>Spatial Relations</u>. The rules in these games do not fix the physical relationships among the variables. For example, a game involving shelter sites in a park simply states that certain shelters are one day's hike from each other. Using this information allows the test taker to ascertain the relationship among the variables, but not their exact positions. Whether a variable is north or south of another variable is generally meaningless in games of this type. The best approach for these games is to diagram the relationships with arrows or lines (as detailed on the next page).

2. <u>Directional</u>. These games involve a fixed point, and all other variables are placed North, East, South, and West of that point. For example, one game fixes City Hall as the center of a town and then proceeds to place all variables directionally by referencing City Hall. The best approach to this type of game is to use the fixed center point and draw each of the four quadrants (NE, SE, SW, and NW) around the center point.

   Although Directional games appeared several times in the 1980s, there has not been a pure Directional game in the 1990s or later. At most, some games have featured directional elements, such as the Park Bench game from the October 1992 LSAT.

3. <u>Supplied Diagram</u>. In these games the makers of the test supply a diagram intended to represent the relationship of the variables. When a diagram is provided as part of the game scenario, plan to quickly redraw it on your scratch paper and use it as the centerpiece of your setup! A good example is the Ski Chalet game from the February 1992 LSAT (game #4).

For a reference
of all games that
have appeared on
LSATs released
since 1991, visit
powerscore.com/
gamesbible.

8

Attacking Mapping Games

When drawing the diagram in a Mapping game, always consider the following three questions, in the order given:

    A. What is the direction of the connection between the variables?

    B. Do the lines have to be straight?

    C. Can the lines intersect?

Although these questions may appear simple, perhaps even obvious, many students make assumptions during the setup of Mapping games that can be deadly. Consider this game scenario:

> In a country, some of seven cities—B, F, J, N, Q, S, and X—are directly connected by highways. None of the cities physically overlap. The cities are connected in accordance with the following rules:
> > Each highway directly connects exactly two and only two cities with each other.
> > A city can be connected by highway to at most two other cities.
> > No highway can intersect with another highway.

The game initially appears to be a drawing exercise connecting the seven cities with highways. Because the highways cannot intersect, most students believe the key will be to arrange the cities in such a way as to make sure there are no intersections. Is that the right approach? Actually, no. The rules never state that the highways are straight. And, of course, if the highways are not straight, they can loop around the other highways and the drawing aspect becomes more or less meaningless. The game is actually a grouping exercise in matching cities to each other.

Let's review the three questions above, and determine how those three questions can help us properly attack this game:

The first of the three questions above, "What is the direction of the connection between the variables," is useful since it indicates whether the connections are one-way or bi-directional. If connections are one-way, draw them with arrows. If connections are bi-directional, just use straight lines. Alternatively, you can draw the lines with double-arrows (◄———►), but note that drawing the arrowheads at each end is a waste of time, hence this is a slightly less efficient approach. In this example, the highways would naturally run both ways, so straight lines would be used to represent the connections.

The second question, "Do the lines have to be straight?" is especially important when there are rules prohibiting intersection. The Highways game demonstrates just how critical this question is, because if straight lines were involved, the game would become more of a drawing exercise than just a pure connection exercise.

The third question is especially important if the lines must be straight. If the lines are straight and there is no intersection, the game will have a limited number of solutions. The last game from the February 1992 LSAT (The Ski Chalets) contains straight lines with no intersection, and there are only six solutions.

To summarize the varying Mapping line combinations and the resulting difficulty:

- Games with one-way connections between the variables will usually have more variables connected than if the direction goes both ways (because bi-directional connections are really double connections—for example, A to B, and B to A).

- If the lines are straight but intersection is allowed, the game is not especially limited.

- If the lines do not have to be straight but intersection is prohibited, the game is not especially limited.

- If the lines must be straight and there is no intersection, the game is limited and there are likely a limited number of solutions.

The last game from February 1992 is a classic Mapping game with no true numerical element. This, in part, explains why the rules about the lines are so important in that game.

8

The Grouping Element

Mapping elements are sometimes used to hide Grouping games. The Highways game discussed above appears to be a Mapping game, but closer analysis reveals that it is a Grouping game about connections where the map has little meaning. As you analyze a game that appears to contain Mapping, ascertain if there are grouping elements (who can and cannot go with each other). If you discover Grouping is present, immediately attack that element and use the map only if necessary.

The last released LSAT Mapping game appeared in June 1995. That game is presented on the next page. Prior to June 1995, Mapping appeared five times on the modern LSAT. In Appendix One we have listed each Mapping game and also noted when the game contained strong grouping elements. At times, questions of classification can arise with Mapping since some games like the Highways game are really Grouping games.

8

The country of Zendu contains exactly four areas for radar detection: R, S, T, and U. Each detection area is circular and falls completely within Zendu. Part of R intersects T; part of S also intersects T; R does not intersect S. Area U is completely within R and also completely within T. At noon exactly four planes—J, K, L, M—are over Zendu, in a manner consistent with the following statements:

Each plane is in at least one of the four areas.
J is in area S.
K is not in any detection area that J is in.
L is not in any detection area that M is in.
M is in exactly one of the areas.

7. Which one of the following could be a complete listing of the planes located in the four areas at noon, with each plane listed in every area in which it is located?

(A) R: J, L;   S: J, M;   T: L;   U: L
(B) R: J, L;   S: K;   T: M;   U: none
(C) R: K;   S: J;   T: L;   U: M
(D) R: K, M;   S: J, L;   T: J;   U: none
(E) R: M;   S: J, K;   T: J, L;   U: none

GO ON TO THE NEXT PAGE.

8. If at noon K is within exactly two of the four areas, then which one of the following CANNOT be true at that time?

(A) J is within area T.
(B) K is within area R.
(C) K is within area T.
(D) L is within area R.
(E) L is within area T.

9. Which one of the following is a complete and accurate list of those planes any one of which could be within area T at noon?

(A) M
(B) J, L
(C) J, L, M
(D) K, L, M
(E) J, K, L, M

10. Which one of the following statements CANNOT be true at noon about the planes?

(A) K is within area T.
(B) K is within area U.
(C) L is within area R.
(D) M is within area R.
(E) M is within area U.

11. It CANNOT be true that at noon there is at least one plane that is within both area

(A) R and area T
(B) R and area U
(C) S and area T
(D) S and area U
(E) T and area U

12. If at noon M is within area T, then which one of the following statements CANNOT be true at that time?

(A) J is within area T.
(B) L is within area R.
(C) L is within area S.
(D) K is within exactly two areas.
(E) L is within exactly two areas.

13. If at noon plane L is within exactly three of the areas, which one of the following could be true at that time?

(A) J is within exactly two of the areas.
(B) J is within exactly three of the areas.
(C) K is within area S.
(D) M is within area R.
(E) M is within area T.

GO ON TO THE NEXT PAGE.

Analysis of Mapping Game #1: June 1995 Questions 7-13

On the surface this game appears to be a drawing exercise, and most students diagram the game as follows:

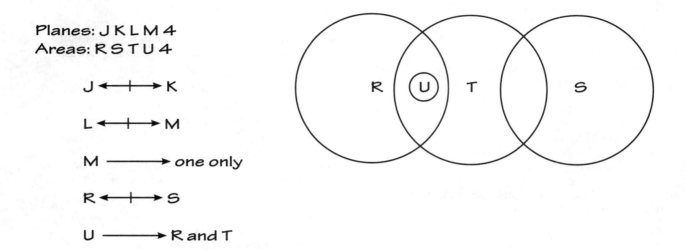

Planes: J K L M 4
Areas: R S T U 4

J ◄———► K

L ◄———► M

M ———► one only

R ◄——┤—► S

U ———► R and T

However, much like the Highways game discussed previously, this is actually a Grouping game masquerading as a Mapping game. Especially indicative are the third and fourth rules, both of which are negative Grouping rules. Since grouping is such an important principle on the LSAT, we felt it worthwhile to examine a game that has mapping elements but is controlled by grouping principles.

Although every student inevitably draws out the detection areas, it is probably easier to understand this game when it is set up in a more Linear fashion:

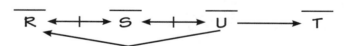

In this setup, we convert the radar areas into a grouping relationship. For example, since U is inside of R and T, in our setup we show U with arrows heading towards R and T, meaning that any variable that is in U must also be in R and T. The game scenario indicates R and S do not overlap; our diagram puts a double-not arrow between R and S to indicate that any variable in one of R or S cannot be in the other. The same relationship holds for S and U.

Note that the grouping rules involving areas R, S, T, and U are easily displayed internally within this diagram. Also, since the detection areas are now represented linearly, it is easier to show the Not Laws that apply to each plane. The game is now diagrammed in a much more familiar format and should therefore be easier to attack.

With the setup structure in hand, let's take a moment to examine the rules and generate the remainder of the diagram. In considering this setup, remember that the game is about where each plane is at exactly noon, and thus this is a snapshot at a given time.

The first rule establishes that planes J, K, L, and M are all in a zone, and thus all four are "in" the game, and no plane is "out." This does not mean, however, that each zone contains a plane. It is possible for a zone to have no planes in it, or more than one plane in it.

The second rule places plane J in area S, and because area S does not overlap with R or U according to the game scenario, J Not Laws can be placed on areas R and U

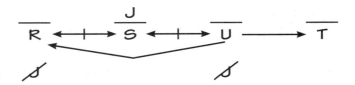

The third rule creates a negative grouping relationship between K and J. Because we have now introduced the possibility of a vertical component in the game, this can be diagrammed with a vertical not-block. Additionally, a K Not Law now appears on area S because J is already in S:

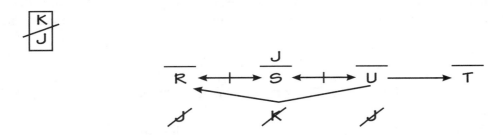

The fourth rule creates another vertical not-block:

No Not Laws immediately follow from this rule, because neither L nor M is placed in any area yet.

The fifth rule limits plane M to exactly one of the areas, which immediately eliminates M from being in U (since U is inside R and T), leading to the final diagram for the game:

Planes: J K L M⁴
Areas: R S T U⁴

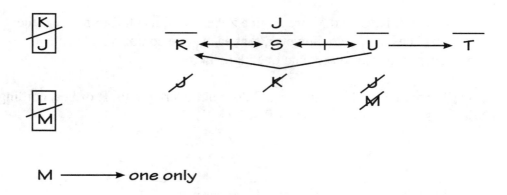

M ──────▶ one only

Before moving to the questions, take a moment to consider how the "overlapping" aspect of the areas affects the planes. For example, J is known to be in area S. However, area S also overlaps with area T, so J *could* also be in area T (but does not have to be in area T). Areas R and T also overlap, so a plane in one could be in the other (unless the plane is in U, in which case it must be in R and T). This overlapping aspect lends a Could Be True element to the placement of the planes, and makes the game more challenging.

Finally, remember that many games that would generally be classified as Mapping games are actually Grouping games, and so often the best approach is to diagram the Grouping relationship as your primary diagram.

Question #7: Global, Could Be True, List. The correct answer choice is (D)

This is a straightforward List question, and a great way to start a difficult game.

Answer choice (A) is incorrect because J cannot be in area R (J is already in area S, and S and R do not overlap according to the game scenario).

Answer choice (B) is incorrect because from the second rule J must be in area S, and because J cannot be in area R (as explained in answer choice (A)).

Answer choice (C) is incorrect because, due to the last rule, M cannot be in area U.

Answer choice (D) is the correct answer.

Answer choice (E) is incorrect because, due to the second and third rules, K cannot be in area S.

8

Question #8: Local, Cannot Be True. The correct answer choice is (A)

If K is within exactly two areas, K cannot be in area U, since area U is also within areas R and T. Because K also cannot be in area S from the game setup, K must be in areas R and T:

$$\frac{K}{R}\cancel{J} \quad \frac{J}{S}\cancel{K} \quad \frac{\ }{U}\cancel{K} \quad \frac{K}{T}\cancel{J}$$

Because K is in area T, from the third rule J cannot be in area T, and answer choice (A) is correct.

Question #9: Global, Could Be True, List. The correct answer choice is (E)

A perfect situation to refer to earlier work. According to question #7, answer choice (D), J can be in area T. Thus, answer choices (A) and (D)—which fail to include J—must be incorrect.

According to the work in question #8, K can be in area T, and thus answer choices (B) and (C)—which fail to include K—must be incorrect. Answer choice (E) is proven correct by process of elimination.

Question #10: Global, Cannot Be True. The correct answer choice is (E)

According to the Not Laws in the initial setup, M cannot be in area U, and thus answer choice (E) is correct.

Question #11: Global, Cannot Be True. The correct answer choice is (D)

Again, according to the relationships diagrammed in the initial setup, no individual plane can be within areas S and U at the same time, and thus answer choice (D) is correct.

Question #12: Local, Cannot Be True. The correct answer choice is (E)

The information in the "if" statement can be diagrammed as follows:

$$\frac{\ }{R}\cancel{M} \quad \frac{J}{S}\cancel{M} \quad \frac{\ }{U}\underset{\cancel{K}}{\cancel{M}} \quad \frac{M}{T}\cancel{K}$$

From the fifth rule, M is in exactly one detection area. Thus, when M is in T, M cannot be in R, S, or U. From the fourth rule, L cannot be in any area that M is in, and so L cannot be in area T. Additionally, because any plane in area U is also in area T, because L cannot be in area T then it also cannot be in area U (and hence the L Not Law on area U). This is essentially a result of the contrapositive of the U $\longrightarrow$ T area relationship.

L is now limited to areas R and S, and because the game scenario specifies that R does not intersect S, no plane can simultaneously be in both areas R and S. Thus, L can be in only one detection area (R or S), and answer choice (E) cannot be true and is correct.

Remember, this is a Cannot Be True question, and thus the four incorrect answer choices could occur. For example, answer choice (D) could be true because K could be in both areas R and T.

Question #13: Local, Could Be True. The correct answer choice is (A)

If L is within exactly three areas, L cannot be in area S (if L were in S, then it could only be in S and T) and therefore L must be in areas R, U, and T:

$$
\begin{array}{cccc}
 & M & & \\
L & J & L & L \\
\hline
R & S & U & T \\
\cancel{M} & \cancel{K} & \cancel{M} & \cancel{M}
\end{array}
$$

Since L and M cannot be in the same detection areas, M cannot be in areas R, U, and T, and therefore answer choices (D) and (E) are incorrect. Since M must be in at least one detection area, it follows that M must be in area S. According to the Not Laws in our initial setup, K can never be in area S, and therefore answer choice (C) is incorrect. In answer choice (B), it is impossible for J to be in three areas since any plane in area S cannot be in area R and U (and plane J is in area S from the second rule). Thus, J can only be in at most two areas. Since answer choice (B) is incorrect, answer choice (A) is proven correct by process of elimination.

When you begin a Logic Game, you should read through all of the rules *before* you begin diagramming. As you read, consider the true nature of the game. LSAC is often able to confuse test takers who fail to completely examine the nature of the rules and their interrelationships. This game provides a fine example of how a thorough and knowledgeable test taker can gain a significant advantage by recognizing the true nature of the rules.

Chapter Nine: Advanced Features and Techniques

Chapter Nine: Advanced Features and Techniques

Two Difficult Question Types ▉

In Chapter Three, we discussed six specific question types (such as List, Maximum/Minimum, etc.) and mentioned that two of the types would be explored in more detail later. These two types—Justify and Rule Substitution—are generally harder than other question types, and they involve more complicated solution strategies.

Justify Questions

Justify questions ask you to select an answer choice that forces a specified result. The question stem states the result you are seeking, and the answers provide possible ways to make that result occur. The correct answer is the one that produces the exact result specified.

These questions have a signature form, so they are usually easy to recognize. One part of the question will state the outcome the test makers wish to force, and the other part of the question will direct you to consider the answer choices to be true. This is one common form of this question:

Justify questions can appear in any type of game.

[Desired result] if which one of the following is true?

Examples:

Q must be third, if which one of the following is true?

The group of astronauts chosen is completely determined if which one of the following is true?

The two questions above are Global, but Justify questions can be Local as well:

If Grigoriev is selected, then which one of the following completely determines the group of parents selected for the panel?

9

In Chapter Three, we discussed taking two basic steps to solve a Justify question. In this section, we will expand and refine those two steps into the following:

Step 1: Isolate the result specified in the question stem.

This piece of advice should make sense. Because producing the result in the question stem is the goal of the question, you must first understand exactly what you are seeking to do.

Step 2: Glance at the answer choices and ascertain the general nature of the answers provided.

Seeing the type of answers provided gives you an understanding of the direction the test makers are taking with the relationships that will lead to the correct answer. This technique works because most Logic Game answers to individual justify questions are of roughly the same sort. For example, the answers to a single question may all read in a similar style, such as "Variable X is placed in slot Y."

Thus, for example, if all the answers contain sequences, you can begin thinking in those terms, whereas if all the answers place individual variables in certain positions, you might think differently about possible solutions.

Step 3: Identify any rules or restrictions relevant to elements named in the specified result.

The result specified in the question stem will reference at least one variable, corresponding space, or group of variables. Quickly examine those variables and spaces for any related rules or inferences.

Step 4: Look for "next level" connections to those elements.

While isolating each related rule or inference is necessary, the solution to these questions usually requires connecting "secondary" inferences, or those inferences that relate to variables that are connected to the variables mentioned in the rule.

Part of this process typically centers around which variables are the most powerful (the variables that have the greatest impact on other variables) and which spaces are the most restricted (spaces with more restrictions are often at the center of question solutions).

Step 5: Identify any occurrences that would force the desired result.

As you work through step 3, identify any situations or events that would force the condition in the question stem to occur. If you do not see any likely candidates, move to the answer choices.

Step 6: Analyze the answer choices, and look for answers that match what you found in step 5.

When analyzing the answers, focus on the one(s) that relates most closely to the areas you've identified as relevant to creating the desired outcome.

Let's now look at an example and see how these steps work in action. Consider the following game scenario and rule set:

> A festival organizer schedules four musical groups—Ariadne, Bender, Crossbow, and Dorado—to play over a period of four days—Thursday, Friday, Saturday, and Sunday. Each day exactly one musical group plays, and each group plays exactly one style: two groups play rock and two groups plays jazz. The groups are scheduled subject to the following constraints:
> Dorado does not play on Sunday.
> Jazz is played on Friday.
> Ariadne plays rock.

The setup to this game is rather simple:

R R J J⁴
A B C D⁴

Let's now add in a straightforward Justify question:

Justify questions can appear as any question number in a game. In other words, they could be the second, or fourth, or sixth question in a game. This is notable because some question types—such as Suspension questions—are always the last question in a game when they appear.

9

Crossbow must be scheduled for Sunday if which one of the following is true?

(A) Ariadne and Bender play on Thursday and Saturday, respectively.

(B) Ariadne and Dorado play on Thursday and Friday, respectively.

(C) Ariadne and Dorado play on Thursday and Saturday, respectively.

(D) Bender and Dorado play on Thursday and Saturday, respectively.

(E) Bender and Dorado play on Friday and Saturday, respectively.

For explanatory purposes, let's look at each of the steps in detail:

Step 1: Isolate the result specified in the question stem.

In this question, the goal is to force Crossbow to be scheduled for Sunday.

Step 2: Glance at the answer choices and ascertain the general nature of the answers provided.

Each answer assigns two groups to two different days. Thus, every answer will address two of the four variables, and place them definitively. This is helpful because we are looking at the placement of one variable, and each answer fixes 50% of the variable set. Because Crossbow is not mentioned explicitly, the correct answer must somehow indirectly affect Crossbow's placement (which is the normal procedure in these questions).

Step 3: Identify any rules or restrictions relevant to the elements named in the specified result.

While Crossbow has no direct restriction or rule involvement, Dorado cannot play on Sunday. Thus, only Ariadne, Bender, and Crossbow are candidates for Sunday.

Step 4: Look for "next level" connections to those elements.

This game is relatively simple and has only a few rules, so there does not appear to be any immediately obvious next-level connections. That won't be the case for most questions of this type, but this question was designed to be a very basic example.

Step 5: Identify any occurrences that would force the desired result.

In this case, because only Ariadne, Bender, and Crossbow are candidates for Sunday, removing Ariadne and Bender from Sunday would force Crossbow to play on Sunday.

Step 6: Analyze the answer choices, and look for answers that match what you found in step 5.

Answer choice (A) removes Ariadne and Bender from Sunday, and is thus the correct answer.

In a real game, you would not stop and methodically take each step; you'd simply apply the succession of steps like a waterfall—very quickly and seemingly at once.

Now, let's look at a slightly more difficult version of the same question type:

The group playing on Thursday is determined if which one of the following is true?

(A)   Ariadne plays earlier than Crossbow.
(B)   Bender plays earlier than Crossbow.
(C)   Dorado plays earlier than Ariadne.
(D)   Crossbow plays later than Bender.
(E)   Dorado plays later than Ariadne.

Again, let's look at each step in detail:

9

Step 1: Isolate the result specified in the question stem.

In this question, the goal is to establish the group playing on Thursday. This is a broader goal than in the previous question, because that question focused on a specific group playing on a specific day; this question focuses on any of the groups being forced to play on a specific day.

Step 2: Glance at the answer choices and ascertain the general nature of the answers provided.

In this question, each answer is sequential in nature, and two groups are placed relative to each other. Thus, we will need to think about a sequence of variables that creates issues or limitations on Thursday. One note of interest is that the first three answers use "earlier than" and the last two answers use "later than." This is easy enough to handle, but it is one more element to have to think about.

Step 3: Identify any rules or restrictions relevant to the elements named in the specified result.

Thursday itself has no restrictions. The other part of the question involves all the groups, so every rule applies.

Step 4: Look for "next level" connections to those elements.

Whereas the first question was rather simple and the solution focused on adding more variables to the preexisting restriction in place for Sunday, this question is more challenging. Accordingly, a deeper analysis is required.

We can dispense with any concern about the type of music played Thursday, because the answers focus on group placement (regardless, even knowing music type would not force a particular group to play Thursday because each type of music is played by two groups). Thus, we can jump directly to looking at the music groups.

While Thursday itself has no restriction, Friday must feature a jazz group, which isolates Thursday to some extent. The Friday jazz stipulations also directly impacts Ariadne. If there is a way to force Ariadne in front of Friday, that would result in Ariadne playing Thursday.

9

Step 5: Identify any occurrences that would force the desired result.

> The only way to force Ariadne into a Thursday placement is
> to eliminate it from Saturday and Sunday. The only restriction
> on those two days is that Dorado cannot play on Sunday. So,
> connecting Dorado to Ariadne creates an opportunity to force
> Ariadne onto Thursday, an opportunity that can be explored in the
> next step.

Step 6: Analyze the answer choices, and look for answers that match what
you found in Step 5.

> Answer choices (A), (C) and (E) each involve Ariadne, but (C)
> and (E) connect Ariadne and Dorado and thus they should be the
> starting points in this question.

> Answer choice (C) creates a D ——— A sequence. Because A
> can play Saturday or Sunday, D could play Thursday, Friday,
> or Saturday. That leaves multiple options for Thursday, and this
> answer fails to justify the condition in the stem.

> Answer choice (E) creates an A ——— D sequence. Because D
> cannot play on Sunday, D must play on Friday or Saturday. If
> D plays on Friday, then A plays on Thursday, and if D plays on
> Saturday, A must still play on Thursday. Thus, when A ——— D, A
> must play on Thursday, and this answer choice is correct.

Because real games have more variables and more rules than our example,
the process of identifying the occurrences that can ensure the desired result
can be more challenging, but the basic process is the same: isolate the end
result, and then look for connections that can be used to lead to that result.

9

Rule Substitution Questions

The other type of question we will discuss in this chapter involves Rule Substitution. These questions ask you to first suspend one of the original rules of the game, and then replace that rule with a substitute that has *exactly* the same effect as the original rule.

Rule Substitution questions are a combination of Suspension and Justify questions: first the original rule is suspended (the Suspension part), and then it is replaced with a new rule that forces the exact same result (this is the Justify component).

The search for a perfect equivalent should not intimidate you. In the *LSAT Logical Reasoning Bible*, we talk about how the test makers can reword a concept in different ways but still arrive at the same meaning. For example, the following two sentences appear to be different at first glance, but each means the same thing:

> All of the men are absent from the meeting.
>
> None of the men are present at the meeting.

In a sense, Rule Substitution questions ask you to achieve the same effect, but because the source material relates to rules and variables, they have a wider range of possible wordings and connections to choose from in achieving this result.

Similar to Justify questions, to solve these questions you must analyze what is under consideration, and then consider the relationships that can lead to the desired outcome. However, because the answer choices must have an identical effect, there are different types of answers, and a greater limitation on the kinds of correct answers that can be presented.

These questions have only appeared on the LSAT since 2009.

Let's begin by discussing how to recognize these questions. They are usually easy to recognize: one part of the question directs you to replace a specific rule with one of the answer choices, and the other part of the question directs you to create the same result as the suspended rule. Here is the typical language you will encounter:

> Which one of the following, if substituted for the [condition/ restriction/information] that [wording of one of the rules], would have the same effect in determining the [order/group/selections in the game]?

Here is an example:

> Which one of the following, if substituted for the condition that Ronald must sing with Lucinda, would have the same effect in determining the pairings of the singers?

9

As you can see from the typical language used, this type of question can appear in any game type—Linear, Grouping, Sequencing, etc. However, when this question has appeared, it has always appeared as the last question in the game.

Rule Substitution questions can appear in any game type.

With an understanding of how to recognize these questions, let's discuss the steps necessary to solve them:

Step 1: Isolate the rule being replaced and analyze its effects.

Because your goal is to replace the rule perfectly, you must first identify the *exact* effects of the rule, including its effect on other variables. Consider the nature of the rule (Is it a block? A conditional relationship? A sequence? ...and so on) and how it impacts the variables in the rule, and limits the placement of other variables.

Step 2: Identify any rules or restrictions that connect to the rule in question and the variables involved in those rules.

The rule specified in the question stem will reference at least one variable and corresponding space or group. Quickly examine those variables and spaces for any related rules or inferences.

Step 3: Move to the answer choices, and examine each to see whether its effects perfectly match those of the rule in question.

In Rule Substitution questions, the test makers have a great deal of latitude in how they can phrase the correct answer, and thus these answers can be extremely difficult to prephrase. Thus, you should not spend much, or any, time trying to come up with what would be a suitable substitute.

Even glancing at the answer choices is not typically fruitful (as it would be in a Justify question) because often the nature of the answers is quite disparate (for example, within the same set of answer choices, some might be conditional and others might be sequential in nature).

The first two steps here make some obvious sense: know the rule under examination, and re-acquaint yourself with the rules and variables that connect to it. The last step requires further discussion. In these questions there are certain types of correct and incorrect answer choices, and thus a deeper discussion of those elements is warranted.

Let us start by discussing incorrect answer choices in these questions, because seeing the range of wrong answers will help provide a more solid understanding of how these questions operate.

Incorrect Answer Choice Types

1. Rearrangement

   These answers feature the exact same variables as the rule in question, but rearrange the relationship. Because Rule Substitution questions are often difficult, students gravitate towards the known. Thus, an answer that features the exact same variables as the rule being replaced will initially be appealing. However, these answers are almost always incorrect.

2. Partial Match

   These answers match a portion of the effects of the rule, but do not match every part of the rule.

   When these answers are in play, the rule being replaced typically has multiple parts or multiple effects. Because you must select an answer with identical effects, one attractive incorrect answer type matches just a portion of the rule, but not all of the rule. Here's a sample rule:

   Abigail plays after Eduardo, but Abigail does not play fifth.

   This rule contains two separate aspects:

   Abigail plays after Eduardo.
   and
   Abigail does not play fifth.

   Thus, a classic wrong answer would fully address one of these aspects (for example, the E ——— A portion) but then fail to address the other portion (A not fifth). Because you must match all of the effects of the rule, these answer choices are automatically incorrect.

9

3. Additional Effects

These answers create additional restrictions that go beyond the restrictions in the rule. In this sense, these answers contain an error that is the opposite of the error in point 2. Instead of failing to meet all aspects of the rule, these answers go beyond the stipulations of the rule, and create new restrictions that did not originally exist. Consider the following example:

H cannot be selected to perform with the first group.

This rule is fairly straightforward, and thus we need to replace it with another rule that knocks H out of group 1. However, an incorrect answer might eliminate H not just from group 1, but from another group (or groups) as well. Because you must match all of the effects of the rule and not add any new effects, these answer choices are automatically incorrect.

4. Shell Game

These answers connect variables that could—when configured properly—lead to a correct answer, but they connect them improperly.

Shell Game answers can be tricky because all of the pieces needed are present, they are just arranged incorrectly. Thus, you must be careful when considering answers to make sure that the relationships stated in the answer accord with what is needed.

We will discuss variable and rule linkage further in the next section, because this area often leads to the correct answer as well.

With a better understanding of the types of incorrect answers that are likely to appear, let's now examine the different types of correct answers.

For the discussion of **Correct Answer Choice Types** in these problems, visit the digital book site using the code on the inside front cover of this book.

9

Numerical Distributions ▮▮▮▮▮▮▮

Recognizing distributions is critical to solid games performance.

A Numerical Distribution allocates one set of variables among another set of variables. Since the distribution controls the placement of variables, the distribution is a basic, but critical, element in the game. Because of their importance, Numerical Distributions were naturally discussed in previous chapters. In Chapter Three the discussion of Basic Linear games introduced the "one-to-one" distribution: the number of variables to be assigned matches the number of spaces to be filled. The following game scenario is an example:

> A tutor is planning a daily schedule of individual tutoring sessions for each of six students—S, T, W, X, Y, and Z. The tutor will meet with exactly one student at a time, for exactly one hour each session. The tutor will meet with students starting at 1 P. M., for six consecutive hours.

The six students are each assigned to one of six hours, a Numerical Distribution of 1-1-1-1-1-1. At this level, the distribution is so basic as to appear obvious. As the discussion in Chapter Three progressed, the distributions became more complex, as in one of the games discussed:

These two examples produce one distribution each. Some game scenarios produce multiple distributions.

> An apartment building has five floors. Each floor has either one or two apartments. There are exactly eight apartments in the building.

The "eight apartments into five floors" scenario produces a 2-2-2-1-1 distribution. This distribution requires more attention than the 1-1-1-1-1-1 distribution since there is variation in the number: some floors have one apartment and others have two apartments. That imbalance is an element that must be tracked throughout the game.

Let us take a moment to examine the composition of the distributions above. In the 1-1-1-1-1-1 example, there are six hours and thus there are six separate numbers. There are also six students assigned to those six hours and so the numbers add up to six. In the 2-2-2-1-1 example, there are five floors and so there are five separate numbers. There are eight apartments assigned to those five floors, and so the numbers add up to eight. Therefore, each separate number represents apartments on a floor. Three floors have two apartments, and two floors have one apartment. Numerical Distributions follow this rule: the numbers add up to an amount equal to the total number of variables in the set being allocated; the number of separate numbers is equal to the number of elements "receiving" the allocated set.

Distributions occur with any two sets of variables; one of the sets is allocated across the other set. The set being allocated will have an equal or greater number of variables than the receiving set, as in the following examples:

1. The variable sets are of equal size.

> Six drivers will be assigned to six cars numbered consecutively 1 through 6. Exactly one driver is assigned to each car.

The six drivers are distributed among six cars. Since there are six drivers and six cars, the distribution is 1-1-1-1-1-1.

2. One variable set is larger than the other variable set.

> Six chefs will cook four dishes. Each chef cooks exactly one dish, and each dish is cooked by at least one of the six chefs.

The six chefs are distributed among the four dishes. Since each chef cooks one dish and there are four dishes to cook, there will be four separate numbers that add up to six. Since there are more chefs than dishes, at least one dish must be cooked by two or more chefs. This scenario creates two distributions: 2-2-1-1 and 3-1-1-1. In the first distribution two different dishes are cooked by two chefs each, and two other dishes are cooked by one chef each. In the second distribution one dish is cooked by three different chefs, and the other three dishes are each cooked by one chef each.

Numerical Distributions appear within a variety of game types, as illustrated by the two examples to the right: the first distribution example is from a Linear game, the second distribution example is from a Grouping game.

9

Creating Distributions Systematically

An extreme distribution has the greatest variance in the numbers, such as 5-1-1.

An average or "middle" distribution is the one closest to the center, with the least variance in numbers, such as 3-2-2.

Because some games have three or more distributions, you must use a systematic approach to find every distribution. To find all the distributions in a game, follow these steps:

1. Satisfy the minimum requirements for the receiver set.

2. Examine the remaining or "extra" variables in the allocated set and count the number of ways the remaining variables can be distributed.

3. Create a distribution for each configuration in Step 2 by adding the minimum requirements to each configuration. Work from the extreme to the "middle."

Consider the following example:

> Five students are assigned to three separate groups. Each group must be assigned at least one student.

Since there are three groups, there will be three separate numbers, and since there are five students, the numbers will add up to five. The minimum requirements are:

	Group	Group	Group	
Minimums:	1	1	1	= 3

Note that the groups have not been numbered since the groups are not ordered. Since each group must be assigned at least one student, the minimum requirements claim three of the five students. This leaves just two "extra" students to consider. The two students can be distributed in only two ways: both can be assigned to the same group or they can be assigned to different groups.

	Group	Group	Group	
Minimums:	1	1	1	= 3

Distribution 1: (both students assigned to same group—the extreme)	3	1	1	= 5
Distribution 2: (the two students assigned to different groups— the middle)	2	2	1	= 5

"Numerical Distribution" refers to both single distributions and multiple distributions within a game.

Since the two "extra" students can be configured only two ways (together or separate), there are exactly two distributions. In Distribution 1 the two students are added to the minimum requirements to create a 3-1-1 distribution. In Distribution 2 the two students are separated and then added to the minimum requirements to create a 2-2-1 distribution. These two distributions represent the only two ways that the students can be assigned to the three groups when at least one student must be assigned to each group.

Please note that you cannot determine that there are two distributions just because there are two "extra" variables beyond the minimum requirements. Consider another example:

There is no rule that allows you to immediately determine the number of possible distributions. Cases must be examined on an individual basis.

> Seven assignments are given to two workers. Each worker must be given at least two assignments.

The seven assignments are distributed between two workers, so there will be two separate numbers that add up to seven. The minimum requirements claim four of the seven assignments:

	Worker	Worker	
Minimums:	2	2	= 4

There are just three "extra" assignments to consider. The three assignments can be distributed in only two ways: all three can be assigned to the same worker or two can be assigned to one worker and one can be assigned to the other worker:

	Worker	Worker	
Minimums:	2	2	= 4

	Worker	Worker	
Distribution 1: (all three assignments to one worker)	5	2	= 7
Distribution 2: (two assignments to one worker and one assignment to the other worker)	4	3	= 7

The most extreme distribution is usually the easiest to identify. Thereafter you work inwards to the least concentrated, or "most average," distribution.

Generally, when you create distributions, it is easier to start by examining extremes. First establish the minimum requirements and then assign the extra variables in maximum-sized groups. In the example immediately above, the first distribution allocates all three extra assignments to one worker, and then divides the three assignments into smaller groups for the second distribution.

Fixed versus Unfixed Distributions

Numerical Distributions are either *fixed* or *unfixed*; that is, the allocated set may or may not be attached to a specific variable in the receiver set. In this chapter each distribution has so far been unfixed. In the last example the 5-2 distribution contains two possibilities: worker 1 is given five assignments and worker 2 is given two assignments; or worker 1 is given two assignments and worker 2 is given five. Since writing out every variation of a complex distribution would waste an incredible amount of time, distributions that can move around are called unfixed. Thus a 5-2 unfixed distribution immediately implies that the "5" and "2" are not assigned to any particular worker (and so the distribution could actually be 5-2 or 2-5). The same is true for the 4-3 distribution above. Either worker could be given the four assignments. The unfixed designation is useful because it delivers a significant amount of information in a compact form and saves time in doing so.

In a 5-2, 4-3 unfixed distribution, there are really four fixed distributions: 5-2, 2-5, 4-3, and 3-4. The order of presentation is irrelevant.

Numerical Distributions can also be fixed, but there must be at least one rule that specifies a relationship among specific variables. Consider the previous example about students and groups:

Five students are assigned to three separate groups. Each group must be assigned at least one student.

Now add a rule that states:

Group 1 must be assigned exactly twice as many students as Group 2.

In games with fixed distributions, it is often best to Identify the Templates. This strategy will be discussed at the end of this chapter.

The rule connects two of the variables in the receiver set and as such it will fix the distribution in place:

	Group 1	Group 2	Group 3	
Minimums:	1	1	1	= 3
Distribution 1: (Group 1 with twice as many students as Group 2)	2	1	2	= 5

In our Advanced
LSAT Logic
Games Course,
we cover the
various types
of Numerical
Distributions in
greater detail.

If Group 2 has one student, then Group 1 must have two students, and the remaining two students are assigned to Group 3. If Group 2 has two students, then Group 1 would have four students, but Group 1 cannot have four students since that adds up to six students and there are only five total. Thus, only the 2-1-2 fixed distribution exists. The *fixed* designation signifies that the 2-1-2 student distribution is assigned to Groups 1, 2, and 3, respectively.

Numerical Distribution Identification and Use

Numerical Distributions occur in almost every game. Often the distribution is so clearly stated that no analysis is necessary. Games that contain a one-to-one distribution are a good example. Other games, however, demand that you recognize and understand the distributions present. To recognize Numerical Distributions other than one-to-one relationships, look for:

Always be on
the lookout
for Numerical
Distributions!

1. A greater number of variables being distributed over a fewer number of variables. Examples include pets to cages, players to teams, and college students to dorm rooms.

A Numerical
Distribution is
a game feature,
not a separate
game type. Most
games with
a significant
distribution
element are
classified
as Linear or
Grouping.

2. Rules that include numbers. Since distributions are numerical in nature, it is necessary that the rules establish those relationships. Look for phrases such as "at least," "exactly," and "at most," as in the following examples:

   At least one adult must be on each committee.

   Each referee must work exactly one game.

   At most five movies are shown.

   File 1 has twice as many documents as File 2.

Rules that specify exact relationships in the receiver set, such as the file/document rule example above, almost always yield fixed distributions.

Note that when rules fail to establish minimums, the number of distributions increases dramatically. For example, consider this game scenario:

9

A television executive is deciding the scheduling for five advertisements—A, B, C, D, and E—to be aired during one week, from Monday through Friday. The schedule must accord with the following:

Exactly one advertisement is scheduled to air each day.

No advertisement can air more than two days per week.

To many students, this appears to be a standard 1-1-1-1-1 distribution, where each advertisement airs once, and each day a different advertisement is aired. From the perspective of the advertisements-to-days, yes, a single advertisement is aired each day (1-1-1-1-1). But, nowhere in the rules does it state that *each advertisement* must be aired, and so some advertisements can air more than once and other advertisements do not have to air at all. This is a critical piece of information, and it creates three distributions of *days to advertisements*:

Distribution #1:   2-2-1-0-0
(two advertisements air twice, one advertisement airs once, and two advertisements do not air)

Distribution #2:   2-1-1-1-0
(one advertisement airs twice, three advertisements air once, and one advertisement does not air)

Distribution #3:   1-1-1-1-1
(each advertisement airs once)

Recognizing the three possible distributions is critical; otherwise you will make faulty inferences about the use and placement of the advertisements on the Monday-though-Friday linear base. The key to triggering the recognition that these distributions exist—and are important—is the lack of a condition specifying that each advertisement must be aired.

Numerical Distributions are important because they fundamentally define all the variations a game can assume. As such, the distributions are a powerful and ultimately controlling force. Always check the distribution in a Logic Game, even if it is a basic one. The more complex the distribution, the more likely that you will be directly tested on your ability to identify the distribution.

When attacking the Games section, keep in mind the Hierarchy of Game Power™, first discussed in Chapter Six, modified now to include a numerical aspect:

A game like this one could also include a seemingly simple but dangerous rule such as: "Advertisement A is never aired later in the week than Advertisement B."

This rule appears to be a straight sequential rule (A ———— B), and some students automatically create Not Laws for A on Friday and for B on Monday. This is a major mistake because neither A nor B necessarily must air. For example, if A does not air during a given week, then B could air on Monday.

Mapping Games, which are non-numerical, fall outside the Hierarchy.

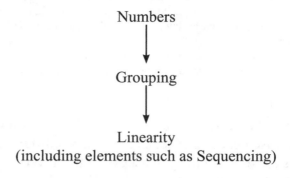

The diagram above indicates that the higher terms dominate the lower terms. When you set up a game, always consider the dominant terms first. Thus, first consider the numerical aspect of the game, then the grouping aspect, and finally the linear aspect. Let us also revisit the example used in Chapter Six, again modified to include the consideration of numbers:

> Suppose you are offered free Super Bowl tickets. Your first reaction wouldn't be to start putting people in the first seat, or second seat, or sixth seat, etc. Instead you would first establish how many free tickets you are being given. Then you would select the group of people to attend the game, and finally, once at the game, you would consider how to line up the individuals in seats.

Operationally, the Hierarchy provides a logical order of analysis for any Logic Game. By examining the most potent areas first, you increase your chances of identifying the key inferences of the game and thus improving your performance.

Final Pre-Drill and Game Note ▬▬▬

The following pages include a short Numerical Distribution identification drill, and thereafter two games that revolve around Numerical Distributions.

As always, please read the explanations to each drill and game carefully, as they will give you a true sense of how to best attack each item. Plus, the explanations always include points that expand the previous discussion.

If you would like to test yourself under timed conditions, you should give yourself 8 minutes and 45 seconds for each game. Good luck on the games!

> In doing these games, **use scratch paper instead of writing directly on the game!** This will prepare you for the Digital LSAT format where you cannot write directly on the screen.

Numerical Distribution Identification Drill

Each of the following game scenarios contain rules that lead to one or more numerical distributions. For each problem identify each of the possible fixed or unfixed numerical distributions created by the rules. *Answers on page 553*

1. Six speakers must participate in a speech contest. Each speaker participates exactly once, and no two speakers speak at the same time.

2. Seven dog biscuits are given to three dogs—a Dalmatian, a Doberman, and a Great Dane. Each dog must be given at least one biscuit, and the Great Dane is given exactly twice as many biscuits as the Dalmatian.

3. Eight drinks are given to two bar patrons. Each patron is given at least three drinks and no more than five drinks.

4. Seven animals are placed into cages containing anywhere from one to three animals. At most one of the cages contains three animals. At least one of the cages contains exactly two animals. At most two of the cages contain exactly one animal each.

5. Eight students are assigned to five different floors in a dormitory. At least one student is assigned to each floor, and at most three students are assigned to a floor.

6. Fourteen vitamin pills are placed into six bottles. At least two vitamin pills are placed in each bottle.

7. Ten cars are assigned to five different mechanics—mechanics A, B, C, D, and E. Each mechanic is assigned at least one car. Mechanic B is assigned two cars. Mechanic C is assigned more cars than Mechanic D. Mechanic B is assigned more cars than Mechanic A. Mechanic E is assigned the same number of cars as Mechanic D.

8. An unknown number of toys are given to four charities. Charity 1 is given three times as many toys as Charity 2. Charity 3 is given one more toy than Charity 4. Charity 2 is given at least one toy. Charity 3 is always given more toys than Charity 2. Charity 4 is given at most two toys.

Numerical Distribution Identification Drill Answer Key

1. Six speakers must participate in a speech contest. Each speaker participates exactly once, and no two speakers speak at the same time.

   Six speakers distributed into six time slots.
   Fixed: 1-1-1-1-1-1 (All one-to-one distributions are automatically fixed.)

2. Seven dog biscuits are given to three dogs—a Dalmatian, a Doberman, and a Great Dane. Each dog must be given at least one biscuit, and the Great Dane is given exactly twice as many biscuits as the Dalmatian.

   Seven dog biscuits distributed to three dogs.
   Fixed: 1-4-2, 2-1-4

3. Eight drinks are given to two bar patrons. Each patron is given at least three drinks and no more than five drinks.

   Eight drinks distributed to two bar patrons.
   Unfixed: 5-3, 4-4

4. Seven animals are placed into cages containing anywhere from one to three animals. At most one of the cages contains three animals. At least one of the cages contains exactly two animals. At most two of the cages contain exactly one animal each.

   Seven animals distributed into an unknown number of cages.
   Unfixed: 3-2-2, 3-2-1-1, 2-2-2-1

5. Eight students are assigned to five different floors in a dormitory. At least one student is assigned to each floor, and at most three students are assigned to a floor.

    Eight students distributed to five floors.
    Unfixed: 3-2-1-1-1, 2-2-2-1-1

6. Fourteen vitamin pills are placed into six bottles. At least two vitamin pills are placed in each bottle.

    Fourteen vitamin pills distributed into six bottles.
    Unfixed: 4-2-2-2-2-2, 3-3-2-2-2-2

7. Ten cars are assigned to five different mechanics—mechanics A, B, C, D, and E. Each mechanic is assigned at least one car. Mechanic B is assigned two cars. Mechanic C is assigned more cars than Mechanic D. Mechanic B is assigned more cars than Mechanic A. Mechanic E is assigned the same number of cars as Mechanic D.

    Ten cars distributed to five mechanics.
    Fixed: 1-2-5-1-1, 1-2-3-2-2

8. An unknown number of toys are given to four charities. Charity 1 is given three times as many toys as Charity 2. Charity 3 is given one more toy than Charity 4. Charity 2 is given at least one toy. Charity 3 is always given more toys than Charity 2. Charity 4 is given at most two toys.

    An unknown number of toys distributed to four charities.
    Fixed: 3-1-2-1, 3-1-3-2, 6-2-3-2

Note in items #4 and #8 the number in the allocated set or the receiver set is unknown; in spite of this, each item contains enough other information to allow distributions to be identified.

A reporter is trying to uncover the workings of a secret committee. The committee has six members—French, Ghauri, Hsia, Irving, Magnus, and Pinsky—each of whom serves on at least one subcommittee. There are three subcommittees, each having three members, about which the following is known:

> One of the committee members serves on all three subcommittees.
> French does not serve on any subcommittee with Ghauri.
> Hsia does not serve on any subcommittee with Irving.

17. If French does not serve on any subcommittee with Magnus, which one of the following must be true?

(A) French serves on a subcommittee with Hsia.
(B) French serves on a subcommittee with Irving.
(C) Irving serves on a subcommittee with Pinsky.
(D) Magnus serves on a subcommittee with Ghauri.
(E) Magnus serves on a subcommittee with Irving.

GO ON TO THE NEXT PAGE.

9

18. If Pinsky serves on every subcommittee on which French serves and every subcommittee on which Ghauri serves, then which one of the following could be true?

   (A) Magnus serves on every subcommittee on which French serves and every subcommittee on which Ghauri serves.
   (B) Magnus serves on every subcommittee on which Hsia serves and every subcommittee on which Irving serves.
   (C) Hsia serves on every subcommittee on which French serves and every subcommittee on which Ghauri serves.
   (D) French serves on every subcommittee on which Pinsky serves.
   (E) Hsia serves on every subcommittee on which Pinsky serves.

19. If Irving serves on every subcommittee on which Magnus serves, which one of the following could be true?

   (A) Magnus serves on all of the subcommittees.
   (B) Irving serves on more than one subcommittee.
   (C) Irving serves on every subcommittee on which Pinsky serves.
   (D) French serves on a subcommittee with Magnus.
   (E) Ghauri serves on a subcommittee with Magnus.

20. Which one of the following could be true?

   (A) French serves on all three subcommittees.
   (B) Hsia serves on all three subcommittees.
   (C) Ghauri serves on every subcommittee on which Magnus serves and every subcommittee on which Pinsky serves.
   (D) Pinsky serves on every subcommittee on which Irving serves and every subcommittee on which Magnus serves.
   (E) Magnus serves on every subcommittee on which Pinsky serves, and Pinsky serves on every subcommittee on which Magnus serves.

21. Which one of the following must be true?

   (A) Ghauri serves on at least two subcommittees.
   (B) Irving serves on only one subcommittee.
   (C) French serves on a subcommittee with Hsia.
   (D) Ghauri serves on a subcommittee with Irving.
   (E) Magnus serves on a subcommittee with Pinsky.

22. Which one of the following must be true?

   (A) Every subcommittee has either French or Ghauri as a member.
   (B) Every subcommittee has either Hsia or Irving as a member.
   (C) No subcommittee consists of French, Magnus, and Pinsky.
   (D) Some committee member serves on exactly two subcommittees.
   (E) Either Magnus or Pinsky serves on only one subcommittee.

GO ON TO THE NEXT PAGE.

This game was widely considered the most difficult of the June 2005 exam. After three linear-based games, the test makers saved a Grouping game for last on that exam.

At first, this game appears to be a straightforward Grouping game: six committee members serving on three subcommittees. However, the game scenario and rules indicate that there are nine subcommittee spaces, and that some committee members serve on multiple subcommittees. If each member served on only one subcommittee, the game would be considerably easier because the assignment of a member to a subcommittee would eliminate that member from further consideration. Thus, the Underfunded aspect of this game gave test takers more to consider as they looked at the composition of each subcommittee.

Note that since the subcommittees do not have formal names, we have labeled them as "SC."

The game scenario provides us with the following basic setup:

FGHIMP^6

$$\begin{array}{ccc} \underline{\quad} & \underline{\quad} & \underline{\quad} \\ \underline{\quad} & \underline{\quad} & \underline{\quad} \\ \underline{\quad} & \underline{\quad} & \underline{\quad} \\ SC & SC & SC \end{array}$$

Now, let us examine each rule.

Rule #1. With six committee members filling in nine spaces, and with the game scenario stating that each member serves on at least one subcommittee, you should be on the lookout for rules that reveal a specific Numerical Distribution. The first rule is just such a rule. But, what is the most beneficial distribution? Is it the nine spaces allocated among the six members, or the six members distributed across the nine spaces?

The latter distribution (six members into nine spaces) is a workable distribution, but it isn't that helpful. Why? Because it creates a 1-1-1-1-1-1-1-1-1 distribution (which is then divided into three groups of three). This occurs because each of the nine spaces is filled by exactly one member. The filling numbers add up to nine instead of six because some of the six members can be on more than one committee. So, although it is a correct distribution, it is not one that tells us anything new.

On the other hand, the nine into six distribution tells us how many spots each member can fill (with a maximum of three because there are only three committees), and thus this distribution shows the possibilities for which members can be on more than one committee.

9

The first rule establishes that one of the committee members serves on all three subcommittees, and thus the remaining five members must fill the remaining six subcommittee spaces. Since every member must serve on at least one subcommittee, the five members automatically fill five of the six spaces. The remaining subcommittee space can be assigned to any one of the committee members (aside from the one member serving on all three committees, of course). Thus, the game is controlled by a 3-2-1-1-1-1 distribution of spaces to committee members. Note that the numbers add to nine (for the nine spaces), and that there are a total of six separate numbers (for the six committee members).

Rules #2 and #3. These two rules establish the following not-blocks:

While these not-blocks may appear standard, when combined with the 3-2-1-1-1-1 numerical distribution there is an important implication. First, because F, G, H and I are involved in the not-blocks, none of those four members can serve on all three subcommittees (otherwise there would be an overlap that would conflict with the not-block). Thus, only M or P can be the member who serves on all three subcommittees.

With the information on the previous page, the complete game diagram is:

FGHIMP⁶
     * *

Dist: 3 - 2 - 1 - 1 - 1 - 1
     M/P

SC   SC   SC   ← M/P

Question #17: Local, Must Be True. The correct answer choice is (C)

The condition in the question stem affects the Numerical Distribution discussed in the setup analysis. If F and M cannot serve on the same subcommittee, then M cannot be the member who serves on all three subcommittees, and P must serve on all three subcommittees:

$$
\begin{array}{ccc}
\underline{\quad} & \underline{\quad} & \underline{\quad} \\
\underline{\text{P}} & \underline{\text{P}} & \underline{\text{P}} \\
\text{SC} & \text{SC} & \text{SC}
\end{array}
$$

Because P serves on all three subcommittees, every other member serves with P, and answer choice (C) is correct.

Question #18: Local, Could Be True. The correct answer choice is (C)

This is the most difficult question of the game. The wording of the conditions in the question stem is quite tricky, and you must carefully consider the meaning of each statement. The phrase, "P serves on every subcommittee on which F serves," means that when F serves on a subcommittee, then P also serves on that subcommittee. This relationship is diagrammed as:

$$
F \longrightarrow P
$$

The second condition is worded in a similar fashion, and can be diagrammed as:

$$
G \longrightarrow P
$$

Consequently, since F and G must serve on at least one subcommittee each, we know the following:

$$
\begin{array}{ccc}
\underline{\quad} & \underline{\quad} & \underline{\quad} \\
\underline{\text{F}} & \underline{\text{G}} & \underline{\quad} \\
\underline{\text{P}} & \underline{\text{P}} & \underline{\quad} \\
\text{SC} & \text{SC} & \text{SC}
\end{array}
$$

Answer choice (A): This answer is incorrect because if M serves on the same subcommittees as F and G, then H and I would be forced to serve on the same subcommittee, a violation of the third rule.

Answer choice (B): This answer is incorrect because there is not enough room for M to serve with both H and I (M can serve on one subcommittee with either H or I, but the other two subcommittees already have P and F, or P and G, and hence there is not space for two more members on those subcommittees.).

Answer choice (C): This is the correct answer. H could be the member who serves on two committees.

Answer choice (D): This answer is incorrect because if P serves on all three subcommittees then F would have to serve on three subcommittees, a violation of the numerical distribution; if P serves on two subcommittees, then F would have to serve on two subcommittees, and M would have to serve on all three subcommittees, creating a 3-2-2-1-1 distribution, which also violates the previously established numerical distribution.

Answer choice (E): This answer is incorrect for the same reasoning used to disprove answer choice (D).

Question #19: Local, Could Be True. The correct answer choice is (B)

Like question #18, the wording of the condition in the question stem is quite tricky, and you must carefully consider the meaning of the statement. The phrase, "I serves on every subcommittee on which M serves," means that when M serves on a subcommittee, then I also serves on that subcommittee. This relationship is diagrammed as:

$$M \longrightarrow I$$

This condition means that M cannot serve on all three subcommittees (if M did serve on all three, then I would have to serve on all three also, a violation of the numerical distribution). Consequently, we can deduce that P must serve on all three subcommittees. We can also infer that M will not serve on two subcommittees (again, I would serve on two as well, a violation of the distribution) and that M serves on only one subcommittee:

I		
M		
P	P	P
SC	SC	SC

Because F and G are in a not-block, we know that F and G must serve on different subcommittees:

$$
\frac{\text{I}}{\text{M}} \quad \frac{}{\text{F}} \quad \frac{}{\text{G}}
$$

I		
M	F	G
P	P	P
SC	SC	SC

The only remaining uncertainty is the placement of H, and whether H or I is doubled:

I	H/I	I/H
M	F	G
P	P	P
SC	SC	SC

Answer choice (A): As discussed in the question analysis, M cannot serve on all three subcommittees, and this answer choice is incorrect.

Answer choice (B): This is the correct answer because I could be the member who serves on two subcommittees.

Answer choice (C): This answer choice is incorrect because I cannot serve on all three subcommittees.

Answer choice (D): This answer choice is incorrect because, as shown above, F and M cannot serve on the same subcommittee.

Answer choice (E): This answer choice is incorrect because, as shown above, G and M cannot serve on the same subcommittee.

Question #20: Global, Could Be True. The correct answer choice is (D)

Answer choices (A) and (B): As established in the game analysis, either M or P must be the sole member who serves on all three subcommittees. If either F or H served on all three, there would be a violation of one of the last two rules. Consequently, both of these answer choices are incorrect.

Answer choice (C): If G serves on every subcommittee that M and P serve on, and we know that one of M and P serves on all three subcommittees, then G must serve on all three subcommittees as well. This scenario violates the numerical distribution, and is therefore incorrect.

Answer choice (D): This is the correct answer.

Answer choice (E): This answer choice creates a scenario where M and P serve on exactly the same subcommittees. Since only one of M and P serves on all three subcommittees, and the other serves on fewer subcommittees, this answer choice is incorrect.

Question #21: Global, Must Be True. The correct answer choice is (E)

This question trades on the M/P inference produced by the combination of the Numerical Distribution and the last two rules. As established in the discussion of the rules, either M or P must serve on all three subcommittees. Since one of the two must be on all three subcommittees, there must be an overlap between M and P, and consequently answer choice (E) is correct.

Question #22: Global, Must Be True. The correct answer choice is (D)

Again, we can use the distribution to quickly and easily destroy this question. As we have previously established, the game contains a 3-2-1-1-1-1 distribution, and exactly one of the committee members serves on two subcommittees. Hence, (D) is the correct answer choice.

9

Exactly seven film buffs—Ginnie, Ian, Lianna, Marcos, Reveka, Viktor, and Yow—attend a showing of classic films. Three films are shown, one directed by Fellini, one by Hitchcock, and one by Kurosawa. Each of the film buffs sees exactly one of the three films. The films are shown only once, one film at a time. The following restrictions must apply:

> Exactly twice as many of the film buffs see the Hitchcock film as see the Fellini film.
>
> Ginnie and Reveka do not see the same film as each other.
>
> Ian and Marcos do not see the same film as each other.
>
> Viktor and Yow see the same film as each other.
>
> Lianna sees the Hitchcock film.
>
> Ginnie sees either the Fellini film or the Kurosawa film.

13. Which one of the following could be an accurate matching of film buffs to films?

(A) Ginnie: the Hitchcock film; Ian: the Kurosawa film; Marcos: the Hitchcock film

(B) Ginnie: the Kurosawa film; Ian: the Fellini film; Viktor: the Fellini film

(C) Ian: the Hitchcock film; Reveka: the Kurosawa film; Viktor: the Fellini film

(D) Marcos: the Kurosawa film; Reveka: the Kurosawa film; Viktor: the Kurosawa film

(E) Marcos: the Hitchcock film; Reveka: the Hitchcock film; Yow: the Hitchcock film

GO ON TO THE NEXT PAGE.

14. Each of the following must be false EXCEPT:

    (A)   Reveka is the only film buff to see the Fellini film.
    (B)   Reveka is the only film buff to see the Hitchcock film.
    (C)   Yow is the only film buff to see the Kurosawa film.
    (D)   Exactly two film buffs see the Kurosawa film.
    (E)   Exactly three film buffs see the Hitchcock film.

15. Which one of the following could be a complete and accurate list of the film buffs who do NOT see the Hitchcock film?

    (A)   Ginnie, Marcos
    (B)   Ginnie, Reveka
    (C)   Ginnie, Ian, Reveka
    (D)   Ginnie, Marcos, Yow
    (E)   Ginnie, Viktor, Yow

16. If exactly one film buff sees the Kurosawa film, then which one of the following must be true?

    (A)   Viktor sees the Hitchcock film.
    (B)   Ginnie sees the Fellini film.
    (C)   Marcos sees the Fellini film.
    (D)   Ian sees the Fellini film.
    (E)   Reveka sees the Hitchcock film.

17. Which one of the following must be true?

    (A)   Ginnie sees a different film than Ian does.
    (B)   Ian sees a different film than Lianna does.
    (C)   Ian sees a different film than Viktor does.
    (D)   Ian, Lianna, and Viktor do not all see the same film.
    (E)   Ginnie, Lianna, and Marcos do not all see the same film.

18. If Viktor sees the same film as Ginnie does, then which one of the following could be true?

    (A)   Ginnie sees the Fellini film.
    (B)   Ian sees the Hitchcock film.
    (C)   Reveka sees the Kurosawa film.
    (D)   Viktor sees the Hitchcock film.
    (E)   Yow sees the Fellini film.

19. Each of the following could be a complete and accurate list of the film buffs who see the Fellini film EXCEPT:

    (A)   Ginnie, Ian
    (B)   Ginnie, Marcos
    (C)   Ian, Reveka
    (D)   Marcos, Reveka
    (E)   Viktor, Yow

GO ON TO THE NEXT PAGE.

Analysis of Numerical Distribution Game #2: December 1998 Questions 13-19

This a Defined-Moving, Balanced Grouping game. It has been chosen for this section since it features two Numerical Distributions that control the placement of film buffs to films. Although virtually all games contain a Numerical Distribution, the distribution becomes an especially significant element if there are multiple distributions, or if the single distribution is unusual. This game is one of the former.

The information in the game scenario establishes that there are seven film buffs attending a showing of three movies. Each film buff sees exactly one film. The first rule then establishes two fixed distributions:

	Fellini	Hitchcock	Kurosawa
Fixed Distribution #1:	1	2	4
Fixed Distribution #2:	2	4	1

The two fixed distributions create two distinctly different scenarios. And since each scenario requires a different analysis, the best strategy is to create two templates, one for the 1-2-4 distribution, and another for the 2-4-1 distribution:

```
    1   2   4              2   4   1
            __                 __
            __                 __
        __  __             __  __
    __  __  __         __  __  __
    F   H   K          F   H   K
```

The rules can now be considered. The second and third rules establish not-blocks, and the fourth rule establishes a regular block:

These negative grouping rules are shown as blocks due to the presence of a vertical element in the game.

The VY block is especially useful, because when L is assigned to Hitchcock in the fifth rule, VY must then see the Kurosawa film in the 1-2-4, and must see the Hitchcock film in the 2-4-1. Those inferences, along with the not blocks and the sixth rule, strongly impact each template:

GILMRVY[7]

Let us analyze the two diagrams in more detail. The fifth rule states that L sees the Hitchcock film. In the 1-2-4 this leaves one open space at Fellini, one open space at Hitchcock, and four open spaces at Kurosawa. But the third rule states that V and Y see the same film as each other, so in the 1-2-4 it can be inferred that V and Y see the Kurosawa film. In the 2-4-1 we can infer that V and Y see either the Fellini film or the Hitchcock film, but at the moment it is uncertain which one. G cannot see the Hitchcock film, and so Not Laws are drawn on both templates, and G split-options are placed on Fellini and Kurosawa.

The two negative grouping rules help fill in both templates. In the 1-2-4, there are four remaining spaces for G, R, I, and M: one space at Fellini, one space at Hitchcock, and two spaces at Kurosawa. Since G and R, as well as I and M, cannot see the same film, it can be inferred that one of G and R must see the Kurosawa film, and one of I and M must see the Kurosawa film.

In the 2-4-1 there are still six open spaces: two at Fellini, three at Hitchcock, and one at Kurosawa. Of the six remaining variables, two—V and Y—must see the same film. If V and Y see the Fellini film, then there would be three open spaces at Hitchcock and one open space at Kurosawa. Since G and R cannot see the same film, one must see Hitchcock and the other must see Kurosawa. That leaves two spaces at Hitchcock for I and M. But wait, I and M cannot see the same film, and so this scenario causes a violation of the rules. Essentially, when V and Y see the Fellini film, there are not enough remaining spaces to properly separate G, R, I, and M. It can therefore be inferred that in the 2-4-1 distribution V and Y see the Hitchcock film.

In both templates there are still several possible solutions, and in the next section we will discuss Identifying the Templates further. For now, it will be important to be aware of G, R, I, and M since they are the only variables still in play.

Question #13: Global, Could Be True, List. The correct answer choice is (D)

Answer choice (A) is incorrect because G cannot see the Hitchcock film. Answer choices (B) and (C) are incorrect because V can never see the Fellini film. Answer choice (E) is incorrect because M and R could never see the Hitchcock film at the same time. Answer choice (D) is therefore correct. Overall a much more difficult List question than usual, but easy if you have used the distributions to identify the two templates!

Question #14: Global, Could Be True. The correct answer choice is (A)

Remember, convert false into true when you analyze the question stem. Answer choices (D) and (E) are eliminated by applying the distributions. Answer choice (C) is eliminated by applying the templates, and answer choice (B) is eliminated by the fifth rule that states that L sees the Hitchcock film. Answer choice (A) is correct.

Question #15: Global, Could Be True, List. The correct answer choice is (C)

The first step is to apply the VY block rule because, if one does not see Hitchcock, it is certain the other will not see Hitchcock either. Answer choice (D) contains Y, but not V, and is incorrect.

The second step is to consider the Numerical Distributions. In the 1-2-4 distribution, two film buffs see the Hitchcock film, and five film buffs do not see the Hitchcock film. In the 2-4-1 distribution, four film buffs see the Hitchcock film, and three film buffs do not see the Hitchcock film. Thus, since this question stem asks for a complete and accurate list of the film buffs who do NOT see the Hitchcock film, the correct answer choice must contain either three or five film buffs. Since answer choices (A) and (B) contain only two film buffs, they can both be rejected without further analysis.

Since answer choices (C), (D), and (E) each contain three film buffs, it is apparent that they are each generated by the 2-4-1 distribution. In the 2-4-1 distribution we have already ascertained that L, V, and Y each see the Hitchcock film, and so any answer choice that contains L, V, or Y will be incorrect. This eliminates answer choice (D) (again!) and also eliminates answer choice (E). Answer choice (C) is therefore correct.

Question #16: Local, Must Be True. The correct answer choice is (A)

According to the information in the question stem, the film buffs are in the 2-4-1 fixed distribution. Accordingly, answer choice (A) is correct. Again, note the usefulness of the distributions and templates.

Question #17: Global, Must Be True. The correct answer choice is (E)

This question can be solved by either referring to the templates or by using the rules.

If the rules are used, the final two rules indicate that G and L must see different films. Consequently, answer choice (E) is proven correct.

If the templates are used, nothing in either template suggests that answer choice (A), (B), or (C) is correct. In answer choice (D), I, L, and V could all see the Hitchcock film under the 2-4-1. The templates ultimately show that answer choice (E) must be true.

Question #18: Local, Could Be True. The correct answer choice is (B)

V and G can only see the same film under the 1-2-4 template:

```
    1      2      4

                 I/M
                 ───
                  G
                 ───
                  Y
           ───   ───
            L     V
    ───    ───   ───
     F      H     K
```

The final two spaces are filled by R and the remainder of I/M. Accordingly, answer choice (B) is correct.

Question #19: Global, Cannot Be True, List. The correct answer choice is (E)

Since each answer choice contains two film buffs, the 2-4-1 fixed distribution applies. Under that distribution we have already inferred that L, V, and Y each see the Hitchcock film, and so any answer choice that contains L, V, or Y would be correct (remember, this is an Except question). Answer choice (E) contains V and Y and is therefore correct.

This game provides an excellent example of how the test makers use Numerical Distributions. Many of the questions force you to examine the templates created by each distribution and then attack the answer choices. The distributions are central to understanding this game: if you do not identify the distributions, the questions in this game cannot be answered correctly.

9

Limited Solution Set Games ▮▮▮

Certain Logic Games are so restricted that only a limited number of solutions conform to the rules. In these games the best approach is to diagram each possibility before attacking the questions. With all of the possibilities in hand, the questions are easy.

Limited Solution Sets are a feature that appears in many different game types, including Grouping and Linear games, but there is no specific type of game that *always* uses this feature. Typically, the number of possibilities is constrained by some type of restriction or limitation that leads to just a few solutions.

Each year, there are usually several LSAT games that contain a limited number of solutions, and students who learn the best approach have a significant advantage. Because of their importance, games with limited solutions have already been previewed several times in this book. For example, in Chapter Three several of the problems in the Linear Setup Practice Drill have a reduced number of possible solutions. In this chapter, the Numerical Distribution game features two basic templates based on two distributions. When you attack Limited Solution Set Games, use one of the following two approaches: Identify the Templates™ or Identify the Possibilities™. Although similar, each leads to a different diagram and requires different decisions.

Pure Sequencing games and Pattern games are two types of games that rarely feature Limited Solution Sets. Both game types depend on a lack of certainty regarding variable placement, and it is therefore not surprising that they rarely have an extremely limited number of solutions.

9

Identify the Templates™ ▬▬▬

Identify the
Templates and
Identify the
Possibilities are
not game types;
rather, they are
techniques for
attacking certain
games.

When a game is attacked by Identifying the Templates, the major possibility templates are diagrammed, but the exact possibilities within each template are not fully displayed. This approach is excellent for games where two or three major directions appear. In the Fellini/Hitchcock/Kurosawa game on page 563, two templates were generated by two fixed Numerical Distributions, 1-2-4 and 2-4-1. Since these distributions created two separate scenarios in the game, it made sense to create basic diagrams for each option. And because these basic diagrams provided a considerable amount of information, there was no need to show every single possibility. The templates were sufficient. Consider one of the templates from that game:

$$
\begin{array}{ccc}
 & \dfrac{Y}{\overline{V}} & \\
\dfrac{G/}{F} & \dfrac{L}{H} & \dfrac{/G}{K}
\end{array}
$$

The diagram is considered a template because it does not show all of the information regarding the placement of the variables.

Identifying the Templates does not have to be connected to Numerical Distributions. For example, assume a rule states, "Marshall drives on either Wednesday or Thursday." If there are several other limiting rules, it might be wise to diagram the two possible templates: one where Marshall drives Wednesday and another where Marshall drives Thursday. The decision to show the templates is normally made when the rules that suggest a major component of the game is limited to just two or three options. This major component could be a variable, a powerful block, a numerical distribution, or some other element.

Focus on
identifying
limiting
elements!

9

Identify the Possibilities™ ▬▬▬▬▬

Identify the Possibilities is an extension of Identify the Templates. Instead of creating basic templates to capture the general direction of the game, each possibility is written out. This usually takes more time during the setup, but since it results in perfect information the questions can be answered incredibly fast.

The difference between showing templates and possibilities is one of degree. Identifying the Templates exposes the major directions of the game; Identifying the Possibilities explores those directions in detail. Because Identifying the Templates is less detailed, it tends to take less time to apply. On the contrary, Identifying the Possibilities takes longer because it is more detailed.

When showing the possibilities, you should use some of the diagramming shortcuts discussed in earlier chapters. Dual-options are a great example. The following diagram uses dual-options to efficiently display two possibilities:

E/F	F/E
C	D
A	B
1	2

The example to the right would be called a template that contains two possibilities.

The two possibilities are based on whether E or F is in group 1 or 2. It would be a waste of time to draw each possibility separately when the dual-option can perfectly capture the same idea.

It can be quite difficult to identify Limited Solution Set games because there is no obvious feature that always leads to just a few possibilities. And consequently it can be difficult to know when to Identify the Templates or Identify the Possibilities.

9

How to Recognize Limited Solution Set Games

There is no single type of rule or game that invariably produces a limited number of solutions. Instead, it is a combination of factors that leads to limited solutions and thus the decision to Identify the Templates or Possibilities. Typically, the number of solutions is constrained by a large number of disparate rules, some limiting principle in the game (such as a numerical distribution), or variable configurations such as unwieldy blocks that have reduced placement possibilities. In part, an understanding of the restrictions comes from examining different games that are limited. In each instance there will be a controlling rule or set of rules that affects certain areas of the game in such a way as to suggest that only a few options are presented. You must examine each Limited Solution Set game to better understand why it is limited.

The following list covers the elements that can help you identify a Limited Solution Set game:

Numerical Limitations

1. A Numerical Distribution.

2. Either a small number of variables or a small number of available spaces.

3. A scenario that creates multiple groups and then leaves only one or two spaces available in one or more of the groups.

4. A game that fixes a significant number of variables and leaves only a few free to move.

Duality

5. A scenario that creates a two-value system, and then uses conditional rules.

6. A rule that creates duality for any variable, such as, "R must be third or fifth."

7. A rule that creates duality for a space, such as, "Either P or Q must be first."

8. Games where the linear base is divided in "half," creating a limited number of spaces on each side.

Overlap Between Rules or Variables

9. A variable that appears in three or more rules.

10. Multiple rules addressing just a limited number of variables.

11. A large number of rules.

Power Blocks

12. One or more sizable or unwieldy blocks. The more blocks present, the more likely the number of solutions is limited.

13. Multiple negative blocks.

14. A combination of three or more blocks and not-blocks.

Limited Randoms

15. No randoms in the game, or a single random in a game with six or fewer total variables.

Note that the mere presence of any one of these elements does not automatically lead one to Identify the Templates or Possibilities, but it does suggest that you should at least consider the option. And, the more elements from the list that you encounter, the more likely it is that there is a limited number of solutions to the game.

9

The Dangers of Misapplication

Identifying the Possibilities is a dangerous weapon: when it is used at the right time, it will result in absolute success; when it is used on the wrong game (one that has too many possibilities) it can waste time. Keep in mind that identifying all of the possibilities forces you to spend extra time during the setup, but that lost time is then regained during your swift demolition of the questions. Remember, though, this technique should be applied only to games with eight or fewer possibilities.

With Identifying the Templates the risk seems to be less: even if you decide that showing all the templates is not feasible, usually the process of looking at the various options increases your game knowledge. Identify the Templates should be used only in games with four or fewer major directions.

Since it can be difficult to determine which approach is best, you can always show the basic templates and then make the decision to explore each possibility. In this way you protect yourself against losing too much time by making an error in judgment.

Final Pregame Note ▮▮▮▮▮▮▮▮▮

There are four games in this section. Two use Identify the Templates and two use Identify the Possibilities. Three of the games feature Numerical Distributions. The explanation for each game will illuminate the reasons for choosing the appropriate technique. Good luck!

> In doing these games, **use scratch paper instead of writing directly on the game!** This will prepare you for the Digital LSAT format where you cannot write directly on the screen.

Identifying the Possibilities is a very seductive technique. Since it shows all the solutions to a game and makes the questions easy, some students try to apply it to every single game. That will be fatal over the course of a Games section because some of the games will have too many possibilities. Imagine trying to show all the possibilities in a game with 50 solutions. Remember, Identify the Possibilities cannot be applied to every game!

During a single week, from Monday through Friday, tours will be conducted of a company's three divisions—Operations, Production, Sales. Exactly five tours will be conducted that week, one each day. The schedule of tours for the week must conform to the following restrictions:

Each division is toured at least once.

The Operations division is not toured on Monday.

The Production division is not toured on Wednesday.

The Sales division is toured on two consecutive days, and on no other days.

If the Operations division is toured on Thursday, then the Production division is toured on Friday.

14. Which one of the following CANNOT be true of the week's tour schedule?

(A) The division that is toured on Monday is also toured on Tuesday.

(B) The division that is toured on Monday is also toured on Friday.

(C) The division that is toured on Tuesday is also toured on Thursday.

(D) The division that is toured on Wednesday is also toured on Friday.

(E) The division that is toured on Thursday is also toured on Friday.

GO ON TO THE NEXT PAGE.

15. If in addition to the Sales division one other division is toured on two consecutive days, then it could be true of the week's tour schedule both that the

(A) Production division is toured on Monday and that the Operations division is toured on Thursday

(B) Production division is toured on Tuesday and that the Sales division is toured on Wednesday

(C) Operations division is toured on Tuesday and that the Production division is toured on Friday

(D) Sales division is toured on Monday and that the Operations division is toured on Friday

(E) Sales division is toured on Wednesday and that the Production division is toured on Friday

16. If in the week's tour schedule the division that is toured on Tuesday is also toured on Friday, then for which one of the following days must a tour of the Production division be scheduled?

(A) Monday
(B) Tuesday
(C) Wednesday
(D) Thursday
(E) Friday

17. If in the week's tour schedule the division that is toured on Monday is not the division that is toured on Tuesday then which one of the following could be true of the week's schedule?

(A) A tour of the Sales division is scheduled for some day earlier in the week than is any tour of the Production division.

(B) A tour of the Operations division is scheduled for some day earlier in the week than is any tour of the Production division.

(C) The Sales division is toured on Monday.

(D) The Production division is toured on Tuesday.

(E) The Operations division is toured on Wednesday.

18. If in the week's tour schedule the division that is toured on Tuesday is also toured on Wednesday, then which one of the following must be true of the week's tour schedule?

(A) The Production division is toured on Monday.
(B) The Operations division is toured on Tuesday.
(C) The Sales division is toured on Wednesday.
(D) The Sales division is toured on Thursday.
(E) The Production division is toured on Friday.

GO ON TO THE NEXT PAGE.

9

This is a Defined, Unbalanced: Underfunded Linear game. The game is Underfunded because three division tours—O, P, and S—must be toured five times (3 into 5). The Underfunded aspect leads to a Numerical Distribution:

Because S is toured exactly twice and each division is toured at least once, the five tours are distributed among the three divisions in a 2-2-1 partially fixed distribution. The distribution is partially fixed since S is toured twice, but the remaining three tours are assigned to P or O in a 2-1 unfixed distribution:

Partially	2	2	1
Fixed	S	O/P	P/O
Distribution			

One of the challenges of the game is to keep track of the distribution of O and P.

Initially, most students diagram the game as follows:

$O P S^3$

Because S is toured twice and the tours are consecutive, the placement options of the SS block are limited to four positions: Monday-Tuesday, Tuesday-Wednesday, Wednesday-Thursday, and Thursday-Friday. These four options split the game in four directions and are the basis for Identifying the Templates:

9

1. SS on Mon-Tue:	S	S	O	O/P	O/P
2. SS on Tue-Wed:	P	S	S	O/P	P/O
3. SS on Wed-Thu:	P	O/P	S	S	O/P
4. SS on Thu-Fri:	P	O/P	O	S	S
	M	Tu	W	Th	F

Although it is not necessary to number each template during the game, we do so here for purposes of the discussion to follow. Let us examine each template in greater detail:

1. SS on Mon-Tue: Since P cannot be toured on Wednesday, and the two tours of S are already scheduled, it can be inferred that O is toured on Wednesday. The only uncertain days are Thursday and Friday. Since neither can be S, O/P options have been placed on each. Note, however, that there are several possibilities for Thursday and Friday, such as O-P, P-O, and P-P. O-O is impossible because of the last rule.

2. SS on Tue-Wed: Since O cannot be toured on Monday, and the two tours of S are already scheduled, it can be inferred that P is toured on Monday. The only uncertain days are Thursday and Friday. Since neither can be S, dual O/P options have been placed on each. There are only two possibilities for Thursday and Friday, O-P and P-O. O-O is impossible because of the last rule, and P-P is impossible since O must be toured at least once during the five days.

3. SS on Wed-Thu: Since O cannot be toured on Monday, and the two tours of S are already scheduled, it can be inferred that P is toured on Monday. The only uncertain days are Tuesday and Friday. Since neither can be S, O/P options have been placed on each. There are three possibilities for Tuesday and Friday, O-P, P-O, and O-O. P-P is impossible since O must be toured at least once during the five days.

4. SS on Thu-Fri: Since O cannot be toured on Monday, and the two tours of S are already scheduled, it can be inferred that P is toured on Monday. Since P cannot be toured on Wednesday, it can be inferred that O is toured on Wednesday. The only uncertain day is Tuesday, which has either tour O or P.

This setup highlights the difference between Identify the Templates and Identify the Possibilities: The templates capture the four major directions of the game but do not map out every single possibility. With the templates in hand, there is sufficient information to attack the questions effectively.

When using the templates, you simply need to scan each to find the correct information. The questions will naturally direct you towards using some templates and away from using others.

Question #14: Global, Cannot Be True. The correct answer choice is (C)

Template #1 eliminates answer choice (A). Template #2 or #3 can be used to eliminate answer choice (B). Checking all four templates proves that answer choice (C) is correct. Template #1 eliminates answer choice (D). Template #4 (and, less resoundingly, template #2) eliminates answer choice (E).

Question #15: Local, Could Be True. The correct answer choice is (B)

The conditions in the question stem eliminate template #2 from consideration. Since there are still three templates in consideration and thus a considerable number of possibilities, it is best to consider each answer choice against all remaining templates. For answer choice (A), only templates #3 and #4 have P toured on Monday; but neither have O on Thursday, and so answer choice (A) is incorrect. For answer choice (B) only templates #3 and #4 could have P toured on Tuesday, and template #3 allows S to be toured on Wednesday, so answer choice (B) is correct. For answer choice (C) only templates #3 and #4 have O toured on Tuesday. Template #4 does not have P toured on Friday, and so it does not apply; template #3 could have P toured on Friday, but to do so would violate the condition in the question stem requiring one other division beside S to be toured twice. Consequently, answer choice (C) is incorrect. For answer choice (D), only template #1 applies, and if O were toured on Friday again, the condition in the question stem requiring one other division beside S to be toured twice would be violated. So answer choice (D) is incorrect. Finally, for answer choice (E) only template #3 applies, but if P were toured on Friday, the condition in the question stem requiring one other division beside S to be toured twice would be violated. So answer choices (C), (D), and (E) each can be eliminated by the condition in the question stem. In this question it is easier to find the correct answer than it is to eliminate the incorrect answers.

Question #16: Local, Must Be True. The correct answer choice is (A)

Only template #3 allows the tours on Tuesday and Friday to be identical (O on both days). Therefore answer choice (A) is correct.

9

Question #17: Local, Could Be True. The correct answer choice is (E)

Template #1 is eliminated from consideration by the condition in the question stem, and for templates #3 and #4 to apply, O must be toured on Tuesday. If necessary, write out the three templates in consideration:

2. SS on Tue-Wed:	P	S	S	O/P	P/O
3. SS on Wed-Thu:	P	O	S	S	O/P
4. SS on Thu-Fri:	P	O	O	S	S

The first four answer choices can each be rejected by scanning the three remaining templates. Template #4 proves answer choice (E) correct.

Question #18: Local, Must Be True. The correct answer choice is (A)

Only templates #2 and #4 meet the condition in the question stem. Consequently answer choice (A) is correct.

The decision to diagram the four templates results in large part from the SS block, but it is also important to consider the impact of the O, S, and P trio. When the LSAT supplies only three options for a space the situation is inherently limited. If just one of the options were removed, then a dual-option would result automatically, making the situation easier to handle.

In this game the benefit of Identifying the Templates is obvious. And spending a bit more time during the setup simplifies the process of answering the questions.

Morrisville's town council has exactly three members: Fu, Gianola, and Herstein. During one week, the council members vote on exactly three bills: a recreation bill, a school bill, and a tax bill. Each council member votes either for or against each bill. The following is known:

Each member of the council votes for at least one of the bills and against at least one of the bills.

Exactly two members of the council vote for the recreation bill.

Exactly one member of the council votes for the school bill.

Exactly one member of the council votes for the tax bill.

Fu votes for the recreation bill and against the school bill.

Gianola votes against the recreation bill.

Herstein votes against the tax bill.

19. Which one of the following statements could be true?

   (A)   Fu and Gianola vote the same way on the tax bill.

   (B)   Gianola and Herstein vote the same way on the recreation bill.

   (C)   Gianola and Herstein vote the same way on the school bill.

   (D)   Fu votes for one of the bills and Gianola votes for two of the bills.

   (E)   Fu votes for two of the bills and Gianola votes for two of the bills.

GO ON TO THE NEXT PAGE.

9

20. If the set of members of the council who vote against the school bill is the same set of members who vote against the tax bill, then which one of the following statements must be true?

    (A) Fu votes for the tax bill.
    (B) Gianola votes for the recreation bill.
    (C) Gianola votes against the school bill.
    (D) Herstein votes against the recreation bill.
    (E) Herstein votes against the school bill.

21. If Gianola votes for the tax bill, then which one of the following statements could be true?

    (A) Fu and Gianola each vote for exactly one bill.
    (B) Gianola and Herstein each vote for exactly one bill.
    (C) Fu votes for exactly two bills.
    (D) Gianola votes for the recreation bill.
    (E) Herstein votes against the recreation bill.

22. If Gianola votes for exactly two of the three bills, which one of the following statements must be true?

    (A) Fu votes for the tax bill.
    (B) Gianola votes for the recreation bill.
    (C) Gianola votes for the school bill.
    (D) Gianola votes against the tax bill.
    (E) Herstein votes for the school bill.

23. If one of the members of the council votes against exactly the same bills as does another member of the council, then which one of the following statements must be true?

    (A) Fu votes for the tax bill.
    (B) Gianola votes for the recreation bill.
    (C) Gianola votes against the school bill.
    (D) Gianola votes for exactly one bill.
    (E) Herstein votes for exactly one bill.

GO ON TO THE NEXT PAGE.

This is an Advanced Linear game with four variables sets: the three bills, R, S, and T; the three votes of Fu; the three votes of Gianola; and the three votes of Herstein. Notably, either the three bills or the three voters could be chosen as the base. Operationally they will produce no difference. We have chosen to use the three bills as the base and create stacks for Fu, Gianola, and Herstein:

```
H:  ___  ___  ___
G:  ___  ___  ___
F:  ___  ___  ___
     R    S    T
```

The choice of voting for (F) or against (A) will fill each space. Applying the rules creates the following basic diagram:

```
H:  ___  ___   A      (at lst 1F)
G:   A   ___  ___     (at lst 1F)
F:   F    A   ___
     R    S    T
   (2F,  (1F,  (1F,
    1A)  2A)   2A)
```

The rules provide a considerable amount of specific information: the number of "for" and "against" votes each bill receives; the minimum "for" and "against" votes by Fu, Gianola, and Herstein; and certain votes each voter casts. From the supplied information several inferences can be made. First, since there are two votes for the Recreation bill and one vote against the Recreation bill, and it has already been established that Fu votes for the bill and Gianola votes against the bill, it can be inferred that Herstein votes for the Recreation bill:

```
H:   F   ___   A
G:   A   ___  ___
F:   F    A   ___
     R    S    T
```

Furthermore, since only two voting options exist (F or A), dual-options can be placed on the remaining open spaces:

```
H:    F    F/A    A
     ___   ___   ___
G:    A    F/A   F/A
     ___   ___   ___
F:    F     A    F/A
     ___   ___   ___
      R     S     T
```

Of course, further information about some of the dual-options would affect the choices in other dual-options. Regardless, examining the diagram makes it apparent that the voting possibilities are limited. Since there are only four uncertain spaces and even those have restrictions, why not try to show every possibility? Although there are several ways to identify each possibility, the first step we will take is to look at the votes for the school bill. If Gianola votes against the school bill and Herstein votes for the school bill, only one solution exists:

```
H:    F     F     A
     ___   ___   ___
G:    A     A     F
     ___   ___   ___
F:    F     A     A
     ___   ___   ___
      R     S     T
      Possibility #1
```

In the diagram above, Gianola must vote for the tax bill since each council member votes for at least one bill; since there must be two votes against the tax bill, it can then be inferred that Fu votes against the tax bill.

The other scenario with the school bill switches the votes of Gianola and Herstein:

```
H:    F     A     A
     ___   ___   ___
G:    A     F    F/A
     ___   ___   ___
F:    F     A    F/A
     ___   ___   ___
      R     S     T
```

Unfortunately, this information does not completely determine the votes of Fu and Gianola on the tax bill. One must vote for the bill and the other must vote against. Since this produces only two scenarios, show each one:

```
H:   F    A    A              H:   F    A    A
G:   A    F    A              G:   A    F    F
F:   F    A    F              F:   F    A    A
     R    S    T                   R    S    T
    Possibility #2               Possibility #3
```

Thus, since all the options for the school bill have been explored, it follows that all the options for the entire voting record have been explored. These three solutions comprise the final setup to the game:

```
H:  F   F   A         H:  F   A   A         H:  F   A   A
G:  A   A   F         G:  A   F   A         G:  A   F   F
F:  F   A   A         F:  F   A   F         F:  F   A   A
    R   S   T             R   S   T             R   S   T
  Possibility #1        Possibility #2        Possibility #3
```

With all of the possibilities fully realized, the questions can be destroyed at light speed.

Question #19: Global, Could Be True. The correct answer choice is (D)

Possibility #3 proves that answer choice (D) could be true and is therefore correct.

Question #20: Local, Must Be True. The correct answer choice is (E)

Only Possibility #3 meets the criteria in the question stem. Possibility #3 confirms that answer choice (E) is correct.

9

Question #21: Local, Could Be True. The correct answer choice is (A)

Possibilities #1 and #3 meet the condition established in the question stem. Possibility #2 does not meet the condition and is not considered while attacking the question. Possibility #1 proves that answer choice (A) could be true and is therefore correct.

Question #22: Local, Must Be True. The correct answer choice is (C)

Only possibility #3 meets the condition in the question stem. Consequently, it can be determined that answer choice (C) is true.

Question #23: Local, Must Be True. The correct answer choice is (E)

As with question #22, only possibility #3 meets the condition in the question stem. Consequently, it can be determined that answer choice (E) is true.

The test makers build the game around the two-value system of the votes and then provide a considerable amount of information about the game. Since there are only four undetermined votes and each vote has only two options, it follows that there cannot be a large number of possibilities. This inherently restricted situation leads to the decision to Identify the Possibilities.

9

A clown will select a costume consisting of two pieces and no others: a jacket and overalls. One piece of the costume will be entirely one color, and the other piece will be plaid. Selection is subject to the following restrictions:

If the jacket is plaid, then there must be exactly three colors in it.

If the overalls are plaid, then there must be exactly two colors in them.

The jacket and overalls must have exactly one color in common.

Green, red, and violet are the only colors that can be in the jacket.

Red, violet, and yellow are the only colors that can be in the overalls.

1. Which one of the following could be a complete and accurate list of the colors in the costume?

	Jacket	Overalls
(A)	red	red
(B)	red	violet, yellow
(C)	violet	green, violet
(D)	violet	red, violet
(E)	violet	red, violet, yellow

GO ON TO THE NEXT PAGE.

9

2. If there are exactly two colors in the costume, then which one of the following must be false?

   (A) At least part of the jacket is green.
   (B) At least part of the jacket is red.
   (C) The overalls are red and violet.
   (D) The overalls are red and yellow.
   (E) The overalls are violet and yellow.

3. If at least part of the jacket is green, then which one of the following could be true?

   (A) The overalls are plaid.
   (B) No part of the jacket is red.
   (C) No part of the jacket is violet.
   (D) At least part of the overalls are yellow.
   (E) At least part of the overalls are violet.

4. Which one of the following must be false?

   (A) Both green and red are colors used in the costume.
   (B) Both green and violet are colors used in the costume.
   (C) Both green and yellow are colors used in the costume.
   (D) Both red and violet are colors used in the costume.
   (E) Both violet and yellow are colors used in the costume.

5. If there are exactly three colors in the costume, the overalls must be

   (A) entirely red or else red and violet plaid
   (B) entirely yellow or else violet and yellow plaid
   (C) entirely violet or else red and violet plaid
   (D) entirely red or else entirely yellow
   (E) entirely red or else entirely violet

GO ON TO THE NEXT PAGE.

9

This is a Grouping game, with colors assigned to two distinct groups, the jacket and the overalls. One of the initial steps in any grouping game is to attempt to establish, if possible, the number of elements in each group. In this instance, it takes a combination of the game scenario and rules to determine how many elements are in each group.

The second sentence of the game scenario establishes that one of the two items will always be entirely one color, and then the first two rules establish the number of colors in each costume piece if the piece is plaid. Each rule creates a separate fixed numerical distribution:

Distribution #1

This distribution comes from the first rule, which states that "If the jacket is plaid, then there must be exactly three colors in it."

The first rule states that if the jacket is plaid, then it must have exactly three colors. From the second sentence in the game scenario, then, the overalls must be exactly one color. This creates a 3-1 fixed distribution:

$$\begin{array}{cc} \underline{} & \\ \underline{} & \\ \underline{} & \underline{} \\ \text{Jacket} & \text{Overalls} \end{array}$$

Distribution #2

This distribution comes from the second rule, which states that "If the overalls are plaid, then there must be exactly two colors in them." From the second sentence in the game scenario, then, the jacket must be exactly one color. This creates a 1-2 fixed distribution:

$$\begin{array}{cc} & \underline{} \\ \underline{} & \underline{} \\ \text{Jacket} & \text{Overalls} \end{array}$$

Because all the possibilities are established when each costume piece is plaid (or, alternately, when each costume piece is entirely one color), these are the only two possible distributions in the game.

With all the numerical possibilities established, you must now focus on the contents of each grouping. In this case, the contents are the colors, and the last three rules of the game address the colors of each piece of the costume. Accordingly, we will examine each of the last three rules against the two numerical possibilities.

Rule #3

This rule states that "The jacket and overalls must have exactly one color in common." From a representational standpoint, an easy way to diagram this rule would be:

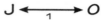

However, this diagram, while useful, is not the best possible representation. A better approach would be to use internal diagramming and represent this rule directly on the diagram of each numerical possibility:

In examining rules #4 and #5, we will keep in mind the operating effects of this rule.

Rule #4

This rule specifies that the colors of the jacket can only be green, red, and violet. In the 1-2 distribution, there is not an immediate impact from this rule (there will be an impact when this rule is combined with rules #3 and #5). In the 3-1 distribution, however, since the jacket is a total of three colors, all three slots are filled:

Note that at this point we have not yet considered the effects of the last rule, but even so we are not going to fill in the remaining slots with options that will ultimately be impossible. For example, in the 3-1 distribution, from rule #3 and rule #4, one could assume that the overalls must be either green, red, or violet. While this is true from those two rules, rule #5 will alter those possibilities to only red or violet, and so we will refrain from diagramming further at this time in order to avoid confusion.

Rule #5

This rule specifies that the colors of the overalls can only be red, violet, and yellow. A comparison of the color sets of the jacket and overalls shows that they share only two colors: red and violet. Thus, in the 3-1 distribution, because the jacket has already been determined to be green, red, and violet, the effect of rule #3 is that the overalls can only be red or violet:

The 3-1 distribution:

$$
\begin{array}{c}
\underline{G} \\
\underline{R} \\
\underline{V} \\
\text{Jacket}
\end{array}
\qquad
\begin{array}{c}
\underline{R/V} \\
\text{Overalls}
\end{array}
$$

In the 1-2 distribution, the jacket must be red or violet (it cannot be green because it would not have a color in common with the overalls). Thus, one color selection for the overalls must be red or violet. The other color selection for the overalls can be any color (except green, and the color the jacket and overalls have in common, of course):

The 1-2 distribution:

$$
\begin{array}{ccc}
 & & \underline{R/V/Y} \\
\underline{R/V} & \longleftrightarrow & \underline{R/V} \\
\text{Jacket} & & \text{Overalls}
\end{array}
$$

This representation, while helpful, is not entirely satisfactory because it creates the possibility that an interpretation mistake could be made (for example, accidentally selecting the same color for both color selections for the overalls while visually scanning the arrangement). Since the jacket can only be two colors, a better approach is to create a template for each color option:

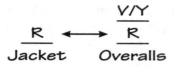

$$\underset{\text{Jacket}}{\underline{R}} \longleftrightarrow \underset{\text{Overalls}}{\overset{V/Y}{\underline{R}}} \qquad\qquad \underset{\text{Jacket}}{\underline{V}} \longleftrightarrow \underset{\text{Overalls}}{\overset{R/Y}{\underline{V}}}$$

Overall, there are three templates containing six solutions: two solutions in the 3-1 scenario, and four solutions in the 1-2 scenario (two solutions when red is the common color, two solutions when violet is the common color).

In reviewing the color contents of the six templates, the controlling effect of the color sets and rule #3 becomes apparent: red and violet are featured prominently, whereas green and yellow do not appear as much. In fact, green and yellow cannot appear in the same costume together, an inference that is tested in question #4.

Combining all of the information above leads to the following optimal setup for the game:

Jacket: G, R, V
Overalls: R, V, Y

$$\text{Jacket}_{\text{Plaid}} \longrightarrow 3 \text{ colors}$$

$$\text{Overalls}_{\text{Plaid}} \longrightarrow 2 \text{ colors}$$

$$J \xleftrightarrow{\ _1\ } O$$

$$G \longleftrightarrow\!\!\!| \longleftrightarrow Y$$

Template #1

The 3-1 distribution:

$$\underset{\text{Jacket}}{\overset{\displaystyle\overline{\overset{G}{\underline{R}}}}{\underline{V}}} \qquad \underset{\text{Overalls}}{\underline{R/V}}$$

Template #2

The 1-2 distribution, jacket is red:

$$\underset{\text{Jacket}}{\underline{R}} \longleftrightarrow \underset{\text{Overalls}}{\overset{V/Y}{\underline{R}}}$$

Template #3

The 1-2 distribution, jacket is violet:

$$\underset{\text{Jacket}}{\underline{V}} \longleftrightarrow \underset{\text{Overalls}}{\overset{R/Y}{\underline{V}}}$$

At this point we are ready to attack the game with confidence since the setup elegantly captures all six solutions to the game.

9

Question #1: Global, Could Be True, List. The correct answer choice is (D)

As with any List question, simply apply the rules to the answer choices. In this game, the easiest approach is to apply the rules in the order given. Note that rule #1 does not eliminate any answer choices because none of the answers feature a plaid jacket.

Answer choice (A): This answer choice is eliminated by the rule in the game scenario that indicates that one of the pieces will be plaid (and thus contain multiple colors). Always remember that in a List question the game scenario might contain conditions that can eliminate answer choices.

Answer choice (B): This answer choice is eliminated by rule #3 because the pieces do not have a color in common.

Answer choice (C): This answer violates rule #5 because the overalls cannot be green.

Answer choice (D): This is the correct answer choice.

Answer choice (E): This answer violates rule #2 because when the overalls are plaid they only contain two colors.

Question #2: Local, Cannot Be True. The correct answer choice is (A)

The first item to attend to is converting the "false" statement in the question stem into terms of "true." "Must be false" is functionally equivalent to "cannot be true," and thus this is really a Cannot Be True question.

Proceeding, the condition in the question stem indicates there are only two colors in the costume. Thus, the only applicable scenarios feature the 1-2 fixed distribution (because the 3-1 distribution features three colors in the jacket). Before attacking the answers, quickly scan templates #2 and #3, which feature the 1-2 distribution, and then use those templates to attack the answer choices.

Answer choice (A): This is the correct answer choice. None of the solutions in templates #2 and #3 contain green as a color, and thus it cannot be true that green is a part of the jacket.

Answer choice (B): This answer choice is incorrect. Template #2 has a red jacket.

Answer choice (C): This answer choice is incorrect. Both templates #2 and #3 allow for red and violet overalls.

Answer choice (D): This answer choice is incorrect. Template #2 allows for red and yellow overalls.

Answer choice (E): This answer choice is incorrect. Template #3 allows for violet and yellow overalls.

9

Question #3: Local, Could Be True. The correct answer choice is (E)

The condition in the question stem establishes that part of the jacket is green, and that can only occur in the 3-1 fixed distribution. Accordingly, refer to template #1 to answer this question.

Answer choice (A): This answer choice is incorrect. In template #1, the jacket is plaid, not the overalls.

Answer choice (B): This answer choice is incorrect. In template #1, part of the jacket is red.

Answer choice (C): This answer choice is incorrect. In template #1, part of the jacket is violet.

Answer choice (D): This answer choice is incorrect. In template #1, the overalls must be red or violet.

Answer choice (E): This is the correct answer choice. In template #1, the overalls must be red or violet, and therefore it could be true that the overalls are violet.

Question #4: Global, Cannot Be True. The correct answer choice is (C)

This is the most difficult question of the game, and one that is not easy to answer from a quick glance at the rules.

First, convert the "false" statement into terms of "true." "Must be false" is functionally equivalent to "cannot be true," and thus this is really a Cannot Be True question.

Second, because this is a Global question, refer to your inferences for any negative deductions. In this case, when discussing the effects of rule #3, rule #4, and rule #5, we arrived at the inference that green and yellow cannot appear in the same costume together:

This inference is directly tested in the correct answer, answer choice (C).

However, consider for a moment the approach to take if you did not see that inference while creating the setup. In this game, that would involve two separate steps:

1. Refer to the templates and eliminate incorrect answer choices. Template #1 (the 3-1) quickly eliminates answer choices (A) and (B), template #2 eliminates answer choice (D), and template #3 eliminates answer choice (E). Thus, answer choice (C) is the only remaining answer choice and must be correct.

2. Refer to the hypotheticals created in other questions. This approach is often helpful in Global questions with no obvious answer, and the hypothetical in question #1 eliminates answer choice (D). This approach could be used if step 1 failed to eliminate all incorrect answer choices.

Answer choice (A): This answer choice is incorrect. Template #1 proves that both green and red can be used in the costume together.

Answer choice (B): This answer choice is incorrect. Template #1 proves that both green and violet can be used in the costume together.

Answer choice (C): This is the correct answer choice. As discussed in the game setup, green and yellow can never appear in the costume together.

Answer choice (D): This answer choice is incorrect. Template #2 proves that both red and violet can be used in the costume together.

Answer choice (E): This answer choice is incorrect. Template #3 proves that both violet and yellow can be used in the costume together.

9

Question #5: Local, Must Be True. The correct answer choice is (E)

The question stem states that there must be exactly three colors in the costume. Templates #2 and #3 feature exactly two colors, and therefore template #1 is the template that applies to this question. The question stem also references the overalls, and since in template #1 the overalls are either red or violet, the correct answer must indicate that the overalls are red or violet, or indicate that the overalls are *not* yellow.

Answer choice (A): This answer choice is incorrect. In template #1, the overalls cannot be plaid.

Answer choice (B): This answer choice is incorrect. In template #1, the overalls cannot be plaid (or yellow, for that matter).

Answer choice (C): This answer choice is incorrect. In template #1, the overalls cannot be plaid.

Answer choice (D): This answer choice is incorrect. In template #1, the overalls cannot be yellow.

Answer choice (E): This is the correct answer choice.

Overall, this game is relatively easy as long as you use the numerical distribution to produce templates, which should enable you to complete the game very quickly with perfect accuracy.

9

On a Tuesday, an accountant has exactly seven bills—numbered 1 through 7—to pay by Thursday of the same week. The accountant will pay each bill only once according to the following rules:

Either three or four of the seven bills must be paid on Wednesday, the rest on Thursday.

Bill 1 cannot be paid on the same day as bill 5.

Bill 2 must be paid on Thursday.

Bill 4 must be paid on the same day as bill 7.

If bill 6 is paid on Wednesday, bill 7 must be paid on Thursday.

1. If exactly four bills are paid on Wednesday, then those four bills could be

(A)   1, 3, 4, and 6
(B)   1, 3, 5, and 6
(C)   2, 4, 5, and 7
(D)   3, 4, 5, and 7
(E)   3, 4, 6, and 7

GO ON TO THE NEXT PAGE.

2. Which one of the following is a complete and accurate list of the bills any one of which could be among the bills paid on Wednesday?

(A) 3, 5, and 6
(B) 1, 3, 4, 6, and 7
(C) 1, 3, 4, 5, 6, and 7
(D) 2, 3, 4, 5, 6, and 7
(E) 1, 2, 3, 4, 5, 6, and 7

3. If bill 2 and bill 6 are paid on different days from each other, which one of the following must be true?

(A) Exactly three bills are paid on Wednesday.
(B) Exactly three bills are paid on Thursday.
(C) Bill 1 is paid on the same day as bill 4.
(D) Bill 2 is paid on the same day as bill 3.
(E) Bill 5 is paid on the same day as bill 7.

4. If bill 6 is paid on Wednesday, which one of the following bills must also be paid on Wednesday?

(A) 1
(B) 3
(C) 4
(D) 5
(E) 7

5. If bill 4 is paid on Thursday, which one of the following is a pair of bills that could also be paid on Thursday?

(A) 1 and 5
(B) 1 and 7
(C) 3 and 5
(D) 3 and 6
(E) 6 and 7

6. Which one of the following statements must be true?

(A) If bill 2 is paid on Thursday, bill 3 is paid on Wednesday.
(B) If bill 4 is paid on Thursday, bill 1 is paid on Wednesday.
(C) If bill 4 is paid on Thursday, bill 3 is paid on Wednesday.
(D) If bill 6 is paid on Thursday, bill 3 is also paid on Thursday.
(E) If bill 6 is paid on Thursday, bill 4 is also paid on Thursday.

GO ON TO THE NEXT PAGE.

9

This is a Defined-Moving, Balanced Grouping game. Even though the bills appear to have a numerical order, it quickly becomes apparent that they can be paid in any order or configuration. More important are the groups of bills paid on the two days, and the key to the game is the Numerical Distribution of the bills to the days. There are seven bills that must be paid on Wednesday and Thursday, and the first rule establishes that three or four will be paid each day. This leads to two fixed distributions:

	Wednesday	Thursday
Fixed Numerical	3	4
Distributions	4	3

These two fixed distributions suggest Identifying the Templates. We will initially set the game up that way and then discuss the decision to Identify the Possibilities. Let us begin by creating a basic diagram:

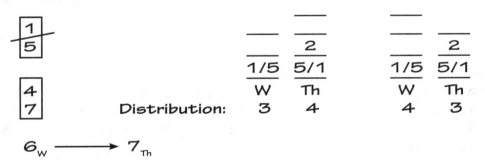

This game also contains a two-value system: all bills must be paid on Wednesday or Thursday. Since bill 1 and bill 5 cannot be paid on the same day, they must be paid on different days. But it is uncertain on which day each is paid, and so a 1/5 dual-option is placed on each day.

The two-value system also affects the last rule. The contrapositive of the last rule is:

$$7_{Th} \longrightarrow \cancel{6}_W$$

Of course, if bill 7 is not paid on Thursday it must be paid on Wednesday, and if bill 6 is not paid on Wednesday, it must be paid on Thursday:

$$7_W \longrightarrow 6_{Th}$$

An examination of the final two rules suggests that the number of solutions is limited. Both rules contain bill 7, and especially important is the power of the 4-7 block. When the 4-7 block is applied to the 4-3 distribution, it has only one placement option; when the 4-7 is applied to the 3-4 distribution, it has only two placement options. On the basis of this limitation, a decision should be made to show all the possibilities of those three options. Each appears as follows:

Possibilities #1 and #2:	Possibilities #3 and #4:	Possibilities #5 and #6:

Possibilities #1 and #2:	Possibilities #3 and #4:	Possibilities #5 and #6:
3	7	3
7 6	3 4	7 6
4 2	6 2	4 2
1/5 5/1	1/5 5/1	1/5 5/1
W Th	W Th	W Th
3 4	3 4	4 3
(4-7 on Wed.)	(4-7 on Thu.)	(4-7 on Wed.)

Each of the three templates includes two possibilities, each dependent on the placement of bill 1 and bill 5. Overall the game has only six solutions. Let us examine each of the three templates in more detail:

Possibilities #1 and #2: 3-4 Numerical Distribution. When the 4-7 block is placed on Wednesday, no other bills can be paid on Wednesday, and they must all be paid on Thursday. The only remaining uncertainty involves bill 1 and bill 5. Since there are only two options for bill 1 and bill 5, this template contains two solutions.

Possibilities #3 and #4: 3-4 Numerical Distribution. When the 4-7 block is placed on Thursday, no other bills can be paid on Thursday, and they must all be paid on Wednesday. The only remaining uncertainty involves bill 1 and bill 5. Since there are only two options for bill 1 and bill 5, this template contains two solutions.

Possibilities #5 and #6: 4-3 Numerical Distribution. The 4-7 block must be placed on Wednesday since there is only one open space on Thursday. When 7 is paid on Wednesday, it can be inferred from the contrapositive of the last rule that bill 6 is paid on Thursday. Since three bills are now paid on Thursday, bill 3 must be paid on Wednesday. The only remaining uncertainty involves bill 1 and bill 5. Because there are only two options for bill 1 and bill 5, this template contains two solutions.

Note that the use of templates to show two possibilities each reduces the amount of set up time required. The templates compactly display the uncertainty about bill 1 and bill 5, and there is no need to draw each of the six solutions out individually.

THE POWERSCORE LSAT LOGIC GAMES BIBLE

Question #1: Local, Could Be True, List. The correct answer choice is (D)

Possibility template #5 and #6 proves answer choice (D) correct. Using the templates for this question is actually somewhat difficult since the bills are listed in numerical order. Glancing at the 4-3 template, it is apparent that bills 3, 4, and 7 must be paid on Wednesday. Thus, any answer choice that does not contain bills 3, 4, and 7 can be eliminated. That leaves only answer choices (D) and (E). Since answer choice (D) contains bill 5, it is correct. Another approach is to realize that any answer choice that contains bill 2 or 6 must be incorrect. That eliminates every answer choice except answer choice (D).

Question #2: Global, Could Be True, List. The correct answer choice is (C)

The question requests a complete list of the bills that could ever be paid on Wednesday. From possibility template #1 and #2 it can be determined that bills 1, 4, 5, and 7 can be paid on Wednesday. Furthermore, from possibility template #3 and #4 it can be determined that bills 3 and 6 can be paid on Wednesday. Possibility template #5 and #6 does not add any insight. Thus, bills 1, 3, 4, 5, 6, and 7 can be paid on Wednesday and answer choice (C) is correct.

Question #3: Local, Must Be True. The correct answer choice is (A)

Only possibility template #3 and #4 meets the condition in the question stem. Accordingly answer choice (A) is correct. Answer choices (C) and (E) could be true, but they do not *have* to be true.

Question #4: Local, Must Be True. The correct answer choice is (B)

Only possibility template #3 and #4 meets the condition in the question stem. Accordingly answer choice (B) is correct. Answer choices (A) and (D) could be true, but they do not *have* to be true.

Question #5: Local, Could Be True. The correct answer choice is (B)

For the third question in a row, only possibility template #3 and #4 meets the condition in the question stem. Accordingly answer choice (B) is correct. Answer choice (A) could never occur since bill 1 and bill 5 cannot be paid on the same day.

Question #6: Global, Must Be True. The correct answer choice is (C)

This question requires checking all of the possibility templates. Answer choice (A) can be eliminated by possibility template #1 and #2. Answer choice (B) can be eliminated by possibility template #3 and #4. Answer choice (C) is proven correct since only possibility template #3 and #4 pays bill 4 on Thursday, and it is also the case that bill 3 is paid on Wednesday. Answer choice (D) can be eliminated by possibility template #5 and #6. Answer choice (E) can be eliminated by possibility template #1 and #2 and possibility template #5 and #6.

This game is a perfect display of the limiting power of Numerical Distributions. The two fixed distributions in combination with the grouping rules lead to the decision to Identify the Possibilities. And since this is the first game on the October 1999 LSAT, getting off to a good start is critical. Identifying the Possibilities in this game not only allows the smart test taker to answer the questions correctly, but, equally important, also allows the questions to be answered quickly.

It is also interesting to note that the Limited Solution Set games in this section featured one Basic Linear game, one Advanced Linear game, and one Grouping game. The advanced techniques of Identify the Templates and Identify the Possibilities can be used in a variety of games, and you should always examine the setup of a game to determine if the situation is limited.

9

Chapter Ten:
Section Strategy
and Management

Chapter Ten: Section Strategy and Management

Approaching the Section Strategically

For many students, the Logic Games section is the most challenging section on the LSAT. How you approach the section depends in part on how good you are at Games. If Logic Games is your strength, and if anything less than completion of the section means failure to you, then much of what is contained in this chapter will not apply to you. On the other hand, if you are one of the many students who has difficulty with the Logic Games section, then the following advice is designed to assist you.

The Games section is often a bellwether of LSAT performance: the Games section tends to affect the rest of the test. If things go well on Games, most students feel as if the test has gone well.

Time Management

Time management is critical to your success on this section. Each section of the LSAT is 35 minutes in length, and since there are always four games per section, you have 8 minutes and 45 seconds to complete each game and transfer your answers. However, this assumes you will complete all four games. For many students that is not possible or advisable. Strong performance on the LSAT depends on two factors: speed and accuracy. If you rush to complete every question but miss most of them, you will not receive a high score. On the other hand, if, by slowing down, you increase your accuracy, you *may* be able to increase your score despite doing fewer questions. Consider the following comparison:

	Student #1	Student #2	Student #3
Questions completed in section	24	20	16
Accuracy Rate	50%	75%	100%
Total Correct Answers	12	15	16

Obviously, actual performance in a section depends on a variety of factors, and each student must assess their own strengths and weaknesses. Regardless, the message is the same: you might benefit from slowing down and attempting fewer games. The following table displays the amount of time that should be allotted to each game, depending on how many are attempted:

10

CHAPTER TEN: SECTION STRATEGY AND MANAGEMENT   605

On the digital
LSAT, the
time remaining
appears in the
upper right
corner of the
screen.

# Games Attempted	Time per Game Attempted
2	17 minutes and 30 seconds
3	11 minutes and 40 seconds
4	8 minutes and 45 seconds

If you rush through four games and only get 12 correct, then perhaps a better choice would be to attack only three games, spend more time on each game, and try for a higher accuracy rate. Practice will dictate which strategy is superior. Keep in mind though that there is a point of diminishing returns. Spending 35 minutes on one game and answering all six questions correctly does not lead to a very high LSAT score! Instead, you must seek the level that provides you with the best combination of speed and accuracy. We strongly believe that you should attempt at least three games unless there is a compelling reason to the contrary.

Doing Fewer Games

Apply this
strategy after
you have proven
that you cannot
complete four
games with
accuracy.

Prior to the test, if you decide to attempt three games or fewer, it would make sense to select the games according to your test-taking strengths. This requires two steps:

1. Know your personal strengths and weaknesses in the Games section. Assess which types of games you prefer, and be detailed in your assessment. For example, do you like Defined Grouping games but dislike Undefined Grouping games?

2. Choose the best games to work on when you begin the section. As the section begins, look for the game types you prefer. Usually a quick reading of the game scenario reveals the game type. Of course, to apply this, you must be intimately familiar with the various game types and corresponding rules.

At the beginning of each Logic Games section, quickly scan the scenario of the first game. If it looks like a game you would like to do or one that seems easy to do, start with that game. If, on the other hand, the first game appears hard or is of a type you dislike, move to the second game (use the navigation bar at the bottom of the screen to quickly jump to the first question of the next game) and scan the scenario. Complete the same analysis to decide if you want to do the game.

10

One factor to keep in mind when analyzing games is the number of questions in a game. Suppose two games appear equally attractive to you. In this case you should do the game with the greater number of questions, the theory being you get "more for your money" when there are more questions.

All else being equal, do the game with more questions.

Your actions within each game are also important. As discussed in previous chapters, some questions are inherently more time-consuming than others, while certain questions tend to be more difficult. Perhaps the most time-consuming question is the one where each answer choice begins with the word "if." These "5 if" questions are like five questions in one since you typically have to create a new diagram for each answer choice. If you are particularly slow with Games, or if you are behind in a section, it makes sense to skip these questions. Also mentioned earlier, the last question in a game is often the most difficult question. The test makers do this for a variety of reasons. Many students arrive at the last question anxious to finish the question and complete the game. When the question proves difficult, they become unsettled and frustrated, and, as a result, often miss the question. Even worse, this frustration carries into the next game, and they begin the next game without the focus necessary to perform well. This in turn can lead to more missed questions. Keep this in mind whenever you approach the last question in a game. It is imperative that you keep your concentration, and if you do not see a clear path to solving the question, move on.

Avoid "5 if" questions if you are slow on Games.

10

Using a Timer

The LSAT itself has a built-in timer on the tablet and timing is done automatically, and so practicing under timed conditions is critically important. PowerScore has online tools that allow you to experience the digital environment while practicing, but you will also likely use different paper resources while you are preparing. In those cases, one of the most important tools for preparation success is a timer. When not working online, your timer should be a constant companion during your LSAT preparation, and, as will be discussed in the next section, you should use your timer to help construct an accurate Pacing Guideline.

Although not all of your practice efforts should be timed, you should attempt to do as many questions as possible under timed conditions in order to acquaint yourself with the difficulties of the test. After all, if the LSAT was a take-home test, no one would be too worried about it.

Practice doing as many games as possible with your timer so that you can develop a comfortable and familiar pace.

A timer is invaluable because it is an odometer for the section. With sufficient practice you will begin to establish a comfortable test-taking speed and the timer allows you to make sure you are maintaining this appropriate speed. If you go too quickly or too slowly you can then make adjustments during the test. Memorize the following time-markers:

Memorize these marking points!

# Games Attempted	Timer Marking Points (counting up from 0 to 35:00 minutes)
2	Move to game #2 at 17 minutes and 30 seconds
3	Move to game #2 at 11 minutes and 40 seconds; Move to game #3 at 23 minutes and 20 seconds;
4	Move to game #2 at 8 minutes and 45 seconds; Move to game #3 at 17 minutes and 30 seconds; Move to game #4 at 26 minutes and 15 seconds

The prior table assumes that each game is done in exactly the allotted time. If you spend more time on one of the games (which is perfectly acceptable and expected at times), you must make up that time in another game to stay on pace. If you do one of the games more quickly, that gives you the luxury of spending more time on a later game.

10

Note also that the Digital LSAT provides you with a visual "5 minutes remaining" warning that pops up onscreen during the exam. The timer bar in the upper right hand corner will also turn from green to red when 5 minutes remains.

Remember, the LSAT is what is known as a "speeded" test. The test makers presume that the average student cannot finish each section in the allotted time (i.e., that they are "speeded" up). So, most people do not finish all the questions in any of the sections. Increasing speed usually requires a lot of practice and analysis of your performance. The tools we use—Not Laws, knowledge of question and game types, diagrammatic representations, etc.—are designed to help you increase your speed once you are familiar with them. Yes, they take some time to adjust to at first, but this is true of any organized system. Keep practicing and work on becoming comfortable with the timed aspect of the test, and your LSAT score will improve.

10

Pacing Guidelines

Every test taker must have a plan of action before they start a section. As you practice, you should strive to determine your personal Pacing Guideline. For example, how much time do you generally plan to spend on the first game? The first two games? How much time do you expect will have elapsed when you reach question #10? Question #20? Before you pick up a pencil and take the actual test, you should be able to answer these questions.

The header at the beginning of every Logic Game section tells you how many questions are in the section.

First off, we are not advocating that you create a strict timeline that controls where you are every moment in the section or that dictates when you quit working on a question. Instead, you must create a loose blueprint for completing the section—one that uses your particular strengths to create an achievable set of goals. To give you a better sense of how the idea works, here is an example of a complete Pacing Guideline for a high scorer:

Games with eight questions are exceedingly rare, but they have appeared before and could again.

> Complete each game in eight minutes or less, unless a game has seven or eight questions.
>
> Last three minutes of the section: double-check work; return to any question noted as especially challenging.

Clearly, this Guideline is an aggressive one that is based on the assumption that the test taker is good enough to complete all the questions accurately and still have time remaining. Your personal Guideline does not have to be the same! Take a moment, however, to review the above Guideline:

- The test taker assumes that he or she can work fast, but makes an adjustment for the number of questions.

- Despite being good enough to expect to finish all the questions, the test taker doesn't just sit back and relax for the last few minutes. Instead, he or she uses that time to re-check troublesome problems.

- The Guideline is relatively loose and contains a minimum of components.

10

Here is how to create and use your own Pacing Guideline:

1. During your practice sessions, focus on determining how fast you can do a typical Logic Game while still retaining a high degree of accuracy. To do this, you will need to time yourself habitually.

2. Set a benchmark for roughly where you should be after the first and second games you attack.

3. Try to take into account the difficulty level of a game, and a high or low number of questions.

4. Do not make your Pacing Guideline too detailed. The difficulty of the questions (and entire sections) varies, so you do not want to create a rigid Guideline that cannot account for these differences. For example, do not make a Guideline that specifies where you will be at 5, 8, 12, 15 minutes, etc, or one that indicates where you will be after question 4, 6, 8, etc. Those are too specific and will be unusable if you run into a hard (or very easy) game early in the section. Try to make your Guideline broad enough to characterize several different points in the section. If you have more than four or five elements to your Guideline, it is getting too detailed!

5. Make sure you are comfortable with your plan and that your goals are achievable. This is not a plan of what you hope will happen, but rather what your practice has proven you can do.

6. Use the Guideline to help monitor your performance during the test. If you end up working more quickly than expected and you are beating your goals, then you will know that things are going exceedingly well and that should bolster your confidence. On the other hand, if you find yourself falling behind the marker points, then you will know that you must bear down and work a bit more quickly.

Implementing the steps above should not be too difficult, but you would be surprised by how many people fail to prepare even the most basic plan of action for each section. In many ways, it is as if they have been asked to run a triathlon but they practice only infrequently and do not keep track of how fast they can go without burning out. Athletes at all levels measure their performance frequently, and the LSAT is just a triathlon for the mind. The important thing is that you create a Guideline that works for you and that you have confidence in. Then, follow it on test day and always remember that you might have to be flexible to account for the unexpected.

You should have a different Pacing Guideline for each section.

10

Question Attack Strategies ▮▮▮▮▮

Students often ask about the existence of an optimal question approach strategy, wondering if there is a certain approach that always yields the best results. Before discussing the best overall strategy, let's first talk about two flawed strategies you may have run across.

<u>Flawed Strategy I: Local First</u>

A Local First strategy dictates that you answer every single Local question (the questions starting with "if") in the game first, and then move on to the Global questions (the questions that do not specify that a variable is placed in a particular space). The idea behind this strategy is that by working out the questions that require you to manipulate the variables and form partial and complete solutions, you will learn about the fundamental operation of the game and find inferences that might otherwise be hard to see. That will position you to quickly answer the remaining Global questions. It sounds interesting and has a catchy name, so what could be the possible downside?

Here are two examples from real LSAT Logic Games in this book where application of this strategy would cause issues:

1. Page 266, the Yamata game. The first question, #8, is a Global Must Be True question that relies on the inference that Yamata must always Lecture on Tuesday afternoon. The inference tested here is critical, and if you do not identify it early in the game, your ability to successfully solve the remainder of the game is severely hampered. If you use the Local First strategy and start the game by skipping directly to Question #11, the first Local question in the game, you waste time and are likely to get frustrated in your attempt to answer #11.

2. Page 344, Library Budget Reductions game. The first question in this game (#6) is a Global question that can be used to help solve question #10, which is probably the hardest Local question in the game. Skipping question #6 would not stop you from solving the game, but it would slow you down on question #10, and create unnecessary frustration.

Those are just two quick examples from the games in the Logic Games Bible, and there are numerous other examples from the many LSATs that have been released. The bottom line is that in *some* cases a Local First strategy would be great, but in other cases it would create serious

10

problems. Unfortunately, there is no way to tell at the outset of a game when the strategy would work and when it would create issues. And because of that problem, this is not a strategy that can be reliably used in every case.

Let's now take a look at the other flawed strategy.

Flawed Strategy II: Global First

In a Global First strategy, you answer all of the Global questions first, and then move on to solving the Local questions. The theory is that by attacking the Global questions first you will learn about the absolute truths of the game and discover any global constants within the game. Then, armed with that information, you can more comfortably attack the Local questions, which will require you to manipulate the variables.

Just as with the Local First strategy, a Global First strategy can be effective, but it can also fail. Here's a classic example where it would cause issues, using one of the games referenced previously:

1. Page 344, the Library Budget Reductions game. Using the Global First strategy on this game, you would solve question #6 first, and then question #12. Completing question #6 is helpful (but you probably would have done it first anyway, as it is the first question of the game), but try to do question #12 without having seen how this game really operates. To solve question #12 before attacking Local question #7 wastes time, especially because the solution to question #7—a solution that is very easy to identify—helps solve question #12.

Local questions have the advantage of making you work with the variables and create hypotheticals, so in answering the Local questions you actually produce information that can then help answer the Global questions. In a game that contains an extremely deep inference, like the Library Budget Reductions, a Global First strategy usually slows you down, and then causes frustration.

There are other considerations that are problematic as well. For example, a number of Suspension questions are Global, and doing them adds little to no value to your understanding of the Local questions. Suspension questions also tend to be time-consuming, meaning that you are taking on lengthier questions earlier in the game, which causes you to feel pressure to move even faster as you approach the 8 minute and 45 second time marker.

10

So, if looking for Global questions first or Local questions first isn't consistently helpful, what is the best strategy? It's one we call the Modified Order strategy, and it allows you to make decisions based on the circumstances of each game.

Modified Order Strategy

1. In general, do the questions in the order given. The first question is usually a List question, and that type of question provides you with valuable information about the game, and almost everyone gets those questions correct.

2. Be smart and know when to skip certain questions in order to return to them later. Global Could Be True questions are often wise to save until the end of the game (because they are based on possibilities that are often best understood after seeing as many solutions as possible). Or, for example, imagine that the second question in a game asks you for all the possible spaces where P could appear. A question like that is much more easily answered after you have seen different solutions to the game, so skip that question and return to it later.

3. If you encounter any "5 if" questions, which are almost always quite time-consuming, skip them and return to them at the end of the game. The same goes for any Maximum/Minimum and Justify questions.

4. If the game contains a Suspension or Rule Substitution question, you will typically encounter it at the end of the game. But, if you skipped any prior questions, return to those questions before attacking the Suspension or Rule Substitution questions.

There are, of course, exceptions to this general order. For example, in a Pattern game, if you cannot deduce the pattern of the game, the best strategy is to immediately go to the Local questions and attack those first, as they produce hypotheticals that can provide insight into the game. Thus, you have to consider the nature of the game itself, as well as the type of question you encounter, in order to make the best decisions as to which questions to attack.

10

Limited Time Strategies ▮▮▮▮▮

Within each Pacing Guideline there is room to make decisions during the test. With practice you will discover your strengths and weaknesses, and you can alter your approach during the test to maximize its effectiveness. Despite all efforts, however, you might find yourself running out of time as you approach your last game. If this occurs, you can handle this situation by employing the special, broad-based strategy described below.

Please keep in mind that this strategy should be applied only if you arrive at the last game and clearly do not have time to complete the entire game (for example, if you have only 2-4 minutes remaining).

Limited Time Approach

Skim the game scenario and rules, answer any List questions, and then answer any attractive question.

This approach does not yield a classic setup and corresponding diagram of each rule; instead, you skim through the game scenario and rules to get a general sense of the type of game, the nature of the rules, and how the rules interact. Then, if the first question is a List question, you immediately attack that question and use the rules to eliminate each incorrect answer choice (which is standard List question strategy). Thereafter, you move to attractive-looking questions and attempt to solve those questions quickly. For example, if you saw a Local question that seemed simple, you could attack that question. Or, if you noticed an interesting Not Law that followed from a rule, you could check to see if there is a Cannot Be True question that might use that Not Law as the correct answer. In other words, if during your review of the rules you deduced an inference, you would then scan the questions for one that might make use of that inference.

Overall, you attempt to solve as many questions as possible, and then guess on the remaining questions. You would typically avoid the following question types: "5-if," Justify, Suspension, and Rule Substitution questions, as these question types are often time-consuming.

The more time you have remaining, the more time you can spend making a setup. For example, with only two minutes remaining, you don't have time to create a setup, but with four minutes remaining, you can take a bit longer to assess how the game works.

This is not the time to wait for the "Big Inference" to hit you! Instead, get right to work on the questions.

10

This is a general strategy, and one that is dependent on the nature of the questions. If you know you are low on time, after scanning the game and the questions, you might need to make some adjustments to your approach. For example, if there are few Local questions, that may mean the game trades on Limited Solution Sets or a major inference. Use that information to adjust your strategy accordingly.

Even if you are able to attack the last game and complete all, or nearly all, of the questions, there are still mini-strategies you can employ within the last game.

The following two "endgame" strategies can save valuable time at the *end of a section*:

1. When you find an attractive answer, choose it and move on

    As time winds down, you can make allowances in your approach to the questions. For example, if you are on question #22 (of 24 total) with only one minute remaining in the section and you find that answer choice (A) is extremely attractive, you should choose it and move on to the next question. Normally you would read all the answer choices, but when time is short, you can alter that approach if it is expedient to do so.

2. Avoid questions that are designed to be time-consuming

    Another example of "endgame" management would be if you only have one minute left, but two questions to complete. In this instance, you would avoid any problem that is designed to be time-consuming (such as a "5-if" or Suspension question). Then, you can return to the problem if time allows. Of course, if the only questions remaining are inherently time-consuming, simply pick the one that appears the most attractive to you.

Remember, good test takers are flexible in their approach and they adapt to changing circumstances. And, even when circumstances change, they maintain focus and a positive attitude.

The Answer Choices

As you know, every LSAT question contains five answer choices. When you complete each problem, your response will be entered as soon as you select the lettered bubble to the left of your chosen answer. That question will then darken correspondingly in the navigation bar, indicating you have answered it. The navigation bar will *not* show which answer you selected, however, so you cannot see your exact choices when working on other questions, or whether any particular answer has appeared with an unusual frequency in the section.

As mentioned previously in this book, you can flag problems you find difficult or wish to review as you work through the section, and we strongly recommend doing so as needed. That allows you to then jump to those problems instantly using the navigation bar. This process is a significant time-saver over the old paper-and-pencil format where you had to transfer your answers to an answer sheet, and then include separate indications about which problems you found difficult and wanted to review.

Four in a row?

Unlike the SAT, the LSAT often has three identical answer choices to consecutive questions (such as three Ds), and on several occasions, four identical answer choices in a row have appeared. On the June 1996 LSAT, it even occurred that six of seven answer choices in one section were (C). The use of multiple answer choices in a row is one of the psychological weapons employed by the test makers to unnerve test takers. Any test taker seeing four (D)s in a row on their answer sheet understandably thinks they have made some type of error, primarily because most tests avoid repetition in their answer choices. If you see three or four answer choices in a row, do not become alarmed, especially if you feel you have been performing well on the section. We are still waiting for the day that the LSAT has five identical correct answers in a row, but we will not be too surprised when it happens.

The test makers have many tricks to keep you psychologically off-balance.

10

Guessing Strategy

Never leave an answer blank on the LSAT! There is no penalty for wrong answers and so it is in your best interest to guess on any problem you cannot complete.

Because the LSAT does not assess a scoring penalty for incorrect answer choices, you should always guess on every question that you cannot complete during the allotted time. However, because some answer choices are more likely to occur than others, you should not guess randomly. The following tables indicate the frequency of appearance of Logic Game answer choices over the years.

All Logic Games Answer Choices June 1991 - November 2022*					
% appearance of each answer choice throughout the entire section	A%	B%	C%	D%	E%
	19.8	**20.6**	19.7	20.1	19.8

These statistics do not include nondisclosed LSAT administrations.

We discuss guessing strategy and many other LSAT concepts on our podcast and in the Free LSAT Help Section of the powerscore. com website.

The table above documents the percentage each answer choice appeared as a percentage of all Logic Game answer choices between June 1991 and November 2022 inclusive. If history holds, when guessing on the LSAT Logic Games section, you would be best served by always guessing answer choice (B). Do not choose random answer choices; do not put in a pattern such as A-B-C-D-E etcetera. Although guessing answer choice (B) does not guarantee you will get the questions correct, if history is an indicator then guessing answer choice (B) gives you a better chance than guessing randomly. Consider the following comparison of students guessing on five consecutive answer choices:

Correct Answer Choice	Student #1 Answer Choices (Pattern)	Student #2 Answer Choices (Random)	Student #3 Answer Choices (All Bs)
B	A	D	B
D	B	C	B
E	C	A	B
A	D	E	B
C	E	B	B
# Correct	0	0	1

Although one question may not seem significant, it adds up over four sections, and depending on where you are in the scoring scale, it can increase your score several points. And every point counts! By guessing answer choice (B), you increase your chances of getting an answer correct.

The next table summarizes the percentage appearance of correct answer choices in just the last five questions of the Logic Games section.

Last Five Answer Choices Per Logic Games Section June 1991 - November 2022*					
% appearance of each answer choice in the last five answer choices of the Logic Games section	A%	B%	C%	D%	E%
	22.6	20.4	19.2	19.2	18.6

*These statistics do not include nondisclosed LSAT administrations.

Within the last five questions, the guessing strategy changes to dictate that you should guess answer choice (A). Notice the significant statistical deviation of answer choice (E). Answer choice (E) is not a good answer choice to guess in the last five questions!

The next table summarizes the percentage appearance of the correct answer of the last question in each *game* over the years, just for fun.

Last Answer Choice Per Game June 1991 - November 2022*					
% appearance of each correct answer choice for the last question of each game	A%	B%	C%	D%	E%
Game #1:	15.0	20.0	**26.0**	23.0	17.0
Game #2:	17.0	**25.0**	17.0	19.0	23.0
Game #3:	17.0	22.0	19.0	**24.0**	19.0
Game #4:	20.0	19.0	**26.0**	22.0	14.0
Average	17.0	21.0	**22.0**	**22.0**	18.0

*Rounded to the nearest whole number. These statistics do not include nondisclosed LSAT administrations.

10

Please keep in mind that the above advice holds only for pure guessing. If you are attempting to choose between two answer choices, do not choose on the basis of statistics alone!

On a related note, if you are a strong test taker who correctly answers most questions but occasionally does not finish a section, quickly review the answer choices you have previously selected and use the answer that appears least as your guessing answer choice. For example, if you have completed twenty questions in a section, and your answers contain a majority of (A)s, (C)s, (D)s, and (E)s, guess answer choice (B) for all of the remaining questions.

10

Final Note ■■■■■■■■■■■

We would like to take a moment to thank you for choosing to purchase the *PowerScore LSAT Logic Games Bible*. We hope you have found this book useful and enjoyable!

For more information relating to Logic Games, including important supplements to this book, please visit:

 powerscore.com/lsatprep

Once there, create an account and then use the code on the inside front cover of this book to gain access.

And check out the PowerScore LSAT PodCast at:

 powerscore.com/lsat/podcast

We talk regularly about all things LSAT, including Logic Games concepts and methods. Also available via iTunes, Spotify, Stitcher, and YouTube.

If you wish to ask questions about items in this book, please visit our free LSAT discussion forum at:

 forum.powerscore.com

10

The forum offers thousands of answers to student questions, including many lengthy explanations and conceptual discussions from the author of this book.

Study hard, and best of luck on the LSAT!

10

Logic Games
ReChallenge

Logic Games ReChallenge

Logic Games ReChallenge ████████

This chapter contains each of the games presented earlier in this book. The games are mixed into seven sections of four games each, allowing you the opportunity to retake each game without seeing any of the work you did when you first encountered the game. If you wish to time yourself, each block of four games should be completed in 35 minutes total. Alternatively, if you choose to do each game one at a time, each game should be completed in 8 minutes and 45 seconds.

A brief answer key is presented at the end of the chapter, and in addition to the answers, the page number for the complete explanation of the game is also given.

Note: In order to most closely emulate the current LSAT Logic Games format, each ReChallenge game is presented on two pages.

R

R

Logic Games ReChallenge
Set #1

R

During a period of six consecutive days—day 1 through day 6—each of exactly six factories—F, G, H, J, Q, and R—will be inspected. During this period, each of the factories will be inspected exactly once, one factory per day. The schedule for the inspections must conform to the following conditions:

   F is inspected on either day 1 or day 6.
   J is inspected on an earlier day than Q is inspected.
   Q is inspected on the day immediately before R is
     inspected.
   If G is inspected on day 3, Q is inspected on day 5.

1. Which one of the following could be a list of the factories in the order of their scheduled inspections, from day 1 through day 6?

   (A)   F, Q, R, H, J, G
   (B)   G, H, J, Q, R, F
   (C)   G, J, Q, H, R, F
   (D)   G, J, Q, R, F, H
   (E)   J, H, G, Q, R, F

GO ON TO THE NEXT PAGE.

R

2. Which one of the following must be false?

   (A)   The inspection of G is scheduled for day 4.
   (B)   The inspection of H is scheduled for day 6.
   (C)   The inspection of J is scheduled for day 4.
   (D)   The inspection of Q is scheduled for day 3.
   (E)   The inspection of R is scheduled for day 2.

3. The inspection of which one of the following
   CANNOT be scheduled for day 5?

   (A)   G
   (B)   H
   (C)   J
   (D)   Q
   (E)   R

4. The inspections scheduled for day 3 and day 5,
   respectively, could be those of

   (A)   G and H
   (B)   G and R
   (C)   H and G
   (D)   R and J
   (E)   R and H

5. If the inspection of R is scheduled for the day
   immediately before the inspection of F, which one of
   the following must be true about the schedule?

   (A)   The inspection of either G or H is scheduled
          for day 1.
   (B)   The inspection of either G or J is scheduled for
          day 1.
   (C)   The inspection of either G or J is scheduled for
          day 2.
   (D)   The inspection of either H or J is scheduled for
          day 3.
   (E)   The inspection of either H or J is scheduled for
          day 4.

6. If the inspections of G and of H are scheduled, not
   necessarily in that order, for days as far apart as
   possible, which one of the following is a complete and
   accurate list of the factories any one of which could
   be scheduled for inspection for day 1?

   (A)   F, J
   (B)   G, H
   (C)   G, H, J
   (D)   F, G, H
   (E)   F, G, H, J

7. If the inspection of G is scheduled for the day
   immediately before the inspection of Q, which one of
   the following could be true?

   (A)   The inspection of G is scheduled for day 5.
   (B)   The inspection of H is scheduled for day 6.
   (C)   The inspection of J is scheduled for day 2.
   (D)   The inspection of Q is scheduled for day 4.
   (E)   The inspection of R is scheduled for day 3.

GO ON TO THE NEXT PAGE.

R

To prepare for fieldwork, exactly four different researchers—a geologist, a historian, a linguist, and a paleontologist—will learn at least one and at most three of four languages—Rundi, Swahili, Tigrinya, and Yoruba. They must learn the languages according to the following specifications:

Exactly one researcher learns Rundi.
Exactly two researchers learn Swahili.
Exactly two researchers learn Tigrinya.
Exactly three researchers learn Yoruba.
Any language learned by the linguist or paleontologist is not learned by the geologist.
Any language learned by the geologist is learned by the historian.

6. Which one of the following could be true?

(A) The linguist learns three languages—Rundi, Swahili, and Tigrinya.

(B) The linguist learns three languages—Swahili, Tigrinya, and Yoruba.

(C) The historian learns three languages—Rundi Swahili, and Tigrinya.

(D) The historian learns three languages—Swahili, Tigrinya, and Yoruba.

(E) The paleontologist learns three languages—Rundi, Swahili, and Tigrinya.

GO ON TO THE NEXT PAGE.

7. If the linguist learns three of the languages, then which one of the following must be true?

   (A)   The linguist learns Tigrinya.
   (B)   The linguist learns Rundi.
   (C)   The linguist learns Swahili.
   (D)   The paleontologist learns Rundi.
   (E)   The paleontologist learns Swahili.

8. Each of the following could be true of the researcher who learns Rundi EXCEPT:

   (A)   The researcher also learns Tigrinya but not Swahili.
   (B)   The researcher learns neither Tigrinya nor Swahili.
   (C)   The researcher also learns Tigrinya but not Yoruba.
   (D)   The researcher also learns both Tigrinya and Yoruba.
   (E)   The researcher also learns Yoruba but not Tigrinya.

9. Each of the following could be a complete and accurate list of the researchers who learn both Swahili and Yoruba EXCEPT:

   (A)   the historian
   (B)   the paleontologist
   (C)   the historian, the linguist
   (D)   the historian, the paleontologist
   (E)   the linguist, the paleontologist

10. If the geologist learns exactly two of the languages, then which one of the following could be true?

   (A)   The paleontologist learns Rundi.
   (B)   The paleontologist learns Swahili.
   (C)   The historian learns Rundi.
   (D)   The paleontologist learns exactly three of the languages.
   (E)   The historian learns exactly two of the languages.

11. Which one of the following must be true?

   (A)   Fewer of the languages are learned by the historian than are learned by the paleontologist.
   (B)   Fewer of the languages are learned by the geologist than are learned by the historian.
   (C)   Fewer of the languages are learned by the geologist than are learned by the linguist.
   (D)   Fewer of the languages are learned by the paleontologist than are learned by the linguist.
   (E)   Fewer of the languages are learned by the paleontologist than are learned by the historian.

12. If exactly two of the languages are learned by the historian, then which one of the following must be true?

   (A)   The paleontologist does not learn Rundi.
   (B)   The geologist does not learn Swahili.
   (C)   The linguist does not learn Rundi.
   (D)   The historian does not learn Rundi.
   (E)   The paleontologist does not learn Swahili.

GO ON TO THE NEXT PAGE.

R

Exactly six trade representatives negotiate a treaty:
Klosnik, Londi, Manley, Neri, Osata, Poirier. There are
exactly six chairs evenly spaced around a circular table.
The chairs are numbered 1 through 6, with successively
numbered chairs next to each other and chair number 1
next to chair number 6. Each chair is occupied by exactly
one of the representatives. The following conditions apply:

Poirier sits immediately next to Neri.

Londi sits immediately next to Manley, Neri, or both.

Klosnik does not sit immediately next to Manley.

If Osata sits immediately next to Poirier, Osata does
  not sit immediately next to Manley.

1. Which one of the following seating arrangements of
    the six representatives in chairs 1 through 6 would
    NOT violate the stated conditions?

(A)   Klosnik, Poirier, Neri, Manley, Osata, Londi
(B)   Klosnik, Londi, Manley, Poirier, Neri, Osata
(C)   Klosnik, Londi, Manley, Osata, Poirier, Neri
(D)   Klosnik, Osata, Poirier, Neri, Londi, Manley
(E)   Klosnik, Neri, Londi, Osata, Manley, Poirier

GO ON TO THE NEXT PAGE.

R

2. If Londi sits immediately next to Poirier, which one of the following is a pair of representatives who must sit immediately next to each other?

(A) Klosnik and Osata
(B) Londi and Neri
(C) Londi and Osata
(D) Manley and Neri
(E) Manley and Poirier

3. If Klosnik sits directly between Londi and Poirier, then Manley must sit directly between

(A) Londi and Neri
(B) Londi and Osata
(C) Neri and Osata
(D) Neri and Poirier
(E) Osata and Poirier

4. If Neri sits immediately next to Manley, then Klosnik can sit directly between

(A) Londi and Manley
(B) Londi and Poirier
(C) Neri and Osata
(D) Neri and Poirier
(E) Poirier and Osata

5. If Londi sits immediately next to Manley, then which one of the following is a complete and accurate list of representatives any one of whom could also sit immediately next to Londi?

(A) Klosnik
(B) Klosnik, Neri
(C) Neri, Poirier
(D) Klosnik, Osata, Poirier
(E) Klosnik, Neri, Osata, Poirier

6. If Londi sits immediately next to Neri, which one of the following statements must be false?

(A) Klosnik sits immediately next to Osata.
(B) Londi sits immediately next to Manley.
(C) Osata sits immediately next to Poirier.
(D) Neri sits directly between Londi and Poirier.
(E) Osata sits directly between Klosnik and Manley.

7. If Klosnik sits immediately next to Osata, then Londi CANNOT sit directly between

(A) Klosnik and Manley
(B) Klosnik and Neri
(C) Manley and Neri
(D) Manley and Poirier
(E) Neri and Osata

GO ON TO THE NEXT PAGE.

R

Five candidates for mayor—Q, R, S, T, and U—will each speak exactly once at each of three town meetings—meetings 1, 2, and 3. At each meeting, each candidate will speak in one of five consecutive time slots. No two candidates will speak in the same time slot as each other at any meeting. The order in which the candidates will speak will meet the following conditions:

Each candidate must speak either first or second at at least one of the meetings.

Any candidate who speaks fifth at any of the meetings must speak first at at least one of the other meetings.

No candidate can speak fourth at more than one of the meetings.

19. Which one of the following could be the order, from first to fifth, in which the candidates speak at the meetings?

(A)   meeting 1: Q, U, R, T, S
        meeting 2: S, T, R, U, Q
        meeting 3: T, U, Q, R, S
(B)   meeting 1: R, S, Q, T, U
        meeting 2: U, T, S, R, Q
        meeting 3: Q, R, T, U, S
(C)   meeting 1: S, Q, U, T, R
        meeting 2: U, T, Q, R, S
        meeting 3: R, Q, S, T, U
(D)   meeting 1: T, R, S, U, Q
        meeting 2: Q, R, S, T, U
        meeting 3: U, S, R, Q, T
(E)   meeting 1: U, T, R, S, Q
        meeting 2: Q, R, S, T, U
        meeting 3: S, T, U, Q, R

GO ON TO THE NEXT PAGE.

R

20. If R speaks second at meeting 2 and first at meeting 3, which one of the following is a complete and accurate list of those time slots any one of which could be the time slot in which R speaks at meeting 1?

    (A)   fourth, fifth
    (B)   first, second, fifth
    (C)   second, third, fifth
    (D)   third, fourth, fifth
    (E)   second, third, fourth, fifth

21. If the order in which the candidates speak at meeting 1 is R, U, S, T, Q, and the order in which they speak at meeting 2 is Q, R, U, S, T, which one of the following could be true of meeting 3?

    (A)   Q speaks first.
    (B)   R speaks third.
    (C)   S speaks first.
    (D)   T speaks second.
    (E)   U speaks fifth.

22. If R speaks first at meetings 1 and 2, and S speaks first at meeting 3, which one of the following must be true?

    (A)   R speaks second at meeting 3.
    (B)   R speaks fourth at meeting 3.
    (C)   S speaks second at at least one of the meetings.
    (D)   S speaks fifth at exactly one of the meetings.
    (E)   S speaks fifth at exactly two of the meetings.

23. It could be true that at all three meetings T speaks

    (A)   first
    (B)   second
    (C)   in some time slot after the time slot in which R speaks
    (D)   in some time slot after the time slots in which S and U speak
    (E)   in some time slot before the time slots in which R and U speak

24. If S, T, and U speak second at meetings 1, 2, and 3, respectively, which one of the following must be true?

    (A)   The fifth speaker at at least one of the meetings is either Q or R.
    (B)   Either Q speaks first at exactly two of the meetings or else R does so.
    (C)   Neither S nor T speaks fifth at any of the meetings.
    (D)   Q speaks third at one of the meetings, and R speaks third at another of the meetings.
    (E)   Q speaks fourth at one of the meetings, and R speaks fourth at another of the meetings.

GO ON TO THE NEXT PAGE.

R

Logic Games ReChallenge
Set #1 Answer Key

Game #1: June 1996 Questions 1-7   *1. B 2. E 3. C 4. E 5. D 6. D 7. C*

Explanations begin on page 178

Game #2: June 1999 Questions 6-12   *6. D 7. B 8. C 9. B 10. A 11. B 12. D*

Explanations begin on page 374

Game #3: June 1991 Questions 1-7   *1. B 2. A 3. B 4. E 5. E 6. C 7. E*

Explanations begin on page 512

Game #4: October 1997 Questions 19-24   *19. D 20. D 21. B 22. E 23. C 24. A*

Explanations begin on page 486

R

Logic Games ReChallenge
Set #2

R

Each of seven television programs—H, J, L, P, Q, S, V—is assigned a different rank: from first through seventh (from most popular to least popular). The ranking is consistent with the following conditions:

J and L are each less popular than H.
J is more popular than Q.
S and V are each less popular than L.
P and S are each less popular than Q.
S is not seventh.

1. Which one of the following could be the order of the programs, from most popular to least popular?

(A)   J, H, L, Q, V, S, P
(B)   H, L, Q, J, S, P, V
(C)   H, J, Q, L, S, V, P
(D)   H, J, V, L, Q, S, P
(E)   H, L, V, J, Q, P, S

GO ON TO THE NEXT PAGE.

R

2. If J is more popular than L, and S is more popular than P, then which one of the following must be true of the ranking?

   (A)   J is second.
   (B)   J is third.
   (C)   L is third.
   (D)   Q is third.
   (E)   P is seventh.

3. Which one of the following programs CANNOT be ranked third?

   (A)   L
   (B)   J
   (C)   Q
   (D)   V
   (E)   P

4. If V is more popular than Q and J is less popular than L, then which one of the following could be true of the ranking?

   (A)   P is more popular than S.
   (B)   S is more popular than V.
   (C)   P is more popular than L.
   (D)   J is more popular than V.
   (E)   Q is more popular than V.

5. If Q is more popular than L, then each of the following must be true of the ranking EXCEPT:

   (A)   H is first.
   (B)   L is fourth.
   (C)   V is not fourth.
   (D)   J is not third.
   (E)   Q is third.

GO ON TO THE NEXT PAGE.

R

An apartment building has five floors. Each floor has either one or two apartments. There are exactly eight apartments in the building. The residents of the building are J, K, L, M, N, O, P, and Q, who each live in a different apartment.

J lives on a floor with two apartments.

K lives on the floor directly above P.

The second floor is made up of only one apartment.

M and N live on the same floor.

O does not live on the same floor as Q.

L lives in the only apartment on her floor.

Q does not live on the first or second floor.

6. Which one of the following must be true?

(A) Q lives on the third floor.
(B) Q lives on the fifth floor.
(C) L does not live on the fourth floor.
(D) N does not live on the second floor.
(E) J lives on the first floor.

GO ON TO THE NEXT PAGE.

7. Which one of the following CANNOT be true?

   (A)   K lives on the second floor.
   (B)   M lives on the first floor.
   (C)   N lives on the fourth floor.
   (D)   O lives on the third floor.
   (E)   P lives on the fifth floor.

8. If J lives on the fourth floor and K lives on the fifth floor, which one of the following can be true?

   (A)   O lives on the first floor.
   (B)   Q lives on the fourth floor.
   (C)   N lives on the fifth floor.
   (D)   L lives on the fourth floor.
   (E)   P lives on the third floor.

9. If O lives on the second floor, which one of the following CANNOT be true?

   (A)   K lives on the fourth floor.
   (B)   K lives on the fifth floor.
   (C)   L lives on the first floor.
   (D)   L lives on the third floor.
   (E)   L lives on the fourth floor.

10. If M lives on the fourth floor, which one of the following must be false?

   (A)   O lives on the fifth floor.
   (B)   J lives on the first floor.
   (C)   L lives on the second floor.
   (D)   Q lives on the third floor.
   (E)   P lives on the first floor.

11. Which one of the following must be true?

   (A)   If J lives on the fourth floor, then Q does not live on the fifth floor.
   (B)   If O lives on the second floor, then L does not live on the fourth floor.
   (C)   If N lives on the fourth floor, then K does not live on the second floor.
   (D)   If K lives on the third floor, then O does not live on the fifth floor.
   (E)   If P lives on the fourth floor, then M does not live on the third floor.

12. If O lives on the fourth floor and P lives on the second floor, which one of the following must be true?

   (A)   L lives on the first floor.
   (B)   M lives on the third floor.
   (C)   Q lives on the third floor.
   (D)   N lives on the fifth floor.
   (E)   Q lives on the fifth floor.

GO ON TO THE NEXT PAGE.

R

Bird-watchers explore a forest to see which of the following six kinds of birds—grosbeak, harrier, jay, martin, shrike, wren—it contains. The findings are consistent with the following conditions:

> If harriers are in the forest, then grosbeaks are not.
> If jays, martins, or both are in the forest, then so are harriers.
> If wrens are in the forest, then so are grosbeaks.
> If jays are not in the forest, then shrikes are.

6. Which one of the following could be a complete and accurate list of the birds NOT in the forest?

(A) jays, shrikes
(B) harriers, grosbeaks
(C) grosbeaks, jays, martins
(D) grosbeaks, martins, shrikes, wrens
(E) martins, shrikes

GO ON TO THE NEXT PAGE.

7. If both martins and harriers are in the forest, then which one of the following must be true?

(A) Shrikes are the only other birds in the forest.
(B) Jays are the only other birds in the forest.
(C) The forest contains neither jays nor shrikes.
(D) There are at least two other kinds of birds in the forest.
(E) There are at most two other kinds of birds in the forest.

8. If jays are not in the forest, then which one of the following must be false?

(A) Martins are in the forest.
(B) Harriers are in the forest.
(C) Neither martins nor harriers are in the forest.
(D) Neither martins nor shrikes are in the forest.
(E) Harriers and shrikes are the only birds in the forest.

9. Which one of the following is the maximum number of the six kinds of birds the forest could contain?

(A) two
(B) three
(C) four
(D) five
(E) six

10. Which one of the following pairs of birds CANNOT be among those birds contained in the forest?

(A) jays, wrens
(B) jays, shrikes
(C) shrikes, wrens
(D) jays, martins
(E) shrikes, martins

11. If grosbeaks are in the forest, then which one of the following must be true?

(A) Shrikes are in the forest.
(B) Wrens are in the forest.
(C) The forest contains both wrens and shrikes.
(D) At most two kinds of birds are in the forest.
(E) At least three kinds of birds are in the forest.

12. Suppose the condition is added that if shrikes are in the forest, then harriers are not. If all other conditions remain in effect, then which one of the following could be true?

(A) The forest contains both jays and shrikes.
(B) The forest contains both wrens and shrikes.
(C) The forest contains both martins and shrikes.
(D) Jays are not in the forest, whereas martins are.
(E) Only two of the six kinds of birds are not in the forest.

GO ON TO THE NEXT PAGE.

R

A reporter is trying to uncover the workings of a secret committee. The committee has six members—French, Ghauri, Hsia, Irving, Magnus, and Pinsky—each of whom serves on at least one subcommittee. There are three subcommittees, each having three members, about which the following is known:

> One of the committee members serves on all three subcommittees.
> French does not serve on any subcommittee with Ghauri.
> Hsia does not serve on any subcommittee with Irving.

17. If French does not serve on any subcommittee with Magnus, which one of the following must be true?

(A) French serves on a subcommittee with Hsia.
(B) French serves on a subcommittee with Irving.
(C) Irving serves on a subcommittee with Pinsky.
(D) Magnus serves on a subcommittee with Ghauri.
(E) Magnus serves on a subcommittee with Irving.

GO ON TO THE NEXT PAGE.

18. If Pinsky serves on every subcommittee on which French serves and every subcommittee on which Ghauri serves, then which one of the following could be true?

    (A) Magnus serves on every subcommittee on which French serves and every subcommittee on which Ghauri serves.
    (B) Magnus serves on every subcommittee on which Hsia serves and every subcommittee on which Irving serves.
    (C) Hsia serves on every subcommittee on which French serves and every subcommittee on which Ghauri serves.
    (D) French serves on every subcommittee on which Pinsky serves.
    (E) Hsia serves on every subcommittee on which Pinsky serves.

19. If Irving serves on every subcommittee on which Magnus serves, which one of the following could be true?

    (A) Magnus serves on all of the subcommittees.
    (B) Irving serves on more than one subcommittee.
    (C) Irving serves on every subcommittee on which Pinsky serves.
    (D) French serves on a subcommittee with Magnus.
    (E) Ghauri serves on a subcommittee with Magnus.

20. Which one of the following could be true?

    (A) French serves on all three subcommittees.
    (B) Hsia serves on all three subcommittees.
    (C) Ghauri serves on every subcommittee on which Magnus serves and every subcommittee on which Pinsky serves.
    (D) Pinsky serves on every subcommittee on which Irving serves and every subcommittee on which Magnus serves.
    (E) Magnus serves on every subcommittee on which Pinsky serves, and Pinsky serves on every subcommittee on which Magnus serves.

21. Which one of the following must be true?

    (A) Ghauri serves on at least two subcommittees.
    (B) Irving serves on only one subcommittee.
    (C) French serves on a subcommittee with Hsia.
    (D) Ghauri serves on a subcommittee with Irving.
    (E) Magnus serves on a subcommittee with Pinsky.

22. Which one of the following must be true?

    (A) Every subcommittee has either French or Ghauri as a member.
    (B) Every subcommittee has either Hsia or Irving as a member.
    (C) No subcommittee consists of French, Magnus, and Pinsky.
    (D) Some committee member serves on exactly two subcommittees.
    (E) Either Magnus or Pinsky serves on only one subcommittee.

GO ON TO THE NEXT PAGE.

R

Logic Games ReChallenge
Set #2 Answer Key

Game #1: December 2000 Questions 1-5   *1. C 2. A 3. E 4. D 5. B*

Explanations begin on page 458

Game #2: October 1991 Questions 6-12   *6. D 7. E 8. A 9. E 10. C 11. B 12. C*

Explanations begin on page 210

Game #3: December 2000 Questions 6-12   *6. D 7. E 8. D 9. C 10. A 11. A 12. B*

Explanations begin on page 380

Game #4: June 2005 Questions 17-22   *17. C 18. C 19. B 20. D 21. E 22. D*

Explanations begin on page 564

R

Logic Games ReChallenge
Set #3

Eight physics students—four majors: Frank, Gwen, Henry, and Joan; and four nonmajors: Victor, Wanda, Xavier, and Yvette—are being assigned to four laboratory benches, numbered 1 through 4. Each student is assigned to exactly one bench, and exactly two students are assigned to each bench. Assignments of students to benches must conform to the following conditions:

Exactly one major is assigned to each bench.

Frank and Joan are assigned to consecutively numbered benches, with Frank assigned to the lower-numbered bench.

Frank is assigned to the same bench as Victor.

Gwen is not assigned to the same bench as Wanda.

1. Which one of the following could be the assignment of students to benches?

    (A) 1: Frank, Victor; 2: Joan, Gwen; 3: Henry, Wanda; 4: Xavier, Yvette

    (B) 1: Gwen, Yvette; 2: Frank, Xavier; 3: Joan, Wanda; 4: Henry, Victor

    (C) 1: Henry, Wanda; 2: Gwen, Xavier; 3: Frank, Victor; 4: Joan, Yvette

    (D) 1: Henry, Xavier; 2: Joan, Wanda; 3: Frank, Victor; 4: Gwen, Yvette

    (E) 1: Henry, Yvette; 2: Gwen, Wanda; 3: Frank, Victor; 4: Joan, Xavier

GO ON TO THE NEXT PAGE.

2. If Victor is assigned to bench 2 and Wanda is assigned to bench 4, which one of the following must be true?

   (A)   Frank is assigned to bench 1.
   (B)   Gwen is assigned to bench 1.
   (C)   Henry is assigned to bench 3.
   (D)   Xavier is assigned to bench 1.
   (E)   Yvette is assigned to bench 3.

3. If Gwen and Henry are not assigned to consecutively numbered benches, which one of the following must be true?

   (A)   Victor is assigned to bench 2.
   (B)   Victor is assigned to bench 3.
   (C)   Wanda is assigned to bench 1.
   (D)   Wanda is assigned to bench 3.
   (E)   Wanda is assigned to bench 4.

4. If Henry and Yvette are both assigned to bench 1, which one of the following could be true?

   (A)   Gwen is assigned to bench 3.
   (B)   Joan is assigned to bench 2.
   (C)   Wanda is assigned to bench 2.
   (D)   Wanda is assigned to bench 3.
   (E)   Xavier is assigned to bench 3.

5. If Gwen is assigned to bench 4 and Xavier is assigned to bench 3, then any one of the following could be true EXCEPT:

   (A)   Gwen is assigned to the same bench as Yvette.
   (B)   Henry is assigned to the same bench as Wanda.
   (C)   Henry is assigned to the same bench as Xavier.
   (D)   Joan is assigned to the same bench as Xavier.
   (E)   Joan is assigned to the same bench as Yvette.

6. If Wanda is assigned to a lower-numbered bench than is Joan, then Henry must be assigned to a

   (A)   lower-numbered bench than is Frank
   (B)   lower-numbered bench than is Gwen
   (C)   lower-numbered bench than is Xavier
   (D)   higher-numbered bench than is Victor
   (E)   higher-numbered bench than is Yvette

7. Which one of the following could be the assignments for bench 2 and bench 4 ?

   (A)   2: Gwen, Xavier
         4: Henry, Yvette
   (B)   2: Henry, Yvette
         4: Joan, Xavier
   (C)   2: Joan, Victor
         4: Gwen, Xavier
   (D)   2: Joan, Wanda
         4: Gwen, Xavier
   (E)   2: Joan, Xavier
         4: Henry, Yvette

GO ON TO THE NEXT PAGE.

R

A clown will select a costume consisting of two pieces and no others: a jacket and overalls. One piece of the costume will be entirely one color, and the other piece will be plaid. Selection is subject to the following restrictions:

> If the jacket is plaid, then there must be exactly three colors in it.
> If the overalls are plaid, then there must be exactly two colors in them.
> The jacket and overalls must have exactly one color in common.
> Green, red, and violet are the only colors that can be in the jacket.
> Red, violet, and yellow are the only colors that can be in the overalls.

1. Which one of the following could be a complete and accurate list of the colors in the costume?

	Jacket	Overalls
(A)	red	red
(B)	red	violet, yellow
(C)	violet	green, violet
(D)	violet	red, violet
(E)	violet	red, violet, yellow

GO ON TO THE NEXT PAGE.

2. If there are exactly two colors in the costume, then which one of the following must be false?

   (A)   At least part of the jacket is green.
   (B)   At least part of the jacket is red.
   (C)   The overalls are red and violet.
   (D)   The overalls are red and yellow.
   (E)   The overalls are violet and yellow.

3. If at least part of the jacket is green, then which one of the following could be true?

   (A)   The overalls are plaid.
   (B)   No part of the jacket is red.
   (C)   No part of the jacket is violet.
   (D)   At least part of the overalls are yellow.
   (E)   At least part of the overalls are violet.

4. Which one of the following must be false?

   (A)   Both green and red are colors used in the costume.
   (B)   Both green and violet are colors used in the costume.
   (C)   Both green and yellow are colors used in the costume.
   (D)   Both red and violet are colors used in the costume.
   (E)   Both violet and yellow are colors used in the costume.

5. If there are exactly three colors in the costume, the overalls must be

   (A)   entirely red or else red and violet plaid
   (B)   entirely yellow or else violet and yellow plaid
   (C)   entirely violet or else red and violet plaid
   (D)   entirely red or else entirely yellow
   (E)   entirely red or else entirely violet

GO ON TO THE NEXT PAGE.

An album contains photographs picturing seven friends: Raimundo, Selma, Ty, Umiko, Wendy, Yakira, Zack. The friends appear either alone or in groups with one another, in accordance with the following:

Wendy appears in every photograph that Selma appears in.

Selma appears in every photograph that Umiko appears in.

Raimundo appears in every photograph that Yakira does not appear in.

Neither Ty nor Raimundo appears in any photograph that Wendy appears in.

13. Which one of the following could be a complete and accurate list of the friends who appear together in a photograph?

(A) Raimundo, Selma, Ty, Wendy
(B) Raimundo, Ty, Yakira, Zack
(C) Raimundo, Wendy, Yakira, Zack
(D) Selma, Ty, Umiko, Yakira
(E) Selma, Ty, Umiko, Zack

GO ON TO THE NEXT PAGE.

R

14. If Ty and Zack appear together in a photograph, then which one of the following must be true?

   (A)   Selma also appears in the photograph.
   (B)   Yakira also appears in the photograph.
   (C)   Wendy also appears in the photograph.
   (D)   Raimundo does not appear in the photograph.
   (E)   Umiko does not appear in the photograph.

15. What is the maximum number of friends who could appear in a photograph that Yakira does not appear in?

   (A)   six
   (B)   five
   (C)   four
   (D)   three
   (E)   two

16. If Umiko and Zack appear together in a photograph, then exactly how many of the other friends must also appear in that photograph?

   (A)   four
   (B)   three
   (C)   two
   (D)   one
   (E)   zero

17. If exactly three friends appear together in a photograph, then each of the following could be true EXCEPT:

   (A)   Selma and Zack both appear in the photograph.
   (B)   Ty and Yakira both appear in the photograph.
   (C)   Wendy and Selma both appear in the photograph.
   (D)   Yakira and Zack both appear in the photograph.
   (E)   Zack and Raimundo both appear in the photograph.

GO ON TO THE NEXT PAGE.

R

A soloist will play six different guitar concertos, exactly one each Sunday for six consecutive weeks. Two concertos will be selected from among three concertos by Giuliani—H, J, and K; two from among four concertos by Rodrigo—M, N, O, and P; and two from among three concertos by Vivaldi—X, Y, and Z. The following conditions apply without exception:

If N is selected, then J is also selected.

If M is selected, then neither J nor O can be selected.

If X is selected, then neither Z nor P can be selected.

If both J and O are selected, then J is played at some time before O.

X cannot be played on the fifth Sunday unless one of Rodrigo's concertos is played on the first Sunday.

19. Which one of the following is an acceptable selection of concertos that the soloist could play on the first through the sixth Sunday?

	1	2	3	4	5	6
(A)	H	Z	M	N	Y	K
(B)	K	J	Y	O	Z	N
(C)	K	Y	P	J	Z	M
(D)	P	Y	J	H	X	O
(E)	X	N	K	O	J	Z

GO ON TO THE NEXT PAGE.

R

20. If the six concertos to be played are J, K, N, O, Y, and Z and if N is to be played on the first Sunday, then which one of the following concertos CANNOT be played on the second Sunday?

(A) J
(B) K
(C) O
(D) Y
(E) Z

21. If J, O, and Y are the first three concertos to be played, not necessarily in the order given, which one of the following is a concerto that CANNOT be played on the fifth Sunday?

(A) H
(B) K
(C) N
(D) P
(E) X

22. If O is selected for the first Sunday, which one of the following is a concerto that must also be selected?

(A) J
(B) K
(C) M
(D) N
(E) X

23. Which one of the following is a concerto that must be selected?

(A) J
(B) K
(C) O
(D) Y
(E) Z

24. Which one of the following is a concerto that CANNOT be selected together with N?

(A) M
(B) O
(C) P
(D) X
(E) Z

GO ON TO THE NEXT PAGE.

R

Logic Games ReChallenge
Set #3 Answer Key

Game #1: September 1998 Questions 1-7   *1. C 2. B 3. A 4. D 5. E 6. A 7. D*

Explanations begin on page 242

Game #2: December 2006 Questions 1-5   *1. D 2. A 3. E 4. C 5. E*

Explanations begin on page 596

Game #3: December 2004 Questions 13-17   *13. B 14. E 15. D 16. B 17. A*

Explanations begin on page 362

Game #4: February 1994 Questions 19-24   *19. B 20. C 21. E 22. B 23. D 24. A*

Explanations begin on page 422

R

Logic Games ReChallenge
Set #4

R

On a Tuesday, an accountant has exactly seven bills—numbered 1 through 7—to pay by Thursday of the same week. The accountant will pay each bill only once according to the following rules:

Either three or four of the seven bills must be paid on Wednesday, the rest on Thursday.

Bill 1 cannot be paid on the same day as bill 5.

Bill 2 must be paid on Thursday.

Bill 4 must be paid on the same day as bill 7.

If bill 6 is paid on Wednesday, bill 7 must be paid on Thursday.

1. If exactly four bills are paid on Wednesday, then those four bills could be

(A)   1, 3, 4, and 6
(B)   1, 3, 5, and 6
(C)   2, 4, 5, and 7
(D)   3, 4, 5, and 7
(E)   3, 4, 6, and 7

GO ON TO THE NEXT PAGE.

2. Which one of the following is a complete and accurate list of the bills any one of which could be among the bills paid on Wednesday?

(A) 3, 5, and 6
(B) 1, 3, 4, 6, and 7
(C) 1, 3, 4, 5, 6, and 7
(D) 2, 3, 4, 5, 6, and 7
(E) 1, 2, 3, 4, 5, 6, and 7

3. If bill 2 and bill 6 are paid on different days from each other, which one of the following must be true?

(A) Exactly three bills are paid on Wednesday.
(B) Exactly three bills are paid on Thursday.
(C) Bill 1 is paid on the same day as bill 4.
(D) Bill 2 is paid on the same day as bill 3.
(E) Bill 5 is paid on the same day as bill 7.

4. If bill 6 is paid on Wednesday, which one of the following bills must also be paid on Wednesday?

(A) 1
(B) 3
(C) 4
(D) 5
(E) 7

5. If bill 4 is paid on Thursday, which one of the following is a pair of bills that could also be paid on Thursday?

(A) 1 and 5
(B) 1 and 7
(C) 3 and 5
(D) 3 and 6
(E) 6 and 7

6. Which one of the following statements must be true?

(A) If bill 2 is paid on Thursday, bill 3 is paid on Wednesday.
(B) If bill 4 is paid on Thursday, bill 1 is paid on Wednesday.
(C) If bill 4 is paid on Thursday, bill 3 is paid on Wednesday.
(D) If bill 6 is paid on Thursday, bill 3 is also paid on Thursday.
(E) If bill 6 is paid on Thursday, bill 4 is also paid on Thursday.

GO ON TO THE NEXT PAGE.

R

A messenger will deliver exactly seven packages—L, M, N, O, P, S, and T—one at a time, not necessarily in that order. The seven deliveries must be made according to the following conditions:

> P is delivered either first or seventh.
>
> The messenger delivers N at some time after delivering L.
>
> The messenger delivers T at some time after delivering M.
>
> The messenger delivers exactly one package between delivering L and delivering O, whether or not L is delivered before O.
>
> The messenger delivers exactly one package between delivering M and delivering P, whether or not M is delivered before P.

8. Which one of the following is an order in which the messenger could make the deliveries, from first to seventh?

(A)   L, N, S, O, M, T, P
(B)   M, T, P, S, L, N, O
(C)   O, S, L, N, M, T, P
(D)   P, N, M, S, O, T, L
(E)   P, T, M, S, L, N, O

GO ON TO THE NEXT PAGE.

R

9. Which one of the following could be true?

   (A)   N is delivered first.
   (B)   T is delivered first.
   (C)   T is delivered second.
   (D)   M is delivered fourth.
   (E)   S is delivered seventh.

10. If N is delivered fourth, which one of the following could be true?

   (A)   L is delivered first.
   (B)   L is delivered second.
   (C)   M is delivered third.
   (D)   O is delivered fifth.
   (E)   S is delivered first.

11. If T is delivered fourth, the seventh package delivered must be

   (A)   L
   (B)   N
   (C)   O
   (D)   P
   (E)   S

12. If the messenger delivers M at some time after delivering O, the fifth package delivered could be any one of the following EXCEPT:

   (A)   L
   (B)   M
   (C)   N
   (D)   S
   (E)   T

GO ON TO THE NEXT PAGE.

R

A tour group plans to visit exactly five archaeological sites. Each site was discovered by exactly one of the following archaeologists—Ferrara, Gallagher, Oliphant—and each dates from the eighth, ninth, or tenth century (A.D.). The tour must satisfy the following conditions:

The site visited second dates from the ninth century.

Neither the site visited fourth nor the site visited fifth was discovered by Oliphant.

Exactly one of the sites was discovered by Gallagher, and it dates from the tenth century.

If a site dates from the eighth century, it was discovered by Oliphant.

The site visited third dates from a more recent century than does either the site visited first or that visited fourth.

13. Which one of the following could be an accurate list of the discoverers of the five sites, listed in the order in which the sites are visited?

(A) Oliphant, Oliphant, Gallagher, Oliphant, Ferrara

(B) Gallagher, Oliphant, Ferrara, Ferrara, Ferrara

(C) Oliphant, Gallagher, Oliphant, Ferrara, Ferrara

(D) Oliphant, Oliphant, Gallagher, Ferrara, Gallagher

(E) Ferrara, Oliphant, Gallagher, Ferrara, Ferrara

GO ON TO THE NEXT PAGE.

R

14. If exactly one of the five sites the tour group visits dates from the tenth century, then which one of the following CANNOT be a site that was discovered by Ferrara?

    (A)   the site visited first
    (B)   the site visited second
    (C)   the site visited third
    (D)   the site visited fourth
    (E)   the site visited fifth

15. Which one of the following could be a site that dates from the eighth century?

    (A)   the site visited first
    (B)   the site visited second
    (C)   the site visited third
    (D)   the site visited fourth
    (E)   the site visited fifth

16. Which one of the following is a complete and accurate list of the sites each of which CANNOT be the site discovered by Gallagher?

    (A)   third, fourth, fifth
    (B)   second, third, fourth
    (C)   first, fourth, fifth
    (D)   first, second, fifth
    (E)   first, second, fourth

17. The tour group could visit at most how many sites that were discovered by Ferrara?

    (A)   one
    (B)   two
    (C)   three
    (D)   four
    (E)   five

GO ON TO THE NEXT PAGE.

R

The country of Zendu contains exactly four areas for radar detection: R, S, T, and U. Each detection area is circular and falls completely within Zendu. Part of R intersects T; part of S also intersects T; R does not intersect S. Area U is completely within R and also completely within T. At noon exactly four planes—J, K, L, M—are over Zendu, in a manner consistent with the following statements:

Each plane is in at least one of the four areas.

J is in area S.

K is not in any detection area that J is in.

L is not in any detection area that M is in.

M is in exactly one of the areas.

7. Which one of the following could be a complete listing of the planes located in the four areas at noon, with each plane listed in every area in which it is located?

(A) R: J, L;   S: J, M;   T: L;   U: L
(B) R: J, L;   S: K;   T: M;   U: none
(C) R: K;   S: J;   T: L;   U: M
(D) R: K, M;   S: J, L;   T: J;   U: none
(E) R: M;   S: J, K;   T: J, L;   U: none

GO ON TO THE NEXT PAGE.

8. If at noon K is within exactly two of the four areas, then which one of the following CANNOT be true at that time?

    (A)   J is within area T.
    (B)   K is within area R.
    (C)   K is within area T.
    (D)   L is within area R.
    (E)   L is within area T.

9. Which one of the following is a complete and accurate list of those planes any one of which could be within area T at noon?

    (A)   M
    (B)   J, L
    (C)   J, L, M
    (D)   K, L, M
    (E)   J, K, L, M

10. Which one of the following statements CANNOT be true at noon about the planes?

    (A)   K is within area T.
    (B)   K is within area U.
    (C)   L is within area R.
    (D)   M is within area R.
    (E)   M is within area U.

11. It CANNOT be true that at noon there is at least one plane that is within both area

    (A)   R and area T
    (B)   R and area U
    (C)   S and area T
    (D)   S and area U
    (E)   T and area U

12. If at noon M is within area T, then which one of the following statements CANNOT be true at that time?

    (A)   J is within area T.
    (B)   L is within area R.
    (C)   L is within area S.
    (D)   K is within exactly two areas.
    (E)   L is within exactly two areas.

13. If at noon plane L is within exactly three of the areas, which one of the following could be true at that time?

    (A)   J is within exactly two of the areas.
    (B)   J is within exactly three of the areas.
    (C)   K is within area S.
    (D)   M is within area R.
    (E)   M is within area T.

GO ON TO THE NEXT PAGE.

R

Logic Games ReChallenge
Set #4 Answer Key

Game #1: October 1999 Questions 1-6   *1.* D *2.* C *3.* A *4.* B *5.* B *6.* C

Explanations begin on page 606

Game #2: September 1998 Questions 8-12   *8.* C *9.* E *10.* A *11.* C *12.* A

Explanations begin on page 186

Game #3: October 2004 Questions 13-17   *13.* E *14.* C *15.* A *16.* E *17.* D

Explanations begin on page 250

Game #4: June 1995 Questions 7-13   *7.* D *8.* A *9.* E *10.* E *11.* D *12.* E *13.* A

Explanations begin on page 524

R

Logic Games ReChallenge
Set #5

R

At a benefit dinner, a community theater's seven sponsors—K, L, M, P, Q, V, and Z—will be seated at three tables—1, 2, and 3. Of the sponsors, only K, L, and M will receive honors, and only M, P, and Q will give a speech. The sponsors' seating assignments must conform to the following conditions:

> Each table has at least two sponsors seated at it, and each sponsor is seated at exactly one table.
>
> Any sponsor receiving honors is seated at table 1 or table 2.
>
> L is seated at the same table as V.

1. Which one of the following is an acceptable assignment of sponsors to tables?

    (A)   Table 1: K, P; Table 2: M, Q; Table 3: L, V, Z
    (B)   Table 1: K, Q, Z; Table 2: L, V; Table 3: M, P
    (C)   Table 1: L, P; Table 2: K, M; Table 3: Q, V, Z
    (D)   Table 1: L, Q, V; Table 2: K, M; Table 3: P, Z
    (E)   Table 1: L, V, Z; Table 2: K, M, P; Table 3: Q

GO ON TO THE NEXT PAGE.

R

2. Which one of the following is a list of all and only those sponsors any one of whom could be among the sponsors assigned to table 3 ?

    (A) P, Q
    (B) Q, Z
    (C) P, Q, Z
    (D) Q, V, Z
    (E) P, Q, V, Z

3. If K is assigned to a different table than M, which one of the following must be true of the seating assignment?

    (A) K is seated at the same table as L.
    (B) L is seated at the same table as Q.
    (C) M is seated at the same table as V.
    (D) Exactly two sponsors are seated at table 1.
    (E) Exactly two sponsors are seated at table 3.

4. If Q is assigned to table 1 along with two other sponsors, which one of the following could be true of the seating assignment?

    (A) K is seated at the same table as L.
    (B) K is seated at the same table as Q.
    (C) M is seated at the same table as V.
    (D) M is seated at the same table as Z.
    (E) P is seated at the same table as Q.

5. If the sponsors assigned to table 3 include exactly one of the sponsors who will give a speech, then the sponsors assigned to table 1 could include any of the following EXCEPT:

    (A) K
    (B) M
    (C) P
    (D) Q
    (E) Z

6. If three sponsors, exactly two of whom are receiving honors, are assigned to table 2, which one of the following could be the list of sponsors assigned to table 1 ?

    (A) K, M
    (B) K, Z
    (C) P, V
    (D) P, Z
    (E) Q, Z

7. Which one of the following conditions, if added to the existing conditions, results in a set of conditions to which no seating assignment for the sponsors can conform?

    (A) At most two sponsors are seated at table 1.
    (B) Any sponsor giving a speech is seated at table 1 or else table 2.
    (C) Any sponsor giving a speech is seated at table 2 or else table 3.
    (D) Exactly three of the sponsors are seated at table 1.
    (E) Any table at which both L and V are seated also has a third sponsor seated at it.

GO ON TO THE NEXT PAGE.

R

Six hotel suites—F, G, H, J, K, L—are ranked from most expensive (first) to least expensive (sixth). There are no ties. The ranking must be consistent with the following conditions:

H is more expensive than L.

If G is more expensive than H, then neither K nor L is more expensive than J.

If H is more expensive than G, then neither J nor L is more expensive than K.

F is more expensive than G, or else F is more expensive than H, but not both.

6. Which one of the following could be the ranking of the suites, from most expensive to least expensive?

(A)   G, F, H, L, J, K
(B)   H, K, F, J, G, L
(C)   J, H, F, K, G, L
(D)   J, K, G, H, L, F
(E)   K, J, L, H, F, G

GO ON TO THE NEXT PAGE.

R

7. If G is the second most expensive suite, then which one of the following could be true?

(A) H is more expensive than F.
(B) H is more expensive than G.
(C) K is more expensive than F.
(D) K is more expensive than J.
(E) L is more expensive than F.

8. Which one of the following CANNOT be the most expensive suite?

(A) F
(B) G
(C) H
(D) J
(E) K

9. If L is more expensive than F, then which one of the following could be true?

(A) F is more expensive than H.
(B) F is more expensive than K.
(C) G is more expensive than H.
(D) G is more expensive than J.
(E) G is more expensive than L.

10. If H is more expensive than J and less expensive than K, then which one of the following could be true?

(A) F is more expensive than H.
(B) G is more expensive than F.
(C) G is more expensive than H.
(D) J is more expensive than L.
(E) L is more expensive than K.

GO ON TO THE NEXT PAGE.

R

A locally known guitarist's demo CD contains exactly seven different songs—S, T, V, W, X, Y, and Z. Each song occupies exactly one of the CD's seven tracks. Some of the songs are rock classics; the others are new compositions. The following conditions must hold:

S occupies the fourth track of the CD.

Both W and Y precede S on the CD.

T precedes W on the CD.

A rock classic occupies the sixth track of the CD.

Each rock classic is immediately preceded on the CD by a new composition.

Z is a rock classic.

11. Which one of the following could be the order of the songs on the CD, from the first track through the seventh?

(A)   T, W, V, S, Y, X, Z

(B)   V, Y, T, S, W, Z, X

(C)   X, Y, W, S, T, Z, S

(D)   Y, T, W, S, X, Z, V

(E)   Z, T, X, W, V, Y, S

GO ON TO THE NEXT PAGE.

12. Which one of the following is a pair of songs that must occupy consecutive tracks on the CD?

    (A) S and V
    (B) S and W
    (C) T and Z
    (D) T and Y
    (E) V and Z

13. Which one of the following songs must be a new composition?

    (A) S
    (B) T
    (C) W
    (D) X
    (E) Y

14. If W precedes Y on the CD, then which one of the following must be true?

    (A) S is a rock classic.
    (B) V is a rock classic.
    (C) Y is a rock classic.
    (D) T is a new composition.
    (E) W is a new composition.

15. If there are exactly two songs on the CD that both precede V and are preceded by Y, then which one of the following could be true?

    (A) V occupies the seventh track of the CD.
    (B) X occupies the fifth track of the CD.
    (C) Y occupies the third track of the CD.
    (D) T is a rock classic.
    (E) W is a rock classic.

GO ON TO THE NEXT PAGE.

R

Morrisville's town council has exactly three members: Fu, Gianola, and Herstein. During one week, the council members vote on exactly three bills: a recreation bill, a school bill, and a tax bill. Each council member votes either for or against each bill. The following is known:

> Each member of the council votes for at least one of the bills and against at least one of the bills.
> Exactly two members of the council vote for the recreation bill.
> Exactly one member of the council votes for the school bill.
> Exactly one member of the council votes for the tax bill.
> Fu votes for the recreation bill and against the school bill.
> Gianola votes against the recreation bill.
> Herstein votes against the tax bill.

19. Which one of the following statements could be true?

   (A)   Fu and Gianola vote the same way on the tax bill.
   (B)   Gianola and Herstein vote the same way on the recreation bill.
   (C)   Gianola and Herstein vote the same way on the school bill.
   (D)   Fu votes for one of the bills and Gianola votes for two of the bills.
   (E)   Fu votes for two of the bills and Gianola votes for two of the bills.

GO ON TO THE NEXT PAGE.

20. If the set of members of the council who vote against the school bill is the same set of members who vote against the tax bill, then which one of the following statements must be true?

    (A) Fu votes for the tax bill.
    (B) Gianola votes for the recreation bill.
    (C) Gianola votes against the school bill.
    (D) Herstein votes against the recreation bill.
    (E) Herstein votes against the school bill.

21. If Gianola votes for the tax bill, then which one of the following statements could be true?

    (A) Fu and Gianola each vote for exactly one bill.
    (B) Gianola and Herstein each vote for exactly one bill.
    (C) Fu votes for exactly two bills.
    (D) Gianola votes for the recreation bill.
    (E) Herstein votes against the recreation bill.

22. If Gianola votes for exactly two of the three bills, which one of the following statements must be true?

    (A) Fu votes for the tax bill.
    (B) Gianola votes for the recreation bill.
    (C) Gianola votes for the school bill.
    (D) Gianola votes against the tax bill.
    (E) Herstein votes for the school bill.

23. If one of the members of the council votes against exactly the same bills as does another member of the council, then which one of the following statements must be true?

    (A) Fu votes for the tax bill.
    (B) Gianola votes for the recreation bill.
    (C) Gianola votes against the school bill.
    (D) Gianola votes for exactly one bill.
    (E) Herstein votes for exactly one bill.

GO ON TO THE NEXT PAGE.

Logic Games ReChallenge
Set #5 Answer Key

Game #1: June 1997 Questions 1-7   *1. D 2. C 3. E 4. B 5. E 6. B 7. B*

Explanations begin on page 354

Game #2: December 2006 Questions 6-10   *6. B 7. C 8. A 9. D 10. D*

Explanations begin on page 464

Game #3: December 2006 Questions 11-15   *11. D 12. E 13. D 14. D 15. E*

Explanations begin on page 258

Game #4: June 1999 Questions 19-23   *19. D 20. E 21. A 22. C 23. E*

Explanations begin on page 590

R

Logic Games ReChallenge
Set #6

R

Charlie makes a soup by adding exactly six kinds of foods—kale, lentils, mushrooms, onions, tomatoes, and zucchini—to a broth, one food at a time. No food is added more than once. The order in which Charlie adds the foods to the broth must be consistent with the following:

If the mushrooms are added third, then the lentils are added last.

If the zucchini is added first, then the lentils are added at some time before the onions.

Neither the tomatoes nor the kale is added fifth.

The mushrooms are added at some time before the tomatoes or the kale, but not before both.

1. Which one of the following could be the order in which the foods are added to the broth?

(A) kale, mushrooms, onions, lentils, tomatoes, zucchini

(B) kale, zucchini, mushrooms, tomatoes, lentils, onions

(C) lentils, mushrooms, zucchini, kale, onions, tomatoes

(D) zucchini, lentils, kale, mushrooms, onions, tomatoes

(E) zucchini, tomatoes, onions, mushrooms, lentils, kale

GO ON TO THE NEXT PAGE.

R

THE POWERSCORE LSAT LOGIC GAMES BIBLE

2. Which one of the following foods CANNOT be added first?

    (A)   kale
    (B)   lentils
    (C)   mushrooms
    (D)   onions
    (E)   tomatoes

3. If the lentils are added last, then which one of the following must be true?

    (A)   At least one of the foods is added at some time before the zucchini.
    (B)   At least two of the foods are added at some time before the kale.
    (C)   The mushrooms are added third.
    (D)   The zucchini is added third.
    (E)   The tomatoes are added fourth.

4. Which one of the following could be an accurate partial ordering of the foods added to the broth?

    (A)   lentils: second; mushrooms: third
    (B)   mushrooms: fourth; lentils: last
    (C)   onions: second; mushrooms: fifth
    (D)   zucchini: first; lentils: last
    (E)   zucchini: first; mushrooms: second

5. If the zucchini is added first, then which one of the following CANNOT be true?

    (A)   The kale is added second.
    (B)   The tomatoes are added second.
    (C)   The lentils are added third.
    (D)   The lentils are added fourth.
    (E)   The onions are added fourth.

GO ON TO THE NEXT PAGE.

R

Doctor Yamata works only on Mondays, Tuesdays, Wednesdays, Fridays, and Saturdays. She performs four different activities—lecturing, operating, treating patients, and conducting research. Each working day she performs exactly one activity in the morning and exactly one activity in the afternoon. During each week her work schedule must satisfy the following restrictions:

> She performs operations on exactly three mornings.
> If she operates on Monday, she does not operate on Tuesday.
> She lectures in the afternoon on exactly two consecutive calendar days.
> She treats patients on exactly one morning and exactly three afternoons.
> She conducts research on exactly one morning.
> On Saturday she neither lectures nor performs operations.

8. Which one of the following must be a day on which Doctor Yamata lectures?

(A) Monday
(B) Tuesday
(C) Wednesday
(D) Friday
(E) Saturday

GO ON TO THE NEXT PAGE.

R

9. On Wednesday Doctor Yamata could be scheduled to

   (A) conduct research in the morning and operate in the afternoon
   (B) lecture in the morning and treat patients in the afternoon
   (C) operate in the morning and lecture in the afternoon
   (D) operate in the morning and conduct research in the afternoon
   (E) treat patients in the morning and treat patients in the afternoon

10. Which one of the following statements must be true?

   (A) There is one day on which the doctor treats patients both in the morning and in the afternoon.
   (B) The doctor conducts research on one of the days on which she lectures.
   (C) The doctor conducts research on one of the days on which she treats patients.
   (D) The doctor lectures on one of the days on which she treats patients.
   (E) The doctor lectures on one of the days on which she operates.

11. If Doctor Yamata operates on Tuesday, then her schedule for treating patients could be

   (A) Monday morning, Monday afternoon, Friday morning, Friday afternoon
   (B) Monday morning, Friday afternoon, Saturday morning, Saturday afternoon
   (C) Monday afternoon, Wednesday morning, Wednesday afternoon, Saturday afternoon
   (D) Wednesday morning, Wednesday afternoon, Friday afternoon, Saturday afternoon
   (E) Wednesday afternoon, Friday afternoon, Saturday morning, Saturday afternoon

12. Which one of the following is a pair of days on both of which Doctor Yamata must treat patients?

   (A) Monday and Tuesday
   (B) Monday and Saturday
   (C) Tuesday and Friday
   (D) Tuesday and Saturday
   (E) Friday and Saturday

GO ON TO THE NEXT PAGE.

During a single week, from Monday through Friday, tours will be conducted of a company's three divisions—Operations, Production, Sales. Exactly five tours will be conducted that week, one each day. The schedule of tours for the week must conform to the following restrictions:

    Each division is toured at least once.

    The Operations division is not toured on Monday.

    The Production division is not toured on Wednesday.

    The Sales division is toured on two consecutive days, and on no other days.

    If the Operations division is toured on Thursday, then the Production division is toured on Friday.

14. Which one of the following CANNOT be true of the week's tour schedule?

(A)   The division that is toured on Monday is also toured on Tuesday.

(B)   The division that is toured on Monday is also toured on Friday.

(C)   The division that is toured on Tuesday is also toured on Thursday.

(D)   The division that is toured on Wednesday is also toured on Friday.

(E)   The division that is toured on Thursday is also toured on Friday.

GO ON TO THE NEXT PAGE.

R

15. If in addition to the Sales division one other division is toured on two consecutive days, then it could be true of the week's tour schedule both that the

   (A)   Production division is toured on Monday and that the Operations division is toured on Thursday
   (B)   Production division is toured on Tuesday and that the Sales division is toured on Wednesday
   (C)   Operations division is toured on Tuesday and that the Production division is toured on Friday
   (D)   Sales division is toured on Monday and that the Operations division is toured on Friday
   (E)   Sales division is toured on Wednesday and that the Production division is toured on Friday

16. If in the week's tour schedule the division that is toured on Tuesday is also toured on Friday, then for which one of the following days must a tour of the Production division be scheduled?

   (A)   Monday
   (B)   Tuesday
   (C)   Wednesday
   (D)   Thursday
   (E)   Friday

17. If in the week's tour schedule the division that is toured on Monday is not the division that is toured on Tuesday then which one of the following could be true of the week's schedule?

   (A)   A tour of the Sales division is scheduled for some day earlier in the week than is any tour of the Production division.
   (B)   A tour of the Operations division is scheduled for some day earlier in the week than is any tour of the Production division.
   (C)   The Sales division is toured on Monday.
   (D)   The Production division is toured on Tuesday.
   (E)   The Operations division is toured on Wednesday.

18. If in the week's tour schedule the division that is toured on Tuesday is also toured on Wednesday, then which one of the following must be true of the week's tour schedule?

   (A)   The Production division is toured on Monday.
   (B)   The Operations division is toured on Tuesday.
   (C)   The Sales division is toured on Wednesday.
   (D)   The Sales division is toured on Thursday.
   (E)   The Production division is toured on Friday.

GO ON TO THE NEXT PAGE.

R

A university library budget committee must reduce exactly five of eight areas of expenditure—G, L, M, N, P, R, S, and W—in accordance with the following conditions:

If both G and S are reduced, W is also reduced.

If N is reduced, neither R nor S is reduced.

If P is reduced, L is not reduced.

Of the three areas L, M, and R, exactly two are reduced.

6. Which one of the following could be a complete and accurate list of the areas of expenditure reduced by the committee?

(A)   G, L, M, N, W
(B)   G, L, M, P, W
(C)   G, M, N, R, W
(D)   G, M, P, R, S
(E)   L, M, R, S, W

GO ON TO THE NEXT PAGE.

7. If W is reduced, which one of the following could be a complete and accurate list of the four other areas of expenditure to be reduced?

  (A) G, M, P, S
  (B) L, M, N, R
  (C) L, M, P, S
  (D) M, N, P, S
  (E) M, P, R, S

8. If P is reduced, which one of the following is a pair of areas of expenditure both of which must be reduced?

  (A) G, M
  (B) M, R
  (C) N, R
  (D) R, S
  (E) S, W

9. If both L and S are reduced, which one of the following could be a pair of areas of expenditure both of which are reduced?

  (A) G, M
  (B) G, P
  (C) N, R
  (D) N, W
  (E) P, S

10. If R is not reduced, which one of the following must be true?

  (A) G is reduced.
  (B) N is not reduced.
  (C) P is reduced.
  (D) S is reduced.
  (E) W is not reduced.

11. If both M and R are reduced, which one of the following is a pair of areas neither of which could be reduced?

  (A) G, L
  (B) G, N
  (C) L, N
  (D) L, P
  (E) P, S

12. Which one of the following areas must be reduced?

  (A) G
  (B) L
  (C) N
  (D) P
  (E) W

GO ON TO THE NEXT PAGE.

R

Logic Games ReChallenge
Set #6 Answer Key

Game #1: June 2003 Questions 1-5 *1. D 2. C 3. A 4. C 5. D*

Explanations begin on page 194

Game #2: February 1993 Questions 8-12 *8. B 9. C 10. E 11. E 12. E*

Explanations begin on page 268

Game #3: June 2000 Questions 14-18 *14. C 15. B 16. A 17. E 18. A*

Explanations begin on page 584

Game #4: October 1996 Questions 6-12 *6. A 7. E 8. B 9. A 10. A 11. C 12. E*

Explanations begin on page 346

Logic Games ReChallenge
Set #7

R

In the course of one month Garibaldi has exactly seven different meetings. Each of her meetings is with exactly one of five foreign dignitaries: Fuentes, Matsuba, Rhee, Soleimani, or Tbahi. The following constraints govern Garibaldi's meetings:

>   She has exactly three meetings with Fuentes, and exactly one with each of the other dignitaries.
>   She does not have any meetings in a row with Fuentes.
>   Her meeting with Soleimani is the very next one after her meeting with Tbahi.
>   Neither the first nor last of her meetings is with Matsuba.

1. Which one of the following could be the sequence of the meetings Garibaldi has with the dignitaries?

    (A)   Fuentes, Rhee, Tbahi, Soleimani, Fuentes, Matsuba, Rhee

    (B)   Fuentes, Tbahi, Soleimani, Matsuba, Fuentes, Fuentes, Rhee

    (C)   Fuentes, Rhee, Fuentes, Matsuba, Fuentes, Tbahi, Soleimani

    (D)   Fuentes, Tbahi, Matsuba, Fuentes, Soleimani, Rhee, Fuentes

    (E)   Fuentes, Tbahi, Soleimani, Fuentes, Rhee, Fuentes, Matsuba

GO ON TO THE NEXT PAGE.

2. If Garibaldi's last meeting is with Rhee, then which one of the following could be true?

   (A) Garibaldi's second meeting is with Soleimani.
   (B) Garibaldi's third meeting is with Matsuba.
   (C) Garibaldi's fourth meeting is with Soleimani.
   (D) Garibaldi's fifth meeting is with Matsuba.
   (E) Garibaldi's sixth meeting is with Soleimani.

3. If Garibaldi's second meeting is with Fuentes, then which one of the following is a complete and accurate list of the dignitaries with any one of whom Garibaldi's fourth meeting could be?

   (A) Fuentes, Soleimani, Rhee
   (B) Matsuba, Rhee, Tbahi
   (C) Matsuba, Soleimani
   (D) Rhee, Tbahi
   (E) Fuentes, Soleimani

4. If Garibaldi's meeting with Rhee is the very next one after Garibaldi's meeting with Soleimani, then which one of the following must be true?

   (A) Garibaldi's third meeting is with Fuentes.
   (B) Garibaldi's fourth meeting is with Rhee.
   (C) Garibaldi's fifth meeting is with Fuentes.
   (D) Garibaldi's sixth meeting is with Rhee.
   (E) Garibaldi's seventh meeting is with Fuentes.

5. If Garibaldi's first meeting is with Tbahi, then Garibaldi's meeting with Rhee could be the

   (A) second meeting
   (B) third meeting
   (C) fifth meeting
   (D) sixth meeting
   (E) seventh meeting

6. If Garibaldi's meeting with Matsuba is the very next meeting after Garibaldi's meeting with Rhee, then with which one of the following dignitaries must Garibaldi's fourth meeting be?

   (A) Fuentes
   (B) Matsuba
   (C) Rhee
   (D) Soleimani
   (E) Tbahi

GO ON TO THE NEXT PAGE.

R

Exactly seven film buffs—Ginnie, Ian, Lianna, Marcos, Reveka, Viktor, and Yow—attend a showing of classic films. Three films are shown, one directed by Fellini, one by Hitchcock, and one by Kurosawa. Each of the film buffs sees exactly one of the three films. The films are shown only once, one film at a time. The following restrictions must apply:

> Exactly twice as many of the film buffs see the Hitchcock film as see the Fellini film.
> Ginnie and Reveka do not see the same film as each other.
> Ian and Marcos do not see the same film as each other.
> Viktor and Yow see the same film as each other.
> Lianna sees the Hitchcock film.
> Ginnie sees either the Fellini film or the Kurosawa film.

13. Which one of the following could be an accurate matching of film buffs to films?

(A) Ginnie: the Hitchcock film; Ian: the Kurosawa film; Marcos: the Hitchcock film

(B) Ginnie: the Kurosawa film; Ian: the Fellini film; Viktor: the Fellini film

(C) Ian: the Hitchcock film; Reveka: the Kurosawa film; Viktor: the Fellini film

(D) Marcos: the Kurosawa film; Reveka: the Kurosawa film; Viktor: the Kurosawa film

(E) Marcos: the Hitchcock film; Reveka: the Hitchcock film; Yow: the Hitchcock film

GO ON TO THE NEXT PAGE.

14. Each of the following must be false EXCEPT:

(A) Reveka is the only film buff to see the Fellini film.
(B) Reveka is the only film buff to see the Hitchcock film.
(C) Yow is the only film buff to see the Kurosawa film.
(D) Exactly two film buffs see the Kurosawa film.
(E) Exactly three film buffs see the Hitchcock film.

15. Which one of the following could be a complete and accurate list of the film buffs who do NOT see the Hitchcock film?

(A) Ginnie, Marcos
(B) Ginnie, Reveka
(C) Ginnie, Ian, Reveka
(D) Ginnie, Marcos, Yow
(E) Ginnie, Viktor, Yow

16. If exactly one film buff sees the Kurosawa film, then which one of the following must be true?

(A) Viktor sees the Hitchcock film.
(B) Ginnie sees the Fellini film.
(C) Marcos sees the Fellini film.
(D) Ian sees the Fellini film.
(E) Reveka sees the Hitchcock film.

17. Which one of the following must be true?

(A) Ginnie sees a different film than Ian does.
(B) Ian sees a different film than Lianna does.
(C) Ian sees a different film than Viktor does.
(D) Ian, Lianna, and Viktor do not all see the same film.
(E) Ginnie, Lianna, and Marcos do not all see the same film.

18. If Viktor sees the same film as Ginnie does, then which one of the following could be true?

(A) Ginnie sees the Fellini film.
(B) Ian sees the Hitchcock film.
(C) Reveka sees the Kurosawa film.
(D) Viktor sees the Hitchcock film.
(E) Yow sees the Fellini film.

19. Each of the following could be a complete and accurate list of the film buffs who see the Fellini film EXCEPT:

(A) Ginnie, Ian
(B) Ginnie, Marcos
(C) Ian, Reveka
(D) Marcos, Reveka
(E) Viktor, Yow

GO ON TO THE NEXT PAGE.

R

An art teacher will schedule exactly six of eight lectures—fresco, history, lithography, naturalism, oils, pastels, sculpture, and watercolors—for three days—1, 2, and 3. There will be exactly two lectures each day—morning and afternoon. Scheduling is governed by the following conditions:

> Day 2 is the only day for which oils can be scheduled.
> Neither sculpture nor watercolors can be scheduled for the afternoon.
> Neither oils nor pastels can be scheduled for the same day as lithography.
> If pastels is scheduled for day 1 or day 2, then the lectures scheduled for the day immediately following pastels must be fresco and history, not necessarily in that order.

12. Which one of the following is an acceptable schedule of lectures for days 1, 2, and 3, respectively?

   (A) Morning: lithography, history, sculpture
        Afternoon: pastels, fresco, naturalism
   (B) Morning: naturalism, oils, fresco
        Afternoon: lithography, pastels, history
   (C) Morning: oils, history, naturalism
        Afternoon: pastels, fresco, lithography
   (D) Morning: sculpture, lithography, naturalism
        Afternoon: watercolors, fresco, pastels
   (E) Morning: sculpture, pastels, fresco
        Afternoon: lithography, history, naturalism

GO ON TO THE NEXT PAGE.

R

13. If lithography and fresco are scheduled for the afternoons of day 2 and day 3, respectively, which one of the following is a lecture that could be scheduled for the afternoon of day 1?

(A) history
(B) oils
(C) pastels
(D) sculpture
(E) watercolors

14. If lithography and history are scheduled for the mornings of day 2 and day 3, respectively, which one of the following lectures could be scheduled for the morning of day 1?

(A) fresco
(B) naturalism
(C) oils
(D) pastels
(E) sculpture

15. If oils and lithography are scheduled for the mornings of day 2 and day 3, respectively, which one of the following CANNOT be scheduled for any day?

(A) fresco
(B) history
(C) naturalism
(D) pastels
(E) sculpture

16. If neither fresco nor naturalism is scheduled for any day, which one of the following must be scheduled for day 1?

(A) history
(B) lithography
(C) oils
(D) pastels
(E) sculpture

17. If the lectures scheduled for the mornings are fresco, history, and lithography, not necessarily in that order, which one of the following could be true?

(A) Lithography is scheduled for day 3.
(B) Naturalism is scheduled for day 2.
(C) Fresco is scheduled for the same day as naturalism.
(D) History is scheduled for the same day as naturalism.
(E) History is scheduled for the same day as oils.

GO ON TO THE NEXT PAGE.

R

Three boys—Karl, Luis, and Miguel—and three girls—
Rita, Sarah, and Tura—are giving a dance recital. Three
dances—1, 2, and 3—are to be performed. Each dance
involves three pairs of children, a boy and girl partnering
each other in each pair, according to the following
conditions:

Karl partners Sarah in either dance 1 or dance 2.
Whoever partners Rita in dance 2 must partner Sarah
in dance 3.
No two children can partner each other in more than
one dance.

14. If Sarah partners Luis in dance 3, which one of the
following is a complete and accurate list of the girls
any one of whom could partner Miguel in dance 1?

(A) Rita
(B) Sarah
(C) Tura
(D) Rita, Sarah
(E) Rita, Tura

GO ON TO THE NEXT PAGE.

15. If Miguel partners Rita in dance 2, which one of the following could be true?

   (A)   Karl partners Tura in dance 1.
   (B)   Luis partners Sarah in dance 2.
   (C)   Luis partners Sarah in dance 3.
   (D)   Miguel partners Sarah in dance 1.
   (E)   Miguel partners Tura in dance 3.

16. If Miguel partners Sarah in dance 1, which one of the following is a pair of children who must partner each other in dance 3?

   (A)   Karl and Rita
   (B)   Karl and Tura
   (C)   Luis and Rita
   (D)   Luis and Tura
   (E)   Miguel and Tura

17. If Luis partners Sarah in dance 2, which one of the following is a pair of children who must partner each other in dance 1?

   (A)   Karl and Rita
   (B)   Karl and Tura
   (C)   Luis and Rita
   (D)   Luis and Tura
   (E)   Miguel and Rita

18. If Miguel partners Rita in dance 1, which one of the following must be true?

   (A)   Karl partners Rita in dance 2.
   (B)   Karl partners Sarah in dance 3.
   (C)   Karl partners Tura in dance 1.
   (D)   Luis partners Rita in dance 2.
   (E)   Luis partners Tura in dance 3.

GO ON TO THE NEXT PAGE.

R

Logic Games ReChallenge
Set #7 Answer Key

Game #1: October 2004 Questions 1-6   *1. C 2. D 3. E 4. E 5. D 6. A*

Explanations begin on page 200

Game #2: December 1998 Questions 13-19   *13. D 14. A 15. C 16. A 17. E 18. B 19. E*

Explanations begin on page 572

Game #3: December 1994 Questions 12-17   *12. B 13. A 14. E 15. D 16. B 17. E*

Explanations begin on page 428

Game #4: October 1993 Questions 14-18   *14. D 15. B 16. B 17. C 18. D*

Explanations begin on page 496

R

Appendix One

Comprehensive Game Classification ▮▮▮▮▮▮

We recommend that you complete as many released LSATs as possible; working through more tests increases the opportunities you have to apply the techniques learned in this book, and exposes you to more of the variations LSAC uses in language, presentation, and rule combinations.

Released LSATs are tests created by LSAC, the producers of the LSAT. The tests are called PrepTests, and they are sold individually, and in books (often of 10 exams each). The LSATs most useful to you are the ones from the "modern" era (June 1991 to the present). Tests prior to that date were administered in a different format (and are virtually impossible to find anyways). In general, we do not recommend that you study simulated LSATs if possible.

Where can you find these tests? Released LSATs can be purchased from LSAC through their website, www.lsac.org. We recommend buying a Prep Plus subscription as that is the most cost effective way to get tests.

As you practice with past LSATs, one great benefit is to know what types of game were presented on each exam. This helps solidify your knowledge, and confirms that your understanding of Logic Games is correct, or alternately can be used as a guide to finding more games of each specific type. Accordingly, on the website for this book we have identified every released LSAT from the modern era and listed the LSAC publication identifier. Each game is then classified according to the PowerScore system.

The classification can be found on the book website at:

 powerscore.com/lsatprep

Once there, create an account and then use the code on the inside front cover of this book to gain access.

Thanks and happy practicing!

Appendix Two

Consolidated Answer Key ▮▮▮▮▮▮▮▮▮▮

The *PowerScore LSAT Logic Games Bible* contains 28 games, each of which appeared on a previously released LSAT, and the answers to every LSAT game used in this book are found in the game explanations. The consolidated answer key in this section contains two parts: the first part provides a quick chapter-by-chapter answer key for students who need to find the answers quickly, and the second part provides a comprehensive listing of the source of all LSAT questions used in this book. The second part is especially helpful for students who are taking practice LSATs and want to know ahead of time which questions we have used in this book. They can then skip those questions ahead of taking the test, or avoid taking certain tests until later.

Chapter-by-Chapter Answer Key ▮▮▮▮▮▮▮▮▮▮

The chapter-by-chapter answer key lists every game in this book in the presented order and proves the correct answer for each question in each game. You can use this answer key as a quick reference when you are solving problems. Each problem is explained in more detail in the text of the chapter.

Note: Games from recently administered LSATs have been avoided in order to preserve those tests for use as fresh practice exams.

Chapter Three: Linear Games

Game #1: PrepTest 19, June 1996 Questions 1-7
  1. B   2. E   3. C   4. E   5. D   6. D   7. C

Game #2: PrepTest 26, September 1998 Questions 8-12
  8. C   9. E   10. A   11. C   12. A

Game #3: PrepTest 40, June 2003 Questions 1-5
  1. D   2. C   3. A   4. C   5. D

Game #4: PrepTest 44, October 2004 Questions 1-6
  1. C   2. D   3. E   4. E   5. D   6. A

Game #5: PrepTest 2, October 1991 Questions 6-12
  6. D   7. E   8. A   9. E   10. C   11. B   12. C

Chapter-by-Chapter Answer Key

Chapter Four: Advanced Linear Games

Game #1: PrepTest 26, September 1998 Questions 1-7
   1. C   2. B   3. A   4. D   5. E   6. A   7. D

Game #2: PrepTest 44, October 2004 Questions 13-17
   13. E   14. C   15. A   16. E   17. D

Game #3: PrepTest 51, December 2006 Questions 11-15
   11. D   12. E   13. D   14. D   15. E

Game #4: PrepTest 7, February 1993 Questions 8-12
   8. B   9. C   10. E   11. E   12. E

Chapter Five: Grouping Games

Game #1: PrepTest 20, October 1996 Questions 6-12
   6. A   7. E   8. B   9. A   10. A   11. C   12. E

Game #2: PrepTest 22, June 1997 Questions 1-7
   1. D   2. C   3. E   4. B   5. E   6. B   7. B

Game #3: PrepTest 45, December 2004 Questions 13-17
   13. B   14. E   15. D   16. B   17. A

Game #4: PrepTest 28, June 1999 Questions 6-12
   6. D   7. B   8. C   9. B   10. A   11. B   12. D

Game #5: PrepTest 33, December 2000 Questions 6-12
   6. D   7. E   8. D   9. C   10. A   11. A   12. B

Chapter Six: Grouping/Linear Combination Games

Game #1: PrepTest 10, February 1994 Questions 19-24
   19. B   20. C   21. E   22. B   23. D   24. A

Game #2: PrepTest 13, December 1994 Questions 12-17
   12. B   13. A   14. E   15. D   16. B   17. E

Chapter-by-Chapter Answer Key

Chapter Seven: Pure Sequencing Games

Game #1: PrepTest 33, December 2000 Questions 1-5
> *1. C   2. A   3. E   4. D   5. B*

Game #2: PrepTest 51, December 2006 Questions 6-10
> *6. B   7. C   8. A   9. D   10. D*

Chapter Eight: The Forgotten Few

Pattern Game #1: PrepTest 23, October 1997 Questions 19-24
> *19. D   20. D   21. B   22. E   23. C   24. A*

Pattern Game #2: PrepTest 9, October 1993 Questions 14-18
> *14. D   15. B   16. B   17. C   18. D*

Circular Linearity Game #1: PrepTest 1, June 1991 Questions 1-7
> *1. B   2. A   3. B   4. E   5. E   6. C   7. E*

Mapping Game #1: PrepTest 15, June 1995 Questions 7-13
> *7. D   8. A   9. E   10. E   11. D   12. E   13. A*

Chapter Nine: Advanced Features and Techniques

Numerical Distribution Game #1: PrepTest 46, June 2005 Questions 17-22
> *17. C   18. C   19. B   20. D   21. E   22. D*

Numerical Distribution Game #2: PrepTest 27, December 1998 Questions 13-19
> *13. D   14. A   15. C   16. A   17. E   18. B   19. E*

Limited Solution Set Game #1: PrepTest 31, June 2000 Questions 14-18
> *14. C   15. B   16. A   17. E   18. A*

Limited Solution Set Game #2: PrepTest 28, June 1999 Questions 19-23
> *19. D   20. E   21. A   22. C   23. E*

Limited Solution Set Game #3: PrepTest 51, December 2006 Questions 1-5
> *1. D   2. A   3. E   4. C   5. E*

Limited Solution Set Game #4: PrepTest 29, October 1999 Questions 1-6
> *1. D   2. C   3. A   4. B   5. B   6. C*

This section contains a reverse lookup that cross references each game according to the source LSAT. The tests are listed in order of the PrepTest number (if any). The date of administration is also listed to make the process easier. If a test is not listed, then no questions from that exam were used in this book.

Games listed under each test begin by listing the *Logic Games Bible* chapter the game appears in, the game date, and then the question numbers.

For information on obtaining the publications that contain the LSATs listed below, please visit our Free LSAT Help area at www.powerscore.com/lsat/help.

PrepTest 1—June 1991 LSAT

> Chapter 8, Page 510, Circular Linearity Game #1: June 1991 Questions 1-7

PrepTest 2—October 1991 LSAT

> Chapter 3, Page 208, Game #5: October 1991 Questions 6-12

PrepTest 7—February 1993 LSAT

> Chapter 4, Page 266, Game #4: February 1993 Questions 8-12

PrepTest 9—October 1993 LSAT

> Chapter 8, Page 494, Pattern Game #2: October 1993 Questions 14-18

PrepTest 10—February 1994 LSAT

> Chapter 6, Page 420, Game #1: February 1994 Questions 19-24

PrepTest 13—December 1994 LSAT

> Chapter 6, Page 426, Game #2: December 1994 Questions 12-17

PrepTest 15—June 1995 LSAT

> Chapter 8, Page 522, Mapping Game #1: June 1995 Questions 7-13

Test-by-Test Game Use Tracker

PrepTest 19—June 1996 LSAT

Chapter 3, Page 176, Game #1: June 1996 Questions 1-7

PrepTest 20—October 1996 LSAT

Chapter 5, Page 344, Game #1: October 1996 Questions 6-12

PrepTest 22—June 1997 LSAT

Chapter 5, Page 352, Game #2: June 1997 Questions 1-7

PrepTest 23—October 1997 LSAT

Chapter 8, Page 484, Pattern Game #1: October 1997 Questions 19-24

PrepTest 26—September 1998 LSAT

Chapter 4, Page 240, Game #1: September 1998 Questions 1-7
Chapter 3, Page 184, Game #2: September 1998 Questions 8-12

PrepTest 27—December 1998 LSAT

Chapter 9, Page 563, Numerical Distribution Game #2: December 1998 Questions 13-19

PrepTest 28—June 1999 LSAT

Chapter 5, Page 372, Game #4: June 1999 Questions 6-12
Chapter 9, Page 581, Limited Solution Set Game #2: June 1999 Questions 19-23

PrepTest 29—October 1999 LSAT

Chapter 9, Page 597, Limited Solution Set Game #4: October 1999 Questions 1-6

PrepTest 31—June 2000 LSAT

Chapter 9, Page 575, Limited Solution Set Game #1: June 2000 Questions 14-18

Test-by-Test Game Use Tracker

PrepTest 33—December 2000 LSAT

> Chapter 7, Page 456, Game #1: December 2000 Questions 1-5
> Chapter 5, Page 378, Game #5: December 2000 Questions 6-12

PrepTest 40—June 2003 LSAT

> Chapter 3, Page 192, Game #3: June 2003 Questions 1-5

PrepTest 44—October 2004 LSAT

> Chapter 3, Page 198, Game #4: October 2004 Questions 1-6
> Chapter 4, Page 248, Game #2: October 2004 Questions 13-17

PrepTest 45—December 2004 LSAT

> Chapter 5, Page 360, Game #3: December 2004 Questions 13-17

PrepTest 46—June 2005 LSAT

> Chapter 9, Page 555, Numerical Distribution Game #1: June 2005 Questions 17-22

PrepTest 51—December 2006 LSAT

> Chapter 9, Page 587, Limited Solution Set Game #3: December 2006 Questions 1-5
> Chapter 7, Page 462, Game #2: December 2006 Questions 6-10
> Chapter 4, Page 256, Game #3: December 2006 Questions 11-15

Reminder: Games from the LSATs that were administered in recent years have been avoided in order to preserve those tests for use as fresh practice exams.